MEXICAN REVOLUTION

The Constitutionalist Years

THE TEXAS PAN AMERICAN SERIES

Mexican Revolution

The Constitutionalist Years

by CHARLES C. CUMBERLAND

With an Introduction and Additional Material by

DAVID C. BAILEY

UNIVERSITY OF TEXAS PRESS, AUSTIN & LONDON

FOR JANEY

from her Father

and her Mother—

and from David

The Texas Pan American Series is published with the assistance of a revolving publication fund established by the Pan American Sulphur Company and other friends of Latin America in Texas.

Library of Congress Cataloging in Publication Data

Cumberland, Charles Curtis.
Mexican Revolution: the constitutionalist years.

Bibliography: p.
1. Mexico—History—1910–1946. I. Title.
F1234.C976 972.08'2 74-38506
International Standard Book Number 0-292-75000-5 (cloth)
0-292-75016-1 (paper)

Manufactured in the United States of America
Second Printing, 1974
First paperback printing, 1974

CONTENTS

FOREWORD

Nearly twenty-five years ago Charles Cumberland began work on a history of Mexico after 1910. He completed one volume, which appeared in 1952 under the title *Mexican Revolution: Genesis under Madero*, and immediately began plans for a second. But other projects kept intervening, and although he finished research for this second volume and devoted most of his last two years to its writing it was unfinished when he died on March 25, 1970.

Mrs. Emily Cumberland Whitaker asked me to complete the manuscript for publication. This entailed writing the last third of chapter 10, adding information on Emiliano Zapata in chapters 2, 5, and 6, making minor changes elsewhere throughout the work, composing an introduction and epilogue, and supplying a title for the book. A bibliographical essay would have been desirable, but one that did not reflect Professor Cumberland's own assessment of the literature would be of marginal interest to the reader, and I therefore decided only to list the materials cited in the footnotes.

Mrs. Whitaker gave invaluable help and encouragement. She edited and proofread the text, organized the bibliography, and assisted in selecting pictures. Professor Michael Meyer of the University of Nebraska read the manuscript and made wide-ranging and excellent suggestions. Professor Justin Kestenbaum of Michigan State University furnished the picture of the author that appears on the jacket.

Only Professor Cumberland could have provided a complete list of his own acknowledgments, but I am sure he would have wished to include the following: Research for this book was supported by generous grants from the Henry L. and Grace Doherty Foundation and the Social Science Research Council. The University of California at Berkeley contributed funds for filming Mexican archival materials, and several All-University Research grants from Michigan State University helped defray typing and duplicating expenses. The staffs of the Secretaría de Defensa Nacional, the Archivo General de la Nación, and the Hemeroteca Nacional in Mexico City, and the National Archives in Washington, D.C., helped resolve many research problems with kindness and efficiency.

An undertaking of this scope is aided by many people who supply information or inspiration, or who facilitate progress in other ways. The author, I know, would want to express particular gratitude to George P. Hammond, former director of the Bancroft Library; to two close friends and colleagues at Michigan State, Professors Paul A. Varg and John F. A. Taylor; and to his favorite typist, Mrs. Ann Brown, whose expertise he so much admired. He would also want to say thank you in a special way to Generoso Garzafox of Mexico City and his wife, Guadalupe Fonseca de Garzafox (a relative of Venustiano Carranza), to their son, Arturo, and his wife, Martha Zolezzi de Garzafox, and to their two daughters and sons-in-law, Guadalupe and Salvador Guerrero and Olga and Manuel de la Tijera; to Charles Cumberland these friends of many years represented the best of the Mexico that the Revolution created.

RALEIGH, NORTH CAROLINA DAVID C. BAILEY

INTRODUCTION

The revolution that began in Mexico in the autumn of 1910 seemed unexceptional enough in its aims. A group of dissidents led by a wealthy *hacendado*, Francisco I. Madero, launched an insurrection to overthrow Porfirio Díaz, the octogenarian dictator who had ruled the country for thirty-four years. They wanted to end despotism and establish political democracy.

The ousting of Díaz proved surprisingly easy; Don Porfirio resigned and fled into exile in May, 1911. Madero was elected president, and the revolution, so it appeared, was over. To be sure, Madero realized that much more had to be done before the new Mexico he dreamed of could become a reality. He knew that most of his countrymen lived in degradation and poverty; rich Mexicans shamefully exploited their unfortunate brothers, and arrogant foreigners helped themselves to the nation's treasures and rode roughshod over national sensibilities. Madero meant to change all this—from a base of honest elections, education, and a new national cohesion.

He failed—or more exactly, he was not allowed to try. Checked at every turn by creatures of the old regime who refused to tolerate even his modest proposals for reform, sniped at incessantly by others who demanded immediate and drastic changes that the moderate Madero could not accept, he was immobilized and then overwhelmed. In fifteen months he was dead, and with him died any hope that Mexico would join the twentieth century the easy way. Even had he enjoyed the support of Mexicans who were in a position to help him, the odds against success were far greater than he realized. No stable and prosperous twentieth-century national state achieved its status easily, but some were able to do it in stages, building on a series of plateaus that were somehow set in place along the way. Mexico in 1910 had barely begun such a process. Its past was still oppressively alive; change would exact a price that none foresaw and that probably few Mexicans would have been willing to pay had they known what it would be.

Most Mexicans had lived an unhappy history. Conquering Spaniards destroyed the ancient cultures and imposed their style of European civilization: a paternal and absolutist political structure, a capitalistic economic system that benefited the few and impoverished the many, and a caste society that relegated the Indian and mixed-blood majority to subservience. With the conquerors came Christianity, in its militant and mystical Iberian form. Almost alone among the institutions of the colony, the Church provided a degree of protection and dignity for the subject races, but the declining zeal of the clergy after the first generation of the conquest coupled with the Church's alliance with the crown diluted much of its effectiveness for promoting human justice. Spanish rule proved inept and oppressive, and Mexico remained largely outside the mainstream in which the rest of the Western world moved after the Renaissance. The war for independence began as a movement to change society, but in the end it changed nothing. The abortive uprising of Miguel Hidalgo and his rampaging Indian mobs in 1810 and the temporary success of José María Morelos in appealing to lower-class resentments thoroughly frightened upper-class colonials, and when liberal ideas seemed to be winning out in Spain itself in 1820, the Creole aristocrats moved for separation from Spain as the best way to preserve themselves from the horrors unleashed on the world by the French Revolution. They wanted their own colony, and so in 1821 they cut the imperial tie in order to preserve the past.

But from the moment of political separation the old ways came under attack. The strife after 1810 destroyed lives and property, unsettled patterns of living, and weakened the social fabric. The new rulers, inexperienced in the exercise of political power, faced obstacles that would have baffled wiser men. Independent Mexico, it soon became obvious, would not be a simple extension of the colony; but neither would it settle into a healthy national life of its own unless a host of basic adjustments were made.

Some perceived this need from the first. By the mid-1820's a liberal party had appeared, drawing its inspiration from the philosophers of the Enlightenment and determined to erase the Spanish colonial past and build anew. The liberals collided with the beneficiaries of the past, and the result was half a century of chaos. Chronic civil upheavals prevented the setting up of a viable political life. Fifty governments held sway in as many years. Fiscal mismanagement made governmental insolvency the norm. Foreign nations intervened almost at will. The bottom came in the 1840's, when Mexico lost nearly half its national territory after a war with the United States and all but collapsed as a national entity.

The liberals seized power in 1855 and set out to impose political and social standards that more advanced nineteenth-century nations were then adopting. But despite the work of intelligent and devoted leaders—Benito Juárez, Melchor Ocampo, and others of them are still honored by Mexicans—their attempt at national transformation failed. After two decades of bloodshed, during which they first subdued their conservative enemies in civil war and then fought back an attempt by the French to impose a European monarchy, they fell back exhausted and the liberal dream soured amid cynical politicking and country-wide lawlessness.

Peace finally came in the last quarter of the nineteenth century, when Porfirio Díaz imposed his praetorian rule. He presided over a stability and a certain growth that many interpreted as progress. And progress there was for some. By 1900 railroads connected the important cities, and factory chimneys here and there evinced the start of industrialization. Mining flourished and exports of raw materials climbed steadily. To foreigners, mainly American and British, whose money financed most of the development, Díaz's Mexico was a haven; there were occasional irritants, but capital was safe and enormously productive, living was gracious, the government treated them royally, and other Mexicans showed them deference. A select minority of Mexicans—the big landowners, the professional military, and the small but prospering business and banker class—also liked the system. It gave the good things of life to those who knew how to appreciate them and ordered all strata of society in a way that was really best for everyone. Díaz's Mexico was in fact a neocolonial society where the old abuses were becoming worse. Land, which meant life to most Mexicans, gravitated to fewer and fewer people. The haciendas, encouraged by benevolent laws and compliant officials, swallowed up small private holdings and even *ejidos*—the Indian communities that had survived centuries of attempts to destroy them. Debt peonage increased and so did hunger; the inherent tendency of the hacienda to produce at minimum levels meant that most Mexicans ate less each year. In many ways this new colonialism was more sinister than the earlier one. The few restraints of the old Spanish system were largely gone. The crown had always insisted that at least potentially the Indian was the equal of his masters, but the "scientific" managers of the *porfiriato* knew better: Indians and most mestizos were born inferior. The Church, which once had furnished an occasional shield to the underdog, was now largely powerless. It survived the liberal onslaught of the mid-nineteenth century to retain the nominal and sometimes devoted allegiance of most Mexicans, but it was deprived of any voice in national affairs by the officially anticlerical Díaz regime—although, somewhat ironically, it remained for some a symbol of repression.

Certainly there was dissatisfaction with the state of things. Under the calm surface of the *paz porfiriana* opposition fermented. Some of it was intellectual and radical, more of it the inarticulate resentment of the desperately poor. It was neither coherent nor effective, but it germinated attitudes and ideas that quietly undermined the regime and had the potential to erupt in a multitude of disparate ways.

Francisco Madero inherited this sad and dangerous situation, which he hoped to remedy gradually through a process of reform. But it was too late; his revolt against Díaz had awakened appetites for immediate and fundamental change. Madero's overthrow and murder by rightists in February, 1913, started an avalanche. The governor of the state of Coahuila, Venustiano Carranza, rallied opposition to the usurpation, and within weeks the country had engulfed itself in civil war.

The seven years from 1913 to 1920, which this book describes and analyzes, were at once majestic and terrible. They were a period of anarchy and destruction—of lives and property, and also of basic and long-held assumptions. But in the midst of the upheaval, out of conflicting tendencies and movements, fairly coherent directions appeared. They were little more than aspirations in 1920; their fruition would come later, after most of the protagonists in the great drama of the teens were dead. Mexico today lives in the wake of what happened during those years; they marked the birth of the modern Mexican nation.

MEXICAN REVOLUTION

The Constitutionalist Years

1. PRELUDE TO CONFLICT

When Charles Flandrau once inquired of a Mexican lady whether it rained more in the summer than in the winter, she replied: "No hay reglas fijas, señor."[1] And, said the young reporter writing during the Díaz dictatorship, the lady's statement epitomized the Mexico of the period. Certain it is that the rules were fluid—applied one way for some groups and another way for others—and just as certainly one of the issues in the 1910 Madero revolution was the correction of this condition. But fixed rules are difficult to impose upon a people accustomed to freewheeling, as Madero soon found.[2]

In both Mexico and the United States the Madero period was seldom recognized for what it actually was, and Madero himself was the subject of violent differences of opinion. A relatively insignificant man with limited intellectual endowments, Francisco Madero

1 "There are no fixed rules, sir" (Charles Macomb Flandrau, *Viva Mexico!* p. 20).

2 The first portion of this chapter is a summation of my *Mexican Revolution: Genesis under Madero*.

probably would have lived, in a society with "reglas fijas," the full and peaceful life of a Mexican landowner, untroubled by economic problems and unconcerned with politics. But in the Mexican milieu of the early twentieth century no thoughtful man with social consciousness could stand idly by and watch the continuation of a dangerous anachronism. Díaz's Mexico was an anachronism because the Western world found itself engaged in a kind of political and social experimentation that Mexico could not seal out, because early twentieth-century Mexico was living under eighteenth-century value systems, and because—in an industrial world dedicated to technological progress with concomitant social and political change—the dominant pattern of Mexican life revolved around the retention of a social and an economic system feudal in philosophy. And danger existed—in the potential explosiveness of the Mexican masses, in the bitterness expressed by young intellectuals, in the burning demands from an unorganized, suppressed, but ever-growing labor group.

Anachronism though it might have been, the Díaz period died hard. And Díaz's resignation (in the face of Madero's capture of Ciudad Juárez in early 1911) failed to render to the era the *coup de grâce*. The famous remark attributed to Díaz that Madero had "unleashed a tiger" came closer to the truth than even the aged dictator realized. But the tiger that Díaz feared and the tiger that did the ultimate damage were different animals. To be sure, Madero unleashed desires and ambitions among the population at large, and the presumably apathetic submerged groups suddenly lost their docility and gave to the ensuing revolution a distinctive stamp. This was the group which Díaz feared, while the real "tiger" freed by Madero was the violent reaction to reform on the part of certain vested-interest groups.

All classes of society, and virtually all members, have "vested interests" of one kind or another, and here the term is used in no pejorative sense. Certainly the landholding segment of Mexican society had what it considered a legitimate interest in retaining the basic characteristics of its civilization, and just as certainly it looked with fear and suspicion upon any attempt to introduce fundamental land reform. Whether the land-reform program that the moderate Madero envisaged posed an actual threat is a moot point, but the *hacendados* interpreted any reform program, no matter how tentative or tenuous, as a step in a dangerous direction. Their insistence that no land problem existed may well have been an expression of conviction; from the *hacendados*' point of view there was no problem. But whether from conviction or selfishness, such expression could not erase the irrefutable fact that the vast majority of those whose livelihood was intimately attached to the soil did not own land, that credit and banking facilities rendered impossible private purchase by small proprietors, that compared to other agricultural nations Mexican agriculture was grossly inefficient, and that many communities on the Central Plateau demanding land were determined to seize it if necessary. When the *hacendados* rejected Madero's first hesitant steps toward reform (through purchase of private holdings for resale on easy terms in small plots) as visionary, unrealistic, and needless, even administration moderates began to question the *hacendados*' motives. Since it was apparent that the *hacendado* class had no intention of cooperating freely, and equally apparent that some action was both socially and politically mandatory, the administration began to move in the direction of more radical change through the application of force. Hacienda expropriation and ejidal restoration, actively debated in the Chamber of Deputies in late 1912, was the answer to the *hacendado* challenge.

By late 1912 land reform was obviously inevitable, if the prevailing administrative mentality continued, and the nature of the reform would seriously undermine the social, economic, and political position enjoyed by the *hacendado* class. The hacienda system, and all that it meant to Mexican society, was confronted with ultimate extinction. Justifiably or unjustifiably, to the threatened group Madero became a symbol of destruction; the Coahuila visionary, for whom the *hacendados* had previously held disdain rather than fear, had become a malevolent force that simply had to be removed. Even before that late date many *hacendados* vigorously, albeit surreptitiously, opposed the Madero administration; they, or their paid hacks, reported banditry or corruption or favoritism even when the charges lacked base—and of course they capitalized upon actual weaknesses and any evidence of corruption. These charges undermined public confidence in the administration, but at least some members of the class decided on more direct action. The Chihuahua *hacendados* supported the 1912 Orozco rebellion in that state; Pascual Orozco became their tool and remained such until his death in 1915. Again, they supported Félix Díaz's abortive 1912 revolt. The fact that neither rebellion succeeded was discouraging, but not killing, to *hacendado* hopes; like the tiger, the *hacendado* could be patient if his existence depended upon patience, but he was ready to pounce should the opportunity present itself.

The army-officer class constituted a second powerful vested-interest group, one that had been made to look utterly ridiculous and helpless during the successful anti-Díaz revolution. During the long *paz porfiriana* the officer corps had grown fat and indolent; except for a somewhat leisurely and constant campaign against Sonora Yaquis, the Mexican army for a full generation had scarcely justified its existence. During those years the real profession of the officer corps was political rather than military, and this lack of attention to purely military matters became brutally clear with Madero's victory. To the injury of defeat was added the insult of preterition when Madero assumed the presidency. He was a civilian in every sense of the word; not only had he no military pretension, but also in his scheme of things the military had no political niche to occupy. The professional army officer suddenly found himself in a new and an unattractive role; he was now an observer and not a leader of the passing political parade. Even more devastating to his self-esteem and to his future, nothing in the Madero administration or in the prevailing philosophy of the president's closest advisors pointed to any improvement in the army officer's political status. But his cup of misery was filled to overflowing when the Madero administration elevated, as members of the regular line officer group, officers who had served the revolution against Díaz. To the alumnus of the military academy, appointment to line officer positions of individuals whose only training was encompassed in revolutionary service appeared to be a denigration of officer status—as indeed it was.

Furthermore, regular officer corps morale was scarcely improved by the campaign against Orozco, during which the "irregulars" and the state forces under such men as Francisco Villa, Pablo González, and the president's younger brothers Emilio and Raúl not only carried the brunt of the fighting but also often gained the laurels of victory. It was this complex of factors which so infuriated the officer corps and which Félix Díaz insisted constituted an insult to the army (although he lacked the temerity to specify the nature of the insults). And it was to avenge the insult that Don Porfirio's nephew rebelled in October, 1912. Unfortunately for the pretensions of the officers, the younger Díaz was a "handsome, gallant but dull and indolent army officer . . . with such slight qualifications and such lack of enterprise that he . . . always failed,"[3] and his venture into vengeance scarcely added luster to his cause. But his failure, ignominious as it was, did not discourage the officers; it merely strengthened their determination to return to a position of prestige as soon as opportunity arose.

Even those officers who did not actively, or consciously, resent Madero's relegation of the army to a political cipher had little interest in perpetuating the regime; not eager to revolt against the constitutional government, they had no deep animosity to others who might do so. When the "moment of truth" arrived, they found philosophical justification for supporting the spurious government emanating from Madero's overthrow.

The entrepreneurial class, both national and foreign, also had a strong vested interest in the porfirian system. Mexican nonagricultural economy prior to 1911 was essentially monopolistic, with a tightly intertwined group controlling most financial and industrial institutions; the foreigners were spiritually, even if not physically, a part of the group. Díaz was devoted to the principle of industrial modernization at whatever cost, and the price demanded—and paid —included tax rebates, special concessions of a monopolistic nature,

[3] William Bayard Hale memorandum to President Wilson, July 9, 1913, file 812.00/8203, National Archives, Record Group 59. Hereafter records in the National Archives are indicated by the symbol NA, followed by the record group (RG) number.

favoritism, guaranteed profits, a docile labor force kept in check by criminal syndicalist laws and similar devices, rights of eminent domain, and a host of related concepts. Whether the need for economic development justified such a price is moot, but that the entrepreneurial class in general was convinced of the justification can not be debated seriously. Implicit in the Madero policy—and often explicit—was a rejection of most of the fundamental tenets accepted as gospel by the entrepreneurs. Madero, too, was devoted to the principle of economic development or economic change, but with considerably different emphasis, an emphasis perfectly demonstrated by his support of organized labor (banned during the Díaz period) and by his insistence that Mexican railroads use the Spanish language in publishing orders for the workers. In supporting—even sponsoring—labor organization, the Madero administration gave notice to the entrepreneurs that the Mexican laborer had a stake in economic development, that the policy of special aid to management at the expense of labor had come to an end. In demanding the use of Spanish in railroad orders, the administration was saying in effect that economic development must be evaluated in terms of its benefits to Mexicans; unless such benefits immediately accrued to the national population there would be no excuse for the enterprise. These and other principles—abolition of monopoly, of special privilege, of the dual legal system—shocked to its core the business community. Acceptance of Maderista principles, mild and moderate though they might be in comparison to contemporary industrial policies in western Europe or the United States, meant the disappearance of a way of life that the entrepreneurial class was reluctant to abandon. This group, too, saw in Madero's policies the same threat that the *hacendados* and the officer corps envisaged.

The fourth major interest group was the foreigners, symbolized by U.S. Ambassador Henry Lane Wilson, whose position with respect to the Madero administration certainly did not represent all foreign opinion but just as certainly was not discrete. Citizens of England, Germany, and Spain, as well as the United States, had made heavy investments in Mexican ventures during the Díaz administration, with the expectation that porfirian policies would continue for generations to come. Representatives of these countries, as well as most others, had vied with each other in September, 1910, in extolling the virtues of the Díaz regime and in predicting a rosy future; the collapse of the regime a few months later came as a distinct shock. While Madero took no joy in plucking the Eagle's feather or twisting the Lion's tail, one characteristic of his movement against Díaz was xenophobia—limited, to be sure—and certainly Madero himself was dedicated to Mexican nationalism. While it may be argued that Madero nationalism was not synonymous with antiforeignism, the new administration's emphasis on Mexican values and Mexican development caused serious concern among resident aliens. Added to this general concern, and stimulating it, was the lawlessness that accompanied the revolution and that held on during all the Madero period. Cold statistical analysis shows clearly that the nation's economy under Madero did not suffer—a good case can be made that it improved—but the fact remains that, compared to the *paz porfiriana*, Mexico in 1912 was lawless, and foreigners became fearful. The alien investor was no longer in a favored position vis-à-vis the Mexican, the major powers' diplomatic representatives lost their ability to determine domestic policy through hints and suggestions, and the entire structure under which the foreigner had earlier invested seemed to be crumbling. Henry Lane Wilson was an incredibly blind diplomat, but he was absolutely convinced that the Madero administration and the entire Madero philosophy spelled doom for U.S. interests. He was tragically wrong, but his policy as ambassador was based upon his fallacious understanding of what was happening and not on some narrowly defined personal interest. Wilson, then, and his Spanish, British, and German colleagues, did what they could in their myopic way to preserve—or reinstitute—a pattern of relationships advantageous to their countrymen. Since their primary concern was with protection of their nationals, and not with abstract truth, the diplomatic representatives frequently twisted their instructions when delivering notes to the Mexican foreign office; Wilson, particularly, interpreted literally the "plenipotentiary" portion of his title.

In fine, by early 1913 four powerful interest groups, with generally disparate goals, felt themselves threatened to the point of extinction by Madero's administration. These were the "tiger," and like tigers at bay they were ready to use any trick or stratagem that might assure safety. The groups were neither internally nor externally cohesive, they entered into no cabals or conspiracies, but they had a momentary and dominant concern that gave them a degree of temporary homogeneity. Each was waiting for the opportune moment to act; when the moment came they did not act in concert, but they did all move in the same direction: the removal of Madero, completely and permanently.

Against this backdrop the Tragic Ten Days of February, 1913, the first step in the "rectification" process, must be viewed, and in this setting the developments of 1913 and early 1914 must be analyzed. The Tragic Ten Days were tragic not only for the needless slaughter—the deliberate slaughter—of hundreds of civilians, but also because this period symbolized the inability of the contending parties to meet at a half-way point. These ten days were a microcosm of the epic revolution with its brutality, its uncompromising nature, its opportunity for unbridled ambition leading to treason, and its generally debilitating effect.

Each of the major vested interests found in the *cuartelazo* that began on February 8 the ideal situation for destroying Madero, and each gave what service it could to that goal. The *hacendados* and the entrepreneurs, through their representatives in the Senate, began immediately predicting the downfall of the regime and then aided the accuracy of that prediction by demanding Madero's resignation. The foreign interests, by a wide variety of techniques, helped undermine confidence in the administration; the most effective of these was Henry Lane Wilson's unauthorized statement that the United States planned to intervene to stop the carnage. The senators believed, or feigned to believe, in imminent intervention and became more insistent on Madero's resignation. But when these tactics failed, it was left to the officer corps to consummate Madero's destruction through as callous a bit of treachery as the twentieth century has seen. Victoriano Huerta, chosen by Madero to defend the government after Félix Díaz and General Manuel Mondragón had rebelled, went through the motions of such defense for a number of days; it was during these days that the civilian population was subjected to a deliberate horror through bombardment; an emotionally exhausted public was essential to Huerta's plan. Finally, on the afternoon of February 18, the penultimate steps were taken; the president, the vice-president, a few members of the cabinet, a few officers whose loyalty to the government was unquestioned, and a number of congressmen were arrested, and Huerta became the acting president.

Huerta undertook his seizure of power with the support—expressed or tacit, prior or post—of the vested interests. Whether he also did it with their prior knowledge is subject to debate, but circumstantial evidence suggests it very strongly. Certainly an agent sent to Mexico by Woodrow Wilson in June, 1913, convinced himself—and undertook to convince President Wilson—that Henry Lane Wilson was privy to the plans at least a day before Madero's arrest.[4] Just as certainly most of the ranking army officers in the environs of Mexico City were involved in the plot. The *hacendado* and entrepreneurial groups, through their representatives in the Senate, may or may not have been involved, but there is no doubting their jubilation once the action was complete. One foreign entrepreneur, a British subject, expressed the sentiments of his group when he said, "Bully for Huerta! It is something that ought to have been done long ago. Don Porfirio's system is the system for this country and for these people, it is the only system."[5] The newspapers, little more than hired claques for these groups, lavished praise on the "heroic" and

[4] Wm. Bayard Hale memorandum of June 18, 1913, file 812.00/7798½, NA, RG 59. Hale, sent to Mexico in the guise of a newspaperman but whose real mission was generally suspected by both Mexicans and resident U.S. citizens, came to this conclusion on the basis of reports concerning visits to the embassy by various persons close to Huerta prior to the coup d'état. These visits, some of which were admitted to by the ambassador, coupled with an immediate notification to the ambassador after Madero's arrest, imply—but do not prove—that H. L. Wilson was fully apprised of the plan. Furthermore, the ambassador had made no secret of his conviction that Madero had to go for the good of Mexico.

[5] As reported by Vice-Consul John R. Silliman to SecState, October 16, 1913, file 812.00/9555, NA, RG 59.

"patriotic" officers who had delivered the country from "corruption" and "despotism."

But Madero's overthrow did not constitute the final act in the macabre drama. The frenzied victors had smelled blood when General Bernardo Reyes, the ostensible leader of the February 8 revolt, was killed in the first attack on the National Palace. The appetite for blood was whetted when Francisco Madero's brother Gustavo was seized and subjected to indescribable brutality as a prelude to his death. Madero and most of his friends knew that satiation would come only with his own death, and this conviction led him to resist for some time the pressures for his resignation. The respectable representatives of the vested-interest groups insisted, after the fact, that they knew nothing of the assassination plans, and Francisco León de la Barra even went so far as to proclaim publicly that he would resign if he ever discovered that the Huerta government had ordered Madero's death—but when the evidence was clear he still occupied his office as minister of foreign relations. The U.S. ambassador, speaking for those foreign representatives whom he called the "diplomatic corps," always contended that he had done all he could to assure Madero's safety, but by his own admission he told Huerta to do with Madero what seemed to be best for the country—and this at a time when general public gossip was to the effect that Madero would never leave Mexico alive. Concrete evidence is lacking with respect to the vested interests' desires for Madero's death, but the circumstantial evidence is strong. As one Huertista put it, not speaking for all the vested-interest groups but clearly voicing their feelings, "nobody wanted to leave these dangerous propagandists of violence and anarchy alive, and their deaths were considered . . . a national necessity."[6]

Whether national necessity dictated the permanent elimination of Madero and Vice-President José María Pino Suárez is a conjectural question, but the answer was clear in the minds of Huerta and his immediate military advisors. On the night of February 21–22, the deposed president and his erstwhile vice-president were sacrificed

[6] Carlos Toro, *La caída de Madero por la revolución felicista*, p. 59.

to Mammon and Mars, a blood offering to assure a return to the Mexico of Porfirio Díaz. "The programme [*sic*] . . . to kill all of . . . their kind and thus stamp out democracy in Mexico"[7] was under way.

"Authorized by the Senate, I have assumed the Executive Power, the President and his Cabinet being under arrest."[8] With these words Victoriano Huerta notified the world, including the state governors, of his successful coup d'état on February 18, 1913, and so began his tortuous maneuvers to elevate himself to the presidency. His seizure of power was complete, in spite of the façade of quasi respectability with which the Pact of the Embassy vested it,[9] and in spite of a public manifesto that assured "full guarantees to nationals and foreigners" and "all liberties consistent with order."[10] The new dictator's no-nonsense determination was made perfectly clear a few days later when he closed a wooing manifesto by an emphasized statement: "I will not hesitate a moment in putting into effect whatever rigorous measures are necessary for the rapid reestablishment of the public peace."[11] Furthermore he arrested not only President Francisco Madero and Vice-President Pino Suárez but also virtually all members of the cabinet, some of the loyal military commanders, and a number of the most noted Maderistas in the national Congress. By seizing all administrative offices, he controlled all means of communication and transportation as well as the military and financial resources of the national government. Co-conspirator Félix Díaz found himself in the unenviable position of onlooker, even

[7] Consul Marion Letcher, Chihuahua, to SecState, October 17, 1913, file 812.00/9484, NA, RG 59.

[8] Alfredo Breceda, *México revolucionario, 1913–1917*, I, 142.

[9] The Pact of the Embassy, or, officially, the Pact of the Ciudadela, actually made no concrete provision for the executive power; it stipulated that "Generals Huerta and Díaz are placed in charge of all elements and authorities of every kind" until such time as the legal status of the government had been determined. It also provided that the two generals would cooperate to place Huerta in the legal position of provisional president within seventy-two hours (see file 812.00/11661, NA, RG 59).

[10] Huerta–F. Díaz manifesto, as given in Jesús Acuña, *Memoria de la Secretaría de Gobernación*, p. 74.

[11] Huerta manifesto, February 22, 1913, ibid., p. 95.

though he had—with the help of U.S. Ambassador Henry Lane Wilson—selected Huerta's first cabinet.[12]

Immediately after executing the coup, Huerta notified the president of the Chamber of Deputies of the action and requested that official to convene the Chamber to consider the "interesting state of affairs" that existed,[13] while Félix Díaz and Mondragón soon thereafter urged individual members of Congress to take steps to legalize the seizure.[14] A deputies session called for the morning of February 19 failed to obtain a quorum,[15] but by dint of much exertion and by pressing the *suplentes* into service, Chamber of Deputies leaders were able to gather a quorum for the afternoon. With the legislative hall surrounded by troops, some of whom were actually inside the building, the deputies began the debate concerning Huerta's legal position. During the debate Querido Moheno put the question squarely to the deputies: Huerta was determined to have his position legalized and counted on support from the army, which was "resolved to go ahead, even if principles are destroyed."[16] Moheno and some of his friends gave consistent support to Huerta during these early days not, according to his account, because of any admiration for Huerta, but rather out of fear of Félix Díaz. "Huerta, in effect, was a doubt, while Félix Díaz was a black certainty."[17] The whole tenor of the deliberations changed when it was announced, late in the afternoon, that Madero and Pino Suárez had resigned, for now the question revolved around the acceptance of the resignations. Whether Madero and Pino were forced to resign under duress is tenable but not positive; it is perfectly clear, however, that some members of the Chamber of Deputies and most of

[12] Hale to Wilson, June 18, 1913, file 812.00/7798½, NA, RG 59.

[13] Stenographic report of debate of February 19, in Acuña, *Memoria*, pp. 74–95.

[14] Statement by forty-eight deputies, July 17, 1914, ibid., pp. 41–43.

[15] Some members were in hiding, some simply refused to attend, and some did not receive notice of the meeting called.

[16] Q. Moheno in Chamber of Deputies debate, February 19, 1913, in Acuña, *Memoria*, p. 76.

[17] Querido Moheno, *Mi actuación política después de la decena trágica*, p. 19. Moheno makes no reference to the Chamber debates.

Madero's intimates believed that failure to accept his resignation would mean his death.[18] Presidential and vice-presidential resignations, according to the constitution, put Minister of Foreign Relations Pedro Lascuráin in line for the succession, but it was necessary for him to take the oath of office in the presence of the Chamber of Deputies. At this point the question of Huerta's legality intrudes, even if Madero's resignation is accepted as bona fide. Immediately after the Chamber accepted the tendered resignations, a number of the members left; it is doubtful that a quorum of that body was present to hear Lascuráin take the oath. Within minutes Lascuráin appointed Huerta to head the Ministry of Gobernación and then in turn resigned. Each of these steps, in order to be legal, had to be approved by the Chamber of Deputies, but after each action the number of deputies dwindled; by the time Huerta took the oath of office only a very small number remained in the Chamber.[19] Even on technical legal grounds, then, the Huerta government was not a legal government.[20]

When Huerta sent his February 18 message to the state governors, some of them immediately tendered recognition, while some remained mute; only one state took a categorically negative position. As soon as he received the message, Governor Venustiano Carranza of Coahuila called an emergency session of the state congress, which met late on the night of February 18 and, soon after midnight,[21] passed a resolution denying recognition to Huerta, giving emergency powers to the governor, and inviting other state governments to support Coahuila's actions.[22] Furthermore, the Coahuila governor

[18] A number of speakers, including Alfonso Cravioto, pointed out that probability during the debate.

[19] Statement by forty-eight deputies, July 17, 1914, in Acuña, *Memoria*, pp. 41–43.

[20] A memorandum dated July 14, 1913, drafted by Fred Morris Dearing for the edification of Secretary of State William Jennings Bryan, stated in its original form that Huerta's "accession to power was perfectly legal." Someone a little more sophisticated, or careful, changed the wording to read "is claimed to be perfectly legal" (file 812.00/8066, NA, RG 59).

[21] Breceda, *México revolucionario*, I, 141–145.

[22] File 812.00/6432, NA, RG 59. The resolution is dated February 19, since the official action was taken after midnight.

dispatched messages to the other state governors in the sense of the resolution, but Huerta's control of the means of communication prevented delivery of all but a few. After the "legalization" of his seizure on February 19, Huerta was somewhat disturbed by the failure of the state governments to volunteer submission, and accordingly on February 22 he ordered Minister of Gobernación Alberto García Granados to obtain an immediate reply from all state governors. Some of the governors reluctantly adhered: Ramón Cepeda of San Luis Potosí replied, "I will sacrifice all my patriotism for the reestablishment of peace and order,"[23] and in so replying showed quite clearly his disgust as well as his weakness. Some were noncommittal: Antonio P. Rivera of Veracruz stated simply that he had already taken the necessary steps to assure "order and public tranquility."[24] A few were enthusiastic: F. B. Y. Barrientos of Puebla assured the Huerta government that "with the greatest good will" he would do whatever was in his power to "assist in the reestablishment of peace."[25] The governors of two states, Sonora and Chihuahua, did not answer at all; his failure to answer cost Governor Abraham González of Chihuahua both his post and his life. Arrested and removed from his office on February 23 by General Antonio Rábago on orders from Huerta, González was held a few days and finally subjected to the *ley fuga* (that is, shot on the pretense that he was attempting to escape) at Mapula, Chihuahua, on March 7, 1913. Carranza of Coahuila did answer: on February 25 he proposed to García Granados a conference by means of the telegraph system in order "to bring about a solution in the delicate situation" existing.[26] Even before García Granados's message, Carranza had apparently taken a similar step. On February 22 he had notified Huerta that he

[23] Cepeda to SecGob, February 24, 1914, Acuña, *Memoria*, p. 96.

[24] Rivera to SecGob, February 24, 1913, ibid., p. 96.

[25] Barrientos to SecGob, February 23, 1913, ibid.

[26] Bernardino Mena Brito, *Carranza: Sus amigos, sus enemigos*, p. 647. According to available documents and sources, Carranza received the García Granados message on February 25, three days after its dispatch and over two days after Madero's assassination. Peripheral evidence and the sequence of events, however, suggest that Carranza in actuality received the message on February 22, but for reasons of his own preferred to hide the actual date of reception.

was sending two representatives to discuss with Huerta the existing situation.[27] He closed, "I hope that the affairs with which the said gentlemen will treat will be satisfactorily arranged."[28] Furthermore, according to Consul Philip E. Holland at Saltillo, Carranza had decided at noon on February 21 to recognize Huerta and had so informed the consul, even though only a few hours before he had told the consul that he intended to oppose Huerta with every possible means and that "his opposition meant a revolution of far more import than the country had previously experienced."[29]

Carranza's inconsistencies during the critical days immediately following the coup d'état have left him open to severe criticism, both in Mexico and abroad. Many of his messages were contradictory and at least some of his orders were similarly inconsistent; he ordered his brother Jesús to suspend all military operations in late February, for example, telling him and Pablo González that he had arranged peace with Huerta. But at virtually the same time that he was dictating the mollifying telegram to García Granados he was also dictating a message to Washington; when he was informed—erroneously—that President Taft had recognized Huerta he penned a bitter note to the U.S. government: "The haste with which your government has recognized the spurious government which Huerta is attempting to establish with treason and crime has brought to the State of Coahuila, which I represent, a civil war which soon will be extended to all the nation. The Mexican Nation condemns the villainous *cuartelazo* which has deprived it of its constitutional rulers . . . I hope that your successor will act with greater circumspection with respect to the social and political interest of my country."[30] Furthermore, he ordered that the rail lines between Saltillo and San Luis Potosí and between Saltillo and Torreón be cut.[31]

[27] Eliseo Arredondo, who made the trip from Saltillo to Mexico City for that express purpose, and Rafael Arizpe y Ramos, who lived in Mexico City, were the deputies.

[28] Carranza to Huerta, February 22, 1913, in Breceda, *México revolucionario*, I, 163.

[29] Holland to SecState, February 21, 1913, file 812.00/6472, NA, RG 59.

[30] Breceda, *México revolucionario*, I, 218.

[31] Ibid., p. 219.

Since Carranza's indecision served as a base for a subsequent campaign to bring the Constitutionalist movement into disrepute,[32] the reasons for the vacillation are of some import. First, it must be pointed out that most of the inconsistencies appear in the form of Carranza messages sent over the national telegraphic system to which, of course, the Huerta government had access. In Mexico City rumors were circulating to the effect that Carranza was gathering men, but at the same time not only did Huerta have the two messages sent to his government—one proposing a telegraphic conference with García Granados and the other announcing the imminent arrival of Carranza's emissaries—but he also had copies of the other messages indicating a willingness to come to terms as well as the information from the U.S. Embassy concerning Carranza's conversation with Philip Holland. The key to the question seems to be one of time, which Carranza desperately needed and which he succeeded in obtaining. He needed time not only to make financial arrangements, but also to extricate some of his loyal followers from uncomfortable positions. On February 19, when the original resolution condemning Huerta was passed, the Coahuila "irregulars" were far from Saltillo. Venustiano's brother Jesús, a colonel in the state forces, was stationed in the environs of Torreón, virtually under the eyes of federal General Fernando Trucy Aubert, and would be a logical subject for reprisal in case Huerta became convinced of the necessity for force. By various ruses, including telling General Trucy Aubert that Jesús wanted to confer with the federal general concerning political questions,[33] Carranza was able to give Jesús sufficient time to march his small force beyond the area dominated by the federal forces. Colonel Pablo González, commanding the other

[32] See particularly "El verdadero origen de la revolución constitucionalista" in the June 24, 1917, issue of *Revista Mexicana* and the lengthy polemic carried on in the columns of Mexican newspapers in late 1933 and early 1934. Many of these latter articles are conveniently found in Mena Brito, *Carranza.*

[33] Carranza to Trucy Aubert, February 23, 1913, in Breceda, *México revolucionario*, I, 165. Trucy Aubert guaranteed a safe conduct to Jesús for the conference; Jesús, instead of conferring with the general, used the extra day to slip between posts manned by federal regulars.

principal contingent of state forces, was in northern Chihuahua, where he had been operating with federal forces against the remnants of the Orozco rebellion. On February 11, after the beginning of the Tragic Ten Days but before the coup d'état, and at Carranza's orders, he began a return to Coahuila by an overland march;[34] not until late February was he safely beyond the surveillance of the federal regulars.[35] The combined forces under Jesús and González became the nucleus of the Constitutionalist army, but it appears quite certain that neither force could have reached the relative safety of central Coahuila had Carranza not gained time for them to move.

Quite aside from the problems involved in maneuvering his pitifully small loyal force, Carranza had a major problem of finances. The state treasury itself, subject to Carranza and his immediate group, was not particularly affluent at the moment; cash was scarce and badly needed. The small resources available in the treasury were distributed among various leaders chosen by Carranza; among those to receive money directly from the treasury in order to equip forces were Francisco Coss, Eulalio Gutiérrez, and Jacinto B. Treviño.[36] A much more important source was borrowed money, but borrowing money necessitated considerable negotiation. Even before the coup d'état had taken place, the legislature had authorized the governor to borrow "up to three hundred thousand pesos, under the best repayment and interest conditions which circumstances permit."[37] Using this authorization, Carranza almost immediately began negotiations with local representatives of banking houses, but the bankers were not anxious to become embroiled in the pending revolution. Negotiations consequently dragged on for nearly two

[34] González insists this action was on his own initiative, but the sparse documentation indicates a prior agreement with Carranza.

[35] Pablo González, "Tergiversaciones históricos" in *El Universal*, May 7, 1934; Mena Brito, *Carranza*, pp. 301–309.

[36] G. Espinosa Mireles to Carranza, January 18, 1920, Archivo Histórico de la Secretaría de Defensa Nacional (hereafter abbreviated ADN), DF 1920. Espinosa was seeking reimbursement to Coahuila from the national government.

[37] Decree 1487, February 17, 1913, in Breceda, *México revolucionario*, I, 158.

weeks, and it was during these critical weeks that Carranza kept Huerta at bay with his vacillations. In view of the reports Huerta was receiving from the north, he decided on February 26 to send Colonel Arnoldo Caso López and his troops, then stationed in San Luis Potosí, to Saltillo to force Carranza to define his stand. Eliseo Arredondo in Mexico City adroitly prevented the movement and gained a little more time.[38] On March 3, Carranza completed his arrangements with the banks, pledging the state credit for a loan of 75,000 pesos;[39] four banks were involved in the transactions. Huerta was aware, through a multitude of messages from Saltillo residents, that Carranza was engaged in financial negotiations, and he was quickly informed when the negotiations were completed. On March 4 he sent the following message to Carranza: "Please inform with what object you have removed fifty thousand pesos from the banks, since this Government has no knowledge of the event."[40] The Coahuila governor was ready to make his position absolutely clear: "I have removed no money from banks to which you refer; and had I done so it would not be to you that I should give an accounting."[41] From that point forward there could be no mistake concerning Carranza's intention; three days later, at Anhelo, the governor's forces for the first time engaged in battle with the federals.

In the meantime, Ambassador Henry Lane Wilson in Mexico City was doing all he could to "pacify" Mexico by convincing potential rebel leaders of the futility of rebellion. From the beginning of the Tragic Ten Days he used the power of his office in an attempt to force Madero's resignation,[42] and immediately after the coup d'état he gleefully reported that "a wicked despotism" had fallen, and that the new government was installed "amid great popular demonstra-

[38] Ibid., pp. 173–174.

[39] G. Espinosa Mireles to Carranza, January 18, 1920, ADN-DF 1920.

[40] Huerta to Carranza, March 4, 1913, in Breceda, *México revolucionario*, I, 161.

[41] Carranza to Huerta, March 4, 1913, ibid., p. 161.

[42] Among other things, he virtually convinced a number of important politicians that U.S. intervention was imminent and inevitable unless the bombardment ceased.

tions of approval."[43] Since the new government was in part, at least, a creature of his own devising,[44] he hoped to use his position to obtain recognition for the new regime both abroad and within Mexico. He obliquely urged recognition to Taft on February 20[45] and the following day reported that the "Diplomatic Corps . . . agreed that recognition of the new Government was imperative, to enable it to impose its authority and reestablish order."[46] Not content to urge on Washington recognition by foreign governments, Wilson at the same time circularized all U.S. consuls in Mexico: "General public approval of Congress in this city, which is perfectly quiet; reassuring reports come from other places . . . Senate and Chamber of Deputies in full accord with new administration. You should make this intelligence public, and in the interest of Mexico urge general submission and adhesion to the new Government, *which will be recognized by all foreign governments today*."[47]

His maneuvers came close to success, at least as far as Washington was concerned. Secretary of State Philander C. Knox, influenced by the Wilson telegrams, was "disposed to consider the new Provisional Government as being legally established," but he wanted some conditions imposed as a price for recognition.[48] Furthermore, according to one of the officials in the Department of State, the Taft administration "saw in the situation at that time a possibility that the Mexicans would be able to work out their own problem, [and] there

[43] Ambassador Wilson to SecState, February 20, 1913, file 812.00/6287, NA, RG 59.

[44] Even though the extent of the ambassador's responsibility for the events leading to the coup d'état and the coup d'état itself may be debated, his influence in the choice of the new cabinet cannot be denied.

[45] Wilson to SecState, February 20, 1913, file 812.00/6287, NA, RG 59.

[46] Wilson to SecState, February 21, 1913, file 812.00/6319, NA, RG 59. Márquez Sterling of Cuba and Cologan of Spain both insist that Wilson's reference to the Diplomatic Corps was deliberately erroneous, since in actuality only a few members were consulted.

[47] Wilson to SecState, February 23, 1913, enclosing circular to consuls of February 21, 1913, file 812.00/6325, NA, RG 59 (italics added). Wilson was either deliberately misleading or extraordinarily presumptuous.

[48] SecState to H. L. Wilson, February 21, 1913, file 812.00/6325a, NA, RG 59.

was a strong disposition to lend the new set of men who came to head of affairs . . . every possible moral assistance."[49]

After Madero's assassination, Ambassador Wilson redoubled his efforts. He accepted at face value the Huerta version of the killing, consistently reported all evidence of pacification while playing down evidence of unrest, diplomatically belabored the Department of State for not granting recognition, and pressed the consular officers to exert themselves "without ceasing to bring about the general submission to the Provisional Government."[50] The ambassador was, in his own words, "endeavoring in all possible ways . . . to aid [the Huerta government] to establish itself firmly and to procure the submission and adhesion of all elements in the Republic."[51] If we believe the Carrancista account, "all possible ways" included telling Carranza that Washington had recognized the Huerta government;[52] certainly Carranza believed that recognition had been granted when he wrote his bitter note of February 25. Whether the ambassador was guilty of deliberately falsifying is questionable, but certain it is that he displayed frenetic zeal in upholding the Huerta point of view, whether the question at issue concerned Madero's assassination or peaceful conditions in Mexico.

[49] State Dept. Division of Latin American Affairs memo to SecState, July 14, 1913, file 812.00/8066, NA, RG 59.

[50] Wilson to Louis Hostetter, February 26, as quoted in Hostetter to SecState, March 1, 1913, file 812.00/6521, NA, RG 59.

[51] Wilson to SecState, February 26, 1913, file 812.00/6394, NA, RG 59. Knox and the Department of State did not object to these activities (see SecState to Wilson, February 28, 1913, file 812.00/6394).

[52] Acuña, *Memoria*, pp. 46–47.

2. THE ARMIES ROLL

In the meantime, despite Ambassador Wilson's best efforts, revolutionary or quasi-revolutionary activity spread outside Carranza's Coahuila. Even while the Sonora governor, José María Maytorena, was insisting to Carranza that the northwestern state was tranquil and disposed to recognize Huerta as the legitimate president,[1] U.S. Consul Thomas D. Bowman in Nogales reported resentment and bitterness and prophesied rebellion.[2] Furthermore, local leaders in Fronteras, Nacozari, Cananea, and Agua Prieta took bellicose action immediately after receiving word of Madero's assassination.[3] In order to counteract the threat to Cananea, whose inhabitants, still

[1] Ismael Padilla, Maytorena's secretary, conferred with Carranza in Saltillo on February 25, at which time he insisted that Sonora would recognize Huerta (see Alfredo Breceda, *México revolucionario, 1913–1917*, I, 209–216).

[2] Bowman to SecState, February 24, 1913, file 812.00/6342, NA, RG 59.

[3] Juan Barragán, *Historia del ejército y de la revolución constitucionalista*, I, 132–133.

smarting with the memory of the bitter strike seven years before,[4] had no illusions concerning the implications of Huerta's seizure of power, the Naco federal garrison was dispatched to the mining center. Naco, as a consequence, was left undefended against rebel forces then gathering in the vicinity.[5]

Governor Maytorena was in a quandary. His state was in an obviously ugly mood,[6] but he himself was unwilling to engage in a test of strength with the new dictatorship; taking the easy way out, he asked for sick leave and left immediately for the United States.[7] The state legislature selected Ignacio Pesqueira as acting governor, lengthily debated the question of recognition, and, stimulated by sporadic rebellious activities,[8] agreed on March 5 to reject categorically Huerta's claim to legality.[9] Governor Pesqueira, in both his address to the legislature[10] and his notification to Mexico City,[11] emphasized federal attempts to undermine state sovereignty rather than the constitutionality of the new regime; the Sonora rebellion, therefore, was based upon a different legal assumption than was that in Coahuila under Carranza. Maytorena, after first attempting to "unify the discontented" and to convince Sonora to accept Huerta,[12] ultimately decided to support the action taken by his compatriots. From Tucson, Arizona, he requested the new Wilson administration "not to recognize the usurped Government of Gen-

[4] See Herbert O. Brayer, "The Cananea Incident," *New Mexico Historical Review* 13 (1938): 387–415, and Manuel González Ramírez, *La huelga de Cananea*, passim.

[5] Mexican Consul, Naco, Arizona, to SecRel, February 26, 1913, ADN-Sonora 1913.

[6] Consul Louis Hostetter reported that the majority of the Sonorans objected to Huerta (Hostetter to SecState, February 28, 1913, file 812.00/6434, NA, RG 59).

[7] Bowman to SecState, February 28, 1913, file 812.00/6435, NA, RG 59.

[8] Local leaders like Plutarco Elías Calles and Arnulfo Gómez burned bridges, seized municipalities, and cut rail lines.

[9] Decree 122, March 5, 1913, in Barragán, *Ejército*, I, 133–134.

[10] Pesqueira's message is reproduced in ibid., pp. 638–641.

[11] Pesqueira to SecGob, March 6, 1913, in ibid., p. 134.

[12] Ismael Padilla was again Maytorena's messenger (see José S. Sáenz to SecRel., March 4, 1913, ADN-Sonora 1913).

eral Huerta until the people of the Republic of Mexico have [had] an opportunity to establish a government by the choice of the people."[13]

After March 5 the revolution became an organized movement. Pesqueira designated Alvaro Obregón, a small landowner and municipal president who had proved himself to be a loyal Maderista with military talent during the Orozco rebellion, as the chief of military operations in the state. At the same time he selected steadfast Maderistas Benjamín Hill, Salvador Alvarado, and Juan G. Cabral as *jefes de operaciones* in the southern, central, and northern sectors respectively. The state capital firmly in their hands, within ten days the rebels isolated Guaymas,[14] captured Nacozari,[15] forced the federals to evacuate Agua Prieta,[16] captured Nogales while the federals fled across the international boundary line to the United States,[17] and finally suffered a minor setback at Naco.[18] But Obregón took personal command of the region, isolated federal General Pedro Ojeda in Naco by feinting and skirmishing, and then fell on Cananea; after a listless defense and in the face of a threatened mutiny by his men, the federal commander capitulated on March 25.[19] By that date, then, rebels held virtually all of the state north of Guaymas,[20]

[13] Maytorena to SecState, March 7, 1913, file 812.00/6553, NA, RG 59. Maytorena's actions during the two weeks after Madero's assassination are indeed puzzling, with many indications of moral cowardice. But throughout his career Maytorena demonstrated decision and fidelity to his concepts.

[14] SecHacienda to SecGyM, March 7, 1913, ADN-Sonora 1913.

[15] Mexican Consul, Naco, Arizona, to SecRel, March 11, 1913, ADN-Sonora 1913. The rebel force was about six hundred men.

[16] Mexican Consul, Douglas, Arizona, to SecRel, March 11, 1913, and Mexican Consul, Naco, Arizona, to SecRel, March 12, 1913, both in ADN-Sonora 1913. An estimated two thousand rebels were in the Agua Prieta region; the federals went to Nogales when they evacuated Agua Prieta.

[17] General Miguel Ruelas to SecGyM, April 16, 1913, ADN-Sonora 1913.

[18] General Pedro Ojeda to SecGyM, March 16, 1913, ADN-Sonora 1913.

[19] General E. Camargo to SecGyM, September 6, 1913, ADN-Sonora 1913. Camargo summarized the reports and bitterly criticized the tactics used in the defense.

[20] The Sonora revolutionaries preferred to call themselves "state forces" rather than either rebels or revolutionaries at that date.

including both Agua Prieta and Nogales, the two major ports of entry.[21]

While Sonora was going through the throes of beginning rebellion, neighboring Chihuahua manifested the same discontent but was in a completely different condition. Chihuahua, much more so than Sonora, was gripped by anti-Madero feeling among the upper classes long before the February coup d'état; even though staunch Maderista Abraham González was governor, the capital city was sullen with resentment against the Madero reform plans and generally supported the moribund Orozco rebellion. Immediately after Madero's assassination, the local federal army commander arrested Governor González, dissolved the state government, and installed a Huertista sympathizer in the gubernatorial office. In early March, Huerta minions assassinated González and terrorized[22] other Maderistas to the point that no Maderista of any stature was left to give leadership to a coordinated movement. The Chihuahua revolution consequently was left in the hands of the crude and the feral, of whom Manuel Chao, Tomás Urbina, and Francisco Villa were the best examples. They had not waited for a call from political leaders. They had organized quickly on their own initiative during the last week of February, and on the twenty-eighth one of their contingents had captured Santa Rosalía.[23] Three days later Maclovio Herrera led a successful rebel attack on Namiquipa in the western Chihuahua mountains,[24] and on March 5 Manuel Chao with fifteen hundred

[21] Control of the ports of entry was highly important to the rebels, since they could legally export material to the United States, obtain cash, and surreptitiously bring in arms and ammunition.

[22] On March 6 González was sent under escort to Mexico City; he was removed from the train near Mapula in the southern part of the state and killed (Marion Letcher to SecState, October 17, 1913, file 812.00/9484, NA, RG 59). Among the methods of terror, as described by U.S. Consul Letcher, were frequent arbitrary arrests and a number of summary executions without benefit of trial. Known Madero sympathizers simply disappeared from public view within the first three weeks after the *cuartelazo*.

[23] General Eutiquio Munguía to SecGyM, March 1, 1913, ADN-Chihuahua 1913. A week later General Antonio Rábago retook the village.

[24] General M. Ruelas to Departamento de Infantería, March 23, 1913, ADN-Coahuila 1913.

men attacked Parral, near the Durango border.[25] The federals beat off Chao after a bitter three-day battle, but at a high cost: a third of General Salvador Mercado's command lost in dead or wounded and another major portion lost through desertion.[26] The battle, though a rebel defeat, was an omen of things to come, since it was a perfect demonstration of potential rebel strength. During this battle federal officers murdered González some miles to the east.

At approximately the same hour that Chao withdrew from battle at Parral and Abraham González from life at Mapula, Francisco Villa entered the ranks of the revolution by crossing the border from El Paso with eight men and nine hundred dollars—the money a gift from Adolfo de la Huerta and José María Maytorena—to begin his ten-year career as hero and scourge of the north country.[27] Not yet thirty-five years of age, Villa was a seasoned campaigner with nearly two decades of experience as bandit, rebel, and Maderista "irregular" general;[28] in this last capacity during the 1912 Orozco uprising, Huerta had accused him of insubordination in the field, had subjected him to a drumhead court-martial, and had condemned him to the firing squad. Saved from death by the arrival of a stay-of-execution order from President Madero,[29] Villa was sent to a military prison in Mexico City to await a more formal trial, and from that prison he escaped in November, 1912. Beating his way northwest-

[25] General E. Munguía to SecGyM, March 5, 1913, ADN-Chihuahua 1913 (Marzo). Manuel Chao to General Salvador Mercado, March 5, 1913, ADN-Chihuahua 1913 (Marzo). Chao, who said he had a force of fifteen hundred men, demanded that Mercado either surrender or come outside the town to join battle. When Mercado declined to do either, Chao attacked.

[26] General S. Mercado to General A. Rábago, March 20, 1913, ADN-Chihuahua 1913 (Marzo); General E. Munguía to SecGyM, March 8, 1913, ADN-Coahuila 1913. The deserters were nearly all from a volunteer group from the state of San Luis Potosí.

[27] Roberto Guzmán Esparza, *Memorias de Don Adolfo de la Huerta según su propio dictado*, p. 57.

[28] The "irregulars" during all this period were volunteer groups officered by men who were not in the regular army. The officers' concepts of military discipline were rudimentary, but they were generally tough men who engendered a deep sense of loyalty.

[29] Villa was actually standing before the firing squad, smoking his final cigarette, when the message arrived.

ward by various means, always apprehensive of arrest, Villa crossed into Nogales, Arizona, on January 2. The journey from Nogales to Tucson and thence to El Paso took a few more days; once in El Paso he wired Abraham González in Chihuahua to the effect that he was safe and could be counted upon in case of any need. At the time of the coup d'état Villa had enormous admiration, respect, and devotion for González and Madero; in his particular pantheon the seats of the most select were reserved for these two—pristine, pure, perfect examples of humanity in Villa's eyes. His adulation for Madero and González was equalled by his ferocious hatred for Huerta, the man who had attempted to railroad him into death, and who now betrayed his heroes. Villa entered the revolution with a burning vengeance, which gave a peculiar zest to all his activities.

During the remainder of March, 1913, Villa slowly gathered an army; from community to community, village to village, he made his way through central and western Chihuahua, and everywhere men flocked to his leadership. While Villa recruited, others raided. Chao and the Herreras seized small towns, burned bridges, cut telegraph wires, and harassed the federal forces wherever they might be found in the western mountains.[30] Toribio Ortega threatened Ojinaga on the Río Grande to such an extent that the federal troops demanded to be mustered out—and promptly joined the rebels.[31] Rosalío Hernández and Tomás Urbina in the southeast made life miserable for the federal garrisons, occasionally occupying Jiménez or other smaller places. By the end of the month, reported railroad officials, rebel bands roamed through the southern and western portions, attacked trains, seized gold and silver shipments (extremely valuable to finance the rebel armies), and generally wreaked such havoc on the rail and telegraph lines that communication between Chihuahua and Torreón was nonexistent except for short periods of time.[32] Repair crews sent from Chihuahua or Torreón laboriously reestablished communications periodically, only to see the repairs destroyed and to be forced to scurry back to home base in fear of their lives.

[30] S. Mercado to A. Rábago, April 19, 1913, ADN-Chihuahua 1913 (Marzo).
[31] A. Rábago to SecGyM, April 5, 1913, ADN–Chihuahua 1913 (Marzo).
[32] Luis Riba to SecGyM, April 14, 1913, ADN-Chihuahua 1913 (Abril).

Within six weeks after Huerta seized power, federal control in the state was limited to the major concentrations of population: Chihuahua, Ciudad Juárez, Parral, Jiménez, and a few other places. For the federals, conditions were bad and prospects bleak; they never regained real control of the state.

Torreón, in the heart of the rich Laguna district, was and is the economic and transportation nerve center for most of Mexico north of Zacatecas and east of the Sierra Madre. Its connections with Durango, Zacatecas, Chihuahua, and Saltillo made it of crucial military importance, and here resided the headquarters of a vast military district. Torreón itself was certainly too strongly held to be attacked frontally, but the strength of Torreón did not deter rebel activity in the vicinity, and in early March, federal General Eutiquio Munguía began to reinforce some of his outlying posts. San Pedro de las Colonias, a relatively rich agricultural town a few miles to the east, was then protected by José Jesús "Cheche" Campos, an Orozco sympathizer in rebellion against Madero at the time of *cuartelazo* who had recently sworn to uphold the Huerta government. Pascual Orozco himself had also agreed to support Huerta, and on March 3 the Orozquistas were ordered to San Pedro to reinforce "Cheche" Campos.[33] Before the new force arrived, however, and at the moment Chao attacked Parral two hundred miles away, Roberto Rivas took the town after an hour's battle; his task was made infinitely easier than he expected when most of Campos's men deserted and virtually all the local police joined Rivas's force. Rivas stayed in San Pedro only long enough to collect nearly ten thousand dollars in "loans" and to recruit a few men; on March 7 he rode out one side of San Pedro while federal reinforcements rode in on the other.[34]

While the Sonora, Chihuahua, and Laguna rebels raided and burned, Carranza in the Saltillo region marched and countermarched but did not fight. It was not necessary. Saltillo was, on paper, a

[33] General M. Mondragón to General A. Rábago, March 3, 1913, ADN-Chihuahua 1913 (Marzo). Orozco was then on his way to an interview with Huerta in Mexico City.

[34] Multitudinous reports giving the details of the attack are to be found in ADN–Coahuila 1913 (Marzo).

major garrison point with a general in command—but the garrison was nonexistent and the general had no command, only a staff. A few federal troops were stationed at Múzquiz and Piedras Negras,[35] but they were too small to take effective defensive or offensive action. The Múzquiz garrison simply declared in favor of Carranza,[36] and the Piedras Negras contingent abandoned that city to Jesús Carranza without a fight in late February. A federal force from Monterrey made motions in the direction of Saltillo before the end of February, but the Carrancistas frustrated the federal plan by a ruse,[37] and by the time Carranza had completed his financial transactions he was free to travel in any part of the state save the Laguna district.[38] But his position in Saltillo, between the major garrison points of Torreón and Monterrey, was clearly untenable, since he had neither sufficient men nor enough matériel to withstand an attack. His wanderings in the Saltillo–Arteaga–Ramos Arizpe triangle, designed primarily to keep the federals uneasy,[39] simply had to come to an end, and in early March he decided to abandon Saltillo for a haven in Monclova, less vulnerable to attack. While on this hegira he tasted his first military action when he was completely surprised by General Fernando Trucy Aubert, on the way to Saltillo with eight hundred men, at Anhelo on March 7; after a short, sharp skirmish Carranza withdrew his small force.[40]

[35] The presence of the federal troops in Coahuila had been the subject of a dispute between Carranza and President Madero; and this dispute gave rise to the claim that Carranza planned to rebel.

[36] A. A. Horcasitas to Subdirector de la Comisión Geográfica, April 19, 1913, ADN-Coahuila 1913 (Mayo).

[37] According to Constitutionalist sources, General M. T. Blázquez left Monterrey with a considerable force to occupy Saltillo on February 25. Jacinto B. Treviño and a few men created a dust cloud by dragging trees over the dry ground and convinced Blázquez that he was confronting a major force, whereupon the federals returned to Monterrey (Barragán, *Ejército*, I, 90).

[38] When Ambassador Wilson reported in early March that Carranza was a "fugitive from justice" he was expressing a hope, not a fact.

[39] His maneuvering did prevent Munguía in Torreón from going to the aid of Santa Rosalía on March 1.

[40] General F. Trucy Aubert to SecGyM, March 13, 1913, ADN-Coahuila 1913 (Marzo); Breceda, *México revolucionario*, I, 245–246. In order to create the impression that he had won a major victory, Trucy reported that the Carranza

The federalist press pictured Carranza's Anhelo defeat as a major government victory. In order to counteract the adverse publicity, which would tend to discourage rebel recruitment, Carranza decided to reoccupy Saltillo by force of arms. After spending two weeks gathering and provisioning an army of roughly six hundred men,[41] early on the morning of March 21 Carranza had his force deployed around what he thought was a lightly garrisoned city. Unfortunately for Carranza's hopes, during the night federal Colonel Arnoldo Caso López arrived in Saltillo with over a thousand officers and men, and, according to reports, more were on the the way. From Arteaga, ten miles to the east, Carranza demanded Caso López's surrender; when the federal commander refused, the attack on the city began.[42] Even under the best of circumstances, given Caso López's superior forces and armament,[43] the capture of Saltillo would have been difficult; but the Carranza forces—through poor coordination, poor information, poor scouting, and bad tactics—materially aided the defenders. After fifty-five hours and heavy casualties,[44] Carranza broke off the attack and took his forces northward.[45] Caso López, anxious to impress his superiors with his military prowess, vastly overestimated the size of the attacking force and reported that the revolutionary army had been destroyed.[46] A grateful Huerta-appointed governor, in order to commemorate the event properly, had medals struck for

---

force numbered about nine hundred. In fact, Carranza had less than half that number, and the affair was a minor skirmish, not a battle, in which the casualties were practically nil.

41 Luis Medina Barrón to SecGyM, May 15, 1913, ADN-Coahuila 1913 (Marzo). Medina Barrón, criticized for not reinforcing Caso López, may have underestimated the number.

42 A. Caso López report, March 24, 1913, ADN-Coahuila 1913 (Marzo).

43 The Carrancistas had only one machine gun.

44 Caso López said that the attackers lost 180 men, 180 wounded, and 200 captured; this is certainly an overestimate, but casualties were undoubtedly heavy.

45 Breceda, *México revolucionario*, I, 392. Breceda was on Carranza's staff and a participant in the battle.

46 Caso López estimated that about eighteen hundred rebels were involved. The federal commander virtually always reported that the enemy was "destroyed" as a future force, but somehow they always came back.

all the defenders—gold, silver, and bronze for the senior officers, junior officers, and troops, respectively; the medals were paid for by "popular subscription,"[47] further demonstrating Huerta's popularity in Saltillo.

Carranza, according to one of his doting companions, was pleased at the outcome of the battle. The fact that he had led, however poorly, a sizable force and had managed to threaten a major federal force he interpreted as a moral victory and one that would still for all time any lingering doubts concerning his determination to reinstall constitutional government.[48] In all probability Carranza did crow to his companions in this general vein, but the self-styled chief of the Constitutionalist forces most assuredly recognized the outcome for what it was, a defeat that Huerta could and would use to the utmost for propaganda. Again, as after the Anhelo defeat, Carranza countered with what he considered a bold move of his own. But this time he depended upon pen and ink instead of bullets; the result was the Plan de Guadalupe.

In the neighboring state of Durango revolutionary activity began soon after the coup d'état, but none of the major state officials were overtly involved. To be sure, both Governor Carlos Patoni (on leave from his gubernatorial duties) and Acting Governor Jesús Perea demonstrated a degree of sympathy for the rebels, but they were extremely circumspect. As was the case in Chihuahua, the rebels were led by the untutored and semiliterate: Orestes Pereyra, Calixto Contreras, Domingo and Mariano Arrieta, and, later, Tomás Urbina. In early March the attacks were merely raids, not differing greatly from those in Sonora at the same time—or from bandit raids. By the third week in March both tempo and character had changed materially; the rebels almost completely dominated the environs of both the capital city and the major habitations in the Laguna district.[49]

[47] Decree of April 19, 1913, in *Periódico Oficial del Gobierno del Estado Libre y Soberano de Coahuila de Zaragoza* 21, no. 34 (1913): 1. Ignacio Alcocer was the governor.

[48] Breceda, *México revolucionario*, I, 392–393.

[49] General M. Ruelas to Jefe del Depto. de Caballería, April 19, 1913, ADN-Durango 1913, and other documents in same file.

The situation so alarmed General Munguía in Torreón that he insisted upon the "urgent necessity of sending to Durango a strong garrison" to hold that city.[50] The federals there did hold the city temporarily, but by month's end all the state, save the capital and the towns close to Torreón, was in rebel hands; the capital city was isolated from the rest of the country.[51]

By the end of March, in some of the other states a modicum of rebel activity could be found. Pánfilo Natera busied himself gathering a small band in Zacatecas. Jalisco and Michoacán were almost daily reporting "bandit" activities. Tamaulipas and Nuevo León were generally quiet, but small rebel bands gathered under Luis Caballero and other local leaders. Furthermore, on March 31 Jesús Agustín Castro's Twenty-first Corps of rurales, stationed in Tlalnepantla after being decimated during the Tragic Ten Days,[52] rebelled and began a three-week trek to the comparative safety of Tamaulipas.

One revolutionary group fighting Huerta was a different breed from the others. In the state of Morelos, just south of Mexico City, years of encroachment by the haciendas on the villages had driven the rural populace to desperation. Bands of men rose in revolt early in 1911 to support Madero in the hope that he would help them regain their lands and secure the integrity of the villages. The most important Morelos leader was Emiliano Zapata, a small farmer and livestock dealer and municipal president of Anenecuilco.[53] After

[50] General E. Munguía to SecGyM, March 22, 1913, ADN-Durango 1913.

[51] Memorándum de Sección 1/a de SecGob, March 13, 1913, Archivo General de la Nación (hereafter abbreviated AGN), Gobernación—Varios Ramos 1913–1914 (Estudios y Dictámenes Diversas). This memorandum, written nearly a year later, said that effective control of the state of Durango had been lost in early April, 1913.

[52] The Twenty-first Corps, obviously and enthusiastically Maderista, was considered by Huerta to be a danger to his plans in the early stages of the Tragic Ten Days. In order to weaken this potential threat, he sent the corps into an open frontal attack on the Ciudadela. The Félix Díaz forces cut the attackers to ribbons with machine guns.

[53] Zapata's rebellion was always peripheral to the larger revolution, although he was a constant thorn in the side of one or another national leader. He is

Díaz's fall, Madero tried to persuade Zapata and his rebels to disband and trust him. His efforts fell through when the interim government launched military operations against them; they dug in and fought; Madero finally lost patience, demanding unconditional submission before he would take up their claims.[54] So the Morelos movement settled into permanent rebellion under its own banner, the Plan de Ayala, which branded Madero a traitor and charted a land-reform program.[55] The Morelos insurrection was never a real threat to Madero's government, but it was increasingly troublesome and expensive. The 1913 coup in Mexico City changed nothing. The rebel chiefs considered Huerta (who had once commanded federal troops against them) not only politically illegitimate but also personally despicable.[56] Zapata simply changed the target of his ire and fought on. He was sporadically in touch with the Constitutionalists, sometimes cooperating with them militarily when there was action in his own backyard, but never really trusting them to do right by his people and their needs.

Most of the remainder of the country was fairly well under the control of the Huerta government, but there were indications, as in San Luis Potosí,[57] that a careful check would have to be kept to prevent new outbreaks.

Henry Lane Wilson nevertheless remained optimistic. In summarizing conditions, Ambassador Wilson found no evidences of insurrection in any state except Sonora, Coahuila, Durango, and Nuevo León; but, he concluded, "as to Coahuila, Durango, and

---

dealt with in this study only to the extent necessary to round out the main story. For a history of the Morelos revolution see John C. Womack, Jr.'s excellent and comprehensive *Zapata and the Mexican Revolution.*

[54] Charles C. Cumberland, *Mexican Revolution: Genesis under Madero*, pp. 173–183.

[55] The text of the plan may be found in Manuel González Ramírez, ed., *Planes políticos y otros documentos*, pp. 73–78.

[56] Gildardo Magaña and Carlos Pérez Guerrero, *Emiliano Zapata y el agrarismo en México*, III, 125–137.

[57] Dr. Rafael Cepeda, the Maderista governor of San Luis Potosí, was arrested on March 6, remaining in a federal prison until Carranza entered Mexico City in 1914. The indications are that Cepeda was on the verge of declaring in favor of Carranza.

Nuevo León, I believe conditions will steadily improve. The government expects to suppress at an early date the Sonora rebellion."[58]

Huerta, at least, was more realistic than Wilson, though he too believed his power would in the end prevail. But he recognized full well that not all was tea and toast in the northern states, and that his government would have to make a real effort to suppress the rebellion. In mid-March the dictator reminded the state governors to be prompt in furnishing the monthly quota of army recruits,[59] and two weeks later the central government was in "dire need" of men.[60]

Indeed the need for men was dire. Hacienda owners, military commanders, railroad officials, mining companies, and a multitude of others begged the central government to furnish greater numbers of men to give protection against what most of them called "bandit raids." That many of these activities were in fact mere raids by brigands who hoped to take advantage of the prevailing social and political disorganization admits of little doubt, but that the vast majority were inchoately expressing animosity for the Huerta government is equally true. In many respects the countryside, particularly that vast expanse north of Querétaro, was seething; to prevent a violent explosion Huerta needed men and more men. But even when he got men to serve in his forces, the crude recruiting methods gave no guarantee that the new recruits would actually stay with the government army during battle. The acuteness of the problem was summed up in General Munguía's plaintive wail to a court-martial a few months later: "How could I meet the rebels in the open? They fight in loose formation. I was obliged to keep my troops together. If I did not they would melt away. Desertion is the idea uppermost in almost every soldier's mind. Again, how could I order my officers to lead their men to attack? I knew their men would shoot them down as soon as they got a chance."[61]

[58] H. L. Wilson to SecState, April 4, 1913, file 812.00/7013, NA, RG 59. The ambassador's failure to mention Chihuahua is in itself interesting.

[59] SecGyM to SecGob, March 13, 1913, AGN-Gobernación—Varios Ramos—Prefectos municipales 1913–1914.

[60] Governor Antonio Puig Rivera (Veracruz) to SecGob, April 1, 1913, AGN—Gobernación—Varios Ramos—Prefectos municipales 1913–1914.

[61] As reported by Henry Hamilton Fyfe, *The Real Mexico*, p. 161. There is

In order to be assured of even the minimum number of men necessary to meet the demands, Huerta's government made herculean efforts and greater promises. During March, April, and May, according to government reports, federal recruitment reached a magnitude of fifteen or twenty thousand a month,[62] but like most of the information emanating from the government concerning its own strength and the rebels' weakness, this was an immense exaggeration.[63] Whether accurate or not, the figures represent an approximation of what Huerta thought would be necessary to consolidate his position through force.

Most of the month of April was characterized by the same general pattern as that evident in March, with one major exception: Durango. Rebel leaders Calixto Contreras, Orestes Pereyra, the Arrieta brothers, and Matías Pazuengo with a total of three to four thousand men by mid-April had Durango, with its seven hundred men under timorous General Antonio Escudero,[64] completely surrounded and under virtual siege.[65] So grave was the danger that five hundred of the younger men "from the most influential families of the city" constituted themselves as the Defensa Social to man the outposts and patrol the city in case of attack.[66] The city administration, insisting that Contreras was a bandit, even went so far as to request the U.S. Consulate to approve armed defense by American nationals resident there. Consul Theodore C. Hamm, certainly no champion of the revolutionists, answered with an unequivocal negative; he could not

---

some doubt as to the accuracy of these words attributed to Munguía, but they certainly express a prevailing concern.

[62] H. L. Wilson to SecState, May 15, 1913, file 812.00/7652, NA, RG 59.

[63] William Bayard Hale, President Wilson's representative in Mexico, reported that, in early July, Huerta claimed to have an army of 71,000 but Hale commented that "it may amount to Forty Thousand [*sic*]" (Hale memorandum, July 9, 1913, file 812.00/8203, NA, RG 59).

[64] Escudero, in spite of numerous suggestions, and even orders, to take the field against the rebels, discreetly stayed within the city. Furthermore, for some reason he refused to report conditions to Mexico City.

[65] Consul T. C. Hamm to SecState, May 14, 1913, file 812.00/7720, NA, RG 59. This report is in the form of a diary; Hamm used this technique rather than daily or weekly reports because of the limited lines of communication available.

[66] Ibid., April 17, 1913.

put his compatriots in an untenable position, he said, because, "although many of the acts recently perpetrated by the rebels are of a nature to make the average bandit blush for shame, still the fact remains that these rebel hordes are today in possession of by far the greater portion of the state of Durango and claim to be fighting for the reestablishment of the Madero regime."[67]

On April 20 the rebels severed the last remaining communication link, the telegraph line over the mountains to Mazatlán; the following day the revolutionary leaders issued a troop directive prohibiting looting but promising a forced loan in case the city were captured, and on April 23 they began an attack in force. During the two-day struggle one ugly facet of what was destined to be a dominant characteristic for the next few years emerged. Shortly after the attack began, the defenders captured twenty rebels who were, in Consul Hamm's words, "executed on the spot." Within a matter of hours some city residents, bitterly anti-Huerta, started firing on the government defenders; the influential young men of Defensa Social succeeded in "capturing the men responsible for these outrages; the majority of those captured were promptly executed, and in this manner the rear fire was speedily silenced."[68] The federals set the pattern, and Pereyra and Contreras exacted payment for these wanton executions when the city was finally captured in June. Executions on both sides, particularly of officers, came to be the mode.

On the afternoon of April 25 the rebels, weary, short of munitions, and threatened by the expected arrival of "Cheche" Campos and four hundred men from the Laguna district, broke off the attack. Within a matter of hours Campos arrived with his vanguard of four hundred, and shortly thereafter an additional four hundred arrived to bring the total defenders—including the Defensa Social volunteers—to over two thousand men. For the moment, at least, Durango was safely in federal hands but still isolated and still threatened.

April in Sonora was used to gather arms and men into some sem-

[67] Ibid., April 19, 1913.
[68] Ibid., April 24, 1913.

blance of military organization; by early May, Huerta officials reported that at least seven thousand Sonorans had enlisted in rebel armies. By mid-April the state forces had occupied Empalme without opposition;[69] there they remained until May 2, when Obregón withdrew his men in the face of a threat posed by two recently arrived warships. Taking all available railroad rolling stock and other needed matériel from Empalme, Obregón slowly retreated northward with two thousand men while federal Generals Miguel Gil and Luis Medina Barrón followed him with fifteen hundred.[70] Joined by another thousand men, Obregón made his stand at Santa Rosa, where on May 9 he opened a three-day battle that proved disastrous for the federals. The battle reports are almost unbelievably at variance one with another,[71] but one thing is certain—the federal forces that returned in terror to Guaymas-Empalme numbered less than half those who had confidently departed the region two weeks earlier. A young federal officer summed up: "Tell General Ruelas that the situation here is critical and that we need new forces, cannon, and above all a General with a good head on his shoulders . . . If you could see the panic here among the new troops you would be convinced."[72]

The Santa Rosa disaster, which included a serious wound to Medina Barrón, brought about a command shake-up: General Pedro Ojeda, who had scarcely distinguished himself in March while losing all of northern Sonora, was designated the new commanding officer. Ojeda regrouped his forces, gathered supplies, and then in late May began again the slow advance on Hermosillo to the north. The campaign, lasting virtually a month, was a replica of the earlier one.

[69] Admiral Walter C. Cowles to SecNavy, June 6, 1913, file 812.00/7841 enclosure, NA, RG 59.

[70] Medina Barrón was transferred to Sonora after his quarrel in March with Caso López concerning Saltillo.

[71] For the federal accounts, see ADN-Sonora 1913 (Combate de Santa Rosa); for rebel accounts see Barragán, *Ejército*, Appendix Documents 11 and 12, or Hostetter to SecState, June 10, 1913, file 812.00/7800, NA, RG 59, which is a translation of Obregón's official report.

[72] Captain Enrique Medina Saules to Major Elfego Ruiz, May 11, 1913, ADN-Sonora 1913 (Combate de Santa Rosa).

Obregón retreated slowly, keeping contact, and Ojeda advanced. At the opportune time—Obregón always fought battles of his choosing, rather than leaving the choice to his enemy—the rebels closed in at Santa María on June 25.

The result was even more catastrophic for the federals than had been the battle of Santa Rosa. Of the 2,500 men engaged, the federals lost 600 by Ojeda's own account; the probabilities are that the loss was much greater. More importantly, when it was all over, the rebels were the richer by artillery, machine guns, hundreds of thousands of rounds of ammunition, railroad engines and rolling stock, and a multitude of other items abandoned by the Ojeda army in its mad flight to the sanctuary of Guaymas, with its protecting warships. What proportion of the original army came limping back to Guaymas is uncertain, but Consul Louis Hostetter in Hermosillo estimated that only a third returned; since his major sources of information were the rebels, his figure is probably incorrect. But Ojeda had learned his lesson; he never again got out of sight of Guaymas until he left the state the following year.[73] Obregón, fearing the guns of the warships, failed to follow his advantage for one of the few times in his military—or political—career. Instead of attacking Guaymas immediately while Ojeda was in his weakened condition, Obregón laid siege to the port, which continued in federal hands for another year.

While Obregón cut to pieces the Sonora federals, his distant companions in arms added considerable luster to the revolutionary cause. On the opposite side of the nation, in Tamaulipas, military developments were slow in the first three months. With the exception of an attack on Ciudad Victoria on April 22,[74] the rebels undertook no major campaigns until June 3, when Lucio Blanco with fourteen

[73] For details of the campaign, see documents in ADN-Sonora 1913 (Combate de Santa María); dispatches from F. Simpich and L. Hostetter to SecState in late June and early July, 1913, in the 812.00/7900–8134 series, NA, RG 59; and Barragán, *Ejército*, I, 148–150 and Appendix Document 13; and Alvaro Obregón, *Ocho mil kilómetros en campaña*.

[74] Ciudad Victoria was attacked by Jesús Agustín Castro's rurales, who had rebelled at Tlalnepantla three weeks before. Ciudad Victoria remained in federal hands for another seven months.

hundred men surprised the four-hundred-man federal garrison at Matamoros.[75] Blanco, according to Consul Jesse H. Johnson, was "a very strong man both mentally and phisically [*sic*], and would impress one as being a very strong man." He and his officers, continued Mr. Johnson, were "gentlemen of education and refinement . . . certainly . . . very earnest in the cause they espouse."[76] Beginning the attack at 10:30 A.M., Blanco completed the conquest early the following morning, driving a part of the federals across the boundary into Brownsville, Texas. On the Mexican side, those federal troops who remained alive—casualties were exceedingly heavy—were made prisoners. Blanco's victory was complete.[77] One Mexican consul on the border downheartedly reported: "The spirits of the carrancistas have risen a hundred per cent; and they are all certain that they will have another triumph in Nuevo Laredo."[78]

Scarcely had the Huerta government fabricated plausible excuses for the loss at Matamoros than it had a more serious loss to explain. Pánfilo Natera, in a bold and unexpected stroke, fell upon Zacatecas on June 7 and by the following day controlled the city. The losses of Matamoros, Cananea, Agua Prieta, Naco, and dozens of smaller places in the northern states could be explained away, but Natera's capture of Zacatecas, in the very heart of the country and the northern gateway to the Bajío, created pandemonium. Huerta was understandably furious. After three months of fighting he could point to no major military victory, while the rebels could with justice indicate a long series of successes capped by the capture of the capital of one of the major central states. The sour dictator first looked for a scapegoat, whom he found in the person of War Minister Manuel Mondragón, the mentally and physically decrepit old

[75] To be sure, during April and May, Lucio Blanco had been busy seizing small places in eastern Nuevo León and in Tamaulipas.

[76] Consul Jesse H. Johnson to SecState, June 16, 1913, file 812.00/7781, NA, RG 59.

[77] For details of the battle see series of messages from various officials in ADN-Tamaulipas 1913 in June and July; Barragán, *Ejército*, I, Appendix Document 5; series of messages from Jesse H. Johnson and others in early June, in the 812.00 series, NA, RG 59.

[78] Consul, Eagle Pass, to SecRel, June 6, 1913, ADN-Tamaulipas 1913.

man who had for years played around the edges of outright corruption as a general in the army and who had come from retirement to be one of the titular leaders of the movement against Madero.[79] Mondragón was allowed to "resign" from his ministry within a few days, to be supplanted by Aureliano Blanquet,[80] whose principal claim to the position rested in the fact that it was he who arrested Madero in the coup d'état of February 18. Much more serious than the dubious loss involved in returning Mondragón to private life was the shift of troops from the Coahuila campaign to Zacatecas, but at least the maneuver was successful; on July 16 Natera abandoned the city, which General José Delgado reoccupied with a federal force.

The self-satisfaction engendered by Delgado's reoccupation of Zacatecas was short-lived; the gain of one state capital was balanced by the loss of another. After the abortive rebel attack on Durango in April, the Huerta government bestirred itself to improve the defenses of that important center, and by May 1 the defenders, including regular army, irregulars, state troops, and Defensa Social volunteers, numbered about 2,500.[81] "Cheche" Campos made occasional forays into the countryside to break up concentrations of rebels under Contreras and Pereyra, and by late May optimistically reported: "The enemy is not of the importance we thought. Soldiers are deserting, according to prisoners."[82] Antonio Castellanos, commissioned as a special agent to encourage rebels to lay down their arms, reported in the same rosy vein.[83] By mid-June, Campos was somewhat less sanguine; he reported to Mexico City that his own irregular troops were of dubious loyalty, that most of the state authorities (including the governor) were sympathetic to the rebels,

[79] One of the major artillery pieces used by the Mexican army was the "Mondragón." Mondragón has been accused of having essentially stolen the model of the field piece and of having made a small fortune in manufacturing it for the army.

[80] Blanquet took office on June 13.

[81] Hamm to SecState, April 29, 1913, file 812.00/7720, NA, RG 59.

[82] J. J. Campos to SecGyM, May 24, 1913, ADN-Durango 1913. If the prisoners taken by Campos reported anything, they had to speak fast, since Campos regularly executed all unfortunate enough to fall into his hands.

[83] A. Castellanos to SecGyM, May 25, 1913, ADN-Durango 1913.

that the divisional commander at Torreón was anile and his subordinates disgusted, that there were insufficient arms and ammunition, that it was folly to consider recruiting more men in the region, and that all the small towns between Torreón and Durango were openly antigovernment. Campos's bitterness may be judged from his final recommendation: that since the residents of both Cuencamé and Ocuila[84] were avowedly Carrancista, the villages should be completely razed and the inhabitants forced into the Laguna region.[85] Campos had reason to be morose. About June 13 Tomás Urbina arrived to take charge of the four thousand rebels surrounding Durango,[86] and four days later launched an attack that culminated in the capture of the city on the following day. To the natural confusion flowing from General Escudero's incompetence[87] was added consternation when Carranza sympathizers within the city repeated the tactics of April, but with more precision and organization; one federal officer complained that the Durango fifth column "hunted the [federal] officers like rabbits."[88] When Escudero, in a desperate attempt to save what he could of his disappearing army and matériel,[89] evacuated the city on the afternoon of June 18 the incoming rebels had a field day; they well remembered the summary executions of two months before. The U.S. consul reported: "Scenes following the rebel entry beggar description. Business and private houses [were] thoroughly sacked; [the] main business section burned; prisoners liberated. . . . Foreigners . . . suffered equally with [the] natives. Absolute anarchy prevails."[90] Durango was now permanently lost to Huerta.

[84] About midway between Durango and Torreón.

[85] M. Ruelas to SecGyM, June 14, 1913, submitting report from Campos, ADN-Durango 1913.

[86] Hamm to SecState, June 13, 1913, file 812.00/7793, NA, RG 59.

[87] All reports, including those from the U.S. consul, some of Escudero's subordinates and his superiors, and some private citizens, emphasized the general's incapacity. Escudero, of course, pictured himself as a victim of superior forces and circumstances.

[88] General Ignacio Morelos Zaragoza to Huerta, August 9, 1913, ADN-Durango 1913.

[89] General Ignacio Bravo to SecGyM, July 30, 1913, ADN-Durango 1913.

[90] Hamm to SecState, June 21, 1913, file 812.00/7919, NA, RG 59.

Only a few days earlier the government had received bad news from another source. The Huerta government feigned to believe that the rebels were limited to the north, that, with the exception of Zapata, the people of the southern states remained loyal to the administration. Governor Manuel Castillo Brito of Campeche, even though earlier identified as Maderista, seemed to accept Huerta wholeheartedly. Certainly Castillo, in reply to a request for more recruits for the army, had spoken of his "eagerness [*afán*] to cooperate effectively for the reestablishment of peace in the Republic . . . and seconding the action of the Federal Executive."[91] To be sure, Castillo consistently signed his official letters with the Maderista formula of Sufragio Efectivo—No Reelección instead of the more palatable Libertad y Constitución adopted by the rest of the governors, but there seemed to be no cause for real concern. His defection on June 13,[92] then, robbed Huerta of one propaganda tool, even though Castillo Brito was never able to control the state for the Carranza cause.

As for Zapata and his rebels in Morelos, Huerta had at first paid them little attention—he had far graver problems in the north and west—but in mid-April he decided to try to pacify the unruly little state. On April 14 federal General Juvencio Robles went to Cuernavaca, threw out the helpless state government, and began a crackdown.[93] The effect was to swell rebel ranks and solidify Zapata's leadership. The day after Robles took over in the state, Zapata stormed Jonocatepec and took it after thirty-six hours of hard fighting, capturing a large and much needed store of arms and ammunition.[94] On the twenty-third he laid siege to Cuautla. By May rebels were operating around Cuernavaca itself,[95] and Robles decreed a "reconcentration" of the rural populace, ordering civilians into desig-

[91] M. Castillo Brito to SecGob, April 9, 1913, AGN-Gobernación—Varios—Prefectos municipales 1913–1914.

[92] H. L. Wilson to SecState, June 13, 1913, file 812.00/7777, NA, RG 59. There is virtually no documentation on Campeche in the ADN.

[93] Womack, *Zapata*, pp. 164–165.

[94] Magaña and Pérez Guerrero, *Zapata*, III, 160.

[95] Ibid., p. 179.

nated towns and authorizing the shooting of any person found in the countryside without a permit.[96] Federals leveled whole villages,[97] to no avail whatever. Zapata's prestige soared and his men's fighting efforts became more ferocious. Militarily, matters became a stalemate. Federal pressure slackened after September, Robles was replaced, and after that Huerta held the main towns while the Zapatistas controlled nearly everything else.[98]

Among the Huertistas in early July the pervading gloom was partially and momentarily dispelled by the capture of Monclova, Carranza's personal headquarters and the center of revolutionary command in the northeast. General Arnoldo Caso López in late May took the offensive against the Coahuila rebels and by May 31 was in sight of Monclova;[99] but Natera's capture of Zacatecas halted the advance by forcing the federals to divert troops from the north. Most of June was spent in building up another striking force,[100] and in early July another deliberate advance was begun. A series of battles in the Monclova region, in which the contending armies seem to have been roughly equivalent,[101] culminated in federal success on July 10.[102] General Joaquín Maass, reflecting the optimistic exaggeration that was endemic among the Huerta supporters, reported that the capture of Monclova meant the pacification of the north.[103] But

96 *El Imparcial*, May 10, 1913.

97 Magaña and Pérez Guerrero, *Zapata*, III, 192.

98 Womack, *Zapata*, p. 177.

99 SecRel to SecGyM, May 31, 1913, ADN-Coahuila 1913 (Mayo).

100 While the federals were building up their force, the revolutionaries were virtually running wild over the state, occasionally even threatening Saltillo. The capital was generally isolated, the outlying towns and villages were occupied by rebels, and all the other major cities remained in rebel hands. U.S. Consul Silliman in Saltillo was thoroughly disgusted with Caso López's dilatory methods.

101 Colonel Emilio Salinas of the Carrancista forces reported (Salinas to Carranza, August 6, 1913, ADN-Coahuila 1917) that Maass had three times as many men as he; Maass reported (Maass to SecGyM, July 11, 1913, ADN-Coahuila 1913 [Julio]) that Salinas had three times as many as he. They at least agreed on the factor three.

102 For details, see the documents in ADN-Coahuila 1913 (Julio); those in the 812.00 series, NA, RG 59, numbered 7955, 7972, 7984, and 7985; and Barragán, *Ejército*, I, 190–206.

103 General J. Maass to SecGyM, July 11, 1913, ADN-Coahuila 1913 (Julio).

it took the complacent general another three months to manage the 170 miles to Piedras Negras.

With Monclova in federal hands, Carranza decided to leave the state of Coahuila himself—designating his brother Jesús and others to continue military operations there—and to visit the other sites of revolutionary activity. His first stop was not actually out of his own state, but in the vicinity of Torreón. In that region some 6,500 rebels clashed with about 4,500 federals in a series of battles over a ten-day period beginning on July 21; Carranza's presence may have given the revolutionaries extra spirit, but it did not add to their military prowess, and on July 31 the rebels drew back leaving Torreón still in federal hands. Carranza remained in the Durango vicinity only long enough to make his presence felt and to issue some orders from Canatlán, then he continued his long and tiresome trip over the Sierra Madre to the west coast.

For two months after the unsuccessful Torreón attack, the rebels in the Laguna region licked their wounds—grievous indeed, for the Torreón attack was costly—gathered men and supplies, made occasional attacks on the outposts, and isolated Torreón to the point that by mid-September the city was threatened with an epidemic.[104] Toward the end of the month the rebels were cheered by the arrival of Pancho Villa with over two thousand picked men. The federals, in the meantime, were doing little or nothing. Irregular General Benjamín Argumedo made an occasional foray into the countryside to gather food to succor the city, the war ministry took some belated steps to send reinforcements and supplies—which never arrived—and the command in Torreón changed hands. Seventy-seven–year-old Ignacio Bravo, who had sat in Torreón since March desperately afraid to send any of his troops on the offensive, was replaced on September 1 by the slightly younger and slightly more energetic General Eutiquio Munguía. Munguía, who had been one of Bravo's subordinates, bestirred himself enough to begin tentative offensive operations in late September; but by that time it was too late. On

[104] George C. Carothers to P. Hanna, September 13, 1913, file 812.00/9059 enclosure, NA, RG 59.

September 29 the rebel attack on the outlying posts began, and by October 1 the terrified Huertistas, civilians and military alike, fled the city in panic; among those fleeing early that morning was General Bravo, who saddled his horse and left the city "following the avalanche of soldiers, civilians, carriages and automobiles, etc., which travelled with no semblance of order."[105] And while the defeated fled the city, the reinforcing column under Trucy Aubert was still hundreds of miles away and the supplies for Torreón's defense were at sea between Veracruz and Tampico. For a week the government managed to conceal the loss, but the word got out, and in order to assuage wounded pride Huerta found another scapegoat. General Munguía was arrested, charged with military crimes in the loss of the city, and subjected to a court-martial. The court-martial may have soothed hurt pride, but it did not recapture Torreón.[106]

While the federals were being soundly drubbed in the Laguna district they were a little more successful to the north and east. Joaquín Maass, after his capture of Monclova on July 10, frittered away a month before undertaking the move north on Piedras Negras. Throughout the remaining portion of August, all of September, and the first week of October the careful federals moved north, finally occupying Piedras Negras on October 7. The capture of the border city gave the federals possession of all the major cities and rail connections in eastern and northern Coahuila. Essentially forced out of Coahuila, the revolutionaries there then turned in the direction of Nuevo León and its capital, Monterrey.

At this point a serious quarrel, for a time threatening not only to disrupt the military campaign in the northeast but also to undermine general revolutionary cooperation, developed. Lucio Blanco, early in the movement, had been designated by Carranza as the

[105] General Ignacio Bravo statement, October 12, 1913, ADN-Coahuila 1913 (Defensa y evacuación de Torreón). The statement was made at the behest of a court-martial trying Munguía.

[106] The full story, in all its conflicting details, of events in Torreón may be found in ADN-Coahuila 1913 (Defensa y evacuación de Torreón); ADN-Coahuila 1913 (Octubre); messages from Hamm, Carothers, and Philip Hanna in the 812.00 series, NA, RG 59, particularly 8819, 9059, 9555, and 9774; and Barragán, *Ejército*, I, 263–266, Appendix Documents 18 and 19.

principal military leader in Nuevo León and Tamaulipas; in that capacity Blanco had directed most of the raids on outposts as well as the assault and capture of Matamoros. But as a result of a combination of circumstances he had been quarreling with Jesús Agustín Castro, and by late September the rupture was complete.[107] Almost contemporaneous with the apex of the Blanco-Castro quarrel came the final occupation of Piedras Negras by Maass's Huertistas and the consequent constriction on revolutionary activity in Coahuila. Pablo González, titular leader of the Constitutionalists in Coahuila and a long-time Carranza favorite,[108] found that he had to leave his own state if he were to command a significant army of operations. Under these circumstances Carranza ordered Blanco to attach himself and his men, in the role of subordinates, to González's command and to cooperate in a campaign against Monterrey. Blanco was understandably irritated. He not only considered himself to be superior to González in ability—which he was, since González was a military dullard—but he also resented the conditions under which the command shift was made. He could see no justification for being put under the command of a general who had been so unsuccessful that he had lost to the enemy the military zone originally assigned to him. Blanco simply refused to put himself under González's orders. After some negotiations between Blanco and representatives from Carranza, Carranza gave Blanco a command in Sonora; therefore, Blanco left his own command, and Nuevo León, at a most crucial time. The rupture that threatened revolutionary unity was delayed,[109] but the tensions involving Blanco during September and October had a serious immediate effect.

While the Blanco contretemps was being settled, González developed a plan of operation against Monterrey, assuming that he

[107] Castro refused to cooperate in the assault on Matamoros in the belief that it could not be taken.

[108] González was one of the leaders of the state forces in the Orozco campaign and never hesitated a moment in supporting the break with Huerta.

[109] When the break between Carranza and Villa came in 1914, Blanco finally went with the Convention against Carranza. To what extent his decision was the result of the experience here related is not clear.

would have the use of Blanco's sizable army in the assault. He spent most of October in effectively isolating the Nuevo León capital from the remainder of the country and in building up his army's strength. On October 23 the general assault began without the three thousand men reported to be in Blanco's army; whether the decision to attack was made in the expectation that Blanco's men, now under a new commander, would arrive in time to participate in the first drive, or in indifference to that participation, is not clear. But González's ignorance or obtuseness cost him Monterrey. The first day's attack went extremely well, with the revolutionaries driving the defenders into the very center of the city; the rebels occupied all the environs and most of the important sites within the city itself. The government sent out a desperate call for succor for Monterrey;[110] on October 24 the first reinforcements arrived from Saltillo after forced marching. In view of the federal reinforcements González withdrew, satisfying himself with an immense quantity of military booty but leaving the city in Huerta's hands for another five months.[111]

In Chihuahua the intervening months had been bitter for the Huertistas. Jiménez and Santa Rosalía both fell to the rebels in April,[112] Parral followed in May,[113] and by late June only Ciudad Juárez and Chihuahua remained under federal control. Occasionally a train would get through to Chihuahua from either Torreón or Ciudad Juárez, but these cases were rare, and generally the defenders of the capital city were in dire straits—on short supplies and threatened by the rapidly growing Villa army. General Salvador Mercado, as timorous as Ojeda and as plaintive as Munguía, begged for more supplies and men; without such additions, he insisted, the entire

110 Blanquet to J. Refugio Velasco, October 23, 1913, ADN-Coahuila 1913 (Octubre). Velasco was in Saltillo, preparing an attack on Torreón.

111 Nelson O'Shaughnessy to SecState, October 27, 1913, file 812.00/9400, and Simpich to SecState, October 31, 1913, file 812.00/9496, NA, RG 59. Matériel that could not be transported or used, such as railroad rolling stock, was destroyed.

112 General I. Bravo to SecGyM, April 26, 1913, ADN-Chihuahua 1913 (Mayo).

113 General S. Mercado to SecGyM, May 18, 1913, ADN-Chihuahua 1913 (Mayo).

state would be lost.[114] In view of the perfectly obvious dangers, the government in early July dispatched Pascual Orozco to the beleaguered city. For almost three weeks the doughty irregular fought his way north from Torreón along the railroad line, using the right-of-way as a road but not being able to transport troops or supplies by train. With Maclovio Herrera, Manuel Chao, Trinidad Rodríguez, and Rosalío Hernández dogging his footsteps, Orozco was forced to fight at Jiménez, Estación Díaz, and Santa Rosalía; each of these was momentarily occupied by the government troops, but each was in turn abandoned to the rebels.[115] On July 22 he entered Chihuahua, a welcome but disheveled sight to Mercado and his men, and almost immediately began quarrelling with both Mercado and the city officials.[116]

During August and most of September the federals based in Chihuahua made tentative excursions into the countryside in half-hearted search of rebels, but it was not until late in September that they mounted any semblance of a sustained offensive. Mercado sent slightly more than half his roughly seven thousand men southward, to join with a similar column moving north from Torreón;[117] the object was to enclose the rebels in the Santa Rosalía–Jiménez region in a pincers and so to clear the rail line. Rebel capture of Torreón completely disrupted the plan although it did not prevent federal reoccupation of Santa Rosalía.[118] By this date, early October, Villa had emerged as the undoubted military leader from Torreón north, having overshadowed Herrera, Rodríguez, Chao, and the others

114 General S. Mercado to SecGyM, July 5, 1913, ADN-Chihuahua 1913 (Julio).

115 A number of documents in ADN deal with Orozco's venture. See particularly General S. Mercado to SecGyM, July 19, 1913, ADN-Chihuahua 1913 (Julio); General P. Orozco to Mercado, August 25, 1913, ADN-Chihuahua 1913 (Agosto); and SubJefe Estado Mayor to SecGyM, November 26, 1913, ADN-Chihuahua 1913 (Noviembre).

116 Letcher to SecState, July 22, 1913, file 812.00/8220, NA, RG 59. Orozco consistently believed that he was not being properly rewarded for his excellence and merits; this attitude, probably fully justified, had contributed to the ill-feeling between him and Mercado.

117 Letcher to SecState, September 25, 1913, file 812.00/8979, NA, RG 59.

118 Letcher to SecState, October 3, 1913, file 812.00/9391, NA, RG 59.

who had been operating more or less independently. Villa remained in Torreón long enough to assess and collect a "loan" of about three million pesos,[119] and then on October 20 began a movement toward Chihuahua.

Villa's campaign, which cleared the Huerta forces permanently from the last vestiges of control in Chihuahua, is almost a classic in military improvisation and derring-do. With a force estimated variously at between eight and sixteen thousand, Villa began on November 5 an attack on Chihuahua,[120] defended by an army variously estimated at between four and seven thousand. For five days the Villistas pecked away at the defenders, sometimes attacking frontally but more often hitting at the weakest sectors. On November 11, after one such frontal assault, Villa broke off the attack and, according to Mercado, dispersed in wild confusion. The defending general's pride in his achievement was enhanced when the report circulated, late that night, that the Villistas were fleeing to the southward; Chihuahua was for the moment safe. Three days later Mercado's airy dream was shattered with devastating suddenness. Villa, far from retreating to the south, quietly by-passed Chihuahua, captured some trains between Chihuahua and Ciudad Juárez, and simply rode the trains into the border city with a portion of his army during the night of November 14–15. The relatively small federal garrison, expecting to be reinforced by two thousand men under José Inés Salazar from Chihuahua, gave little heed to the military train arriving at two in the morning; before the sentries were fully aware of what was happening, the train spewed forth its rebel cargo with such precision and rapidity that the garrison, with all its stores and ammunition, fell to Villa after a short struggle. A few of the defenders, fleet of foot and mind, managed to escape into the United States.

Mercado, isolated in Chihuahua and desperate, dispatched the major portion of his force against Villa; Mercado himself remained in Chihuahua with Orozco, entrusting the campaign against Villa to Marcelo Caraveo and José Inés Salazar. In one of the bloodiest

119 Silliman to SecState, October 25, 1913, file 812.00/9391, NA, RG 59.
120 On the route from Torreón to Chihuahua, Villa reoccupied Santa Rosalía.

battles in the entire revolution, on November 23–25, Villa cut the federals to pieces at Tierra Blanca near Ciudad Juárez; federal casualties approximated one-fifth of the total force, and virtually all the federal military supplies, including badly needed artillery, fell to Villa. With half his army battered and tattered, with Chihuahua isolated and supplies scarce, and with the conviction that he would be Villa's next victim, Mercado took immediate steps to abandon Chihuahua in spite of abject pleas by the local merchants who now offered to donate three million pesos to the cause—this offer coming from men who, three weeks before, had refused even to lend money to Mercado. Making hurried preparations, which included the appointment of some provisional officials as well as the execution of all prisoners in the local jail, Mercado began the evacuation on November 27. For three days the refugees straggled out of the city, bound for Ojinaga on the border, making the first part of the journey by train. Broken rails and burned bridges, along with desertion of trainmen, forced Mercado to abandon the trains while still in sight of the city; the remainder of the trip across the inhospitable land was made under conditions that precluded taking all the supplies, and so great stores of arms and ammunition were put to the torch. The march became flight, the flight became rout. By the time the last of the survivors, greatly reduced by desertions, limped into Ojinaga on December 12, the Huerta Chihuahua army had all but disappeared.[121] Mercado did indeed hang on in Ojinaga for another month, and the irregulars under Caraveo, Salazar, and Orozco did strike out into the countryside, but after early December there was never any question as to who controlled the northern state.

While Villa engaged himself in the pleasant task of battering the Huerta forces in the north, Pablo González gained one of his rare

[121] The documentation on the campaign against Chihuahua and Ciudad Juárez is voluminous. The major Huerta documents may be found in ADN-Chihuahua 1913 for October, November, and December. Consuls Letcher in Chihuahua and Edwards in C. Juárez sent frequent messages, to be found in the series, 812.00 NA, RG 59, varying numbers in the 9000's. Villa gives his account in his *Memorias, Libro Segundo*, Caps. 3–7. Barragán gives an account, including a portion of a Villa report (*Ejército*, I, Chapter 10).

major victories in the northeast. After the unsuccessful attack on Monterrey, but with the city still virtually isolated, González projected an attack to the south in Tamaulipas. Gathering all his forces, totaling about five thousand, he first occupied Linares and then began the investment of Ciudad Victoria on November 14 at almost precisely the same hour that Villa began his audacious advance on Ciudad Juárez. The city, defended by Generals Antonio Rábago (removed from his Chihuahua command in June), Juan de Dios Arzamendi (even less able than Rábago), and irregular Higinio Aguilar (crusty, unimaginative octogenarian), was gripped with an inordinate fear of the revolutionaries; Rábago may not have been a particularly good general, but he was an excellent propagandist who convinced a large proportion of the populace that the Constitutionalists were little short of satanic. Some five hundred volunteers from the city gave heroic aid to the thousand-man garrison; the result was a tenacious defense, which González was able to break through only after two days of hard fighting. But numbers told, and early on November 18 González's force entered in triumph to find the city in ruins: large sections burned, public buildings wrecked by explosives, piles of partially cremated bodies, half-buried cadavers of officers, and a general stench of death and destruction. Furthermore, when the federal troops had begun to withdraw in the predawn hours, they had taken with them about two thousand civilians who wished to flee the expected brutalities of the rebels. In the chaos and fear of the flight, the Huertistas abandoned the relatively level road to the southeast and Tampico, choosing instead the rough route over the mountains to Tula. In the mountains the army virtually abandoned the civilians, most of whom returned to Ciudad Victoria, and their arms and ammunition, most of which was gathered up by hotly pursuing revolutionists under Antonio Villarreal and Cesáreo Castro. Dropped military supplies may have served the same purpose as Hippomenes' golden apples; certainly Castro, emulating Atalanta, slowed his pursuit to gather the fruits. Arzamendi gathered his stragglers in Tula, whence they went to Cerritos on the San Luis Potosí–Tampico rail line. While in Cerritos, Arzamendi was ordered to the defense of Tampico, under attack as of December 10 from Pablo

González. On this occasion the defenders were successful,[122] and Tampico remained under Huerta control until the following May.

During the last six months of 1913 the war in the west lacked the drama that the Chihuahua and northeast campaigns exhibited. With Ojeda holed up in Guaymas, unwilling to evacuate and unable to undertake an offensive campaign, military operations in the region for a time took on all the appearances of a stalemate. But with new recruits in the state, including Yaqui Indians by the thousands,[123] and with the help of Durango rebels under the Arrietas, who were freed for other duty after the fall of Durango in late June, Obregón simply bypassed Guaymas and began a slow campaign to the south. General Reynaldo Díaz, commanding the Huerta garrison in Mazatlán, recognized the symptoms of impending disaster; in late July, concerned with the double movement from Sonora and Durango, he urged the Ministry of War to undertake a vigorous campaign in the Fuerte Valley near the boundary between Sonora and Sinaloa. General Díaz was under no delusions, and in order to dispel any remaining illusions in Mexico City he insisted on the military necessity of such a campaign "if you do not want to happen to Sinaloa what has already happened to Sonora and Durango."[124] Less than a week after Díaz expressed his concern, Felipe Riveros threatened the city of Sinaloa,[125] on the edge of the Fuerte Valley, but Riveros's failure to capture the city convinced the central government that Díaz was too pessimistic. Within a month Díaz had additional proof to support his pessimism; a series of small campaigns in the region

[122] The major portion of the available documentation on the capture of Ciudad Victoria is to be found in ADN-Tamaulipas 1913. Of particular value are Higinio Aguilar to SecGyM, November 23, 1913; E. Camargo to SecGyM, January 14, 1914; and Arzamendi to Jefe Div. del Bravo, November 28, 1913. Some of the Constitutionalist reports are reprinted in Barragán, *Ejército*, I, Appendix Documents 20 and 21. With respect to the Tampico attack, see Juan de Dios Arzamendi to Jefe Div. del Bravo, December 15, 1913, and Joaquín Téllez to SecGyM, December 13, 1913, both in ADN-Tamaulipas 1913.

[123] Hostetter to SecState, August 14, 1913, file 812.00/8460, NA, RG 59.

[124] General R. Díaz to SecGyM, July 22, 1913, ADN-Sinaloa 1913.

[125] Felipe Riveros to Com. Militar of Sinaloa, July 31, 1913, ADN-Sinaloa 1913. Riveros was the governor elected during the Madero administration. This document was a surrender demand.

around Topolobampo and San Blas in late August and early September resulted in heavy losses to his command.[126] Still the central government made no serious effort to protect the state, even in the face of reports that the rebels were steadily seizing complete control.[127] By the first week in September, in fact, the Constitutionalists controlled all of the state save Sinaloa, Culiacán, and Mazatlán; the extent of this control was dramatically demonstrated when Carranza traversed the major part of the state in early September and then took a train from Fuerte to Hermosillo, Sonora.[128] Sinaloa fell to the revolutionists on October 5, and Culiacán followed on November 14,[129] with the survivors retreating by land and sea to Mazatlán. The Culiacán victors a week later attacked the port city, but after two days of bitter fighting withdrew;[130] Mazatlán, like Guaymas, remained under Huerta's control until he himself fled the country the following summer. By early December, then, in the states of Sonora and Sinaloa only Guaymas and Mazatlán remained in federal hands.

For the Huertistas, however, Christmas came early in December; General José Refugio Velasco recaptured Torreón.[131] When Villa moved north in late October to begin his maneuvers that ultimately cleared Chihuahua of federals, he left in Torreón a relatively small garrison to protect his rear. General Velasco, in command of the federal army that had been dispatched in late September to rein-

[126] General R. Díaz to General P. Ojeda, September 2, 1913, ADN-Sinaloa 1913.

[127] E.g., Luis F. Molina to SecGyM, September 14, 1913, ADN-Sinaloa 1913.

[128] Josephus Daniels to SecState, October 1, 1913, file 812.00/9283 enclosure, NA, RG 59.

[129] Captain M. R. Alcérreca to General M. Rodríguez, October 10, 1913, and General A. T. Rasgado to SecGyM, November 26, 1913, both in ADN-Sinaloa 1913.

[130] General P. Ojeda to SecGyM, November 25, 1913, ADN-Sinaloa 1913.

[131] General José Refugio Velasco was the youngest, and by far the ablest, of Huerta's field generals in the regular army. A man of considerable integrity and rectitude, he disagreed violently with military mixture into political affairs and objected to the Huerta coup. But as an army officer he believed it incumbent on him to support the government, regardless of the manner through which the government came to power. He is the one important military figure in the Huerta government who was almost universally respected, both as a man and as a military leader, by the Constitutionalists.

force Munguía in Torreón and that was still on the road when the city fell to Villa, began reorganizing his force in October. After some weeks spent in developing the army into a fighting force, Velasco started the advance early in November; while Villa attacked Chihuahua, Velasco made first contact with the rebels holding Torreón, and on November 9 he captured the first important outlying post. He slowly tightened the ring around the city through successive captures of posts in both Coahuila and Durango during the remainder of November; his advance was deliberate, planned with exactitude, and effective. On December 9 he began the frontal attack on the city itself, and on the following day he gained the victory.[132] He defeated but did not destroy the rebels; most of the men escaped to the north, taking their war supplies with them. Since a major victory was rare in the annals of the federal army, all military commanders received orders from Minister of War Blanquet to make a special effort to publicize the event.[133]

Federal jubilation over Velasco's victory may have been real, but Huerta had little cause for optimism. By the end of 1913 the Huertistas were obviously doomed, the victims of their own inefficiency rather than of Constitutionalist genius. The basic military characteristics of the contending forces had become clear, with all the advantages on the side of the revolutionary forces. In the first place, federal military activity reflected the government's political attitude; the commanders were tradition-bound and unimaginative with few exceptions. Untrained revolutionary forces, led by military amateurs, consistently outfought the federals, even though they suffered many setbacks. Second, the federal forces were loath to undertake the offensive and were easily discouraged by defeat. Mercado waited in Chihuahua, Bravo and Munguía waited in Torreón, Escudero waited in Durango, and Ojeda waited first in Naco and then in Guaymas; the safety of the barricades and the cities was certainly more comfortable than the dangers of an open-field campaign, but it was

[132] General José Refugio Velasco to SecGyM, December 10, 1913, ADN-Coahuila 1913 (Diciembre).

[133] A. Blanquet to Jefes de División y Comandantes Militares, December 11, 1913, ADN-Coahuila 1913 (Diciembre).

scarcely conducive to the reconquest of rebel-held territories. Only rarely did the federals bestir themselves sufficiently to undertake an offensive action and even then, such as Maass's advance on Piedras Negras and Nuevo Laredo, the action was so timorous as to be ludicrous; Velasco's Torreón campaign was the only major exception to the general rule. Third, and intimately related to the above, the regular federal forces seemed to be completely unable to operate away from a solid base with railroad transportation. When Escudero was forced to evacuate Durango, when Mercado left Chihuahua, when Munguía found Torreón too hot for comfort, the retreat turned into flight. Mercado, particularly, seemed to be panic-stricken at the thought of marching across country to Ojinaga, and Ojeda stayed in Guaymas primarily through fright of having his retreat cut off. Only the federal "irregulars"—Marcelo Caraveo, Benjamín Argumedo, "Cheche" Campos, Pascual Orozco, and others like them—could and did operate with fluidity. On the other hand, most of the Constitutionalists found no real cause for alarm if they were temporarily separated from a major base; Villa, Chao, Herrera, the Arrietas, Natera, and others consistently combed the open country for supplies and, if necessary, operated for months without a firm base in a major city on a rail line. Even the unimaginative Pablo González, compared to the federal commanders, had a veritable flying column. Fourth, the enlisted men among the federals frequently had little stomach for the fight. Few were volunteers; most were unwilling conscripts impressed into service. This unwillingness to fight was first demonstrated in the battle for Cananea, when the troops simply forced their commander to capitulate; it was the dominant factor in virtually every battle, manifested by wholesale desertion. Only the irregulars, consisting entirely of volunteers, remained relatively steadfast to their commanders; and even among some of the irregulars, particularly "Cheche" Campos's, desertion was a major problem. Finally, and obversely, the ease with which the Constitutionalists could recruit troops and the steadfastness of those troops in battle were important ingredients in the victories. The phenomenal growth of the armies commanded by Obregón, Villa, Blanco, González, and others attests to the willingness to volunteer;

the enlisted man—whether indigene or mestizo,[134] urban laborer or rural peon—knew or thought he knew what he was fighting for.

By the close of 1913 there were no indications of any change in the military characteristics, which had been clear within the first months of the revolution. As long as these characteristics held true, Constitutionalist prospects would continue to brighten.

[134] Many Indian groups took an active and important part in the military campaigns; this was particularly true of the Yaquis of Sonora, who formed a significant part of Obregón's army.

3. ON THE POLITICAL FRONT

Victoriano Huerta, when he took the oath of office as president on February 20, 1913, was not officially a completely free agent in the selection of the personnel with whom he was to work. The Pact of the Embassy[1] had divided the cabinet posts between Huertistas and Felicistas, and Madero's statement of resignation had stipulated that state governors would retain their posts despite a change in national administration. Huerta's first cabinet was made up of generally able men,[2] the members of Congress continued to hold office,[3]

[1] The agreement signed by Huerta and Félix Díaz at the U.S. embassy immediately after Madero's overthrow.

[2] The cabinet included Francisco León de la Barra as minister of foreign relations, Toribio Esquivel Obregón as minister of finance, Rodolfo Reyes as minister of justice, Manuel Mondragón as minister of war and marine, Alberto Robles Gil as minister of *fomento*, Alberto García Granados as minister of *gobernación*, David de la Fuente as minister of communications.

[3] A number of the deputies joined revolutionary forces immediately and therefore did not serve in the Chamber under Huerta. Among these were Francisco Murguía, Roberto V. Pesqueira, Eduardo Hay, Heriberto Jara, and Roque González Garza.

and ostensibly a legal and constitutional government still functioned in Mexico. Even after Madero's assassination, the sycophants surrounding the new administration insisted that events in Mexico City should not be construed as an attack on the political system, and that the even tenor of political life need not be disrupted. One newspaper argued strongly that the coup d'état was designed for one purpose only: to rid Mexico of an evil personality—Madero—and that it did not threaten the federal system and state sovereignty. The editor, furthermore, welcomed the pending investigation into the dual assassination but was confident of the outcome: "[We] congratulate ourselves that there appears to be no culpability attached to the government because [such culpability] would be a black and horrible blot on the Nation's history [and we are sure] . . . that the name of our country will not appear dishonored at home or abroad, at the present or in the future."[4] Huerta promised to remain in office only long enough to hold a presidential election; the national Congress passed a special election law and set October 26, 1913, as election day; partisans of presidential aspirants—the strongest of whom was Félix Díaz[5]—organized political parties; and occasionally a deputy strongly criticized Huerta from the Chamber floor.[6] To the casual observer in Mexico City, governmental business seemed as usual during the first three months of the Huerta period.

But appearances deceived. Huerta's prime problem was pacification; and pacification, as Luis Lara Pardo pointed out in early May,[7] was compounded of political, financial, and military ingredients. In spite of the brave front and the optimistic reports, after ten weeks in office the government was confronted with a serious rebellion obviously growing in strength; men, money, and a quiet political home front were essential to victory. In order to prevent manifestations of political unrest, Huerta began to apply pressure. The government

[4] *El Centinela*, March 2, 1913, pp. 1–3.

[5] The Partido Nacional Felicista, with branches in many of the states, was organized in mid-April (see SecGob to SecGyM, April 15, 1913, ADN-Oaxaca 1913).

[6] Heriberto Barrón made such an attack on May 16. Since he was not considered to be a Maderista, Huerta took no reprisal.

[7] In *El País*, May 3, 1913.

arrested and otherwise harassed deputies who stepped out of line,[8] closed even faintly critical newspapers,[9] and shipped political prisoners out of Mexico City to places distant from the center of government as a means of both getting them out of sight and warning others.[10] Furthermore, Huerta began to have second thoughts about the October election and about his Pact of the Embassy cabinet. By mid-June rumors of trouble between Huerta and Félix Díaz had become so insistent that Díaz felt compelled to call upon Ambassador Henry Lane Wilson to deny them,[11] and shortly thereafter Francisco León de la Barra took leave of his office,[12] to which he never returned.

In order to make repression palatable, Huerta leavened his ever-tightening control with at least a nod in the direction of social reform. In late May, stimulated by crippling strikes resulting from the "agitation of bad elements" and from "unfavorable conditions which . . . [the workers] have had from time immemorial,"[13] Huerta decided to establish labor offices in each state to settle industrial disputes. A month later the Department of Labor, a part of the Ministry of Fomento, began the publication of a monthly bulletin to make the public aware of its work on this "transcendental problem,"[14] and by mid-summer the department was busily collecting data on industrial accidents that would be "of great value for the discussion of the accident law . . . being prepared" for submission to Congress.[15] But

[8] For example, Enrique Bordes Mangel was arrested May 8 and remained in jail two days; the following week Eliseo Arredondo found himself in the same position, but for a longer period.

[9] Both *El Voto* and *La Voz de Juárez* were closed down on May 3, and then all the personnel were arrested. *La Opinión* and *La Unión* of Veracruz soon followed, as did a multitude of other papers.

[10] On May 12, 1913, 110 such prisoners were sent to Quintana Roo (*El Diario*, May 3, 1913).

[11] H. L. Wilson to SecState, June 19, 1913, file 812.00/7833, NA, RG 59.

[12] Carlos Pereyra to SecGob, June 26, 1913, AGN-Gobernación—Varios 1911–1913.

[13] SecGob circular, July 21, 1913, AGN-Gobernación—Diversos 1911–1912–1913.

[14] SecGob circular, June 27, 1913, AGN-Gobernación—Varios Expedientes 1904–1914.

[15] SecFom to SecGob, August 14, 1913, AGN-Gobernación—Varios 1913–1914.

industrial concerns rarely furnished data,[16] and the Huerta government never submitted an accident bill to the national legislature. Whether Huerta ever had any such intention is highly dubious, for while the Department of Labor went through the motions of developing reform and loudly acclaimed its good intentions, the government broke up meetings of the Casa del Obrero Mundial and imprisoned its officials.[17]

The military aspects of pacification depended upon men and money, both difficult to secure. Of men there were plenty in Mexico, but of volunteers there were none. Huerta was forced to devise a scheme for expanding his armies and replacing his losses; his final formula was simple enough. The central government, through the Ministry of Gobernación, assigned to each state a *contingente de sangre*, or quota, based roughly on state population.[18] Each governor then ordered the *jefes políticos* of the municipalities to gather a specified number during a specified time; no set selection system was employed at the local level, the local officials being left free to use their own devices and imaginations in performing the task. Each *jefe político* in turn surrendered the recruits—or impressed men—to the district's ranking police officer, who retained custody until ordered by the governor to surrender them to a designated military official.[19] The army then furnished the new recruit with a uniform and a gun, assigned him to a unit, and sent him to fight; he received no formal combat training prior to actual engagement. Small wonder then, that

[16] Gov. Veracruz to SecGob, December 20, 1913, ibid.

[17] Majorie Ruth Clark, *Organized Labor in Mexico*, p. 25.

[18] Occasionally Huerta's government neglected to take into account Constitutionalist control in some states. The governor of Sonora, for example, was somewhat surprised to find himself responsible for raising a full contingent, even though he controlled only Guaymas and its immediate environs (see Francisco H. García to SecGyM, December 2, 1913, ADN-Sonora 1913 [Diciembre]).

[19] This system is made clear in the documents included in AGN-Gobernación —Varios—Prefectos municipales 1913–1914. One such document reads: "Today I wrote the Chief of Police: 'The Governor orders you to put at the disposition of the Commanding General of the Seventh Military Zone the ten individuals whom the Jefe Político of this district delivered to you as a part of the *contingente de sangre* allocated to this state'" (Juan Carrasco to SecGob, April 5, 1913).

recruits demonstrated a marked sullenness upon which many Huerta officials commented and which was most neatly described by the governor of Querétaro:

> [If the recruits are held for any time there is] great excitement among the families and friends of the recruits, which rapidly extends to the people, who through companionship and compassion make common cause with those conscripted, all this provoking scenes which leave a bad impression . . . ; for these reasons this Government has followed the practice of sending them out rapidly, escorted by state rurales and taking them in small groups in order to call less attention [to the recruitment practices] . . . , and thus provoking the least possible indignation among the lower class, who look on military service with horror, even though it be legal.[20]

Small wonder, too, that special agent William Bayard Hale could write concerning the implications of the system: "The Government forces are made up entirely of conscripts—captured rebels, released jail-birds and impressed peons. They can be handled only when kept together. To dispatch a column of even four or five hundred into the country after the enemy is equivalent to making them a present of so many recruits."[21] Despite the obvious weaknesses of his recruiting system, Huerta retained the same basic pattern throughout his tenure; and federal troop desertion to the Constitutionalist forces characterized the struggle.

Recruits without arms and ammunition were useless, and shortages were endemic. Governor Alcocer of Coahuila complained in May that the rurales had exhausted their scarce supply of ammunition and that "to date they have received not one gun nor one cartridge, and we now find ourselves prevented from pursuing even the smallest [rebel raiding] bands."[22] But ammunition and guns cost money, of which, despite frantic administration efforts, there was always a shortage. The antiquated tax structure brought little income to the government; furthermore, any significant change in the struc-

[20] Governor Carlos M. Loyola to SecGob, May 30, 1913, AGN-Gobernación—Varios—Prefectos municipales 1913–1914.

[21] William Bayard Hale Memorandum, July 9, 1913, file 812.00/8203, NA, RG 59.

[22] Gov. Ignacio Alcocer to SecGob, May 7, 1913, ADN-Coahuila 1913 (Abril).

ture to produce adequate revenues would alienate the very classes that Huerta looked to for support. Under these circumstances, foreign borrowing appeared the only solution, but effective borrowing depended upon recognition. President Wilson's steadfast refusal to grant recognition effectively closed U.S. money markets, but the European markets were opened in early May when England and other countries recognized the new government. Huerta's agents completed the loan in June amid great publicity in Mexico; the government announced with smug satisfaction that it had met the financial problem and would soon suppress the rebellion. But shortly after the completion of the loan, William Bayard Hale, in his own curious style, wrote from Mexico:

> Financially, the prospects of the Government could scarcely be worse. Expenses are greater than ever; not only is the cost of the war inevitably heavy, but wartime conditions multiply all forms of graft.
>
> To meet this heavy deficiency, a loan of 200,000,000 pesos was authorized, and, it was announced, obtained: 60 millions immediately; 50 millions in six months; the balance in a year. In fact, 60 millions immediately was obtained—that is, at 90 cents, 54 millions, less certain commissions, which brought the sum down to 51,400,000, was placed at the Government's disposal. But of this, 40 millions went to Speyer and Company to extinguish an old loan, and at least 3 millions to pay other overdue and pressing debts. The Government actually gets about 8½ million pesos—$4,250,000.
>
> The additional loans of 50 millions in six months and 50 or 90 millions in a year, is optional with the Banks and will never be made. On the day the public reports stated that the Mexican loan had been subscribed twice over in London and three times over in Paris, I saw a cablegram addressed to the Bankers chiefly interested here saying that the London public had actually taken 16 per cent of the offering, the underwriters shouldering the rest. There will be no loan in six months.[23]

One may find fault with Hale's literary style but not his predictions; the remainder of the authorized loan was never completed. Like most of Huerta's military victories, the loan was much more impressive in the newspapers than in fact.

[23] William Bayard Hale Memorandum, July 9, 1913, file 812.00/8203, NA, RG 59.

In spite of Huerta's propaganda, the public seemed to be fully aware of the stringent fiscal situation. The exchange rate (50 centavos to the dollar at the time of negotiation) steadily declined; by the third week in July the exchange had fallen to 42.5 and, according to Chargé d'Affaires Nelson O'Shaughnessy, it was almost impossible to find gold in sufficient amounts to carry on normal business activity.[24] Within a matter of days the peso had declined to a point below 42,[25] where it remained for a few days before continuing its downward trend, reaching 36 by mid-September. In the face of the financial crisis, Huerta's government turned to forced loans; the central government informed governors and other interested personnel of the new policy in this form: "In order to maintain existing conditions, it is fitting to obtain funds for [military] supplies through forced loans; these loans will probably be repaid the 15th or 20th of the month when taxes are due. This should be done energetically, by order of the President."[26] The individual commanders and governors were left free to determine the specific method for allotting and collecting the loan. Some governors simply made a special assessment of 5 percent on all goods and properties,[27] but the military commanders tended to demand from business and banking houses arbitrarily determined sums.[28] Regardless of the system used, the forced loans were not particularly successful and the military field commanders continued to have grave difficulties in finding the funds to pay their men and to buy vitally needed supplies.

The financial crisis was not helped by the political maneuverings in connection with the election scheduled for late October. Félix Díaz, who had refused to take a cabinet position after the coup be-

[24] O'Shaughnessy to SecState, July 22, 1913, file 812.00/8113, NA, RG 59.

[25] O'Shaughnessy to SecState, July 26, 1913, file 812.00/8157, NA, RG 59.

[26] Gobernación to all governors and divisional military commanders, undated but dispatched mid-August, 1913, ADN-Jalisco 1913.

[27] For example, see SecGob to Governor of San Luis Potosí, September 19, 1913, and Governor of Sinaloa to SecGob, November 28, 1913, both in AGN-Gobernación—Asuntos varios 1913–1914.

[28] For example, the federal general in Nuevo Laredo demanded, and received, seventy thousand pesos from local businessmen, the funds to be used to pay the troops. There was always an implicit threat that if the men were not paid they would riot.

cause he wanted to be free to campaign for the presidency, found himself gradually eased into the background. In mid-summer he was dispatched to Europe on a military mission; after completing the mission, but while still in Europe, he was designated as a special envoy to Japan to thank the Japanese for their participation in the 1910 Centennial celebration.[29] But this mission collapsed when the Japanese government notified Mexico that Díaz would not be received at court, and as a consequence Huerta's partner in the coup was forced to dally in Europe in spite of his obvious desire to return to Mexico for the electoral campaign. Since Díaz's stay in Europe was now clearly a political exile and therefore embarrassing to Huerta's government, the Ministry of War "ordered" him to return in September.[30] By that date Huerta could safely allow him to return to Mexico; Huerta had forced the last of the Felicista cabinet members to resign in mid-September.[31] Ardent Huertistas of the stamp of Manuel Garza Aldape, or uncommitted but ambitious "intellectuals" like Querido Moheno,[32] replaced them. Furthermore, Huerta removed civilian governors who might support either Díaz or some other candidate and replaced them with military men who took orders from Huerta henchman Aureliano Blanquet.[33] By late September, then,

[29] In early 1913 Gustavo Madero had been designated to undertake such a mission, but the coup transpired before he left. In the case of both Gustavo Madero and Félix Díaz, the mission was clearly a political exile.

[30] *El Diario* carried the full story in its daily columns. While speculations concerning Díaz's actions were at the height, the Ministry of War pointed out that Díaz was still subject to military orders, and that if he returned to Mexico without specific orders he would be guilty of a breach of military law and therefore subject to a court-martial.

[31] He also removed Orozquista Minister of Communications David de la Fuente, whom he sent to Europe on an undefined mission (Querido Moheno, *Mi actuación política después de la decena trágica*, pp. 39–40). According to Moheno, who broke the news to de la Fuente, the minister had a simple choice: either accept a European assignment or be shot.

[32] Moheno, in his *Mi actuación*, attempts to make his participation in Huerta's government appear to be motivated by the highest principles, but his own words convict him of an overweening ambition as well as a lack of intellectual integrity.

[33] In early September, Minister of Gobernación Aureliano Urrutia blandly announced that three of the few remaining civilian governors were going to resign in a "few days," and that military governors were even then actually performing

Huerta's strategy became clear: unable to be a candidate himself, inasmuch as he held office, he was determined to prevent strong support to any candidate and to keep the vote to a minimum, thus providing an excuse to declare the election void because of insufficient public interest.

But as long as Congress remained in session, there was some danger that Huerta's plans would go awry. The old Maderista group who had retained their seats in the Chamber had formed themselves into a cohesive unit,[34] self-styled as the Bloc Renovador, and had systematically opposed the government. Allied with the Felicistas and partisans of other actual or potential candidates,[35] the Maderistas posed a real threat to Huerta's ambitions. As the first step in bringing the rebellious Congress under control, in mid-August Huerta appointed José María Lozano to the cabinet; Lozano enjoyed considerable prestige in the legislative chambers and could presumably exercise some influence there. When Congress continued to be recalcitrant, Huerta took an additional step the following month: he commissioned Lozano to form a majority bloc in the Chamber of Deputies and at the same time appointed Catholic party Deputy Eduardo Tamariz to the cabinet.[36] Opposition members refused to be gulled by such an obvious ruse; they effectively blocked Tamariz's appointment and in the process irritated Huerta even more.[37] While Huerta and his minions fumed over the failure of the Chamber of Deputies to cooperate, a distinguished senator from

the duties of the three offices. One suspects that the three governors thus first learned that they were going to resign (see *El Diario*, September 7, 1913, for Urrutia's announcement).

[34] Among the most important of this group were Félix Palavicini, José Natividad Macías, Manuel Puig Cassauranc, Luis Cabrera, Serapio Rendón, Luis Manuel Rojas, Alfonso Cravioto, and Luis G. Guzmán.

[35] In addition to Félix Díaz, the most notable candidates were Manuel Calero and Federico Gamboa. Gamboa, whose vice-presidential running mate was the military governor of Yucatán, resigned from the cabinet to be a candidate. Manuel Calero, with Jesús Flores Magón as his running mate, was due to draw heavy liberal support.

[36] Moheno, *Mi actuación*, p. 26.

[37] *El Diario*, September 20, 1913. As an elected member of the Chamber,

Chiapas really belled the cat. Belisario Domínguez, after providing for the future care of his young son, blistered Huerta and shamed Congress in a vitriolic attack in late September.[38] He minced no words:

The truth is this: during the rule of Mr. Victoriano Huerta, not only has nothing been done for the pacification of the country, but the conditions now in the Mexican Republic are infinitely worse than ever before . . . First and before all else [this condition is due to the fact that] the Mexican public will not resign itself to accept Don Victoriano Huerta as President of the Republic, that soldier who snatched power by means of treason and whose first act after coming to the presidency was to assassinate, in the most cowardly manner, the President and Vice President legally consecrated by popular vote . . . Peace we will have at any cost, Don Victoriano Huerta has said. Have you studied, Gentleman, the meaning of these words within the egotistical, ferocious criteria of Don Victoriano? These words mean that Don Victoriano Huerta is willing to spill every drop of Mexican blood, to cover the entire land with cadavers, to convert the entirety of our Motherland into an immense ruin, rather than abandon his power or spill a single drop of his own blood.

The National Assembly has the duty of deposing . . . [Huerta] from the presidency; he is the one against whom our brothers in arms protest with great reason, and consequently, he is the one least able to carry out the pacification . . .

The world is looking on us, Gentlemen of the Mexican National Congress; and the Motherland hopes you will honor her before the world, saving her from the shame of having as Chief Executive a traitor and an assassin.[39]

Tamariz could not, according to the constitution, accept other "employment." Since serving in the cabinet would be "employment," the opposition argued, he could not accept such a post.

[38] On September 23, Domínguez gave a copy of his speech to the secretary of the Senate, asking that it be read. The Senate leaders refused to allow it to be read, but Domínguez gave carbon copies to a number of senators, with the request that it be copied and passed on to others. A few days later the speech was printed and given wide distribution in Mexico City.

[39] For a poor translation, see file 812.00/9320 NA, RG 59. The version here is taken from Jesús Acuña, *Memoria de la Secretaría de Gobernación*, pp. 157–159.

Senator Domínguez disappeared from view. For the first few days his colleagues saw no reason for concern, assuming that he was prudently remaining in hiding until the shock of his speech died down; but when a week and then two weeks passed with no word from him, the Chamber of Deputies, by resolution on October 9, demanded an accounting.[40] At a series of emergency cabinet meetings late into that night and well into the following day, the government decided to dissolve Congress and put under arrest a selected list of opposition deputies.[41] On the morning of October 10, Minister of Gobernación Garza Aldape appeared before the Chamber of Deputies and demanded that the insulting resolution be withdrawn; when it became clear that the Chamber had no intention of doing so, police began apprehending those on the list, and a few moments later Huerta declared the dissolution of Congress and announced that a new Congress would be chosen in the October 26 election.[42]

With a cabinet composed of loyal minions or shallow rationalizers, with his own military appointees occupying the gubernatorial chairs, and with Congress dissolved, Huerta now controlled Mexico. Even prior to the dissolution, Governor John Lind of Minnesota, President Wilson's personal envoy, had become convinced that the election would be either postponed or declared void.[43] As election day approached, a combination of fear and indifference cast a pall over the country. One editor lamented the lack of enthusiasm and then summed up: "In public and private conversations, everyone dodges political questions, and when one asks the question, 'What's new?' everyone answers 'Nothing' with the coldest indifference and continues on his way, refusing to concern himself even for the moment

[40] *El Diario*, October 10, pp. 1 and 8. The following August, Domínguez's body was found in a shallow grave in Coyoacán, the victim of assassination.

[41] Moheno, *Mi actuación*, pp. 41–49. Maderistas, Felicistas, and Gamboistas alike were apprehended; among those who were imprisoned were Palavicini, Macías, Puig, Rojas, Pascual Ortiz Rubio, Rodolfo Reyes, Jorge Vera Estañol, Gerzayn Ugarte, and Juan Sarabia. On the list were 128, of whom 110 were found and imprisoned.

[42] *El Diario*, October 11, 1913, pp. 1 and 7.

[43] Lind to SecState, October 8, 1913, file 812.00/9127, NA, RG 59.

with political events."[44] But Huerta and his advisors left nothing to chance. Deciding that both domestic and international politics demanded at least a pretense of an election, the government decided not to postpone the balloting but to be sure that the election could be declared void; detailed instructions were sent to the state governors on techniques to be used. The plan was threefold. First, each governor was instructed to discourage voting, by careful selection of voting officials and judicious placement of ballot boxes, so that at least two-thirds of all polling places would show no ballots cast. In this event, under existing electoral law, the election could be declared void. But as an insurance against the failure of this technique, the Ministry of Gobernación told the governors to encourage, by any means not flagrantly illegal, write-in ballots for Huerta and Blanquet as president and vice-president; since neither was eligible for office, a significant vote for them would be used as grounds for invalidation. And in case the first two parts of the plan failed, Huerta's government insisted, it was incumbent on the governor, through his *jefes políticos*, to do a sufficient amount of "doctoring" to make the ballot boxes conform to the plan. Governors who failed to carry out the orders not only would be removed from office but also would be subject to "whatever other punishment the government may apply."[45] U.S. consuls in Mexico, in commenting on the election, were

[44] *El Centinela*, October 26, 1913, pp. 1–2.

[45] Governor Lind, through a means he did not divulge, secured a copy of the instructions sent to Governor Joaquín Maass and transmitted a translation to the Department of State. Secretary of State Bryan was understandably interested in the authenticity and asked both Lind and O'Shaughnessy to check carefully. Lind, who observed the elections, replied: "The . . . circular . . . is authentic. Large placards urging election of Huerta and Blanquet were posted through this city [Veracruz] and at the polls yesterday. The election was conducted and arrests were made in exact accordance with the instructions in the circular" (Lind to SecState, October 27, 1913, file 812.00/9406 NA, RG 59). O'Shaughnessy, who was sympathetic to Huerta, reluctantly agreed to the probable authenticity. At any rate, he concluded, the circular as transmitted certainly did convey Huerta's ideas on the election (O'Shaughnessy to SecState, October 27, 1913, file 812.00/9416). For Lind's translation of the circular, see Lind to SecState, October 26, 1913, file 812.00/9392. The circular was dated October 22, 1913.

unanimous in characterizing the event as a complete farce.[46] The ne result was that Huerta continued as provisional president with a sham and completely subservient Congress.[47] Even the blindes could no longer argue honestly that Huerta was a legal and constitutional president; by year's end Huerta had been no more successful in creating a political *ambiente* conducive to pacification than he had been in his military and financial activities.

While ineptitude drove Huerta's government deeper into the morass, Carranza was busy with the same kind of problems in the northern states; his methods were no less crude but they were considerably more effective, probably because most of the population was sympathetic with what they considered to be Carranza's ends. From the very beginning Carranza took the position that he represented constitutional government, inasmuch as the central government and all state governments that recognized that central government were unconstitutional, while he, as the elective chief magistrate of a sovereign state, had a constitutional duty to perform. The doughty northerner, while occasionally paying homage to the martyred President Madero, carefully refrained from identifying himself or his movement with Maderismo; by making his a struggle for constitutionalism rather than Maderista vengeance, he hoped to attract not only the Maderistas but also the anti-Madero intellectuals, who had a philosophical attraction for a constitutional form of government.

His first concrete step in this direction, after the initial declarations at the state level, was the oft-mentioned and highly overrated Plan de Guadalupe of March 26, 1913. Having suffered a major de-

[46] During the last days of October most of the consuls and other officials of the United States in Mexico reported on the elections in their districts; these reports may be found in the 812.00 series, NA, RG 59.

[47] Huerta ultimately found it necessary to use an interesting fiction. Inasmuch as the members of Congress were elected at the same time, it was impossible to declare the elections void on the ground of insufficient participation; to have done so would have voided the congressional elections as well and left Huerta with no legislature at all. For months there was no official announcement concerning the outcome of the presidential election. Huerta finally announced that since those receiving most of the votes for president were ineligible, no president had been elected. The congressional election was not affected by the decision.

feat in his attack on Saltillo on March 21–24, Carranza felt a desperate need to give the Constitutionalist movement a national rather than a purely local cast; even though revolutionary activity was rapidly growing in Chihuahua, Sonora, and Durango, to that date nothing even resembling a unified plan had been proclaimed. The Plan de Guadalupe filled the vacuum. Unlike most revolutionary plans, Carranza's document made no mention whatsoever of any social, economic, or political question other than that of constitutional government; the plan merely disavowed Huerta's government and those state governments which had given fealty to it, designated Carranza as the First Chief of the Constitutionalist army, and stipulated that the First Chief (whether Carranza or by that time some other) would act as *ad interim* president for the purpose of holding elections after victory had been achieved.[48] The document as originally drafted and signed was purely a Coahuila, and an unofficial, instrument; all the signatories were with Carranza's army in the immediate vicinity, and no representatives of the other states were present for either the drafting or the signing ceremonies.

Within a few days after Carranza had completed the Plan de Guadalupe, revolutionaries from other states took the initiative in consolidating the rebellious groups. Juntas had grown like Topsy in the month following Madero's assassination; groups in, or exiled from, the northern states were desperately meeting to give real impetus to military activities, and it was crucial that there be some semblance of unity. Dr. Samuel Navarro, one of the delegates to the Chihuahua legislature who had managed to escape when General Antonio Rábago seized that state government in late February, arrived in Monclova on April 1 to suggest to Carranza that a formal union be established among the various revolutionary forces. As a consequence of the suggestion, and after much traveling by representatives between Coahuila and Sonora, delegates from Sonora, Chihuahua, and Coahuila met in Monclova on April 19 with Carranza to draft and sign a statement of cooperation.[49] The resulting

[48] "Plan de Guadalupe," in *Decretos y demás disposiciones del ejército constitutionalista*, pp. 16–18.

[49] Roberto V. Pesqueira and Adolfo de la Huerta from Sonora, Dr. Samuel

document stipulated that the legal representatives of the three state governments concerned accepted as a basis of operation the Plan de Guadalupe, and that Roberto V. Pesqueira—the brother of Governor Ignacio Pesqueira of Sonora and an elected member of the national Chamber of Deputies—be designated by Carranza as the confidential agent of the Constitutionalist government to work for recognition by the United States.[50] In this fashion the Constitutionalist government, in rudimentary form, was created. In order to reinforce the Constitutionalist aspects of the agreement, the legislatures of Sonora and Coahuila formally accepted the document.[51]

Armed with no more authority than the Plan de Guadalupe and the subsequent acceptance of that plan by Sonora and Chihuahua, Carranza began issuing decrees of paramount importance to the nation's future. As the spirit moved him, or as the need arose, he decreed dispositions regarding fiscal, military, and political or administrative affairs. To be sure, he consulted his advisors prior to issuing any important decree; but in every case the final decision was his. Constitutionalist government in 1913 was an anomaly; although Carranza was careful to retain the flavor of a legal and constitutional government, he was in fact an absolute dictator governing by decree and circular. Using as his authority for decrees the statement, "In use of the extraordinary faculties with which I find myself vested," —these powers presumably inherent in his position as Primer Jefe—Don Venustiano during 1913 and early 1914 constructed a government and developed an army. The decrees exude confidence; Carranza was, in his own mind, the head of state and he functioned as such.

Navarro from Chihuahua, and Alfredo Breceda from Coahuila. Each held an official position with his state government at the time of the Huerta coup and could therefore claim a Constitutionalist position.

[50] Some of the details of the negotiations, and the instrument itself, are given in Juan Barragán, *Historia del ejército y de la revolución constitucionalista*, I, 135–140.

[51] Since the Coahuila legislature was adjourned *sine die*, the legislative Permanent Deputation ratified the Plan de Guadalupe on April 19. In Sonora, where the state government continued to function without interruption, the legislature ratified the Monclova agreement when it met during the summer.

Carranza, like Huerta, was confronted with the threefold problem of military, finance, and politics. Recruitment tended to take care of itself, since the military rank or rate of an individual depended upon the number of men he could persuade to submit to his authority. Natera, Herrera, the Arrieta brothers, Chao, Blanco, Villa, and others of like capacity became recognized field commanders—first by their own men, and then by the Constitutionalist government. For the first few months Carranza made no attempt to formalize the military organization; in his own region—Coahuila, Nuevo León, and Tamaulipas—the Primer Jefe did indeed develop a rough table of organization and personally designated the major command positions, but in Sonora the state government accepted the responsibility. In the other regions, where no Constitutionalist state government existed, units gathered and campaigned on a purely informal and cooperative basis, depending upon the wisdom—or whim—of the local commanders. By early July the Constitutionalist movement had gathered sufficient momentum to warrant at least a modicum of general planning, and consequently Carranza divided the nation into seven areas of military operations, with the military forces in each area designated as a corps commanded by a general.[52] Of these seven, two became of dominant importance and a third assumed considerable military—and major political—significance.[53] The Northeast Corps, including Coahuila, Nuevo León, and Tamaulipas, was commanded by Pablo González; the Northwest Corps, including Sonora, Sinaloa, Chihuahua, and Durango, was commanded by Alvaro Obregón;[54] the Central Corps, including Zacatecas and the states to the south and east, was ultimately commanded by Pánfilo Natera. These three corps, with few exceptions, operated independently of one another during 1913 and well into 1914; they carried the brunt of the fighting and were essentially the victors against Huerta. The

[52] Carranza decree of July 4, 1913, in *Decretos y demás disposiciones*, pp. 87–88.

[53] The Central Corps became a political football between Carranza and Villa in June, 1914, when Zacatecas was under attack.

[54] The Northwest Corps was subsequently split into two divisions, with Villa and Obregón the divisional generals.

other corps—the East, the West, the South, and the Southeast—were expressions of optimism in July, 1913, rather than a ratification of an existing condition; they were of minor significance militarily until late in the movement against Huerta.

Even before the creation of the corps, Carranza made a military decision that gave to the revolution one of its most malignant characteristics. Probably stimulated by the summary executions to which some of the Durango rebels were subjected in late April, and possibly growing out of his rigid concern for law, Carranza on May 14, 1913, put into force a Benito Juárez decree of 1862.[55] According to Juárez's decree, promulgated during the French invasion, anyone guilty of rebellion against constituted authority, rebellion against established political institutions, or attack on the life of the president was to be subject to the death penalty.[56] In practice this meant summary execution of prisoners of war, since all members of the federal forces were, in Carranza's terms, rebelling against established institutions; in theory the Constitutionalists, representative of legal authority, would not be subject to the original Juárez decree.

Carranza, like Huerta, had his money problems. "When the Revolution against the Huerta regime began, it was impossible to follow any regular system of financing, since each military chieftain independently had to gather military supplies wherever he could obtain them,"[57] according to Carranza when he belatedly reported to the national Congress in 1917. Seizing or requisitioning mounts, food, and clothing are effective means of getting immediate control of supplies, but responsible revolutionary leaders early recognized the ultimate chaos—as well as the poor public relations—emanating from such activities. Furthermore, munitions of war could not be requisitioned; cash was needed to buy guns and ammunition from

[55] Carranza decree Number 5, May 14, 1913, in *Decretos y demás disposiciones*, p. 80.

[56] For the text of the Juárez decree, dated January 25, 1862, see ibid., pp. 80–87. When Carranza reissued the Juárez decree, he italicized the pertinent parts.

[57] Venustiano Carranza, *Informe . . . encargado del poder ejecutivo de la República*, p. 166.

foreign sources.[58] The problem confronting the leaders, then, and Carranza in particular as the responsible leader, was to organize a fiscal system that would establish a medium of exchange acceptable within the country and to obtain gold for foreign expenditures. Carranza himself opposed dependence upon loans from individuals or banks, even though he had begun his movement through such a loan, on the grounds that such resources not only would be insufficient but also would put "the Revolution at the mercy of the lenders."[59] Officially, then, financing the revolution depended upon a combination of paper money and export taxes. Operating on the principle that it was the duty "of all Mexicans to contribute in proportional part to financing the Army until constitutional order" was reestablished, Carranza on April 26, 1913, authorized the first emission of paper money;[60] in bills of one, five, ten, fifty, and one hundred pesos, he printed and distributed five million pesos of paper money within the next few months. Before the end of the year it was necessary to augment the supply through the emission of another fifteen million,[61] and in early 1914 an additional ten million was printed.[62] Carranza declared the money to be legal tender and decreed prison sentences for those refusing to accept the money or discounting it; he required that public officials as well as private individuals accept the paper as satisfaction for any and all debts. Furthermore, he prohibited the use of tokens or any other form of medium of exchange.[63] But in spite of decrees and penalties, Gresham's law operated in classical fashion; before the end of the year small coins disappeared from public view and in early 1914 the Constitutionalist government was forced to print five- and ten-centavo bills.[64]

Military commanders operating along the U.S. border early began

[58] To be sure, munitions were captured from federal supplies, but this source at best was uncertain and had to be supplemented by major purchases in the United States.

[59] Carranza, *Informe*, p. 168.

[60] Carranza decree of April 26, 1913, in *Decretos y demás disposiciones*, p. 52.

[61] Carranza decree Number 14, December 28, 1913, ibid., pp. 54–56.

[62] Carranza decree Number 18, February 12, 1914, ibid., pp. 57–58.

[63] Carranza decree Number 14, December 28, 1913, ibid., pp. 54–56.

[64] Carranza decree Number 22, March 4, 1914, ibid., pp. 59–60.

collecting a duty on exports, particularly on cattle, for the purpose of obtaining hard money with which to buy munitions of war. Since each commander enjoyed a marked degree of independence and set the duty arbitrarily at a rate demanded by the immediate situation, before the end of the year wide variations in such duties were the rule. In order to correct the situation, and particularly to create an impression of an organized government properly functioning, by decree in October, Carranza established a uniform duty for various classes of cattle.[65] As Constitutionalist control extended to mineral and petroleum regions, he subjected these products to an export tax. The tax on oil probably was motivated as strongly by a desire to control the industry as the need to collect money for the revolution, for, as Carranza later said, "By this means the Revolutionary Government not only was able to gather funds, but also began to resolve a problem that had been pending for a long time, and that consisted of making petroleum companies, who considered themselves exempt from tax payments, contribute [to government income]."[66] The total amount collected from the oil and mining companies during the struggle against Huerta is unknown, but it appears to have been of some significance.

A tax source of lesser importance, in terms of total income, was the collection of the stamp tax already in existence; in those areas under their control the Constitutionalists simply acted as the federal government for the collection of normal taxes, with the local revolutionary officials responsible for the collection and the accounting. Nothing in the records indicates the magnitude of this source. The Constitutionalists also had another minor source: the income from "intervened" properties. Military commanders commonly seized properties belonging to "enemies of the Revolution," as a means both of obtaining funds and of assuring themselves that the Huerta government would not have access to the income. At no time during the Huerta period did the Constitutional government make any attempt

[65] Carranza decree of October 20, 1913, ibid., p. 54. The first tax was from four to ten pesos an animal, depending upon age and sex; a later decree doubled the duty.

[66] Carranza, *Informe*, p. 171.

to regularize the practice or to establish a system through which the properties would be returned to the owners. Local officials, generally military but on occasion civilian, determined what properties to seize and on what grounds.[67]

Aside from the above sources of Constitutionalist income, in every case presumably "national" in character, each local government or military command used its own methods to obtain funds. "Distance and the independence with which the military chiefs operated, particularly at the beginning of the Revolution, made it impossible for them to be provided with funds by the First Chieftainship."[68] In view of this situation, Carranza early authorized various military leaders to print paper money; before the beginning of 1914 every major field commander, including Obregón, Villa, Pablo González, the Arrieta brothers, Manuel Diéguez, Luis Caballero, and Francisco Murguía, was busily turning out reams of fiat money.[69] Furthermore, the various states themselves, as Constitutionalist government was established, entered into the practice, and by early 1914 six states had bills of their own. In an attempt to bring some order out of the existing chaos, early in 1914 Carranza decreed that all the paper money issued by the Constitutionalist governors be accepted as legal tender in all areas controlled by the Constitutionalists.[70]

Constitutionalist finance during the Huerta period, then, consisted of paper money emitted by Carranza, by dozens of military commanders, and by six states; except for the thirty million pesos issued by Carranza there is no adequate record of the paper money printed, but in 1917 Carranza estimated it at an additional thirty million.[71] Furthermore, each local commander requisitioned whatever available supplies he needed, and as often as not he failed to give the

[67] Ibid., pp. 171–174.

[68] Ibid., p. 177.

[69] Ibid., pp. 177–178.

[70] Carranza decree Number 21, February 28, 1914, in *Decretos y demás disposiciones*, p. 59. The six states were Sonora, Chihuahua, Durango, Sinaloa, Nuevo León, and Tamaulipas; Carranza's own state of Coahuila is conspicuously absent from the list.

[71] Carranza, *Informe*, p. 178.

owner of the requisitioned property a receipt,[72] even though Carranza urged all revolutionaries to be scrupulous in giving such documents.[73] Added to the confusion of paper money and requisition chits, the local commanders seized "enemy" property and only infrequently made any accounting of the income received; haciendas, mines, and business establishments were the favorite targets for intervention. As though this welter of presumably negotiable paper were insufficient, local commanders utilized a special form of requisitioning—forced loans. Bankers and merchants in Torreón, Chihuahua, Durango, Parral, San Pedro, Ciudad Victoria, and all other major towns occupied either temporarily or permanently by Constitutionalist troops were called upon to open their coffers. Villa reportedly relieved Torreón of about three million pesos in gold after he captured that city in September, 1913.

The system, or lack of system, was an open invitation to every possible kind of financial skulduggery, and at least some of the revolutionaries were quick to take advantage of opportunities offered. Reports coming from both Huerta officials and U.S. representatives in Mexico are filled with allusions to questionable transactions and results. José Obregón, the general's dull-witted brother, was reputed to be excessively zealous in appropriating to himself both cash and property. Lorenzo Rosado, an official in the Sonora government under Pesqueira and "one of the most pernicious" of the revolutionaries, was accused of enriching himself in the short space of six months.[74] Other rebel leaders seized, and sold in the United States cattle belonging to individuals and to companies;[75] the Cananea Cattle Company lost most of its herds in this fashion. Revolutionaries frequently used ransom of one form or another as a means of obtaining money. Consul Hamm reported from Durango: "Are still a

[72] For example, see Hostetter to SecState, October 28, 1913, file 812.00/955 and enclosure, NA, RG 59.

[73] Carranza circular of August 10, 1913, in *Decretos y demás disposiciones*, p. 64.

[74] Mexican consul, Nogales, to SecRelEx, August 14, 1913, ADN-Sonora 191 (Septiembre).

[75] SecRelEx to SecGob, November 11, 1913, AGN-Gobernación—Relaciones con los estados 1913–1914.

the mercy and caprice of General Urbina. Citizens constantly arrested and held for ransom. Archbishop placed in cell for a half-million ransom. Foreigners suffering equally with natives."[76] General Hill forced Pascual G. Lamadrid of Alamos, Sonora, to pay forty thousand pesos in ransom,[77] and a U.S. citizen who owned a ranch in the Mexican Big Bend country paid a Constitutionalist officer nearly twenty thousand dollars as a surety that his cattle would not be driven off.[78] Carranza probably had reference to these irregularities when he later stated that "in many cases it was necessary to leave tax-collecting at the disposition of the military authorities, . . . and in the majority of cases the military commanders, obligated by necessity, assumed treasury faculties which extended to imposing special contributions."[79]

Given these circumstances it is impossible to ascertain the total cost of the Constitutionalist effort. Records were ill-kept, even for the expenditure of funds represented by paper money; while Carranza's staff kept an accurate tab on the amount of paper money printed, and the states did the same, the military commanders were lax in record-keeping. Carranza later summed it up: "In the realm of the military, above all, it has been impossible to secure the data necessary to authenticate the expenditures made. In many cases the funds allocated to campaign necessities were made in lump sum, with the money going to the military commanders or to the paymasters accompanying them, and many times there is no record of the expenditure."[80] Constitutionalist fund-raising methods may have been necessary, and certainly were effective, but they saddled the ultimate government with a major fiscal problem productive of economic malaise.

From the outset of the Constitutionalist movement, Carranza ac-

[76] Hamm to SecState, July 9, 1913, file 812.00/8063, NA, RG 59.

[77] P. G. Lamadrid to SecGob, September 10, 1913, and attached documents, AGN-Gobernación—Varios 1911–1913. Lamadrid gave three bank drafts valued at thirty thousand pesos as a part of his ransom; a stop order prevented the actual payment of the drafts.

[78] Consul Ellsworth to SecState, June 12, 1913, file 812.00/7802, NA, RG 59.

[79] Carranza, *Informe*, p. 168.

[80] Ibid., p. 189.

cepted as a responsibility the ultimate repayment of all damages, whether in the form of loans or destruction, resulting from his movement. A decree of May 10, 1913, recognized "the right of all nationals and foreigners to reclaim payment for damages suffered during the Revolution of 1910, being the period between November 21, 1910 and May 31, 1911, . . . [and the] right of all nationals and foreigners to reclaim [payment for] the damages which they have suffered and continue to suffer during the present struggle, being the period from February 19 of the current year until the restoration of constitutional order."[81] Whether this decree stemmed from Carranza's concern for foreign approbation or domestic acceptance, or from principles of governmental responsibility, is questionable. But in this position, the Primer Jefe was absolutely consistent, iterating and reiterating that with the reestablishment of order would come a general accounting during which all legitimate claims would be paid. On the basis of this decree the later claims commissions were established.

In the meantime Carranza decided to move closer to the center of successful Constitutionalist military activity for the purpose of establishing at least a semblance of government. By mid-summer of 1913 he was fully conscious of troubles brewing among the revolutionary forces in Sonora, where Maytorena's return to the governorship was not greeted with tumultuous joy by the Pesqueira partisans, and he therefore determined to visit the state to act as a mediating force. He could have made the trip in ease and comfort by crossing the Texas border and taking a train; there was no particular danger of arrest by U.S. authorities, since the northern government was making no serious attempt to enforce the neutrality statutes and Constitutionalist agents operated openly in all the border cities. But Carranza was a stubborn and prideful man who considered it undignified for the head of a revolution to forsake the national territory even for one moment. Furthermore, were he to leave the country, even temporarily, his opponents could claim that he had thereby divested himself of any claim he might have to constitutional power.

[81] Carranza decree of May 10, 1913, in *Decretos y demás disposiciones*, pp. 52–53.

Rather than take the easy way then, Carranza began the long trip overland, stopping at Torreón in late July to direct the unsuccessful attack on the Laguna city. Traveling by horseback to Pedriceña, Durango, some thirty miles southwest of Torreón, he took a train for Durango City, where he arrived on August 6. Establishing a temporary headquarters at nearby Canatlán, he remained some days consulting with the Arrieta brothers and other revolutionary leaders in the region and issuing a number of decrees concerning fiscal matters. He left Durango toward the middle of August, going to Parral, Chihuahua, by way of Tepehuanes, Durango; he made the two-hundred-mile trip by horseback and by train without incident. Remaining in Parral for only three days, during which he exchanged impressions with Generals Herrera and Chao, he began the tortuous horseback journey over the Sierra Madre Occidental with an escort of slightly more than a hundred men. He covered the first hundred miles southwest to the little mining community of Guadalupe y Calvo, Chihuahua, in torrential rains; for the next ninety miles along the crest northwesterly to Chinobampo, Sinaloa, he rode in better weather but over rougher terrain. When he arrived at Chinobampo on September 12 he wired Governor Felipe Riveros at San Blas;[82] three days later, at El Fuerte, the Primer Jefe was met by Riveros, General Obregón (who had come from Sonora with a special escort), General Hill, and Alfredo Breceda, whom Carranza had sent to Sonora by way of the United States from Coahuila two months earlier to pave the way. A train took Carranza from El Fuerte to San Blas to Navajoa, Sonora, and to Cruz de Piedra, in the vicinity of Guaymas; he stopped at each point to encourage the local revolutionary leaders. With federal General Pedro Ojeda in occupation of Guaymas and attempting to ambush Carranza and his small band,[83] the Pri-

[82] Riveros was constitutional governor of Sinaloa at the time of the Huerta coup and, although he did not take any strong stand against Huerta, was forced to flee to the United States not long after that event. Carranza, always keeping uppermost in mind the question of constitutionality, urged Riveros to return and claim his post. As the Sonora forces moved south, Riveros received sufficient aid from them to return to his state and act as the titular head of the government and of the Constitutionalist forces operating there.

[83] Ojeda to SecGyM, October 11, 1913, ADN-Sonora 1913 (Octubre). At that

mer Jefe and his escort again took off in the rain on horseback guided by Yaquis,[84] to intercept the rail line at Santa María wher Governor Maytorena and other officials of the Sonora governmen met him. He and his party arrived in Hermosillo on September 20 two months and ten days after he had been forced to leave Mon clova.[85]

Whether the Primer Jefe intended originally to remain in Sonor is unknown; the little evidence on the subject leads to the contrar conclusion. But he obviously liked what he found in the northwest ern state: complete control save Guaymas, a fairly efficient and func tioning government dating from the Madero period, ports of entr giving access to the United States and its military supplies, and strong military force under able leadership. By mid-October he ha concluded that Hermosillo would be a suitable temporary capital,[8 and there he remained for the rest of the year.

Shortly after reaching his decision to stay in Sonora, Carranz "considering that the major part of the national territory [was] foun under the domination of forces under . . . [his] command, and fo this reason it . . . [was] necessary to organize a cabinet of all branch es of Public Administration,"[87] by decree established a central gov ernment consisting of eight departments, paralleling those existin in Mexico City.[88] Neither labor nor agriculture was considered c

---

time Ojeda was confident that Carranza would return by the same route an was again making plans for an ambush, but he was not too sanguine as to th result.

84 Ibid. Ojeda lamented the fact that the combination of rain and Yaq guidance prevented him from capturing Carranza.

85 This account of his travels is pieced together from a variety of sources, ir cluding Alvaro Obregón, *Ocho mil kilómetros en campaña*; Manuel Aguir Berlanga, *Revolución y reforma*; Barragán, *Ejército*; and Alfredo Breceda, *Méx co revolucionario, 1913–1917*. U.S. consular reports are inaccurate, as are th documents in ADN, largely because they were based upon rumor.

86 He so informed U.S. Consul Frederick Simpich at Nogales on October 1 (see Simpich to SecState, October 13, 1913, file 812.00/9188, NA, RG 59).

87 Quoted from the preamble of decree Number 10, October 17, 1913, i *Decretos y demás disposiciones*, p. 20.

88 Decree Number 10, October 17, 1913, ibid., pp. 20–24. Carranza had onl the day before returned from an inspection trip to northern and eastern Sonor

sufficient importance to warrant a separate ministry; labor was under the jurisdiction of the Ministry of Gobernación, while agriculture was one of the widely varied functions of the Ministry of Fomento. Furthermore, in filling the positions designated in the decree, Carranza saw no need at that point for a separate secretary of *fomento*; he designated Ignacio Bonillas, with the title of *oficial mayor* rather than either *secretario* or *subsecretario*, to administer both Communications and Fomento.[89] Within a matter of weeks Carranza had his newly formed government operating with relative efficiency in all the northern regions controlled by the Constitutionalists. His government established postal rates, brought a degree of order and consistency to the administration of customs and immigration services, devoted some attention to problems of the mining companies and regularized the terms of their concessions, and established some semblance of control over military operations.

Thus before the end of 1913 Carranza had his "national" capital in Hermosillo and Huerta his in Mexico City. Both men governed in roughly similar fashions, by decree, and both depended upon equivalent sources of power, the military. But Carranza's power was waxing full, and Huerta's was on the wane.

[89] The other cabinet posts: Foreign Relations and Treasury combined, Francisco Escudero; Gobernación, Rafael Zubarán Capmany; and War, Felipe Angeles. Justice and Public Instruction were left unfilled (see Barragan, *Ejército*, I, 219–220).

4. HUERTA AND WILSON

From retirement, several years after the termination of his venturesome tenure at the Mexico City embassy, participant-observer Henry Lane Wilson summed up the trials and tribulations that the Huerta government confronted in the field of diplomacy: "Huerta was a man of strong passions, great courage and patriotism; his ambition was to restore the system of Díaz but he lacked the genius and constructive industry of Díaz. Lacking these qualities he fell a victim to conspiracies and was driven from power by the armies and fleets of the Government of the United States, leaving behind him chaotic conditions which endure to this hour [1920]."[1] Whether these few words accurately represented the situation need not be debated—certainly the Constitutionalists always believed it was they, and not the United States, who drove Huerta from power —but Wilson's words do point up a serious problem facing the

[1] Henry Lane Wilson, "How to Restore Peace in Mexico," in *Mexico and the Caribbean*, ed. George H. Blakeslee, p. 149.

Huerta administration: recognition by foreign governments. U.S. contiguity and a preeminence of economic interests led most of the world momentarily to depend upon that nation to take the lead in the matter of recognition, it being generally assumed that the United States would so act with a minimal delay. But the new Washington administration refused to respond immediately despite Ambassador Wilson's importunities;[2] as President Wilson and Secretary of State Bryan saw it, three major questions had to be answered before they could extend de facto recognition.

First, and probably foremost, the administration was attempting to bring to international affairs the same kind of morality it hoped to instill in domestic politics. As President Wilson phrased it only a few days after his inauguration:

> We hold, as I am sure all thoughtful leaders of republican government everywhere hold, that just government rests always upon the consent of the governed, and that there can be no freedom without order based upon law and upon the public conscience and approval. We shall look to make these principles the basis of mutual intercourse, respect and helpfulness between our sister republics and ourselves. We shall lend our influence to every kind of realization of these principles in fact and in practice, knowing that disorder, personal intrigue and defiance of constitutional rights weaken and discredit government and injure none so much as the people who are unfortunate enough to have their common life and their common affairs so tainted and disturbed. We can have no sympathy with those who seek to seize the power of government to advance their own personal interests or ambition.[3]

One may quarrel with Wilson's basic assumptions in making the policy statement. The question of whether a major power should or can shoulder responsibility for maintaining governmental morality in the smaller nations has vexed men for many generations and has frequently impinged on the question of recognition. Even the British, whose recognition policy was probably the most consistent

[2] The Huerta coup d'état occurred on February 18, Madero's assassination on the night of February 22, and Wilson's inauguration on March 4.

[3] Wilson statement, March 11, 1913, published in the *American Journal of International Law* 7 (1913): 331.

among the major powers, had habitually refused to extend recogni-tion to provisional governments. Immediately after the Huerta co the Foreign Office stipulated that an "election according to duly pr scribed constitutional methods" must precede any recognition of t new Mexican government.[4] State Department Counselor John Ba sett Moore insisted that the United States could not be the judge other nations' morals and pointed out that the United States mai tained relations with many governments of doubtful constitutionali and morality.[5] But once President Wilson had enunciated the prin ples, valid or not, the question of Huerta's constitutional status b came of paramount importance. On the basis of the evidence befo him, he could certainly conclude that Huerta had been guilty "personal intrigue" and had seized power to further his own "pe sonal interests or ambition."

Second, the contiguity of the United States and Mexico, with the roughly fifteen-hundred-mile common border, posed some serio problems. Internal dissension in Mexico inevitably spilled over in the United States, not only raising uncomfortable diplomatic que tions but also endangering lives of U.S. citizens within their ow country; the experiences during the abortive Liberal party revolt 1906 and the Madero movement four years later had made this fa abundantly clear.[6] Furthermore, the very areas in which the Cons tutionalists had become most active by the second week in March- Sonora, Chihuahua, and Coahuila—were regions in which U.S. ci zens invested and lived. Despite the optimistic and soothing repor coming from Ambassador Wilson concerning the nation's accep ance of Huerta, on the basis of reports coming from the consuls the north the administration saw evidence of a serious revolution the making. In view of Carranza's bitter note to Taft on February 2 it seemed clear that a premature recognition of the Huerta regin

[4] Irwin Laughlin (U.S. chargé in London) to SecState, February 25, 191 file 812.00/6372, NA, RG 59.

[5] John Bassett Moore to SecState, May 14, 1913, file 812.00/8378, NA, F 59.

[6] The Maderista attack on Ciudad Juárez in May, 1911, had particularly u fortunate results, since a number of persons in El Paso were killed or wound by bullets coming from the Mexican side.

would make the Constitutionalists hostile to U.S. citizens and interests alike in the northern region. Before granting recognition, therefore, Washington had to be doubly sure of Huerta's ability to suppress the Constitutionalist movement quickly and effectively.

And finally, reports from Mexico indicated quite clearly that Ambassador Wilson had played a role in the events of February. Exactly what the role had been and how it had affected the coup d'état and its bloody sequel were not clear, but the unanswered questions had been put before the U.S. public by a number of newspapers that openly charged the ambassador with complicity in both the coup and the assassinations. In view of a minor reign of terror apparently developing in Mexico,[7] Wilson could scarcely afford to grant recognition to such a government, which his own ambassador had helped to create.

The president, then, was not to be stampeded into granting recognition to Huerta. Before making any move, he felt it incumbent on his administration to determine the legality of Huerta's regime, the acceptance of that government by the Mexican people, the attitude of the Mexicans toward Carranza and his incipient Constitutionalist revolution, the ability of the Huerta government to maintain order and fulfill international obligations, and the part played by Ambassador Wilson. But the information coming from Mexico did more to confuse than to illuminate. The ambassador repeatedly and consistently stressed the strength demonstrated by, and the acceptance accorded to, the Huerta regime while he characterized the revolution as mere bandit activity of no political import. At the same time, consular reports from Hermosillo, Nogales, Mazatlán, Ciudad Juárez, Chihuahua, Saltillo, Monterrey, and Matamoros seriously questioned the validity of the ambassador's judgment.[8] Admiral Cowles reported favorably on the discipline and order among the revolutionists in

[7] In addition to the murders of Gustavo Madero, Francisco Madero, Pino Suárez, and Abraham González, the new government or its agents were guilty of killing at least one political prisoner in Mexico City, of hanging men presumed to be revolutionaries, and of the incarceration of many state officials who had been elected during the Madero administration.

[8] Reports from these consuls, giving their observations of the situation, may be found in the 812.00 series for February, March, and April, NA, RG 59.

Sonora,[9] Consul Gaston Schmutz of Aguascalientes characterized Pánfilo Natera as an intelligent and dedicated man,[10] Consul Jesse Johnson praised Lucio Blanco in glowing terms,[11] and businessman Alexander Dye not only complimented the Constitutionalists on their discipline but also prophesied a Huerta defeat.[12] But Ambassador Wilson was not alone in his evaluation. Consul Theodore C. Hamm of Durango feared the revolutionists as bandits,[13] Consul Luther Ellsworth at Piedras Negras dismissed the Constitutionalists in contemptuous terms,[14] Admiral F. E. Beatty insisted that Huerta was the only alternative to absolute chaos,[15] businessman Thomas L. Carothers from Guanajuato reported that only a military dictatorship would ever be effective,[16] while businessman Delbert J. Haff told the president not only that Huerta honestly wanted free elections but also that "the most influential classes here, both political and social as well as business, are united in support of the Huerta Administration."[17] But these were only a few of those who offered

9 Cowles to SecNavy, June 6, 1913, file 812.00/7841, NA, RG 59. The admiral made a day-by-day report of his observation in the Guaymas region, April 15–May 2.

10 Schmutz to SecState, June 12, 1913, file 812.00/7910, NA, RG 59.

11 Johnson to SecState, June 16, 1913, file 812.00/7781, NA, RG 59.

12 Dye to Fred Morris Dearing, June 10, 1913, file 812.00/7823, NA, RG 59. Dye, who had earlier served as a consul, had what he called "large interests" in Mexico.

13 Hamm to SecState, Diary report, April–May, 1913, file 812.00/7720, NA, RG 59.

14 See particularly Ellsworth to SecState, May 22, 1913, and May 28, 1913, files 812.00/7611 and /7673, NA, RG 59. In the latter report, Ellsworth said: "It might surprise the Department could it hear the expressions of Americans and Mexicans resident in the American Border, regarding the treatment that should be accorded Huerta, Diaz, La Barra, Mondragon, and our Ambassador, Honorable Henry Lane Wilson. The people of the Border use a word 'kill' so frequently that I think they at times forget that to kill is a crime." Ellsworth had his own peculiar grammatical style.

15 Beatty to SecNavy, May 14, 1913, file 812.00/7631 enclosure, NA, RG 59. Beatty estimated that Huerta could last only ninety days without active U.S. aid.

16 Carothers to Attorney General J. C. McReynolds, May 14, 1914, file 812.00/7648, NA, RG 59. Thomas Carothers was the brother of George Carothers, who later played an important role as a Wilson special agent.

17 Haff to Wilson, May 28, 1913, file 812.00/7746, NA, RG 59. Haff had

advice and information on the Mexican situation; the administration was inundated with mail, each writer insisting on his own peculiar sensitivity to the Mexican problem and ridiculing those who might have a contrary view.

Confronted with this welter of contradictions, and doubtful of the capacity of the consular and embassy officers to report accurately, Wilson and Bryan cast about for some individual whom they could trust to make an objective study of the situation. As early as mid-April, Wilson had sounded out William Bayard Hale, a journalist who had supported Wilson in the 1912 campaign; he wanted to know whether Hale would make a trip to "Central and South American states" on a confidential mission to "find out just what is going on down there."[18] A gifted and loquacious, albeit erratic, reporter whose only Latin American experience had been a short trip some years previously, Hale accepted the mission but delayed almost a month before he began his journey with verbal instructions to investigate the part played by Ambassador Wilson; he was cautioned to pose as a newspaperman with no governmental connections.[19]

In the meantime, despite the failure of recognition, Ambassador Wilson continued for a time to work with the Huerta government with considerable harmony, attempting to obtain from the Mexican administration a clear commitment with respect to outstanding claims. But the curious situation could not last indefinitely, and in a fit of pique on May 7 Huerta upbraided the ambassador for the "unfriendly" posture of the United States; three days later he informed H. L. Wilson that thenceforward his government would treat with the embassy only on routine matters.[20] Huerta's action came as a result of a fundamental misconception of the issues as President Wil-

---

previously been in Washington and had left a memorandum on the Mexican situation.

[18] A copy of the letter to Hale is in Ray Stannard Baker, *Woodrow Wilson: Life and Letters, 1913–1914*, pp. 243–244.

[19] In spite of the instruction, Hale let the nature of his mission be known in Mexico City; the ambassador objected strenuously to his activities (see H. L. Wilson to SecState, July 8, 1913, file 812.00/7990, NA, RG 59).

[20] H. L. Wilson to SecState, May 8 and May 10, 1913, files 812.00/7431 and /7454, NA, RG 59.

son saw them; the Mexican assumed that the real stumbling block to recognition was the claims question and hoped that he could force favorable action by posing an implied threat to the extensive U.S. interests in his country. But relegating the U.S. ambassador to an inferior position had no effect on President Wilson; it merely destroyed the effectiveness of Huerta's strongest supporter in the diplomatic service.

But Great Britain, too, had extensive interests in Mexico.[21] Unlike Wilson and Bryan, the officials in the British Foreign Office were unconcerned with the "morality" of the Mexican administration and therefore took a hard "realistic" view of the situation; their only concern was Huerta's legal status and his ability to pacify the country.[22] The question of recognition came to the attention of the Foreign Office immediately after the coup, and within the government there were sharp differences of opinion with regard to the proper course to pursue. In view of past British practice of recognizing only legally constituted governments in Latin America, the question of Huerta's constitutional status initially became an issue as important to the British as to the State Department. Some members of the Foreign Office staff hoped to delay the decision until the U.S. position had become clear, but Huerta forced the British to make a decision even before Wilson's inauguration. Badgered by repeated requests from the Mexican Ministry of Foreign Relations to come to a decision—

[21] Peter Calvert (*The Mexican Revolution, 1910–1914*, pp. 19–20) estimates British investment to have been roughly equivalent in total value to that of the United States. His argument is unconvincing. A more reliable comparison, given by Cosío Villegas (*Historia moderna de México*, vol. VII, part II, pp. 1137, 1140, 1152, and 1154), indicates that British investment was considerably less important than American, although it did run into the hundreds of millions of dollars. Calvert's explanation of Britain's position on recognition is excellent; the following account is taken from his pages 156–166.

[22] Ambassador Walter Hines Page from London frequently vented his wrath at the British for failing to recognize the moral issue involved. On one occasion, after consulting Foreign Office personnel and reading every newspaper account he could find, he wrote that "in this whole wretched waste of comment, I have not seen even an allusion to any moral principle involved nor a word of concern about the Mexican people. It is all about who is stronger, Huerta or some other bandit, and about the necessity of order for the sake of financial interests" (Burton Jesse Hendrick, *Life and Letters of Walter H. Page*, I, 184).

with the implication that failure to render an affirmative decision would constitute an unfriendly act—an official in the Foreign Office observed on the last day of February that "our interests in Mexico are so enormous that it might be imprudent to risk any possible injury to them by too rigid adherence to the custom of not recognizing Provisional Presidents." With this position Foreign Secretary Sir Edward Grey agreed, even to the point of vetoing a suggestion to feel out Germany, France, and the United States on the question; British interests were "so big" that she needed to make her own decision "without making it dependent upon that of other" nations. Once this decision was made on economic-interest grounds—or, as the Foreign Office preferred to call it, "political"—the question of Huerta's legality assumed less and less importance. Even a highly unflattering characterization of Huerta by the British minister in Mexico, which arrived a few days before the formal extension of recognition, failed to alter the decision that had been made by March 3, less than two weeks after the coup d'état. Great Britain extended formal recognition on March 31,[23] to President Wilson's chagrin and Bryan's irritation.

In the meantime, both before and after Huerta's curt treatment of him in early May, Ambassador Wilson continued to bombard Washington with demands for recognition. With his access to the Ministry of Foreign Relations essentially severed, and with William Bayard Hale poking into the events of February, in June the ambassador reached a point of impertinence in his dispatches: "I must again urge upon the President that on the highest grounds of policy, which in this case I understand to be the conserving and extension of our material interests in Mexico, the restoration of peace and the cultivation of sentiments of friendship and respect with a neighboring and friendly nation, that we should without further delay, following the example of all governments accredited here but two, accord offi-

[23] An exchange of letters between the new government and the Crown constituted recognition. The time consumed in sending mail from Mexico to London, and receiving an answer, was responsible for the long delay in official recognition.

cial recognition to the present provisional government."[24] But the president was unimpressed by the ambassador's line of reasoning, as he was unmoved by the actions of other nations with respect to Mexico. A few days later, through Bryan, President Wilson gave his answer: "The interests of the United States are vitally involved with conditions of peace, justice and recognized authority in Mexico, and the Government of the United States can acquiesce in nothing which does not definitely promise these things."[25] The president's message, said Bryan, was not to be construed as the official and public position of the United States and was not to be transmitted to the Huerta government. In the president's view, nothing that had happened in Mexico since his inauguration gave evidence of actual or potential strength by the Huerta government. Rebel strength had grown markedly in the interim, and at about the time that the ambassador and the president exchanged the above views, the Constitutionalists captured Matamoros, Durango, and Zacatecas[26] and effectively controlled all the state of Sonora above Guaymas. The British Foreign Office might insist that Huerta's fall would be "followed by chaos,"[27] but the fact was that chaos then existed and recognition would do nothing to abate it. Furthermore, the president had not yet heard from Hale.

In late June, Hale's first report arrived in Washington, and a disturbing one it was. His evidence was admittedly not the best, much of it being hearsay and most of it being circumstantial, but in a thirty-page letter he made a strong case to support the contention that Ambassador Wilson was privy to and approved of, if indeed he did not help plan, Huerta's coup d'état. In his own distinctive style, Hale concluded:

> It cannot be but a course [source?] of grief that what is probably the most dramatic story in which an American diplomatic officer has ever been involved, should be a story of sympathy with treason, perfidy and assassination in an assault on constitutional government.

[24] H. L. Wilson to SecState, June 9, 1913, file 812.00/7741, NA, RG 59.
[25] Bryan to H. L. Wilson, June 13, 1913, file 812.00/7741, NA, RG 59.
[26] Huerta's forces recaptured Zacatecas within a few days.
[27] This was the consistent British position throughout the year.

And it is particularly unfortunate that this should have taken place in a leading country of Latin America, where, if we have any moral work to do, it is to discourage violence and uphold law.

Trifling, perhaps, in the sum of miseries that have flowed from it, yet not without importance in a way, is the fact that thousands of Mexicans believe that the Ambassador acted on instructions from Washington and look upon his retention under the new American President as a mark of approval and blame the United States Government for the chaos into which the country has fallen.[28]

The president read the report carefully and then, as he was wont to do, typed a short personal note to Bryan: "The document from Hale is indeed extraordinary. I should like, upon my return from my little outing, to discuss with you very seriously the necessity of recalling Henry Lane Wilson in one way or another, perhaps merely 'for consultation' until we have a talk with the man himself."[29]

Faced with Hale's report, even if that report were partly erroneous —nothing in Wilson's correspondence or attitude ever suggested that he doubted its veracity—the president simply could not extend recognition to Huerta. Even had he been able to convince himself of Huerta's legality, or had he been able to overcome his moral compunctions, or had he become convinced that Huerta could control the revolution, recognition was political dynamite. He could scarcely insist upon his progressive government policy at home, or upon the foreign policy principles he had outlined early in his administration, while at the same time granting recognition to a Mexican government created through the devious and "perfidious" intervention of his minister plenipotentiary in that country. Were there a single doubt in the president's mind concerning his failure to grant recognition, the doubt fled when he read the Hale report.

But the ambassador continued his campaign for recognition. He made no effort to authenticate reports handed him by the Huerta government, merely parroting the Huerta line of optimism. He incorrectly reported that Huerta's military recruitment program was

[28] William Bayard Hale to President Wilson, June 18, 1913, file 812.00/7798 1/2, NA, RG 59.

[29] Wilson to SecState, July 1, 1913, file 812.00/7864 1/2, NA, RG 59.

enormously successful, that the Huerta government had been able to borrow all the money it needed, and that the government was extremely popular throughout Mexico. He insisted that the Constitutionalist movement was a fraud and that the revolution was simple brigandage; he substantiated his evaluation by reporting that over fifty "maidens of the best families" in Durango had committed suicide after "being ravished" by revolutionaries when Urbina captured the city on June 18.[30] By early July he was so distraught that he was in "a highly nervous state, raging against the indignity of his position, berating his staff and reviling his own Government."[31] His anomalous position and his own personality had alienated him from both the Mexicans and the foreign residents in the capital, and his dispatches reflected his humiliation. In one of his last reports from Mexico he felt obliged "for the preservation of the harmonious relations which should exist between contiguous and friendly nations; on behalf of the some thirty thousand suffering Americans who are still left in Mexico, the objects of public hatred and without any guarantees of protection for their lives and property . . . , to again urge upon the President the urgent necessity for some action of a drastic and convincing kind."[32]

By that time the ambassador had outlived whatever usefulness he might have had; he had been invited to come to Washington to give his views, and the president had already decided that he would not return to Mexico in any capacity.[33] Leaving Mexico on July 17, the

[30] H. L. Wilson to SecState, June 30, 1913, file 812.00/7933, NA, RG 59. Theodore Hamm, in Durango throughout the period and completely out of sympathy with the revolution, reported all manner of rebel atrocities and near atrocities—but he reported neither rapes nor suicides.

[31] Hale memorandum, July 9, 1913, file 812.00/8203, NA, RG 59.

[32] H. L. Wilson to SecState, July 9, 1913, file 812.00/7999, NA, RG 59. At that point he urged either recognition or a breach of diplomatic relations by closing the embassy, but by the time he reached Washington later in the month he opposed recognition.

[33] I have not been able to find the copy of the dispatch to the ambassador asking him to return to Washington, but apparently President Wilson had given such an order even before he left for his "little outing" to New Hampshire on July 4. The documents do not clearly indicate that the president had decided to ask for the ambassador's resignation, but the tone of his correspondence strongly

ambassador journeyed to Washington by way of Havana and New York, where he arrived on July 25 and embarked immediately for the capital. Once there he handed the president a long memorandum outlining his own proposal for the solution of the Mexican problem.[34] Only on one point did the president and the ambassador see eye-to-eye: unrestricted recognition under the circumstances was out of the question. Henry Lane Wilson proposed that if recognition were to be granted—and this he did not recommend—it should be granted only under the strictest conditions, which would include the settlement of all major claims, a guaranteed free election in October, and a cooperative military endeavor between the United States and the Huerta government to pacify the area to the north of the twenty-second degree of latitude.[35] The ambassador, then, would recommend recognition only if Huerta were willing to accept U.S. military aid for the extirpation of the Constitutionalist forces. But his prime recommendation was that the United States prepare for massive military intervention by concentrating all the standing army and all the border states' militia along the international boundary, and by massing the fleet "at every Mexican port on the Atlantic and Pacific." After such concentration of forces, he urged, the president should appoint a commission consisting of "the ambassador,"[36] the ranking officer in the army invasion force, the ranking officer in the navy invading force, and a member of the Senate Foreign Relations Committee. This commission was first to seek "a reconciliation of all the contending forces in Mexico" in an "urgent, expeditious [manner] and not to be detained by any dilatory methods . . . ;" the failure of such a reconciliation would be followed by full-scale invasion in

suggests it. For a discussion of the episode, see Louis M. Teitelbaum, *Woodrow Wilson and the Mexican Revolution, 1913–1916*, pp. 42–45.

[34] The memorandum, undated, is reproduced by H. L. Wilson in his "How to Restore Peace in Mexico," in *Mexico and the Caribbean*, ed. Blakeslee, pp. 147–155.

[35] The twenty-second parallel runs roughly through Tampico, San Luis Potosí, Aguascalientes, and Tepic, from east to west.

[36] Apparently H. L. Wilson saw himself in that role, since it would have been legally impossible to appoint another ambassador without first granting recognition.

which the commission would act as the military government, "re-establishing the rule of law and dispensing justice and order in the name of the United States." Under no circumstances could this action be interpreted as an aggression; it would be the "discharge of a duty to humanity and civilization," with the troops withdrawing as soon as "constitutional methods and practices [were] re-established and firm government installed."

Ambassador Wilson, who so prided himself on his knowledge of Mexico and the Mexican character and who later castigated the president and all his advisors for their abysmal ignorance, showed his own misunderstanding and naïveté in making the recommendations. It apparently never occurred to him that the combined government and revolutionary forces in Mexico exceeded those of the United States, or that such an invasion would lead to all-out war. He obviously assumed that the Mexicans—federals and rebels alike—would be cowed by a show of force and would welcome the invaders.

Exactly what transpired between the president and the ambassador in their meeting will never be known, but Woodrow Wilson obviously had no taste for the proposals made. Since Henry Lane Wilson took the same proposals to the Senate Foreign Relations Committee a few days later, and then resigned to the accompaniment of a blast directed at the president and his policy,[37] it may be assumed that the conference was not amicable. The situation left the president in a predicament. His refusal to recognize Huerta committed him irrevocably to a course of action; he must, in some manner, eliminate Huerta and encourage the formation of a constitutional government. Since he had no more confidence in Chargé d'Affaires Nelson O'Shaughnessy than he had in Henry Lane Wilson,[38] he felt impelled to designate a special agent, a man whom he

[37] The exact moment at which the president asked for his resignation, and the nature of the communication by which it was done, is in some doubt.

[38] The clearest evidence of this lack of confidence is included in a dispatch from Bryan to John Lind (October 26, 1913, file 812.00/9392, NA, RG 59), in which Lind was asked to authenticate a document damning to Huerta. It was urgent that Lind investigate, said Bryan, since O'Shaughnessy would be likely to

could trust to reflect his own thinking and to report accurately, a man who had sufficient skill to handle the delicate task of forcing Huerta to hold an honest election and to abide by the results. His choice fell on John Lind of Minnesota, to whom he sent a message soon after his conference with Henry Lane Wilson.[39] That the president was concerned more with general competence and trustworthiness than with special qualifications is clear; Lind admittedly knew absolutely nothing about Mexico and could not speak Spanish, but he had been a successful governor and was Wilson's friend. Wilson himself drafted the instructions for his emissary; they were simple and straightforward and deviated not at all from a general line of policy that had shown itself as early as May. Lind was to demand that Huerta negotiate an armistice with Carranza immediately, and that he guarantee an early election in which he himself would not be a candidate and the results of which would be acceptable to the entire Mexican public. But the instructions were simpler than the task, and the Lind mission was doomed to failure before he ever arrived in Mexico, not merely because of his own ignorance but also because of conditions in that country.

Whether the Minnesota ex-governor recognized the hopelessness of his situation is doubtful; he embarked on his mission with rare good will and, unfortunately, fanfare. Lind departed from Washington on August 4, only a week after Wilson had decided to designate him as his special agent. Traveling by train to Galveston and by warship to Veracruz, he arrived in Mexico City on August 10, but by that time the entire world knew the nature of his mission and most of the details of his instructions. Despite an earlier statement by the Mexican Ministry of Foreign Relations that the emissary would not be accepted unless he were a fully accredited minister plenipotentiary, Lind conferred with Secretary of Foreign Relations

"exercize [*sic*] extreme care to conceal proof of such a document." The chargé was openly sympathetic to Huerta.

39 For the details of the Lind mission, see George M. Stephenson, *John Lind of Minnesota*, pp. 208–278, which must be read with some care; for a slightly different view of the mission, see Calvert, *The Mexican Revolution*, pp. 201–215.

Federico Gamboa,[40] on August 12 and, two days later, presented Huerta with the essence of his instructions.

In making the demands for the immediate negotiation of an armistice to be followed by a free election, Lind and Wilson overlooked two salient facts. Huerta, strongly backed by the British and German ministers and basking in the comfort of recognition by those two powerful European nations,[41] was certainly in no mood to knuckle under to a U.S. demand of which the world was fully aware. The military campaign was going badly and rebel strength was growing, but the situation was far from hopeless;[42] the mood in Mexico City was one of general optimism, and Huerta was even then maneuvering to consolidate and increase his power. But even had Huerta, in a momentary display of weakness or statesmanship, accepted the basic premises of the proposal, it is certain that the Constitutionalists would have refused to abide by the results of any election held under Huerta's aegis. Although Carranza did not make clear until November his determination to reject any solution save that by force of arms,[43] it is certain that the Primer Jefe was at that moment urging the Bloc Renovador to step up its campaign to force Huerta to dissolve Congress and thereby divest himself of any claim to constitutional standing.[44] Any action on Huerta's part that could be interpreted as an unconstitutional seizure of power would

[40] The statement was made on August 6 by Acting Secretary Manuel Garza Aldape, who was replaced by Federico Gamboa on August 11 as an incident in Huerta's political maneuvering. Gamboa was no less intransigent than Garza Aldape, but he was more suave.

[41] Peter Calvert makes the case (*The Mexican Revolution*, particularly in Chapters 5, 6, and 7) that the British did not give strong support to Huerta. This may well be true, but Huerta was convinced of that support and acted accordingly.

[42] Calvert (ibid., p. 203), depending upon British and U.S. sources, erroneously concludes that "the tide had turned in favour of the federal forces in the north, following the long build-up of the army there." Only in the state of Coahuila were Huerta arms demonstrating success.

[43] Hale to SecState, November 16, 1913, file 812.00/9769, NA, RG 59.

[44] For a discussion of these Carranza aims, see Félix Fulgencio Palavicini, *Mi vida revolucionaria*, pp. 171–179.

strengthen the Constitutionalist cause, and Carranza would scarcely accept a proposal that would undercut his plans.

Lind apparently believed that Huerta would accept the proposals without demur,[45] and therefore Gamboa's categorical and sarcastic rejection on August 16 must have come as an unpleasant surprise. Gamboa insisted that the federal armies had full control of most of the country, and that any attempt to negotiate a truce with the rebels would be tantamount to a recognition of their belligerency; this the government would never do. Even more importantly, the foreign secretary held, the proposal by the United States was an unwarranted and presumptuous intervention into domestic politics.[46] A few days later Lind attempted to sweeten the pot by saying that if the Huerta government accepted the proposals "then the President will assure the American bankers and their associates that the government of the United States would look with favor upon the negotiation of an immediate loan."[47] But Gamboa coldly rejected this rather clumsy attempt at national bribery and on August 26, two weeks to the day after having first officially presented his proposals, Lind departed for Veracruz, where he remained for the next five months. His "mission" had scarcely been one of outstanding success.[48]

Ambassador Wilson's recall and the Lind appointment, with its known set of demands, created an intervention fever and fear. The utter savagery of the fighting along the international boundary, the

[45] On August 11 Lind asked Bryan what posture he should assume in case "the President's proposal is spurned and I am given to understand that it is considered an unwarranted attempt to dictate in Mexican Domestic affairs? Such action is not likely but it is an eventuality that should be considered" (Lind to SecState, August 11, 1913, file 812.00/8334, NA, RG 59).

[46] Gamboa to Lind, August 16, 1913, file 812.00/10637, NA, RG 59.

[47] As translated from the Lind note to Gamboa in Isidro Fabela, *Historia diplomática de la revolución mexicana, 1912–1917*, I, 215–216.

[48] Calvert (*Mexican Revolution*, p. 297) seems to imply that Lind's personality was a major factor in the failure of his mission. Fabela (*Historia diplomática*, p. 217) correctly points out that the mission never had a chance of success, and thereby he implies that the failure had nothing to do with Lind, but with the impossibility of Wilson's demands.

obvious threat to lives and property of foreigners in Mexico, and the failure of the Wilson administration to take a firm stand all combined to create a demand for positive action—even military intervention. In July the German consul in Chihuahua reportedly took the lead in circulating the rumor that all European nations were pressing the United States to intervene,[49] and Bryan's categorical denial that any such demand had been made did nothing to quiet the fears.[50] In this atmosphere every indication of possible action was magnified and distorted, every private statement by any Mexican official was examined for evidence of hostility, and the U.S. side of the border boiled with stories of an impending attack by Mexico in reaction to a potential intervention.[51] The degree to which Wilson seriously considered intervention in July and August is moot, but the evidence suggests that it was discussed as one alternative and that Wilson agents sought to enlist the aid of the Constitutionalists in the event of such an intervention.[52] While Lind traveled to Mexico City, Wilson requested from the War Department a statement concerning the number of available troops and implied that an invasion of Veracruz was in the offing.[53] The War Department hurriedly prepared detailed plans for an invasion and for the protection of the border[54] and urged the Department of State to give ample advance notification in case a decision to intervene were made.[55] The general tenseness of the atmosphere, particularly along the border, convinced

[49] Letcher to SecState, July 21, 1913, file 812.00/8117, NA, RG 59.

[50] J. B. Moore to Letcher, July 23, 1913, file 812.00/8117, NA, RG 59.

[51] For example, one Otto Winter, who had spent a few days in a northern Mexican jail, reported to U.S. army authorities that he had heard frank talk concerning the concentration of six thousand troops in the vicinity of Nuevo Laredo to invade the United States (see E. P. Brewer to Commanding General, Southern Department, August 9, 1913, file 812.00/8679 enclosure, NA, RG 59. Enclosures in this particular document include five different reports of impending Mexican invasion).

[52] Teitelbaum, *Woodrow Wilson and the Mexican Revolution*, pp. 45–51.

[53] Ibid., p. 48.

[54] Bliss to President of Army War College, August 11, 1913, file 812.00/9122 enclosure, NA, RG 59.

[55] Acting Secretary of War Henry Breckinridge to SecState, August 13, 1913, file 812.00/9122, NA, RG 59. Secretary of War Lindley M. Garrison was vacationing.

General Tasker H. Bliss of the strong possibility of a Huerta invasion as a means of forestalling an attack on Veracruz,[56] and Hale reported from Mexico City that Huerta boasted that he could march "the army to St. Louis without opposition."[57] Henry Lane Wilson's testimony before the Senate Foreign Relations Committee in August did nothing to allay fears on either side of the border, since he recommended massive military intervention. The Huerta consul in San Diego, California, notified his government that U.S. naval officers there openly predicted an invasion in early September, but officials in Mexico City were inclined to give little credence to the report.[58]

As the furor over the possibility of American intervention or an armed attack by Huertistas on the United States reached its height, Wilson did make one major change in his posture toward the Huerta government: he stopped the shipment of arms. A joint resolution of March, 1912, authorized the president to embargo arms to Mexico in case of civil disturbance. The resolution was permissive, not mandatory, and had been used by Taft to prevent the shipment of arms to Orozco and other rebels against the Madero government while allowing that government to purchase arms; Wilson continued that policy after his inauguration, applying the embargo against the rebels but allowing shipments to Huerta.[59] Why Wilson elected to continue the shipment of arms to a de facto government too wicked to merit recognition is not clear, but every request for an export license coming from "the Central Administration in Mexico" received the president's signature without question. Huerta's continued purchase of arms in the United States infuriated the Constitutionalists; one rebel officer was reported to have said in late August that the United States, "violating international law and the rights

[56] Bliss to President of Army War College, August 9, 1913, file 812.00/9122 enclosure, NA, RG 59.

[57] As quoted in Baker, *Life and Letters, 1913–1914*, p. 272.

[58] SecRelExt to SecGob, September 3, 1913, and memo to SecGob, September 5, 1913, in AGN-Gobernación—Varios 1913–1914.

[59] Elton Atwater (*American Regulation of Arms Exports*) examines in some detail the policy regarding Mexico; apropos of the present discussion, see particularly pp. 50–72. Calvert (*The Mexican Revolution*, p. 177) states that Wilson allowed arms to "pass to both sides," but he gives no source.

of the people, has permitted, with our knowledge, Huerta and comrades to introduce arms and ammunition from . . . [the Unit States] to shoot us down."[60] But by this time the president had cided to stop the flow to Huerta. Exactly when and why he reach the decision is not clear,[61] but the rejection of the Lind propos and the possibility of intervention both had an effect. On August he appeared before a joint session of Congress for the ostensi purpose of clarifying the Lind mission, but in fact to review Mexican policy.[62] The United States, he said, could not "be partis to either party to the contest," or act as "the virtual umpire betwe them." He would therefore no longer approve arms shipme either to Huerta or to the revolutionaries.[63] Officially closing t United States as a source of arms supply inconvenienced the Hue forces, but the European nations were no more anxious to foll Wilsonian policy in this respect than in others, and the Europe markets remained open to Huerta. The Constitutionalists, as t president no doubt realized, were inconvenienced even less; th controlled the northern border regions and could smuggle ar with little difficulty.

While Wilson and his administration were seeking ways to o Huerta from his position, and while Washington suspicions w high concerning British motivation and policy,[64] the Foreign Off

[60] Gabriel Calzada, as reported by William Blocker to SecState, August 1913, file 812.00/8786, NA, RG 59.

[61] Calvert (*The Mexican Revolution*, p. 178) says that Wilson made the d sion after an objection was raised by Senator A. O. Bacon on August 23; but quotes a document (p. 209) under date of August 18 in which it appears though shipments had already been stopped.

[62] Wilson was under fire from two sources: those who insisted on the neces for immediate intervention and those who requested immediate recognition.

[63] The most convenient source for Wilson's presentation is *Papers Relating the Foreign Relations of the United States, 1913*, pp. 820–823 (hereafter ci as *Foreign Relations*). Teitelbaum (*Woodrow Wilson and the Mexican Revo tion*, p. 10) states that Wilson reversed his policy, "that is, arms were permit to reach Carranza and Villa, while interdicted from Huerta." He gives no dence.

[64] In March, Bryan had concluded, on the basis of dispatches from Wa Hines Page, that the British would follow the U.S. lead with respect to recog tion. When London announced Huerta's recognition, therefore, Bryan belie

took a step that seemed to U.S. observers to be a calculated insult: London announced in July that Francis William Stronge was being replaced by Sir Lionel Carden as minister to Mexico. "If the British Government had ransacked its diplomatic force to find the one man who would have been most objectionable to the United States, it could have made no better selection."[65] Carden had long served the British in the Caribbean, where his openly anti-United States stance had so infuriated the State Department that protests had been lodged with the Foreign Office, to no avail. He was a man of strong convictions, considerable arrogance, a deep distrust of the United States, and utter contempt for U.S. power; he was also personally committed to supporting Huerta, since "it would be madness at such a juncture to contemplate substituting a new and untried man."[66] Why Sir Edward Grey selected him remains in some doubt,[67] but it certainly was interpreted in Mexico as an indication of British support for Huerta against U.S. demands, and it may have been an important factor in John Lind's cold reception even though Carden had not yet arrived.[68] But in addition to carrying with him a well-deserved reputation for anti-Americanism, Carden also brought along an undeserved notoriety—at least in the United States—of being nothing more than a tool of British oil interests; this being the case, Wilson and Bryan incorrectly assumed that petroleum magnate Lord Cowdray controlled British Mexican policy.[69] Carden himself did nothing to allay U.S. fears. He stopped in New York on his way to Mexico and immediately created a storm by giving an interview in which

that Grey "had changed his mind" and assumed that British oil interests had been responsible. Calvert (*The Mexican Revolution*, Chapter 4) demonstrates the error in Bryan's conclusions.

65 Hendrick, *Life and Letters of Walter H. Page*, I, 197.

66 On Carden, see Calvert, *The Mexican Revolution*, Chapter 7. The quotation is from a Carden memorandum to Grey before leaving England.

67 Calvert (*The Mexican Revolution*, p. 219) indicates conclusively that Grey selected Carden "for his own reasons," but essays no explanation of motivation.

68 Stronge left Mexico City on September 14; Carden arrived on October 8.

69 Weetman Dickinson Pearson, First Viscount Cowdray, was head of the international development firm of S. Pearson and Son, Ltd. He controlled a huge petroleum agglomerate in Mexico, the Compañía Mexicana de Petróleo "El Aguila," S.A.

he was quoted as having said that Wilson was ignorant of Mexico and that Huerta was the only man to control the Mexican situation. He scarcely alleviated the situation when he arrived in Veracruz to be met by Cowdray's representative, thereby more than ever convincing the State Department of his relationship with the oil interests, or by criticizing "Woodrow Wilson, Bryan and the United States in general with utter frankness" in a meeting with Lind.[70] In a series of meetings with Lind on October 7 he pushed hard for Huerta's recognition "on the score of expediency because he is a strong man, a strong man being needed."[71]

But more was to come. In a matter of hours after Huerta had dissolved Congress on October 10 and imprisoned over a hundred deputies, Carden appeared before Huerta to present his credentials. Whether it was a deliberate action to underscore his own support to the Huerta administration is not clear—it probably was, but Carden gave no explanation—but it convinced Lind in Veracruz. He reported to Bryan "that Carden knew what was going to happen on the tenth and that the presentation of credentials was timed with reference to it."[72] Not satisfied with this open irking of the U.S. government, Carden a few days later granted another press interview, with results roughly equivalent to the earlier one in New York; again he was reported to have been publicly critical of U.S. policy.[73]

But Carden either deliberately or mistakenly misrepresented the British position. Grey had never been particularly keen on Huerta, but he believed him to be the least obnoxious of the possible alternatives. He had never wished to challenge the United States on its Mexican policy, even though he disagreed with it,[74] and on frequent occasions he had warned Carden against being drawn into the uncomfortable circumstance of appearing to support Huerta against

[70] According to the British chargé, in Calvert, *The Mexican Revolution*, p. 226.

[71] Lind to SecState, October 8, 1913, file 812.00/9127, NA, RG 59.

[72] Lind to SecState, October 23, 1913, file 812.00/9355, NA, RG 59.

[73] Calvert (*The Mexican Revolution*, pp. 237–243) examines the question of his press statement in some detail.

[74] Grey's unfortunate appointment of Carden might be presumed evidence to the contrary, but Calvert's documentation shows quite clearly that he did not want to make an issue of U.S. policy.

the United States. But Carden's frequently intemperate remarks,[75] plus Grey's apparent reluctance to abide by an implied promise to reconsider recognition after the October 26 elections,[76] tended to create additional tension between the United States and Great Britain over the Mexican question. Wilson, utterly convinced that Huerta's dissolution of Congress and the subsequent electoral fraud demonstrated the dictator's complete degradation, began to sound out the position of governments other than the British. From his point of view, the replies were surprisingly satisfactory. From Guatemala came word that President Estrada Cabrera believed Huerta's most recent action to "be that of an unbalanced man in desperate straits."[77] From Russia came the information that the tsar thought that "the only satisfactory solution is annexation, and this action Russia would see with approval."[78] Chile, Brazil, Panama, and El Salvador, according to the various U.S. ministers, gave strong approval to Wilson's efforts to stabilize the Mexican situation, while Norway was sympathetic but noncommittal. Italy and France preferred to wait for the reactions of other European nations before committing themselves. Germany disavowed any political interest in Mexico, but implied a slight disapprobation of U.S. policy.[79] Before the end of October even the British seemed to be more sympathetic. Grey admitted that the problem faced by the United States was quite dif-

[75] Calvert (*The Mexican Revolution*) gives a number of examples, including some highly undiplomatic remarks made to both the German minister and the U.S. chargé.

[76] In July, Page reported that Grey had pointed out that Huerta's recognition had been conditional "and would terminate in October at [the] Mexican election, when [the] question of recognition would come up again" (Page to SecState, July 11, 1913, file 812.00/8026, NA, RG 59). But Grey quite properly insisted that the dissolution of Congress did not alter the relations between Huerta and the Foreign Office.

[77] Chargé d'Affaires, Guatemala City, to SecState, October 18, 1913, file 812.00/9267, NA, RG 59.

[78] Chargé d'Affaires, St. Petersburg, to SecState, October 27, 1913, file 812.00/9431, NA, RG 59.

[79] The information relayed by these ministers may not always have been accurate, but it was the information upon which Wilson acted. The documents may be found scattered through the 812.00 series for October, NA, RG 59.

ferent from that of other nations,[80] and he finally agreed to make no statement on the British position under the new circumstances occasioned by the election until after he had ascertained the Wilson position.[81]

It was under these circumstances that Wilson decided it to be his "immediate duty to require Huerta's retirement" and to use "such means as may be necessary to secure the result."[82] In the first days of November, Chargé O'Shaughnessy, at Wilson's direction, handed Huerta what amounted to an ultimatum: he was to get out, immediately, or the United States would do everything in its power "to cut the government of Huerta off, if he persists, from all outside aid or countenance."[83] Huerta appeared to be ready to submit—though he may have been playing for time—but the news of the ultimatum somehow reached the press,[84] and Huerta, in a burst of patriotic zeal, notified various governments that he would continue in his post until the nation had been completely pacified. Wilson, sorely tried, then notified all nations who had legations in Mexico that the policy of the United States was irrevocable, and that Huerta must go.

Wilson's belligerent attitude and sharp words brought a new wave of intervention rumor, somewhat justified. The extent to which Wilson seriously considered armed intervention is problematical, but he did instruct Frederick Simpich and William Bayard Hale to determine Carranza's attitude regarding such a step on the part of the United States. The administration should have known what the Primer Jefe's answer would be. He was opposed to intervention on

[80] Page to SecState, October 21, 1913, file 812.00/9310, NA, RG 59.

[81] Page to SecState, October 27, 1913, file 812.00/9408, NA, RG 59.

[82] Circular note sent by Bryan to selected U.S. representatives November 7–10, 1913, file 812.00/9625a, NA, RG 59. Wilson himself drafted the note.

[83] Bryan to O'Shaughnessy, November 1, 1913, as quoted in Arthur S. Link, *Wilson: The New Freedom*, pp. 380–381. Wilson drafted the note. O'Shaughnessy and others read the note to be a clear threat of armed intervention. Mrs. Edith O'Shaughnessy told her mother on November 2: "Last night came what is practically an ultimatum from Washington to Huerta. He is to get out, he, and all his friends, or—intervention" (*A Diplomat's Wife in Mexico*, p. 32).

[84] Edith O'Shaughnessy, almost certainly reflecting her husband's thinking, believed that Lind leaked the note by talking too much. Bryan, on the other hand, believed that Huerta himself leaked it, in order to make a big play.

any grounds; armed action even for the laudable purpose of removing Huerta was abhorrent to the Constitutionalists and would result in "kindling a fire that is extinguished and . . . would surely carry us to an enduring struggle. . . . The whole responsibility would rest upon the United States if upon the grounds of protecting the interests of foreigners they should attempt" intervention.[85] But Huerta still quite obviously depended upon strong support from the British government to the point that, according to the German minister, Carden was Huerta's "acknowledged adviser for internal as well as external policy."[86] In the face of Carden's activities, and to underline the seriousness of Wilson's intentions, Ambassador Walter Hines Page stressed to Grey the importance of British support to U.S. policy; the question, he said, was no longer whether Huerta would go, but whether he was to be eliminated "with or without the moral support" of Great Britain.[87]

The British government had no desire to alienate the United States over the Mexican question. The looming European crisis made U.S. friendship critical to the British, and the Foreign Office, confronted with Wilson's adamant stand, began to take steps to ease the tension between the two nations. In late October, Sir William Tyrrell, Grey's private secretary, sailed for the United States with the object of discussing the Mexican situation with the president. Even before he arrived in Washington conditions had changed. On November 10 Prime Minister Herbert Asquith in a public address made mollifying statements,[88] and the next day Page reported that Grey had assured him that Huerta would be told that he could not depend upon British support against the United States.[89] Tyrrell conferred with Wilson at length on November 13, not only discussing the Mexican

[85] Simpich and Hale to SecState, November 12, 1913, and November 16, 1913, files 812.00/9685 and /9768, NA, RG 59.

[86] As quoted by Calvert, *The Mexican Revolution*, p. 259.

[87] Page to SecState, November 8, 1913, file 812.00/10437, NA, RG 59.

[88] Asquith said very little in fact, but did state that British policy had not been designed to "thwart" U.S. policy (see Calvert, *The Mexican Revolution*, pp. 265–266).

[89] Page to SecState, November 11, 1913, file 812.00/10438, NA, RG 59.

situation with utter frankness but also touching on the Panama Canal tolls controversy,[90] and the following day Carden in Mexico City "led a procession of European diplomats to General Huerta [and] formally advised that warrior to yield to American demands and withdraw from the Presidency of Mexico."[91] Wilson now had a clear hand to deal with Huerta, without threat of opposition from any European nation.[92]

Wilson apparently believed that his successful efforts in eliminating British support for Huerta would force the dictator's retirement from Mexican politics, but he was sadly disappointed. Huerta, far from collapsing, continued to consolidate his own power in Mexico City and gave no sign that he was disposed to leave office. Two weeks after Carden's visit to Huerta, and with Huerta giving no indication of a change in posture, Wilson notified the world that "if General Huerta does not retire by force of circumstances it will become the duty of the United States to use less peaceful means to put him out. It will give other Governments notice in advance of each affirmative or aggressive step it has in contemplation should it unhappily become necessary to move actively against the usurper; but no such step seems immediately necessary."[93] But the threat of armed action was idle, and Huerta knew it, since he was fully aware of Carranza's strenuous objection to Wilsonian intervention. The revolutionaries, in fact, wanted only one thing from the United States in the form of aid: freedom to buy arms and ammunition. The arms embargo prevented the rebels from buying munitions legally, but revolutionary successes in the north quite clearly demonstrated that it did not starve the armies. During December, as Huerta's dictatorship became more clearly naked and as the Constitutionalist forces

[90] Hendrick, *Life and Letters of Walter H. Page*, I, 201–208. The Panama Canal tolls controversy revolved around the question of whether a congressional act exempting U.S. coastal vessels from paying a toll was in contravention of the Hay-Pauncefote Treaty.

[91] Ibid., I, 209.

[92] Both Lind and O'Shaughnessy from Mexico, however, continued to complain of Carden's activities in Huerta's behalf.

[93] Bryan to O'Shaughnessy, November 24, 1913, file 812.00/11443d, NA, RG 59. The dispatch was sent to most embassies and legations.

gained ground,[94] both Lind and O'Shaughnessy urged Washington to take some positive action to bring the impossible situation to an end; at least, they said, the arms embargo should be lifted to allow the revolutionaries to finish the job.[95]

Wilson himself became more and more attracted to the general proposition that the contestants should be allowed to settle the issues between themselves. In late January, Sir Edward Grey approached Wilson with a proposition. He could, he believed, convince the other European powers to support the British in demanding Huerta's resignation, but only on two conditions: that the plan meet with Wilson's approval and that the president submit a definite program for a government to take Huerta's place. Huerta, said the foreign minister, would probably be more amenable to submitting to pressure from a group of powers than he would be to resigning at the behest of the United States only.[96] Such a suggestion in August would have met with the president's enthusiastic approval, but by January it was much too late; the Constitutionalists were now too strong and the issue too clearly delineated as a contest between a group that wished to perpetuate the old regime and one that sought a change in the social as well as the political system. Under these conditions the president could submit no "program" that would be acceptable to both Huerta and Carranza. Wilson's reply was prompt and to the point: "From many sources which it deems trustworthy the Government of the United States has received information which convinces it that there is a more hopeful prospect of peace, of the security of property and of the early payment of foreign obligations if Mexico is left to the forces now reckoning with one another there than there would be if anything by way of a mere change of personalities were effected in Mexico." This being the case, the president continued, the United States planned to lift the arms embargo

94 Edith O'Shaughnessy in early December reported that the members of the cabinet "fill up certain conventional spaces usual in governments, and that is all —a sort of administrative furniture, along with tables and chairs" (*A Diplomat's Wife in Mexico*, p. 76).

95 Baker, *Life and Letters, 1913–1914*, p. 299.

96 Page to SecState, January 28, 1914, file 812.00/10712, NA, RG 59.

within a few days as a means of putting the contenders on an equal footing with respect to availability of arms. "Settlement by civil war carried to its bitter conclusion is a terrible thing, but it must come, whether we wish it or not, unless some outside power is to undertake to sweep Mexico with its armed forces from end to end, which would be the mere beginning of a still more difficult problem."[97]

The president was as good as his word; on February 3 he proclaimed that "as the conditions on which the Proclamation of March 4, 1912, was based have essentially changed, and it is desirable to place the United States with reference to the exportation of arms and munitions to Mexico in the same position as the other Powers, the said Proclamation is hereby revoked."[98] This, thought Wilson, would bring an end to a most trying and difficult diplomatic problem. But in the long run Carranza proved to be much more trying than Huerta.

[97] Bryan to Page, January 29, 1914, file 812.00/10712, NA, RG 59. On January 31 the essence of the dispatch was sent to all U.S. diplomatic missions.

[98] As printed in *Foreign Relations, 1914*, pp. 447–448.

5. FINAL CAMPAIGNS AGAINST HUERTA

Confronted by the pleasing probability that the United States would soon raise the arms embargo against Mexico, in early 1914 the Constitutionalists bent their energies to the reduction of the remaining border ports of entry along the Río Grande. With both Ciudad Juárez and Matamoros—the end points on the river boundary—secure in their hands, the rebels needed only Ojinaga, Piedras Negras, and Nuevo Laredo to control all rail connections between the United States and Mexico. General Mercado, after his mad flight from Chihuahua in late November, retained a precarious hold on Ojinaga, but as a port of entry for the Huerta forces it served no purpose, since the rebels controlled the countryside. Piedras Negras occupied a slightly more important position in Huerta strategy inasmuch as the rail line through Allende, Múzquiz, and Monclova did give central Mexico access to U.S. goods, but the city was not of great commercial importance, and facilities for freight handling on both sides of the river left much to be desired. For the Constitutionalists, Piedras Negras was a minor irritant, not a major point of attack. But Nuevo Laredo, with its excellent rail facilities and its easy connections both with the United States and with those areas in Mexico controlled by the central government, appeared to be crucial to Constitutionalist plans, and it was here that the rebel forces made their first thrust.

Nuevo Laredo had been, since early in the revolution, one of the major ports of entry for the Huerta government, but aside from undertaking a few abortive attempts to cut the line to Monterrey, the Constitutionalists had left the city free from attack. However, inasmuch as movements against the federal forces in his zone of command had brought few victories and little glory to the Constitutionalist cause, in the waning days of 1913 General Pablo González determined to take Nuevo Laredo. General González, unfortunately, had neither Villa's dash nor Obregón's tactical sense. His rather clumsy attempt at a feint against Monterrey served merely to alert the enemy, and his ill-conceived plan to destroy, by a night attack, a crucial bridge between Sabinas Hidalgo and Nuevo Laredo came to nought when the two wings of the attacking force became confused in the dark and literally decimated each other without touching the bridge. The failure of both maneuvers gave the Huerta forces the time and the opportunity to reinforce the target garrison with men and artillery, providing the defenders with a slight advantage in number and an enormous advantage in position and fire power. Instead of withdrawing, as some of his officers suggested in view of conditions, González ordered a head-on attack for the morning of January 1; the result was utter disaster. During the two-day battle the attacking force lost nearly one-fifth of its men in dead, wounded, and missing without inflicting any serious damage on the defenders.[1] During the next few months González's forces harassed the environs of the border city but never renewed the

[1] For accounts of the battle, see SecRelEx to SecGyM, January 5, 1914, ADN-Tamaulipas 1914; Joaquín Téllez to SecGyM, January 3, 1914, in ibid.; Juan Barragán, *Historia del ejército y de la revolución constitucionalista*, I, 293–301, for the general account; and Cesáreo Castro to Pablo González, January 4, 1914, in Barragán, *Ejército*, I, 700–703. The federal sources estimated a Constitutionalist loss of six hundred; but Barragán, a participant, gave the figure of one thousand of a total attacking force of less than five thousand.

frontal assault;[2] Nuevo Laredo remained in Huerta's hands until the capture of Monterrey nearly five months later made the position untenable.[3]

Ojinaga, in Villa's area, suffered a distinctly different fate. On January 4, 1914, Constitutionalist forces under Pánfilo Natera,[4] Rosalío Hernández, and Toribio Ortega began a concerted attack. Mercado, whose career demonstrated an almost total lack of offensive imagination, did know how to construct defensive lines and was therefore able to repel the attack; after a three-day battle the Constitutionalists withdrew. Villa, impatient as the last enemy bastion in Chihuahua held out, decided to take the field himself. Assuming personal command of the troops, and reinforced by Maclovio Herrera, Villa fell on the city on January 10; after an all-day battle in which both sides lost heavily, the victory was his. Marcelo Caraveo and Pascual Orozco with their men managed to slip through the Villa lines in the waning stages of the battle,[5] but Mercado and all the remaining officers and men fled to the safety of the United States, where they surrendered ignominiously to local authorities.[6] Save for a few wandering bands of irregulars still supporting Huerta, the state of Chihuahua was clear of federal troops.

[2] Accounts of these movements may be found in the documents of ADN-Tamaulipas 1914.

[3] Monterrey fell to the Constitutionalists on April 24, and within a matter of hours the federalists evacuated Nuevo Laredo.

[4] Natera, from Zacatecas, happened to be in Ciudad Juárez when the plans were made; he was selected to be "guest conductor" of the operation.

[5] The Constitutionalists were understandably disappointed that these two escaped, but took pride in the fact that it was they, the products of the revolution itself, who escaped while the regular army contingents surrendered.

[6] Mercado's flight to the United States and his internment by U.S. authorities probably saved him from a court-martial; officials in Mexico City, incensed at his flight from Chihuahua, were contemplating an investigation when the battle of Ojinaga disrupted their plans. For accounts of the battle and related items, see documents in ADN-Chihuahua 1914, particularly SecRelExt to SecGyM, January 5, 1914; S. Contreras to SecGyM, January 14, 1914; Enrique Pulido to SecGyM, February 20, 1914; Marcelo Caraveo to SecGyM, March 13, 1914; and Salvador R. Mercado to SecGyM, March 1, 1914. See also Barragán, *Ejército*, I, 271–272. Lieutenant Colonel Pulido's account is particularly interesting, since he indicated that he had lost nearly 60 percent of his troops and a third of his officers in the series of battles initiated by Villa in mid-November.

With the capture of Ojinaga, significant military activity took a two-month holiday. To be sure, minor engagements continued throughout the country, but in general the leaders in the central and southern states remained independent of any direct command from Carranza; their movements were not coordinated with the major campaigns of the north. Continual forays, reported as bandit raids by the federal officers, in Jalisco, Aguascalientes, Michoacán, Puebla, Hidalgo, Guerrero, Oaxaca, and other states far from the centers of military activity tied down Huerta troops and irritated the central government but otherwise had little immediate effect.[7] Obregón, in the northwest, fought an inconclusive battle near Empalme in late January,[8] and González, in the northeast, directed a number of minor engagements designed to interrupt communications between Nuevo Laredo and Monterrey, but most of the period between January 10 and mid-March was devoted to training and munitioning the new recruits, which were swelling the Constitutionalist ranks. President Wilson, in a long-expected move, lifted the arms embargo on February 3, thus giving the revolutionary forces legal access to U.S. munitions, and matériel poured across the border in return for cattle, gold, silver, or anything else of value the Constitutionalist commanders could collect, seize, or borrow. By early March the Constitutionalist forces, for the first time, enjoyed an advantage in the accoutrements of war.

By mid-March the final drive began. Almost simultaneously Obregón began moving from his main camp in Navajoa,[9] Villa started south from Chihuahua against Torreón, Pablo González began a general investment of Monterrey and siege of Tampico, and Constitutionalists in the southern and central states redoubled their harassing activities. The central government, apprised by intercepted

[7] The details of these events may be found in the proper files of the ADN collection; summaries may be found in Barragán, *Ejército*.

[8] The details are given in a series of documents in ADN-Sonora 1914.

[9] For about eight months Obregón hesitated to undertake a major drive to the south as long as Guaymas remained in Huerta's hands, but the existence of a small federal navy made the reduction of the port city impossible. In February, 1914, Obregón decided to leave Salvador Alvarado investing the city while he proceeded south with the bulk of the army.

messages of the Constitutionalist plans,[10] made faint and feeble efforts to counter the moves through reorganization of the command zones, intensified recruitment,[11] and stepped-up counterrevolutionary activities along the border. Pascual Orozco, José Inés Salazar, Carlos García Hidalgo and Benjamín Argumedo (all irregulars who had been among the few successful commanders in the north) were assigned as commanding generals in newly created military zones in Chihuahua and Durango with the duty to interrupt lines of communication and retard Villa's move to the south.[12] The fact that in each case the "headquarters" assigned to the generals was actually occupied by Constitutionalist forces bothered Huerta not at all, since the designations made it appear in the capital that Ciudad Juárez, Chihuahua City, and Parral remained under federal control. To prevent Obregón's deliberate progress to the south, Huerta called on Joaquín Téllez, who had been successful in the northeast, to take over the governorship and military command of Sonora, but that able general recognized the situation as well-nigh hopeless.[13] Probably Huerta's most significant military countermove was to concentrate the cream of his army at Torreón, under the command of José Refugio Velasco, his only imaginative general officer. In addition, the central government expended enormous amounts of

[10] Periodically an officer on the General Staff in Mexico City summarized the information coming from these and other sources; these memoranda will be found scattered throughout the ADN collection.

[11] Huerta always found recruitment difficult, but by early 1914 it was virtually impossible. In order to meet the emergency, Huerta merely ordered each state governor to furnish a specified number of recruits at regular intervals, leaving the actual method to the ingenuity of the individual governor. Numerous documents in AGN-Gobernación—Varios 1913–1914, concern the problem.

[12] E. Carmona to Jefe del Estado Mayor de la División "Distrito Federal," February 9, 1914, and E. Carmona to Jefe de la División del "Ajusco," March 7, 1914, in ADN-Chihuahua 1914.

[13] Joaquín Téllez to SecGob, March 16, 1914, in AGN-Gobernación—Autógrafos de Gobernadores—Varios 1913–1914; Téllez had taken over on the previous day, and he pointed out that the area of his command consisted merely of Guaymas and a "small radius" around the city. The fact that the report did not reach Mexico City until April 13, by which time Obregón was over two hundred miles south of Guaymas, indicates the impossible situation in which Téllez found himself.

money, particularly in the El Paso region, in a vain attempt to develop guerrilla groups that might threaten Villa's rear.[14] But in spite of Huerta's efforts the year-long contest was approaching a climax and Huerta, according to most observers, was doomed.[15]

Torreón, the center of the rich Laguna agricultural district and a major rail point with connections to Chihuahua, Durango, Zacatecas, and Monterrey, suffered from the first major assault. Velasco, with ten to fifteen thousand men under his command,[16] and with adequate military supplies, by early March had developed a strong ring of fortifications extending as far as fifty miles to the north and northeast. But he suffered from one major drawback—his line of communications with the central government was long and tortuous through Saltillo, San Luis Potosí, and Tampico, thence by sea to Veracruz. The Arrieta brothers had long since cut the line to Durango, and Pánfilo Natera returned to his old haunts to interrupt rail service between Zacatecas and San Luis Potosí. Other bands often cut the line between Saltillo and San Luis Potosí, and even the Torreón-Saltillo road suffered periodic damage by flying columns. With Pablo González developing his campaign to the east against Monterrey and thereby forcing the armies in that region to retain their positions, Velasco in Torreón found himself virtually isolated and almost totally surrounded.

In preparing for the attack, Carranza ordered every available

[14] On March 16 Miguel E. Diebold dispatched a long report detailing the efforts and the events, and a multitude of other documents attest not only to the efforts but also to the failures; all these may be found in ADN-Chihuahua 1914. U.S. army personnel and Constitutionalist sources were also aware of the activities, as the voluminous documentation in the U.S. National Archives concerning the "red-flaggers" attests.

[15] U.S. consuls or special agents, such as Louis Hostetter, John R. Silliman, Frederick Simpich, and Theodore Hamm, disagreed with one another concerning the nature of the revolution and the probable ultimate consequences, but they agreed perfectly in their assessment of Huerta's defeat.

[16] It has been impossible to ascertain with any accuracy the number of troops in either command. The federals assessed their own strength at eight thousand, but some sources estimated it at fifteen thousand. Villa gave his own strength as fourteen thousand.

military force in the entire north-central part of the nation to give every possible aid, with one notable exception: the Arrieta brothers in Durango, always distrustful of Villa, begged off.[17] The combined revolutionary forces probably came to fifteen thousand and certainly outnumbered the defenders. The opening gun in the attack came at Bermejillo on the main line to Chihuahua, Velasco's outermost defense post; on March 20 Villa occupied the city and forced the defenders to withdraw to Gómez Palacio. Supreme in the field and overflowing with confidence, Villa demanded that Velasco surrender, but the federal general brusquely rejected the demand, and the concerted attack on Gómez Palacio–Torreón began on March 23. After eleven days of brutal fighting, during which roughly five hundred Constitutionalists and a thousand federals died and about twice that many sustained serious wounds, Velasco began an orderly retreat eastward to Viesca on April 2. In the meantime Huerta had dispatched reinforcements that began arriving at San Pedro, about fifty miles north of Viesca, at about the time that Velasco arrived at the latter point. Villa's attacks on Velasco forced the federal general to undertake an overland march to San Pedro to join the reinforcements there. After a few days of skirmishing, the Constitutionalists began an intensive attack on San Pedro on April 14; the outcome was never in doubt. Velasco's remnant, now whittled down to about four thousand exhausted and demoralized men, had neither the matériel nor the morale to continue the struggle, and a violent quarrel between Velasco and Joaquín Maass over the supreme command further disheartened them. Velasco therefore continued his retreat to the east, leaving Maass with about four thousand men to defend San Pedro; but Maass soon found himself to be no match for the determined Villa. After hurriedly setting fire to the principal buildings (including all the properties belonging to the Madero family),

[17] The basis of the distrust is not clear, but the consequences are. Villa obliquely threatened, a few weeks later, to "restore order" in Durango even if he had to "execute some revolutionary leaders"—a clear reference to the Arrietas. When the break came between Villa and Carranza some months later, the Arrietas supported Carranza.

the federal troops fled eastward in wild confusion. Velasco's withdrawal from Torreón had been a retreat, but the flight from San Pedro was absolute chaos. The federals abandoned arms, ammunition, medical supplies, and even clothing in a mad dash to seeming safety; hundreds of men divested themselves of all identifying insignia and disappeared, many to perish in the arid southern fringes of the Bolsón de Mapimí. Those who escaped death or capture finally straggled into Saltillo, a woefully small segment of what had been only a few weeks before an army of fifteen to twenty thousand men. The road to central Mexico was clear.[18]

The battle for Torreón was of enormous military significance, since it destroyed an army and gave the Constitutionalists control of a key railroad point, but it was also important for other reasons. It was undoubtedly the most destructive engagement to that date, both in lives and property. Considering the entire campaign from March 20 to April 15 as one battle for control of the Laguna city, the campaign probably cost three thousand dead and five or six thousand wounded among contestants and civilian population; Juan Barragán, who traveled from Torreón to Saltillo six weeks later, insists that the stench of death pervaded the atmosphere throughout the long journey.[19] The city of Torreón itself was a complete shambles by April 2, with buildings gutted, heaps of unburied dead in the streets, hundreds of untended wounded, and thousands of terrorized citizens. By April 15, when the Villa forces entered San Pedro, that city of ten thousand was in worse shape: fires burning out of control; citizens starving, since no food had entered for over two weeks; and dead and wounded littering the streets. The total costs were incalculable.

Furthermore, Villa's actions in Torreón boded ill for future U.S.-Mexican relations and for cooperation between Villa and Carranza. During the months previous to the Torreón campaign Villa had

[18] For accounts of the battle, see the documents in ADN-Chihuahua 1914; T. C. Hamm to SecState, April 19, 1914, file 812.00/11703, NA, RG 59; and Barragán, *Ejército*, I, 372–419. The ADN collection did not contain the official reports from federal Generals Velasco, Maass, Maure, or Caso López.

[19] Barragán, *Ejército*, I, 432.

become progressively more hostile to the Spaniards in his district, summarily exiling them and sequestering their property,[20] but it was in Torreón that his hatred for the Spaniards ran wild. In spite of official U.S. protests, undertaken at the behest of the Spanish government, Villa rounded up the Spaniards as though they were so many cattle, shipped them to El Paso, and took ownership of all property; included in the booty were a hundred thousand bales of cotton that belonged to the Spaniards and other "enemies of the popular cause." Although Carranza disagreed with the action,[21] he was powerless to prevent it. This was the first of a long series of actions by Villa that convinced Carranza that Villa would be a continual embarrassment to his plans, but for the moment the Primer Jefe kept his counsel and refused to make an issue of the incident.

While Villa hammered Torreón and the center, the two wings of the overall advance moved according to plan with Obregón advancing down the west coast and Pablo González taking the offensive in the northeast. In the northeast, on March 26 a portion of González's forces, well provisioned through a steady flow of goods coming by way of Brownsville-Matamoros,[22] laid siege to Tampico, where Ignacio Morelos Zaragoza held the port with about two thousand men;[23] the action effectively blocked any possible help to Monterrey from that sector. On April 8 González began his move against

[20] The 812.00 series of documents, NA, RG 59, in February and March, particularly those from Carothers and Cobb, make this clear.

[21] Carothers suggested as much soon after the battle for Torreón and said that "Carranza is really afraid to interfere with Villa . . . and is prepared to leave him entirely alone . . ." (Carothers to SecState, April 12, 1914, file 812.00 /11755, NA, RG 59).

[22] Even before the lifting of the embargo, federal officials along the border reported heavy arms shipments through Matamoros. On January 19, for example, Huerta's consul in Laredo reported, without indicating his source of information, that supplies in Matamoros included over two million rounds of ammunition, and an "infinite number" of rifles, saddles, and the like (Consul, Laredo, to Inspección de Consulados, January 19, 1914, ADN-Tamaulipas 1914; also a series of letters from the consul general in San Antonio to the Jefe, División del Bravo, in the same file).

[23] General Ignacio Morelos Zaragoza to SecGyM, February 27, 1914, ADN-Tamaulipas 1914; he reported that his force consisted of 168 officers and 1,738 men.

Monterrey itself, first by cutting all rail lines that could possibly serve as sources of help to the city. By April 16 González's forces not only occupied strong positions between Monterrey and all the outlying areas—including Saltillo, Nuevo Laredo, and Piedras Negras—but also had the city partially surrounded. The frontal assault began on April 18, and after six days of almost incessant fighting the remnants of the defending force fled to the mountains of the south,[24] abandoning a major portion of their supplies either in the city or on the retreat route. The triumphant González reported to Carranza that the "so-called Division of the Bravo [Río Grande] has been completely annihilated."[25] The loss of Monterrey could not be counted as great a disaster as that of Torreón, but it demonstrated the complete inability of the federals to defend their major cities in the north.

The capture of Monterrey made federal retention of Piedras Negras and Nuevo Laredo impossible. Piedras Negras, in fact, fell to the Constitutionalists a few days before the evacuation of Monterrey, and within a matter of hours after González entered the Nuevo León capital the federal commander at Nuevo Laredo abandoned that port of entry after having destroyed the public buildings by explosives.[26] The successful campaigns in Nuevo León and northern Tamaulipas also freed troops to make an assault on Tampico, and González decided to take advantage of the momentum his forces

[24] Soon after the U.S. occupation of Veracruz on the morning of April 21, a two-hour truce was arranged to allow discussions concerning a possible federal surrender; otherwise the firing was without let-up.

[25] For the campaign against Monterrey see the battle reports submitted by Pablo González and Cesáreo Castro, Appendix Documents 31 and 32 in Barragán, *Ejército*, I, 744–753; Consul Garrett to SecState, April 24, 26, 26, 1914, files 812.00/11691, /11710, and /11716 respectively, and William Blocker to SecState, April 20 and April 29, 1914, files 812.00/11779 and /11808 respectively, NA, RG 59.

[26] U.S. Consul Garrett in Nuevo Laredo "received information from a reliable source" that the order to destroy the buildings came from Mexico City. It appears as though a modified scorched-earth policy had been put into effect, since the Huerta armies destroyed buildings upon evacuating Torreón, San Pedro, Nuevo Laredo, and, later, Saltillo and Zacatecas. The federal commander at Piedras Negras stated that he had been ordered to raze buildings there, but he refused to do so.

then enjoyed. On May 1 he moved an army to the environs of Tampico,[27] with one column of troops tolled off to cut the rail line running west to San Luis Potosí. In the last few days before the actual assault began, a steady stream of foreign representatives, including U.S. Admiral Henry T. Mayo and British Admiral Sir Christopher Cradock as well as a commission of consuls headed by those from Spain and Germany, called on González and Luis Caballero to seek assurances that foreign lives and properties would be fully respected; since Tampico was the major oil shipping point, with expensive and extensive storage facilities operated by nearly two thousand U.S. citizens and probably as many other foreigners, the stakes were indeed great. Had the defense been as tenacious as that at Torreón there is a strong possibility that U.S. naval forces would have been forced to intervene—Mayo suggested as much in his conference with González—but fortunately Morelos Zaragoza had neither the imagination nor the men that Velasco depended upon in his Torreón defense. The city of Tampico itself was scarcely touched. Opening the attack early on the morning of May 11, González's troops moved slowly into the outskirts of the city during that and the next day, when nature in the form of torrential rains came to the aid of the attackers; a rising wall of water during the night of May 12–13 forced the defenders to abandon a strongly fortified ravine and made further defense impossible. The federals began their exodus by train, but Constitutionalist control of Ebano only a few miles away forced Morelos and his men to leave the rails. After a "long and painful march" through the mountains the crippled force straggled into a Puebla mountain hamlet three weeks later, and the defeated general made his doleful report to the central government.[28]

While González moved on Tampico, Carranza and his generals

[27] The size of González's force is impossible to ascertain. Barragán, who had access to some records that since have disappeared from view, gave the number as three thousand, but Morelos Zaragoza reported that "according to his own [the enemy's] sources, after he occupied the Port," the number reached twelve thousand. This is scarcely credible, since it is doubtful that González ever had that many men under arms at any one time until mid-July.

[28] Ignacio Morelos Zaragoza to SecGyM, June 3, 1914, ADN-Tamaulipas 1914; Barragán, *Ejército*, I, 471–475, 754–756.

held a series of war councils in Torreón to decide the next move. I spite of the predilection on the part of Villa and Felipe Angeles t undertake an immediate campaign against Zacatecas,[29] Carranza in sisted on reducing Saltillo first. In Saltillo all the remnants c northern federal forces had concentrated: those who had survive the San Pedro battle, those who had escaped Monterrey, and thos who had abandoned Piedras Negras and Nuevo Laredo. The tot force probably numbered ten thousand men in Saltillo and anoth five thousand guarding Paredón on the rail line to Torreón, bu munitions were in short supply and morale was low; save for thos few who had come from Nuevo Laredo and Piedras Negras, ever man in the defending force had taken part in at least one disastrou flight. According to the plan, Pablo González's men were to move o Saltillo from the north and east,[30] while Villa was to attack from th west and south. But one Villa cavalry charge on Paredón was suff cient; the ten thousand horsemen caught the defenders complete by surprise on May 17, killing, wounding, or capturing over thre fifths of the defending force. The remnant duplicated the flight fro San Pedro, dashing madly to Saltillo and abandoning their few r maining provisions. Three days later the Saltillo defenders bega the three-hundred-mile walk to San Luis Potosí, evacuating the cit without a struggle but setting fire to some of the buildings as the left.[31]

While Villa in the center and González in the east cut the federa to bits, Obregón in the northwest progressed steadily down the coas Unable to capture and hold the major port cities because of a lac of a navy, he attacked, laid siege to, and then by-passed first Topol bampo (April 14) and then Mazatlán (May 5) while his vanguar

[29] By this time the mutual suspicions between Villa and Carranza had reache such a point that Carranza feared Villa's growing popularity and myth.

[30] At the beginning of the campaign, when Villa left Torreón on May 1 González himself was engaged in the reduction of Tampico and therefore cou not take part, but portions of his command under Francisco Coss, Ernesto Sa tos Coy, Andrés Saucedo, and Jesús Dávila Sánchez were ordered to coordina their movements with those of Villa.

[31] Barragán, *Ejército*, I, 475–480; Martín Luis Guzmán, *Memorias de Panch Villa*, pp. 386–406.

under Manuel Diéguez, Rafael Buelna, and Lucio Blanco took in turn Acaponeta, San Blas, and Tepic.[32] None of these engagements on the west coast even approximated those in other sectors insofar as number of men engaged was concerned. The campaign was primarily for the purpose of developing lines of communication with absolute security for the eventual attack on Guadalajara and on central Mexico from the west; as a preparation for the final assault on the Huerta stronghold it was of great significance, but in view of the critical situation in the center and the poor communications to the west, Huerta could take no effective moves to counter Obregón's measured pace of conquest.

But the west coast campaign probably had a greater long-range effect than its importance in Huerta's overthrow. In the almost leisurely move through Sonora, Sinaloa, and Nayarit (then Tepic), Obregón had an opportunity to mature as a military man; it was in this campaign that he learned the basic strategic and tactical lessons that transmuted him from a simple farmer to the greatest military mind in Mexican history. He learned to leave nothing to chance, to be careful or bold as the situation demanded. He learned how and when to use reserves, how to take advantage of the terrain, and how to capitalize on the enemy's weaknesses. Unlike Villa, who in his simplicity committed the totality of his cavalry in the successful attack on Paredón and therefore left himself open to disaster had he misjudged the situation, Obregón came through the western campaign with an amazing degree of military sophistication. From that time forward to the end of his life he never lost a battle.

By the third week in May, 1914, all roads to central Mexico were open to the successful Constitutionalist forces, and the Huerta regime was on the verge of total collapse; it was saved for two additional months by two major developments: the U.S. occupation

[32] Barragán, *Ejército*, I, 485–491; Alvaro Obregón, *Ocho mil kilómetros en campaña*, pp. 106–122. On April 14 one of Carranza's nephews, Gustavo Salinas Carranza, carried out the first aerial bombardment in history when from an altitude of four thousand feet he attempted to disable a Huerta gunboat near Topolobampo. Obregón pridefully reported this "first" to Carranza, but he neglected to mention that the target vessel was unharmed in the attack.

of Veracruz and a growing split among the revolutionaries themselves.

The occupation of Mexico's major port was the outgrowth of an incident at Tampico, where on April 9 a group of U.S. uniformed navy men, including an officer, were arrested by a Huerta officer under conditions that made it appear as though the action were a deliberate affront to the United States.[33] Huerta's failure to accede to U.S. demands for a proper apology, coupled with two minor incidents in Veracruz again interpreted by the United States as insulting to national honor, led President Wilson to determine upon punitive action, with a landing at Tampico probable. But news that the German ship *Ypiranga* was due to arrive in Veracruz with a shipment of arms to Huerta brought about a radical and sudden change of plans; about mid-morning of April 21, U.S. marines and sailors landed at Veracruz and secured the city after a brief but sharp struggle.

Wilson and Bryan both perceived the landing as an aid to the Constitutionalist cause, since the port occupation not only deprived Huerta of the arms shipment but also divested him of his greatest source of ready revenue—the duties at the custom house.[34] Mexican

[33] The background and the actual occupation are detailed in a variety of excellent works; the most convenient is Robert Quirk, *An Affair of Honor*.

[34] The shipment of arms was finally landed in Puerto México on May 27. The general assumption, supported by some newspaper accounts of the time, is that the arms did in fact get into the hands of the Huerta forces and that Wilson's attempt to deprive Huerta of arms was completely ineffectual. The view needs rectification. Huerta officials on April 21 were completely ready to receive the arms and to dispatch them immediately to the front; trains had been assembled, the engines had steam up, and the crews were at the ready to move the two hundred machine guns and the fifteen million rounds of ammunition to Zacatecas, San Luis Potosí, and intervening points—but these arms never arrived at their destinations. When the arms finally reached Puerto México over a month later, neither trains nor crews were available to move the material rapidly, and as a consequence the central military zone starved for munitions. San Luis Potosí put up no defense at all, and when the booty from Zacatecas was counted on June 23, after the capture of all war matériel, it consisted of "twelve thousand Mausers, 12 cannon, a few [*algunas*] machine guns and the normal [*regular*] quantity of munitions." In the context of other reports concerning arms, "a few machine guns" probably meant no more than ten or fifteen; the brigade that had more than ten machine guns was considered to be extremely well off. It therefore appears certain that Zacatecas had received none of the arms supply. Further-

reaction, much to official Washington chagrin, was exactly the converse of what was expected: not only did the Huertistas object violently, but also official statements and actions emanating from the Constitutionalist forces left little room to doubt the depth of Mexican hostility from every quarter.[35] Guerrilla activity against federal forces in the Veracruz-Puebla mountains came to a complete halt; recruits by the thousands poured into Huerta command areas,[36] and in all the areas controlled by the central government Huerta suddenly became the symbol of Mexican national honor. President Wilson unknowingly made of the dour and unattractive dictator a hero.

And in the Constitutionalist camp the occupation brought absolute consternation. Carranza, knowing full well the intent of Wilson's action, could not for a moment afford to allow the incident to pass without vigorous protest. For some months previously he had been engaged in a diplomatic contest with Washington in an attempt to force the northern government to divest itself of the mantle it had assumed as protector to all foreigners who happened to be within the confines of Mexican national territory, and further to impress upon the Department of State the necessity of dealing with him, rather than the field commanders, over questions involving international relations. In spite of Washington's hesitation in both matters, Carranza had almost carried the day before Veracruz. He had impressed upon his own subordinates the necessity for referring to his provisional government, wherever it might be located, all ques-

---

more, the ADN documents show conclusively that at the termination of the conflict great stores of arms and ammunition, not yet distributed to combat units, were surrendered to the Constitutionalists in Salina Cruz and other southern points. General Luis Gamboa, for example, reported that he gave Jesús Carranza custody of twenty unused machine guns and two thousand new rifles, along with four million rounds of 7 mm. ammunition, at Salina Cruz in September. There is a good possibility that some of this came from the *Ypiranga*.

35 The following account is a short summary of my article, "Huerta y Carranza ante la ocupación de Veracruz," *Historia Mexicana*, no. 24 (1957): 534–547. The documentation may be found in that article.

36 One Huerta official estimated the number at seventy thousand, most of whom could not actually be used, because of lack of arms.

tions of an international character,[37] and most Department of State personnel had come to the conclusion that for the purpose of saving time it was necessary to direct the messages to Carranza prior to, or perhaps contemporaneous with, a request for redress from the local officials.[38] In addition Carranza, after the beginning of 1914, consistently refused as a general principle to accept intercession by U.S. officials in behalf of non-U.S. citizens. If a foreigner were in an area not served by an official of his own government he could request aid from a U.S. official, but Carranza would honor such a request only if the government concerned made a *written* request to the U.S. government for such good offices.[39] Carranza had been engaged, in short, in a strenuous and largely successful effort to impress upon the United States the vital necessity for respecting Mexican sovereignty and for recognizing the provisional government as a viable instrumentality in the regions held by Constitutionalist arms.[40] Under these circumstances, allowing the Veracruz occupation to pass unchallenged would have been disastrous both then and later; in order to preserve his own leadership, and the popularity of the revolutionary cause, he was forced to be verbally more bellicose than Huerta.

[37] Obregón demonstrated the greatest punctilio in this respect and Villa the least; Villa, in fact, seemed to be willing to submit such questions to Carranza only if they became so embarrassing that he himself felt incapable of handling them.

[38] The U.S. maintained consuls, vice-consuls, or consular agents in every port and most inland cities of any size, while other major nations had fewer officials. The development of this problem, and its resolution, may be found in the 812.00 series for the last months of 1913 and the early months of 1914, NA, RG 59. A number of documents in ADN-Sonora and Chihuahua, 1913 and 1914 in both instances, also deal with the question. A long dispatch from Carothers to SecState, April 12, 1914, file 812.00/11755, summarizes the situation.

[39] On one occasion Bryan ordered a U.S. consul to "make clear to the [Carranza] authorities that we are obligated to foreign nations to extend to other nationals the same protection that we extend to American citizens and that we therefore demand that all foreigners" remain unmolested (Bryan to AmConsul, Saltillo, October 13, 1913, file 812.00/9275, NA, RG 59). But he was forced to abandon that position.

[40] The documentation concerning this question may be found intermingled with that mentioned in note 38.

The extent to which the incident slowed the Constitutionalist advance remains moot. It certainly did not affect the Monterrey campaign at all, since Pablo González plowed ahead in his conquest of the city, and it probably did not influence the Tampico move. Whether it slowed Obregón's advance is questionable, but, since he advocated a declaration of war against the United States,[41] it is quite probable that, for a few days at least, he temporized. In the case of Villa the situation is a little more clear. He himself was undisturbed by the occupation; as far as he was concerned, he told Consul George C. Carothers, the United States could "keep Vera Cruz [*sic*] and hold it so tight that not even water could get in to Huerta."[42] But with most of his officers in an uproar, and with the United States both threatening to reimpose the arms embargo and actually sending troops to the border, Villa felt it crucial to make a hurried trip to Ciudad Juárez to calm passions and to seek additional arms. How much of the month's delay between San Pedro and Paredón can be ascribed to this cause is uncertain, but it was a month that Huerta used to strengthen his position in the environs of Mexico City.

Much more serious, both for the immediate defeat of Huerta's government and for the pacification of the nation after that defeat, was the growing breach between Carranza and Villa. The two men were poles apart in attitude, education, and personality, and from their first encounter near Ciudad Juárez in 1911 their relations were somewhat strained. Villa was volatile, quixotic, crude, and unlettered in spite of a high intelligence. Carranza was deliberate, cold, thoughtful—scheming, his enemies said—suave, and sophisticated. Villa had a great sense of personal pride and personal honor; Carranza a great sense of Mexican pride and national, as well as personal, honor.[43] And they both had an enormous *don de mando*—the

[41] Obregón to Carranza, April 21, 1914, ADN-Chihuahua 1914. Obregón was fearful that the United States might sign a treaty with Huerta, and that Huerta could use the situation to the disadvantage of the Constitutionalist movement.

[42] As reported by Carothers to SecState, April 23, 1914, file 812.00/11654, NA, RG 59. Villa made known his view publicly in Ciudad Juárez, where he freely and sometimes intemperately talked to members of the press.

[43] One facet of Carranza's personality is revealed by the fact that he utterly refused to step outside the boundaries of Mexico for any reason. In his journey

ability and the need to command. Villa respected most of Carranza's good qualities, but he saw him as a *perfumado* and a *chocolatero*,[44] without either the ability or the audacity to lead troops in the field, but with unlimited ambition.[45] Carranza saw Villa as a semi-savage with delusions of grandeur who could be used by every schemer who happened to be in his good graces, and with unlimited ambition. And since both were partially right but saw themselves in quite different light, the breach was inevitable.

By April, 1914, some of Villa's nonmilitary activities had become a source of serious embarrassment to Carranza's provisional government,[46] and the events of that month added to the mutual distrust. In late February, Carranza had decided to move his government from Hermosillo to Chihuahua; his decision was prompted in part by his misgivings concerning Villa, whom he wished to supervise more directly. Traveling by train when he could and horseback when necessary, he spent almost five weeks in the trip to Ciudad Juárez, arriving in that border city five days before Villa captured Torreón. On April 12 Carranza arrived in Chihuahua City, and he was there to greet Villa after the battle of San Pedro. During the few days the two were together in Chihuahua they had two serious alterca-

---

from Coahuila to Sonora he crossed the forbidding Sierra Madre by horseback rather than take the more comfortable route through the United States, and when he transferred his government from Sonora to Chihuahua he again remained completely within Mexico. He could have made the entire trip to Ciudad Juárez by train, through the United States from Nogales, in one day, but the journey by horseback took over three weeks.

[44] These two terms can be translated roughly as "dandy" and "creampuff." In this evaluation Villa was wrong.

[45] Carranza was careful to identify himself, always, as the First Chief and never as a general. Official Washington, as well as the newspapers, consistently and incorrectly referred to him as General Carranza. He perceived himself to be commander in chief, with no military rank.

[46] The most distressing of these actions was the execution, without trial and apparently without cause other than irritation, of an English subject named William Benton; the incident provoked grave difficulties with both England and the United States. Villa also seized property, mistreated foreigners, and executed Mexicans in a fashion that brought ill repute to the Constitutionalists. Most of the details of these actions may be found in the 812.00 series, NA, RG 59, a good portion of which also appear in *Foreign Relations* for the proper years.

tions, which convinced Carranza that he would be forced to keep Villa in check.

The first came as a result of Carranza's posture regarding the United States. Even before the Veracruz incident, Villa and most of his advisors had become irritated at the First Chief's tone in dealing with the Department of State, and at one time in early April, Villa's principal advisors informed Carothers that if Carranza continued to offend the United States Villa "would not stand for it, but would call a general meeting of the different generals of the Constitutionalist Army, and instruct Carranza to change his policy, or get out."[47] Carranza was undoubtedly aware of Villa's attitude, and he certainly knew that Villa had expelled all Spaniards from Torreón in spite of his explicit instructions to the contrary.[48] When Villa made his statements regarding the U.S. occupation of Veracruz, therefore, Carranza was convinced that the general's military victories had induced him to preempt the political field, which was Carranza's own.[49] The fact that neither Obregón nor Pablo González had ever questioned his political wisdom probably made Carranza even less patient with Villa's attitude. Even though Carothers reported on April 29 that Carranza was completely "in accord with Villa on [the] policy towards the United States,"[50] the accord was merely on the surface.

The second incident was a more direct challenge to Carranza's political authority and resulted in a personal confrontation. Carranza, as the chief political officer of the Constitutionalist forces,

[47] Carothers to SecState, April 12, 1914, file 812.00/11755, NA, RG 59.

[48] Hamm to SecState, April 19, 1914, file 812.00/11703, NA, RG 59.

[49] That Villa differed violently from Carranza on the Veracruz affair, and that Villa resented Carranza's hostile note to Washington, is perfectly clear. Through Carothers, Villa told President Wilson that "the great majority of the Mexican people" knew "that the difficulties between the United States of America and the United States of Mexico have originated from the deliberate intent of the usurper Huerta to force a war." He then continued: "It is true that the situation has been aggravated by the form of the note of the Constitutional Governor of Coahuila and First Chief of the Revolution, but this note was entirely personal . . . " (Carothers to SecState, April 25, 1914, file 812.00/11714, NA, RG 59). By branding Carranza's note as personal, Villa by implication rejected the First Chief's authority to speak for the revolutionists.

[50] Carothers to SecState, April 29, 1914, file 812.00/11770, NA, RG 59.

recognized as such in the Plan de Guadalupe, had designated Manuel Chao as governor of Chihuahua in mid-1913, even though most of the state remained in the hands of the federals. But not long after arriving in Sonora in 1913, Carranza had designated Villa as the commanding general of the Division of the North, with Chihuahua as his field of operations, which created the anomalous situation of having General Chao subordinate to Villa in military affairs and Governor Chao superior to Villa in political affairs. After Villa's capture of Chihuahua City in late 1913 the four generals involved—Chao, Maclovio Herrera, José Rodríguez, and Villa—chose Villa as governor without consulting Carranza and without referring to the earlier designation;[51] Carranza soon pointed out their error and reinstalled Chao as governor, and it was Chao, not Villa, who welcomed the First Chief to the state of Chihuahua. According to Barragán, who was then on Carranza's staff, Villa was unhappy with the situation but made no attempt to change it until after the conquest of the Laguna, but when he came to Chihuahua City in mid-April he came with the determination to force Carranza to remove Chao from the governorship. Without consulting Carranza, however, Villa ordered Chao, as his military subordinate, to take command of his troops immediately and depart for Torreón; if Chao obeyed the command he would be eliminated as governor. Chao, as governor, not only refused to obey the command but did not even answer it, whereupon Villa ordered his summary execution for insubordination. Shortly before the scheduled execution, and somewhat by accident, Carranza became apprised of the situation. Over Villa's protests Carranza countermanded the order immediately, set Chao at liberty, and again confirmed his position as governor.[52] On the surface no

[51] Barragán, *Ejército*, I, 437, reproduces the document by which the agreement was certified.

[52] The account here follows ibid., pp. 437–445. Barragán, a loyal Carrancista, may have gilded the lily a bit, but there seems to be no reason to doubt the essence of the account. Guzmán (*Memorias de Pancho Villa*, pp. 380–382) gives a slightly different account, but he has Villa say to Chao: "You are the governor of the state only through my obedience to a mandate from the First Chief, and because I cannot concern myself with these administrative details [*esos negocios*] while I am carrying the weight of the war. But I want you to know, my friend,

harm was done, for in spite of a harsh exchange of words in which Villa insisted that Chihuahua was his realm to command and Carranza hotly denied Villa's authority, the incident was passed off as only a misunderstanding. But both Villa and Carranza knew that they had come to a parting, and thenceforward each planned his actions as a prelude to an eventual armed conflict.

Even while Villa and Carranza drew apart, another and apparently unconnected split among the revolutionaries developed in Sonora. The Sonora quarrel, in fact, developed at the time of the Huerta coup when Governor José María Maytorena received from the state legislature permission to leave his post for a period of six months for his "health." Maytorena later insisted that he left in order to remove himself from an atmosphere of greedy ambition and intrigue,[53] but most of those who took up arms against Huerta viewed the action as the flight of a coward;[54] they further resented Maytorena's last official act before leaving the state: he extracted from the treasury twelve thousand pesos to pay his own salary and expenses, and those of his aides, while on leave. In late July, 1913, Maytorena determined to return to the state and renew his active governorship, to which he was legally entitled. Most of the field commanders objected strongly to his return, but they consented in order to retain the flavor of constitutionalism that was the heart of the movement.[55]

that here I command, because the fight in which we are all involved demands it. And I want to tell you further that I am going to have you executed right now, so that you don't get any more ideas about undermining respect for me." But Villa, speaking through Guzmán, says he had no intention of carrying out the threat; he simply wanted to underscore the magnitude of his irritation with Chao's attitude.

[53] In 1919, from Los Angeles, Maytorena wrote an unconvincing account of his part in the revolution in which he accused Obregón, Calles, and others of all manner of intrigue and dishonesty (see José María Maytorena, *Algunas verdades sobre el General Alvaro Obregón*).

[54] The most important were Obregón, his brother José J. Obregón, Calles, Salvador Alvarado, Manuel Diéguez, Benjamín Hill, Juan G. Cabral, Ignacio Pesqueira, and Roberto Pesqueira.

[55] A group of the leaders, including Obregón, Hill, Calles, and Ignacio Pesqueira made a special trip to Nogales to try to convince Maytorena not to return. But when he insisted that he had a legal right to the governorship, they all

From the moment of his return trouble developed, particularly between Maytorena, on the one hand, and Calles and Obregón, on the other; whether the quarrel had an ideological or a personal base is not clear—Obregón insisted that Maytorena was sympathetic with the *científico* mentality—but the U.S. consul in Hermosillo was convinced that Maytorena envied Obregón's position as commander of the Northwest Division and worked to undermine his authority.[56] Regardless of the reason, by late March, 1914, Maytorena complained to Carranza that "every day Col. E. P. Calles's attitude toward me as governor becomes more hostile . . . State employees and friends of mine are being expelled [by Calles and Obregón]. This leads me to demand that you tell me categorically how you view my position."[57] Carranza not only replied that he would support Maytorena's authority as governor,[58] but he also dispatched a special agent to Sonora to settle the issue and ordered Calles to allow the governor to retain a special military escort.[59] The situation gradually deteriorated, however, until by early June the state was a divided camp, ready to explode into open warfare. Not only was the atmosphere not conducive to wide recruitment and rapid military advance, but also the quarrel directly affected the military movements. Arms and ammunition that should have flowed to Obregón in his assault on the Huerta bastions remained in Sonora in the hands of both Obregón and Maytorena sympathizers as a guarantee of equilibrium, and troops that should have joined the western military chieftain stayed in the northwest watching one another. Internal dissension had become a strong Huerta weapon.

The differences among the Constitutionalists could be obscured

---

agreed that they would not take any action to prevent his reoccupation of the office (Obregón, *Ocho mil kilómetros*, p. 80).

[56] Hostetter to SecState, May 17, 1914, file 812.00/12056, NA, RG 59.

[57] Maytorena to Zubarán Capmany, May 29, 1914, ADN-Sonora 1914.

[58] Zubarán Capmany to Maytorena, April 2, 1914, ibid.

[59] Carranza sent Ramón Puente as his confidential agent, with verbal instructions. Among Puente's observations was that Calles had ordered, as commandant of the zone, Maytorena's escort to leave Hermosillo; Carranza ordered Calles to send the escort back to the capital, where it would be under Maytorena's direct orders. A series of documents in ibid. deals with the questions.

but not completely hidden; even the federal forces knew of the problem. In Zacatecas, where General Luis Medina Barrón commanded the Huerta garrison, rumors of the quarrel were so current that the general reported the split as a fact, but added sadly that "nevertheless they all collaborate against the country."[60] The lack of collaboration, in fact, allowed Medina Barrón to retain control of Zacatecas for at least a month longer than he should have.

Firm in the conviction that Villa constituted a real threat, Carranza determined that he would prevent, if possible, the northern *caudillo*'s entrance into Mexico City as the hero who had overthrown the Huerta dictatorship; mainly for this reason he insisted that Villa attack Saltillo in mid-May instead of proceeding to the reduction of Zacatecas. Furthermore, he sent one of his most trusted aides to Obregón's headquarters, nearly two thousand miles away by available transportation, to urge that general "to make every effort to speed-up my advance into the center of the nation; because he had begun to suspect the conduct of Villa and Angeles, his idea was that our Army Corps, whose loyalty he had never doubted, should occupy the principal cities in the interior."[61] More importantly, he planned to leave the conquest of Zacatecas to Pánfilo Natera and the Arrieta brothers, all of whom he trusted implicitly. Unfortunately, both he and Natera miscalculated the strength of Medina Barrón's defenses, and the miscalculation brought an open break with Villa.

Zacatecas lies in a slight depression, with the massive Veta Grande mountain slightly to the north, the imposing La Bufa immediately to the northeast, El Grillo guarding the west, and other high places scattered around the entire circle. Although revolutionary activity had been marked in the state for the preceding year, the city itself

[60] L. Medina Barrón to MinGob, May 14, 1914, ADN-Zacatecas 1914. Medina Barrón reported that Villa was in Torreón and Angeles in Monterrey; they were both, in fact, then moving on Paredón. The federal intelligence service was generally poor, consistently erroneous regarding the movements of the enemy and the location of the principal leaders. On one occasion, for example, the government became so convinced that Pablo González was wounded and in the United States that it requested the U.S. government to arrest him. González was neither wounded nor in the United States at the time.

[61] Obregón, *Ocho mil kilómetros*, p. 121.

had been unmolested and the federals had therefore been given ample time to develop their defenses and to provision their troops. With twelve to fifteen thousand troops under his command, General Medina Barrón had dug into the surrounding hills, developed a strong set of inner trenches for secondary positions, and placed his artillery so that any attacking force would be raked by its fire. The federals considered the city to be absolutely impregnable against any possible Constitutionalist assaulting force.[62] But unless the entire attack against Huerta were to be stalled, the Constitutionalists had to occupy the city.

As soon as he had convinced Villa to undertake the Saltillo campaign, Carranza made a trip from Torreón to Durango, where he conferred with the Arrietas, and then in their company he traveled to Sombrerete, where Natera had established his headquarters. There, Natera and the Arrieta brothers insisted to the First Chief that they could and would take Zacatecas without any help from Villa. His normal good judgment impaired by his fear of Villa, Carranza agreed to the plan even though the combined Arrieta-Natera forces scarcely reached six thousand poorly equipped men with almost no artillery.[63] After making the final arrangements for a combined attack, and giving the necessary orders for provisioning, Carranza returned to Torreón in early June, expecting to meet Villa there for further conferences. But Villa, by this time certain that Carranza was deliberately holding him back, found it expedient to be elsewhere; only hours before Carranza's entry into Torreón, Villa left for Chihuahua and Ciudad Juárez, where his general disgust with Carranza, and his suspicions of him, led him to make public statements that widened

[62] Reports from Medina Barrón to the Ministry of War, and public statements by Minister of War Blanquet, indicate that the government had no real fear concerning the fate of Zacatecas. Documents in ADN-Zacatecas 1914 exude confidence. The number of troops included those nearby who came into the city before the big battle began.

[63] Natera badly underestimated the strength of the federals and overestimated his own strength. He believed that Medina Barrón had only about six thousand men, many of whom would join the attackers at the first opportunity and that the attack would attract thousands of recruits to his own forces (Barragán, *Ejército*, I, 477–478).

the breach. He made it clear that he believed himself to be the only powerful general,[64] and that only he could finish the fight against Huerta. Carranza, for his part, decided to starve the Villa war machine as much as possible by holding back ammunition, by preventing the shipment of coal from the Coahuila fields to Villa, and by seizing railroad equipment.[65]

Such was the situation, then, when Natera began his attack on Zacatecas on June 11.[66] After two days of fighting, Natera realized the difficulty of the task before him and requested Carranza to send a reinforcement of three thousand men, whereupon Carranza ordered Villa, again in Torreón, to dispatch a column of his men to give Natera aid. Villa refused by temporizing and then, when Carranza insisted on June 13 that Villa dispatch the reinforcements immediately, the northern general resigned his command in a huff and spread the word that Carranza had ordered him to go to Zacatecas himself and to serve under Natera, which his pride would not allow him to do.[67] Carranza then ordered all the generals who had been serving under Villa to confer and to recommend a successor, but when they met the following day they informed Carranza: "We are going to convince the commander of this Division to continue the fight against the Huerta government as though no disagreeable event has taken place this day and we advise you to proceed in the

[64] Villa was often free in his criticisms of the military acumen of Pablo González and Obregón. His attitude, if not his words, was that he was the commander in chief of the armed forces.

[65] This action was reported as a rumor on June 4 and became certain on June 10, by which time all rolling stock going to Saltillo and Monterrey from Torreón was held at the former points (see Letcher to SecState, June 4, 1914, file 812.00/12160, and Carothers to Z. L. Cobb, June 10, 1914, file 812.00/12219, NA, RG 59).

[66] Barragán indicates that the attack began on June 10, but Medina Barrón reported to Blanquet (Medina Barrón to SecGyM, June 11, 1914, in ADN-Zacatecas 1914) that the attack began at 8:00 P.M. on June 11. The discrepancy probably comes from the difference between a "movement" and an "attack."

[67] It was generally accepted by the Villistas that Carranza demanded that Villa serve under Natera (see Cobb to SecState, June 16, 1914, file 812.00/12266, NA, RG 59). In fact, Carranza not only did not order Villa personally to go to Zacatecas and serve under Natera, but by implication he also ordered him not to go south.

same manner, with the object of defeating the common enemy."[68] This was, of course, an act of rank insubordination on the part of Villa and all the generals involved, and in the exchange of telegraphic correspondence between them and Carranza there was much more: Carranza was accused of making a "malevolent resolution," of "defrauding the hopes of the people by a dictatorial attitude," of being desirous of removing from the revolution any "man of power who is not an unconditional Carrancista," of fomenting "disunion in the states," and of "blunders in the field of international relations."[69] The act was not merely a military insubordination; it was a political rejection in unforgettable terms.

Immediately after having advised Carranza of their determination, Villa's commanders began moving on Zacatecas with nearly twenty thousand men well supported with artillery. On June 19 Toribio Ortega captured the federal positions on the Veta Grande, within artillery range of the city itself, and during the next three days of rain and blustery weather the Constitutionalist forces gradually reduced the outposts and surrounded the city. The frontal assault on the inner defenses began early on the morning of June 23, and by late afternoon Zacatecas had become a hecatomb. The panic-stricken troops, bereft of leadership,[70] attempted to flee but found all avenues of escape closed; Felipe Angeles, who had been primarily responsible for the design of the attack, reported: "Immediately they fled toward Jerez and then fell back. They attempted to leave by way of Veta Grande, on the side we were on, and we ordered our infantry to hunt them down, struggling as they were among our own men. 'Have no fear,' I told them; 'it is not a question of fighting, since

[68] Barragán, *Ejército*, I, 522; the generals involved were Toribio Ortega, Eugenio Aguirre Benavides, Maclovio Herrera, Rosalío Hernández, Severiano Ceniceros, Martiniano Servín, José Rodríguez, Trinidad Rodríguez, Mateo Almanza, Felipe Angeles, José I. Robles, Tomás Urbina, Calixto Contreras, Máximo García, and Orestes Pereyra.

[69] The message is duplicated in ibid., pp. 523–524; Guzmán (*Memorias de Pancho Villa*, pp. 461–462) gives a different version of the telegram but says the same thing generally.

[70] Exactly when Medina Barrón and his staff left seems to be in doubt. One civilian who happened to be in Zacatecas and left soon thereafter reported that the general began the evacuation on the afternoon of June 22.

they are in flight, but only a question of exterminating them.' "[71] In desperation the trapped men pounded eastward on the road to Guadalupe and south to Aguascalientes, running a gauntlet through to the Arrietas' and Natera's brigade, who with enfilading and cross-fire reduced nearly five thousand of their fellow Mexicans to quivering corpses in a matter of moments. When it was over Angeles was jubilant: "I confess without blushing that I saw them annihilated with overflowing joy; because I saw the event from the artistic point of view, as the master work terminated."[72] When the contenders stopped shooting and counted losses, they found a staggering toll: nearly six thousand federals and one thousand Constitutionalists dead, some three thousand federals and two thousand Constitutionalists wounded, uncounted civilians dead or injured through gunfire or by debris flying from public buildings ordered dynamited by the fleeing Medina Barrón,[73] and the city in a shambles.[74] Of the entire federal army, only three or four hundred escaped with Medina Barrón to the haven of Aguascalientes; all others not killed became prisoners.[75]

Had there been perfect accord among the revolutionaries at that point the issue of the Huerta government could have been resolved

[71] Angeles kept a day-by-day account of the battle; it is reproduced in Barragán, *Ejército*, I, 540–564.

[72] Angeles's statement is reminiscent of the Italian aviator who spoke of the beautiful floral effect created by a bomb dropped on concentrated Ethiopian troops in early 1936. One wonders whether Angeles appreciated the beauty of Carranza's "master work terminated" when he himself stood before a firing squad in 1919.

[73] One federal prisoner stated that the entire city was mined by Medina Barrón's order and that the charges had been connected to the electric light plant. Capture of the plant and the cutting of current prevented the full fruition of the plan, but some buildings were blown up (see Carothers to SecState, July 5, 1914, file 812.00/12473, NA, RG 59).

[74] An epidemic of typhus hit the city soon after the battle; one of the victims was Toribio Ortega, who died in mid-July.

[75] For accounts of the battle see Carothers to SecState, July 5, 1914, with appended maps, file 812.00/12473, NA, RG 59; *El Sol*, June 26 and June 27, 1914; Natera to Carranza, June 29, 1914, in Barragán, *Ejército*, I, 756–760. Barragán (pp. 515–516, 536–564) also gives a narrative account. The ADN-Zacatecas 1914 documents include nothing on the battle itself; Medina Barrón presumably made an official report, but I have been unable to locate it.

quickly. Constitutionalist forces moving from Saltillo down the line to San Luis Potosí and Querétaro, along with Villa's forces moving from Zacatecas, could have swept the demoralized federal forces before them with ease. But with conditions as they were, Carranza's loyal men in Saltillo appeared to be ready to move into Torreón instead of San Luis, and Villa drew all his men from the Zacatecas region to fortify the Laguna and the region to the north. From that date forward Villa took no part in Huerta's overthrow;[76] Carranza, not Huerta, was now the enemy. To be sure, an attempt was made to heal the breach. Pressured by a number of men who had not taken part in the Torreón insubordination, Carranza agreed in early July to send a commission to discuss affairs with representatives of the Villa group. The result was an agreement signed on July 8 by the terms of which the Division of the North recognized Carranza's position as First Chief; Villa was recognized as the commanding general of the Division of the North; Carranza agreed to furnish the necessary arms, ammunition, and coal to Villa's forces for an assault to the south; Carranza agreed to call a convention of military leaders as soon as the Constitutionalist forces occupied Mexico City; and Carranza's position as chief civil administrative officer was confirmed.[77] In addition Villa agreed unofficially to release a number of Carranza officials he had earlier arrested in Ciudad Juárez and to return to Carranza a large sum of money he had seized at the same time.[78] But the agreement was façade; neither Carranza nor Villa be-

[76] As late as June 18, Villa intended to press on beyond Zacatecas as soon as possible, but ten days later, after the battle of Zacatecas, he had decided that he could not do so (see Carothers to SecState, June 18, 1914, file 812.00/12305, and Cobb to SecState, June 29, 1914, file 812.00/12370, NA, RG 59).

[77] George Carothers in Torreón received a copy of the agreement from Villa and transmitted it in translation to the State Department (see Carothers to SecState, July 9, 1914, file 812.00/12717 enclosure, NA, RG 59). The agreement was signed by Antonio Villarreal, Manuel Bonilla, Luis Caballero, Miguel Silva, Cesáreo Castro, José Isabel Robles, Ernesto Meade Fierro, and Roque González Garza. None of the men involved could be considered as irrevocably committed to either Carranza or Villa.

[78] Carothers to Cobb, July 8, 1914, file 812.00/12470, NA, RG 59; he sent the message immediately after having conferred with Villa, after the men and money had been returned to Carranza, and after Villa had received a shipment of coal

lieved it settled the major issues,[79] and both took actions on the assumption of probable future conflict.

On the day that the agreement was signed Obregón captured Guadalajara from the federals after an enveloping campaign of almost a month; much of the delay came from the lack of rail transportation between Tepic and Guadalajara, necessitating animal transportation of all equipment, including munitions and artillery, over more than two hundred miles of difficult terrain. In the battle Guadalajara itself was untouched; after the Constitutionalists had defeated a major portion of the federalists at Orendáin, only twenty-five miles to the northwest of the city on July 6–7, the federals attempted to leave by the rail line running to the southeast and thence to Mexico City, only to find that Lucio Blanco, under Obregón's command, had cut the line at El Castillo, some twenty miles from the city. In the ensuing battle there the Constitutionalists mauled the federalist army and closed the escape route; the result was another federalist army destroyed. Of the twelve thousand federals engaged in the Guadalajara defense, nearly two thousand perished and another six thousand became prisoners;[80] the remainder fled on foot in any direction that seemed to offer safety. Obregón's men captured most of the artillery, over five thousand rifles, great stores of ammunition, and, perhaps most importantly, all the railroad rolling stock.

For the next three weeks Obregón devoted his energies to neutralizing federal strength to the south of Guadalajara in Colima; he particularly feared a concentration of all the west coast federals in Manzanillo, thus threatening his lines of supply. After having made the proper dispositions to assure his safety, Obregón began moving to the east along the rail line leading through La Piedad, Irapuato,

---

in return. Alberto J. Pani gives the sum of money as six million pesos in Carranza currency, plus twenty thousand dollars in cash (*Apuntes autobiográficos*, I, 200).

[79] Leon Canova, a special agent who had been sent by Bryan to remain with Carranza, after conferences with both Carranza and González concluded that the split was irreparable (Canova to SecState, July 8, 1914, file 812.00/12474, NA, RG 59).

[80] Among those who died was General José María Mier, a veteran of the French intervention, who at the time of his death was the commanding general of all federal forces in the west.

Celaya, Querétaro, and Tula, Hidalgo, to Mexico City. Leaving Guadalajara on July 26, by easy stages and without serious resistance, he progressed toward Mexico City; by August 10 he was in Teoloyucan, a village some fifteen miles from the outskirts of the city and almost in contact with the advance posts of the 25,000 troops said to be guarding the capital.[81]

While Obregón developed his campaign in the west and Villa sulked in the north, the northeastern division began a two-pronged attack on San Luis Potosí. By July 4 Jesús Carranza had moved from Tampico to Cerritos, sixty miles northeast of San Luis on the rail line, and Pablo González had occupied Charcas, roughly the same distance to the north of the city on the San Luis–Saltillo line. Both commands had incorporated quasi-independent groups that had been operating in the eastern and northern sections of the state, with the consequence that an army of about twenty thousand men was moving slowly on the state capital from the north, while an equal or larger number under Obregón moved from the west. In addition, large numbers of Constitutionalists in scattered groups carried on forays in Veracruz, Puebla, and Hidalgo, while Emiliano Zapata with some fifteen thousand men in Morelos threatened the city from the south.

Zapata had remained his own man, independent and single-minded as ever. At the time of the Veracruz affair he vowed to fight the Americans if necessary, but not in league with Huerta—in fact, his officers shot at least three federal emissaries who tried to woo them to Huerta's side to fight Yankees.[82] As for the Constitutionalists, Zapata remained outside their fold, recognizing them as co-belligerents against the federals but not as having any special legal status. Despite Carrancista efforts to win him over, he continued to treat the First Chief only as an equal among a half dozen other leaders in

[81] The information used in this short summary of Obregón's campaigns from Tepic is in Obregón, *Ocho mil kilómetros*, pp. 126–155. Some reports concerning Obregón's advance may be found in the newspapers, particularly *El Sol*, but none of the official correspondence between the federal Jalisco command and the Ministry of War was found.

[82] Gildardo Magaña and Carlos Pérez Guerrero, *Emiliano Zapata y el agrarismo en México*, IV, 188–196.

the northern movement,[83] and by the summer of 1914 he was demanding that Carranza and all revolutionaries adhere to his Plan de Ayala,[84] which as amended the year before named Zapata supreme chief of the revolution.[85] Militarily he was doing his part to unseat Huerta, although he was chronically short of supplies. In March he took Chilpancingo in Guerrero,[86] and in April his forces were hounding Huertistas in the state of México and southern Puebla.[87] In Morelos, by May, the federals held only Cuernavaca, which was surrounded and helpless,[88] and Zapata was girding for an advance on Mexico City.[89] He hoped to occupy the capital after Huerta's fall, not necessarily with the idea of fighting the Constitutionalists, but because he believed that being at the center of an action so important as liberating the seat of national power was the best way to guarantee that his people and their villages would be secure when the revolution was over.[90]

Since the stunning defeats to his armies in the north, particularly those in April and May, Huerta had been playing for time in the hopes that he could salvage his government without a military victory. In a gesture much like that of the aged Porfirio Díaz three years earlier when his support was gone, in mid-February Huerta decreed the creation of a new ministry, that of Agriculture and Colonization,[91] and a short time later ordered local officials to undertake the "preliminaries in the development of an active agrarian policy, in consonance with the needs and aspirations of the coun-

[83] John Womack, *Zapata and the Mexican Revolution*, pp. 194–195.

[84] Ibid., p. 195.

[85] Manuel González Ramírez, ed., *Planes políticos y otros documentos*, pp. 86–89.

[86] Magaña and Pérez Guerrero, *Zapata*, III, 312–314.

[87] Ibid., IV, 169–170.

[88] Ibid., pp. 217–220.

[89] Womack, *Zapata*, p. 187.

[90] Ibid., pp. 186–187.

[91] SecGob Circular, February 17, 1914, in AGN-Gobernación—Varios 1913–1914. Agriculture had been under the jurisdiction of the Ministry of Development, Colonization, and Industry; with Agriculture and Colonization now enjoying the prestige of a separate ministry, the original was confined to Industry and Commerce.

try."[92] After the Veracruz occupation and the beginning of the Niagara Conference,[93] he banked heavily on an ultimate compromise that would put him in a bargaining position with the Constitutionalists. He was so confident of that ploy's success, or so desperate to grasp at straws, that he asked for a special session of his Congress to be ready to approve the conference recommendation because "by virtue of the good intentions of the mediating powers, and of their efficacious efforts, it is very probable that some arrangements will be made between the *ad interim* Constitutional Government of Mexico and the Carranza revolutionaries conducive to the pacification of the country."[94]

But with his armies disappearing and the Niagara Conference delaying, by early July, Huerta and his minions began taking steps to protect themselves. On July 2 Joaquín Maass and his two brothers left for Europe on a "delicate mission" for Huerta, and the following day Querido Moheno resigned from the cabinet for reasons of "ill health."[95] On the evening of July 9 Supreme Court President Francisco Carbajal was designated as minister of foreign relations in an obvious move to put him in position to take over the government.[96] On July 13 Minister of War Blanquet announced that he was leaving

[92] Jefe Político, Tepic, to SecGob, March 11, 1914, in AGN-Gobernación—Personal—Varios 1913–1914; the *jefe político* assured Gobernación that he was doing all in his power to meet the "needs and aspirations" of the local peasants.

[93] Soon after the occupation of Veracruz, President Wilson requested the mediation of Argentina, Brazil, and Chile; the three nations agreed on April 25, and both the Carranza and the Huerta factions agreed to send commissioners. As soon as it became apparent that the mediators, along with the Huerta commissioners and those from the United States, were intent on working out a solution not only of the Veracruz incident but also of the political affairs in Mexico itself, Carranza refused to have anything further to do with the conference. By the time the conference made its recommendations, which included the formula for the designation of a provisional president in Mexico, both Zacatecas and Guadalajara had fallen and the Huerta government was in collapse.

[94] SecRelExt to SecGob, June 17, 1914, in AGN-Gobernación—Varios 1913–1914. The "Congress" was merely an agglomeration of Huerta sycophants, but Huerta tried to maintain the form of a constitutional government. The special session sat from June 8 until July 8, when the long-awaited conference proposal arrived in Mexico City. By that time it was too late to help Huerta.

[95] *El Sol*, July 4, 1914.

[96] Ibid., July 10, 1914.

for Europe "with the object of studying the organization of the European armies,"[97] and on the same date the minister of communications resigned also to go to Europe "with the object of studying the administrative service and railroad organization of those countries."[98] Then on July 15 Huerta resigned, Carbajal became acting president, and the remainder of the cabinet left their offices. One of the newspapers that had bravely proclaimed its independence of thought but that had been most faithful in parroting the government line, in a bold headline announced: "The Collapse of a Tyranny."[99]

But Huerta's flight did not bring an immediate end to the armed conflict, even though it was in part responsible for the ease with which Obregón moved from Guadalajara to Teoloyucan, and the northeast forces from north of San Luis Potosí to the same spot.[100] Those who had remained in Mexico City and those who still served the government were terrified of the probable vengeance to be meted out by the victorious Constitutionalists; it was incumbent on Carbajal's government to work out with Carranza an understanding that would give some protection. Furthermore, most Mexico City officials would prefer control of the capital by the Constitutionalists rather than the Zapata hordes, whom they looked upon as savages; some method therefore had to be devised to allow Carranza's forces to police the city as the federals abandoned it.

A combination of these two factors led Carbajal to undertake, through the United States as intermediary, negotiations for the surrender of his government to the Constitutionalists; he made no attempt to make a direct contact with Carranza but depended upon U.S. representatives in Saltillo and Monterrey, under instruction from Washington, to make the proper arrangements. From the beginning of these conversations Carranza made it perfectly clear that the subject of discussions was "to agree upon the form of the uncon-

[97] SecGyM to SecGob, July 13, 1914, AGN-Gobernación—Varios 1913–1914.

[98] Ibid.

[99] *El Sol*, July 16, 1914.

[100] Obregón and González met in Querétaro on August 1 and there agreed to the disposition of the troops. Only a portion of the González forces ever reached Teoloyucan.

ditional delivery of the Government at Mexico City," and that the meeting place would have to be Saltillo;[101] Carbajal was so notified. In spite of Carranza's attitude, Carbajal still hoped to impose conditions for the surrender and hoped to select New York as the site for negotiations;[102] the suggestion for the site was so unrealistic that Bryan refused to pass it on to Carranza.[103] Ten days after he had assumed office as provisional president, Carbajal finally appointed Lauro Villar and David Gutiérrez Allende to go to Saltillo as "peace commissioners,"[104] with instructions to demand a number of concessions in return for the surrender of the city.[105] Probably somewhat dubious concerning Carranza's reception of his demands, on the same day he requested and received a telegraphic conference with Obregón, still in Guadalajara but ready to move out, in which he said that he wanted "an understanding with the chiefs of the revolution" and asked for a suspension of all military activities. Obregón replied curtly that any negotiations would have to be done through Carranza, and that until Carranza ordered the contrary the military operations would go on; he promised Carbajal that he would arrive in the vicinity of Mexico City in the middle of August, with all his

[101] The documentation may be found in the 812.00 series for late July and August, NA, RG 59. Since the United States had no diplomatic representative in Mexico City, the Brazilian minister there acted in that capacity, and it was through him that the Mexico City end of the arrangements were made. Carranza first made his position clear in a conversation with U.S. Consuls Hanna, Robertson, and Silliman in Monterrey on July 19 (Silliman to SecState, July 19, 1914, file 812.00/12552).

[102] Brazilian Minister Cardoso de Oliveira (Mexico) to SecState, July 22, 1914, file 812.00/12586, NA, RG 59.

[103] Bryan urged Carbajal, through the Brazilian minister, to drop the New York suggestion and accept Saltillo (Bryan to Cardoso de Oliveira, July 23, 1914, file 812.00/12586, NA, RG 59).

[104] *El País*, July 27, 1914; in the formal note to the Department of State announcing the action, the term "peace commissioner" was not used. Villar, wounded in the first encounter that ushered in the Tragic Ten Days and generally considered to be a Madero supporter, had taken no active military part in the Huerta armies; Gutiérrez Allende, as a justice of the Supreme Court, was presumably apolitical.

[105] No one, other than Carbajal and the commissioners, knew of the existence of the instructions until the first meeting between them and the Carranza representatives.

army.[106] Obregón immediately informed Carranza of the incident and continued his plans to move on the capital.

The journey of the two commissioners to Saltillo was completely sterile. Even though Carranza had suggested a journey by way of San Louis Potosí, the Carbajal commissioners chose to come by way of Tampico and Monterrey;[107] Carranza never made any mention of this failure to follow his suggestion, but the action must have irritated the First Chief. The commissioners were so shabbily treated on the journey between Tampico and Monterrey that they appeared at the U.S. consulate early on the morning of August 1 to request that Consul General Philip C. Hanna escort them to the border; only Hanna's "strongest appeals to their patriotism" induced them to continue.[108] They had been assured that they would talk with Carranza himself,[109] but they found on arriving in Saltillo that he had designated Antonio Villarreal and Luis Caballero to be his agents, and then they soon discovered that they had no basis upon which to confer. Villar and Gutiérrez Allende laid down six conditions for surrender: an immediate armistice, reinstitution of the old Congress dismissed by Huerta, a general and sweeping amnesty to be issued by the Congress, confirmation of existing military ranks in both Constitutionalist and federal forces, designation of a new president by the Congress, and the validation of debts of all parties. Villarreal and Caballero "could not take them into consideration," since the conditions were in "absolute disagreement" with the Plan de Guadalupe and would imply a "recognition of acts executed by the usurping government."[110] To Carranza and the other revolutionists an

[106] Obregón gives a terse account in his *Ocho mil kilómetros*, p. 150.

[107] The commissioners said they could not go by way of San Luis Potosí, since a gap of two hundred kilometers existed on the line between Mexico City and San Luis. Any such gap was between Mexico City and Querétaro and was caused by retreating federals, against which Obregón had warned Carbajal on July 26.

[108] Hanna to SecState, August 1, 1914, file 812.00/12704, NA, RG 59.

[109] So Carranza told Silliman on July 28, and the information had been passed on (Silliman to SecState, July 28, 1914, file 812.00/12643, NA, RG 59).

[110] The statement made by Villarreal and Caballero, including the six demands, may be found in a number of places, in either Spanish or English translation. The most convenient is in *Foreign Relations, 1914*, pp. 579–580.

acceptance of the conditions would have been tantamount to losing the fruits of victory; they were determined to destroy, completely and absolutely, every vestige of the old federal army; they insisted on the right to punish those in high echelons of civil and military command; they themselves were going to determine the nature of the government and to name the man to act as chief magistrate; and they had given ample warning that they had no intention of saddling Mexico with the debts contracted by Huerta. They wanted, and would accept nothing less than, absolute and unconditional surrender. Since the commissioners by instruction could not discuss unconditional surrender, and the Constitutionalists would discuss nothing else, the negotiations came to an end before they started. Discouraged and probably fearful for their lives, the commissioners requested permission to leave by way of the United States; they were told curtly to go back the way they had come.[111]

In the meantime Obregón continued his advance on Mexico City, becoming more and more impatient with what he considered the dilatory tactics of the new government. On August 8, from his headquarters about forty miles from Mexico City, Obregón sent a peremptory demand to Carbajal; he wanted the provisional president to "declare in a concrete manner the attitude you assume as the chief of the Huertista forces who garrison the city; whether you are disposed to surrender or defend the city."[112] He demanded an immediate answer, but while awaiting it he continued to advance slowly. Two days later and over twenty miles closer to the capital, Obregón received his answer: the city would be surrendered without a fight, and the government wished to send representatives to discuss the transfer of power.[113] In the interim between Obregón's demand and Carbajal's answer, Villar and Gutiérrez Allende had returned from their bootless venture to the north, bringing with them the word that Carranza absolutely refused to agree to an order for a general amnesty. The news, which threatened all members of the

[111] Silliman to SecState, August 4, 1914, file 812.00/12746, NA, RG 59. They left Saltillo late on the afternoon of August 4.

[112] Obregón, *Ocho mil kilómetros*, p. 154; he quotes the document in full.

[113] Ibid., p. 155; Barragán, *Ejército*, I, 590–591, has the full text of the reply.

government and all field-grade officers with summary execution, put the city in a panic; wild rumors circulated, the most intriguing of which was that the army would put up a heroic defense, select Angeles as president, and depend upon Villa to come rushing from Chihuahua to save the federal officials from extermination.[114] José Refugio Velasco, who in the general debacle had been handed the unenviable post of minister of war, urged on Carranza a more reasonable attitude regarding amnesty and issued a public statement attempting to clarify his position.[115] The army, he said, was blameless; as an apolitical branch of the government its only choice under any circumstance was to obey the orders emanating from the executive recognized by the legislative and judicial branches, and Huerta had been so recognized. He assured both revolutionists and the general public that the army as an institution would put no obstacle in the way of the successful revolution, but that, in view of the widespread practice of military executions meted out to captured federal officers, military officials could not depend upon the "magnanimity" of the victors. They needed guarantees, and without these guarantees they would be forced to resist.[116] Carranza's consistent position, expressed to John R. Silliman and transmitted to Carbajal, was that no general amnesty could be granted, that those who knew they were guilty of punishable crimes should leave the country, and that those who were innocent had nothing to fear.[117] This was cold comfort to fearful officials. The situation appeared to be exceedingly dangerous, since Mexico City was occupied by over 25,000 federal troops.

[114] Cardoso de Oliveira to SecState, August 9, 1914, file 812.00/12788; the Brazilian was "reliably informed" of this plan.

[115] He sent this word to Carranza via the Brazilian minister and the secretary of state; Cardoso de Oliveira to SecState, August 9, 1914, file 812.00/12787, NA, RG 59, includes the Velasco plea.

[116] The statement, issued by Velasco on August 9, appeared in *El Diario*, August 10, 1914.

[117] Silliman to SecState, undated, received August 9, 1914, file 812.00/12779, NA, RG 59. One of Carranza's major concerns, as he expressed it to Silliman, was that the federals would disband and hide their arms and ammunition. Carranza, looking forward to the probable Villa struggle, was determined to have them.

While these events transpired, Obregón urged Carranza to come as soon as possible to direct the final action—military or political, as the case might be—and Carranza in his turn gave Obregón the authority to enter into negotiations for the military surrender of the city. With the decision made to surrender, Carbajal began to take the final steps in the transfer of the government—but he made one last attempt to salvage something by requesting the Brazilian minister, J. M. Cardoso de Oliveira, to confer with Carranza. On August 11 at Teoloyucan, in what the Brazilian described as a "long" conference and Barragán as "extremely brief," Carranza refused to make any concessions regarding conditions for surrender.[118] With this last hope gone, Carbajal delivered the government of the city to Eduardo Iturbide as governor of the Federal District and, along with most of the remaining members of his cabinet, went into exile on August 12.[119] The following day Iturbide, as the sole civil authority of the extinct Huerta regime, signed an agreement with Obregón for surrendering the control of the city itself, while General Gustavo A. Salas and Admiral Othón P. Blanco, representing Velasco and the military, affixed their signatures to an understanding regarding the military aspects of the problem.[120] The revolution had triumphed.

In the articles of capitulation the revolutionaries held fast to the general principle upon which Carranza had been insisting: unconditional surrender with no mention made of a general amnesty. The first agreement stipulated that Obregón would enter the city with

[118] Cardoso de Oliveira to SecState, August 12, 1914, file 812.00/12834, NA, RG 59; Barragán, *Ejército*, I, 597. Barragán says that Cardoso de Oliveira demanded protection for the foreigners and the nationals in the city, and that Carranza said pointedly that the treatment of Mexicans was no business of a Brazilian. According to Barragán, the interview probably took less than five minutes, but Cardoso de Oliveira was not at all reticent in indicating the importance of his own role, in whatever situation.

[119] Cardoso de Oliveira to SecState, August 13, 1914, file 812.00/12842, NA, RG 59.

[120] The full text of the agreements, popularly known as the "Treaties of Teoloyucan," may be found in a number of places. Both Barragán, *Ejército*, I, 599–602, and Obregón, *Ocho mil kilómetros*, pp. 158–161, quote them in full in Spanish, and *Foreign Relations, 1914*, pp. 586–587, has the English translation, incomplete and sometimes inaccurate.

his troops, that the police force would then come under the jurisdiction of the new government, and that "General Obregón has seen fit to offer" complete guarantees against looting, seizure of private property, or other crimes against the general order; in a word, the general public had nothing to worry about. The military accord was somewhat more complicated. First, the agreement provided for the abandonment of the city by the federals, who would take with them only their rifles; details for the surrender of those arms were to be determined later by the revolutionary government. Second, by virtue of a combination of three articles, all other existing federal forces, both land and sea, were to surrender their arms to officials to be designated by the new government. To guard against the Zapata threat, the agreement provided that the federal forces confronting the Zapatistas would remain in their places until relieved by revolutionary forces, at which time the federals would surrender their arms to those forces. All other military establishments and offices were to continue under the control of the officials then in command, until such time as the new government made provision to take them over. Finally, all officers of the armed services would "remain at the disposition of the First Chief of the Constitutionalists who, on his entrance into the Capital, will become invested with the character of Provisional President of the Republic." In spite of Velasco's earlier plea, the officers would have to depend upon Carranza's magnanimity to escape firing squads.

Under these terms Obregón entered the city with six thousand men on August 15, the remainder of his troops and many of those of the northeastern forces being sent directly to outlying garrisons without entering the city itself. Zapata, although he had sizable forces poised in the southern suburbs, decided not to contest the situation. Five days later Carranza made his majestic entry into the city,[121] at the head of a column of troops and flanked by some of the

121 Carranza never merely "arrived" in a city; he always made an entry on horseback flanked by his staff. On this occasion he began his march from Tlalnepantla, some seven miles from the National Palace, which allowed him to traverse a major portion of the city and receive the enthusiastic welcome of an estimated 300,000 people.

most illustrious of the military leaders in the region. But among those not seen in the triumphal parade was Pablo González, who was irritated because Obregón had not asked him to co-sign the articles of capitulation.

With Carranza in the capital the struggle against the usurpation came to an end. But far to the north, open warfare had begun in Sonora; and in Chihuahua, a U.S. official reported, "Villa is recruiting men and scouring the country for horses as fast as arms can be smuggled from the United States. No body [*sic*] here doubts the purpose of this activity."[122]

[122] Marion Letcher to SecState, July 25, 1914, file 812.00/12614, NA, RG 59; Cobb reported the same kind of activity a few days later (Cobb to SecState, August 1, 1914, file 812.00/12706) and Letcher further reported that Villa had been assured by "high authority" that he would receive support from the United States against Carranza (Letcher to SecState, August 4, 1914, file 812.00/12794).

6. THE WAR OF THE WINNERS

The sixth article of the Plan de Guadalupe, under which the Constitutionalists had been warring against Huerta, stipulated that "the Interim President of the Republic will call general elections as soon as peace has been consolidated, surrendering power to him who will have been elected." But the quarrel with Villa had altered the plan. Villa and his advisors distrusted Carranza's political ambitions, and the rather nebulous wording as to the time for the calling of elections disturbed them; consequently, the Torreón conference in July recommended that "on assuming, in accordance with the Guadalupe platform, the office of provisional president of the Republic, the citizen First Chief of the Constitutionalist army will call a convention whose object will be to discuss and determine the date on which the elections shall be held . . . and other topics of national interest."[1] Even though he was very dubious about Villa's intentions

[1] Carothers to SecState, July 9, 1914, file 812.00/12717 enclosure, NA, RG 59. Carothers, who received a copy of the agreement from Villa, made a quick and unsatisfactory translation.

to cooperate on the other provisions of the understanding, Carranza publicly accepted the recommendation. When he entered Mexico City on August 20, therefore, he considered the calling of such a convention one of the first orders of business. But his first days in the city were filled with myriad problems. The police and the military quarreled to the point of almost open warfare, the Zapatistas demanded an immediate and unqualified acceptance on Carranza's part of the Plan de Ayala,[2] a number of the federal generals refused to lay down their arms,[3] the Sonora situation became critical, and a civil government of some kind had to be established. With his attention devoted to these details, it was not until September 5 that the new chief executive officer—Carranza refused to take the title of provisional or interim president—convoked a "junta of all the governors and Generals who had command of troops"[4] to "agree on the reforms which should be begun and the program needed by the new government";[5] the meeting was to convene in Mexico City on October 1. Long before the generals and governors gathered, however, the breach in the victors' ranks became irreparable.

By the time the Treaties of Teoloyucan had been signed, Villa's acts were suspicious, but Maytorena's were belligerent. Even before all the federal forces had been liquidated on the west coast, Maytorena began to sweep his state clean of civilian and military officials who gave their loyalty to either Carranza or Obregón. He removed Salvador Alvarado from his command of troops and jailed him

[2] The Plan de Ayala, under which Zapata rebelled against Madero in 1911, demanded immediate land distribution and, as amended in May, 1913, named Zapata head of the entire national revolutionary movement.

[3] The most important were Benjamín Argumedo, Juan Andreu Almazán, Higinio Aguilar, Pascual Orozco, and Joaquín Téllez. The first three continued to fight in conjunction with Zapata, Orozco beat his way to the north and the United States, and Téllez ultimately went to El Salvador.

[4] Venustiano Carranza, *Informe . . . encargado del poder ejecutivo de la República*, p. 20. Carranza consistently used the term "junta," rather than "convention," presumably because a junta is advisory and a convention sovereign.

[5] E. Castro to V. Carranza, September 7, 1914, ADN-Chihuahua 1914. Castro, the commandant at Piedras Negras, was answering Carranza's invitation. I have been unable to find a copy of the original summons.

along with other officers and civilians in early July,[6] and then he began making preparations to drive Calles into either Chihuahua or the United States;[7] on August 16 the advance guards of the two groups began battling.[8] In view of these circumstances Obregón, on August 18, requested permission of Carranza to go to Chihuahua and Sonora in an attempt to put an end to the difficulties before the events led to a catastrophic split. Even though he was convinced that no lasting peace would come from "agreements," Carranza concurred, since he was willing to make a gesture toward pacification.[9] He announced to Silliman that Obregón would go to Sonora with a "large force,"[10] to control the "situation," but when Obregón left the city on August 21 his force consisted only of his staff and a fifteen-man escort.[11] Before Carranza's emissary reached Chihuahua, Maytorena not only forced Calles to evacuate Nogales and to retreat to Naco, but he also announced that he was undertaking the campaign under orders from Villa.[12] Obregón discovered soon after arriving at Villa's headquarters on August 24 that the northerner was much more interested in discussing the size and equipment of the forces loyal to Carranza than in contemplating ways of stopping the Sonora fighting. Nevertheless Obregón was able to prevail upon Villa to go to Sonora for a conference with Maytorena. The three conferred in Nogales on August 29,[13] and for the moment they seemed to have solved the problem.

Both George Carothers and Z. L. Cobb reported complete accord,[14] but they erred in their assessment. Immediately after the conference a joint statement signed by the three men, as well as by two of Maytorena's officers, provided that Maytorena would be

[6] Hostetter to SecState, August 10, 1914, file 812.00/13101, NA, RG 59.

[7] Simpich to SecState, August 10, 1914, file 812.00/12803, NA, RG 59.

[8] Simpich to SecState, August 16, 1914, file 812.00/12875, NA, RG 59.

[9] Alvaro Obregón, *Ocho mil kilómetros en campaña*, p. 167.

[10] Silliman to SecState, August 19, 1914, file 812.00/12939, NA, RG 59.

[11] Obregón, *Ocho mil kilómetros*, p. 168.

[12] General Bliss to War Department, August 20, 1914, file 812.00/12973, and Bryan to Carothers, August 21, 1914, file 812.00/12944, NA, RG 59.

[13] Obregón, *Ocho mil kilómetros*, pp. 169–172.

[14] Carothers to SecState, September 1, 1914, file 812.00/13063, and Cobb to SecState, September 1, 1914, file 812.00/13065, NA, RG 59.

recognized as the military commandant of the state as well governor, but that in his military capacity he would be subject Obregón's orders. Within a matter of hours after the accord had be signed, a diatribe against Obregón and Carranza hit the Nogal streets in the form of an unsigned manifesto. Assuming that t publication had come from Maytorena and his friends,[15] Villa a Obregón drew up a new "understanding," which divested Mayt rena of his new position as commandant but left him in comma of his own troops. Furthermore the agreement, made without co sulting Maytorena, provided that Calles's troops would pass to t command of Benjamín Hill, and that all troops would maintain t positions they then occupied.[16] Still concerned over the situati even after they returned to Chihuahua in the first days of Septemb Obregón and Villa signed still another "accord" on September The new understanding, which did not indicate when the eve would transpire, provided that Juan G. Cabral would come Sonora to become both governor and commandant, that the volu teers who had been swelling the anti-Maytorena ranks would d perse, that Cabral would give personal and property protection Maytorena, and that Calles with his troops would leave the state As the final act of his peace mission, Obregón induced Villa— perhaps the converse was true—to sign the fourth in the series documents designed to bring an end to the conflict. In summa the two drafted some "propositions" for Carranza's "consideratio the proposals dealt with the reestablishment of civil governme through the reinstitution of the various ministries,[18] Carranza's desi

[15] Maytorena denied any complicity or knowledge of the publication, but sin he had been carrying on a running newspaper fight in Nogales, Obregón w justified in his assumption.

[16] José María Maytorena (*Algunas verdades sobre el General Alvaro Obreg* pp. 37–38) and Obregón (*Ocho mil kilómetros*, pp. 170–175) agree on the a tions, but not the motives. Obregón reproduces the two conventions and t flysheet.

[17] Obregón, *Ocho mil kilómetros*, p. 176.

[18] Although the various ministries of the national government were functic ing, they were under subsecretaries or first secretaries, not ministers. Villa a his advisors saw this decision on Carranza's part as evidence of an intent maintain a dictatorial regime.

nation as provisional president, the reestablishment of the national and state civil courts that had been suspended as an incident of revolution, and step-by-step elections, beginning at the local level, which would eventuate in the selection of a constitutionally elected president.[19] Since one of the proposals forbade the election of a "provisional" officer to the "constitutional" post, Carranza was ineligible to become constitutional president within the terms of the "propositions." After completing the formalities, Obregón left for Mexico City accompanied by Miguel Silva and Miguel Díaz Lombardo as Villa's agents to present the proposals to Carranza.[20]

By the time Obregón returned to the capital Carranza had already issued his invitation for the "junta," but rumors had begun flying that the convention would be stacked with Carrancistas who would deny, in fact, any voice to Villa or others who questioned Carranza's motives or actions; one evidence of this perfidy, the anti-Carrancistas said, was the invitation to the governors, all of whom owed their positions to Carranza, instead of just the generals, who were divided in their loyalties.[21] In spite of these rumors, Obregón and Villa's commissioners on September 9 presented the "propositions" to Carranza, who promised to give an answer as soon as he had had an opportunity to study the text.[22] Four days later he gave his answer: he would definitely approve the article that gave him the title of provisional president, but the rest of the articles were of such "transcendental importance that they should not be an object of discussion and approbation among three or four persons," but should be referred to the convention due to meet within two weeks.[23] Whether Carranza was merely playing for time, or was convinced that major

[19] Obregón, *Ocho mil kilómetros*, pp. 178–179, gives the document in full.

[20] Cobb to SecState, September 6, 1914, file 812.00/13118, NA, RG 59; Carothers, who accompanied the group to Mexico City, had advised Cobb of the plan.

[21] Paul Fuller to SecState, September 7, 1914, file 812.00/13122, NA, RG 59. Fuller was one of the numerous special agents representing the State Department.

[22] Obregón, *Ocho mil kilómetros*, p. 185.

[23] Ibid., pp. 186–187, gives Carranza's answer in full, addressed to Obregón and Villa.

change should come only from an agreement among those responsible for Huerta's overthrow, is not clear, but he was in an unimpeachable position. Villa's advisors had complained bitterly and frequently that Carranza acted in a dictatorial manner, and certainly an immediate acceptance and implementation of the proposals would have been a violation of the Plan de Guadalupe and the Torreón agreement, as well as an affront to all the leaders who had not been consulted. But even had he agreed fully and honestly to all the proposals, the new revolution then brewing probably could not have been forestalled; Maytorena was in no mood to surrender his authority under any circumstances,[24] and Villa by September 13 had committed himself to support the Sonora governor.

By the terms of the second of the agreements signed by Villa and Obregón, General Hill took command of the Calles troops in the Nogales-Cananea-Naco region into which Maytorena had driven them, and here he was to remain until a final settlement of the problem; Maytorena and his troops were to remain in their position in Nogales itself and along the railroad running to the south. But with tensions running high and with the troops so close together, hostile incidents were almost inevitable, and they occurred. Each side, of course, accused the other of responsibility, but Villa, with his characteristic impatience and apparently believing that Sonora had become his own peculiar province, peremptorily ordered Hill to leave the state. Since Hill was officially a part of Obregón's command, not Villa's, he simply ignored the order.[25] Villa repeated his demand, which Hill again ignored, and then on September 8 sent an urgent message to Obregón: "In conformity with that which we agreed upon, I have repeatedly ordered General Hill to retire to Casas Grandes, with the forces of his command, in order to avert difficulties, for you will understand that, if my efforts in Sonora are

[24] Maytorena insisted, publicly, that the issue was one of state sovereignty and of constitutionalism. Since he was the elected governor, he intended to maintain control of the state, at the head of troops if necessary, and he would brook no interference. At this time Alvarado, along with members of his family and other Maytorena political opponents, remained in jail even though Maytorena told the U.S. Consul in Nogales that they had been released.

[25] Simpich to SecState, September 9, 1914, file 812.00/13137, NA, RG 59.

to be successful, it will be necessary for these forces to leave immediately."[26] None of the four agreements Obregón and Villa had made any reference, even obliquely, to Hill's leaving Sonora, nor did any of them even by implication give Villa the right to send a military order to Hill. The following day—the day upon which he handed Carranza the "propositions"—Obregón sent Villa a temporizing and mollifying message,[27] but on the next day Villa again demanded that Obregón order Hill to leave the state.[28] Under these circumstances Obregón decided to make yet another trip to Villa's headquarters to settle the Sonora issue and to convince Villa to attend the convention called by Carranza. In the meantime he completed arrangements for Cabral to leave for Sonora.

When Obregón arrived in Chihuahua on September 16, Villa's irritation had reached the explosion point. That day passed calmly enough, with Villa entertaining Obregón with a military parade in celebration of Mexican Independence Day. Later that day and on the next, Obregón, in private conversations with many of Villa's generals, urged attendance at the convention, but Villa was far from convinced. On the morning of September 17 Villa "vehemently expressed his dissatisfaction over the existing condition of affairs and his firm belief that Carranza[29] would not permit an honest convention."[30] Later that afternoon Villa, probably resentful over Obregón's private conversations with his generals and certainly furious because of a reported attack by Hill on Maytorena's forces, threatened Obregón with summary execution; intercession by some of his staff calmed Villa sufficiently to allow the restoration of apparently normal conditions.[31] The two generals even attended a dance to-

[26] Obregón, *Ocho mil kilómetros*, p. 183.

[27] Ibid.

[28] Ibid., p. 185.

[29] The telegram used "Decker" as a code word for Carranza.

[30] Carothers to SecState, September 9, 1914, file 812.00/13227, NA, RG 59.

[31] The exact sequence of events during the September 17–24 period is subject to some doubt, since many of the participants have left slightly different versions and some nonparticipants purportedly received "eye-witness" accounts. For the events see Obregón, *Ocho mil kilómetros*, pp. 199–214; Maytorena, *Algunas verdades*, pp. 40–43; Martín Luis Guzmán, *Memorias de Pancho Villa*, pp. 612–632. In addition, messages from George Carothers and Leon Canova from Chi-

gether that night, and their demeanor was such that the U.S. representative there did "not consider the situation as serious."[32] But during the time when Villa held Obregón under threat of death he had forced Obregón to approve a message to Hill ordering a withdrawal from Sonora. Had Hill immediately accepted the order Villa might have been mollified temporarily. Hill, however, suspected the order's validity and refused to comply until Obregón himself arrived on the scene,[33] but Villa held Obregón hostage in Chihuahua until Hill did comply.[34] The situation was further complicated by Cabral's appearance in Sonora, where he demanded the surrender of Maytorena's troops to him even while he accepted the order to Hill as valid.[35] Under these circumstances Obregón remained in a precarious position in Chihuahua.

For the next few days Villa and Obregón seemed to be in perfect accord, with most of their attention centered on the question of the convention. On September 19 Villa reported that he had decided to send a delegation to Mexico City consisting of Eugenio Aguirre Benavides, Raúl Madero, Maclovio Herrera, and José Isabel Robles,[36] but after further discussions he changed his mind and decided to send only Aguirre Benavides and Robles; on September 21 these two, along with Obregón, left for Mexico City under what appeared to be very congenial circumstances. But in Mexico City, Carranza, convinced that Obregón would never be freed from the trap he was in and fearing a rapid Villa move to the south, ordered communications and transportation suspended between Torreón and Aguascalientes at about the time Obregón left Chihuahua. Villa, furious at what he considered a bellicose act on Carranza's part, demanded

---

huahua, and from Frederick Simpich from Nogales, give much information. Unless otherwise indicated, I have followed Obregón's account.

[32] Carothers to SecState, September 19, 1914, file 812.00/13237, NA, RG 59.

[33] Carranza to Obregón, September 19, 1914, ADN-Chihuahua 1914. Carranza transmitted a message from Hill to Obregón, without indicating the date.

[34] Simpich to SecState, September 20, 1914, file 812.00/13231, NA, RG 59. Cabral had reported as much to Simpich.

[35] Simpich to SecState, September 23, 1914, file 812.00/13269, and Carothers to SecState, September 19, 1914, file 812.00/13228, NA, RG 59.

[36] Carothers to SecState, September 20, 1914, file 812.00/13229, NA, RG 59.

an explanation from Carranza, who in reply demanded from Villa an explanation of his treatment of Obregón.[37] Villa's answer made the situation utterly hopeless and further endangered Obregón's life:

In answer to your message, let me tell you that General Obregón and other generals of this Division departed last night for the Capital, with the object of treating of important affairs relating to the general situation in the Republic; but in view of your proceedings, which reveal a premeditated desire to put obstacles in the way of a satisfactory arrangement of all the difficulties and to obtain the peace that all of us desire so much, I have ordered his journey be suspended and that he be retained in Torreón. As a consequence, I notify you that this Division will not be represented at the Convention you have convoked, and I also notify you that I disavow you as the First Chief of the Republic, leaving you free to proceed as you think best.[38]

After a conversation with Villa, Canova reported that "he had stood all he intended to. The suspension of railway communication . . . seems to have been the last straw."[39] But Villa did not detain Obregón in Torreón; he ordered the train to return to Chihuahua, where he and his advisors debated Obregón's fate throughout the day of September 23, and then sent him on his way again late that night. But Obregón was not yet free. Villa ordered that the train be stopped and Obregón executed, but the intercession of Robles and others allowed Obregón to reach the comparative safety of Zacatecas.[40]

While these events transpired in Chihuahua and both Maytorena and Hill in Sonora abandoned any pretense of staying in their own positions, Carranza took steps to shore up his defenses. First he sent Antonio Villarreal to the north as commandant of the Nuevo León–Coahuila district.[41] Next he began an intensive recruiting and munitioning campaign for those forces he considered absolutely loyal to

[37] Carranza to E. Gutiérrez, September 23, 1914, ADN-DF 1914. Gutiérrez had asked Carranza for an explanation of Villa's disavowal.

[38] Obregón, *Ocho mil kilómetros*, p. 208.

[39] Canova to SecState, September 23, 1914, file 812.00/13275, NA, RG 59.

[40] Silliman to SecState, September 19, 1914, file 812.00/13244, NA, RG 59.

[41] Carranza to Eulalio Gutiérrez, September 23, 1914, ADN-DF 1914.

him, such as his brother Jesús and Pablo González.[42] Then he undertook to assure himself of the loyalty of some of the forces in the north central region, and to order them to prevent a rapid and unchallenged Villa move on Mexico City;[43] in his planning he correctly assumed that he could depend upon the Arrieta brothers,[44] but he mistakenly counted on Natera.[45] As he wrote to Eulalio Gutiérrez: "If we are unable to make a peaceful arrangement and the armed struggle begins—not because we want it but because of circumstances—we want to be prepared."[46] Villa's treatment of Obregón, his intemperate disavowal of the First Chieftainship, and his open support to Maytorena already in arms, all but convinced Carranza that the cause was lost. According to Silliman, assigned by the Department of State to accompany Carranza and report his every move and mood:

I understood a few days ago that Carranza, while not in complete accord with the Villa plan for the convention, would not in any way undertake to influence the convention; that he would loyally accept the conclusions of the convention, being content with his part in the triumph of the revolution and the announcement of the evacuation of Vera Cruz [*sic*] . . . He has spoken very seldom [often?] recently of being tired and of wanting to go to the United States for rest. The attitude of Villa toward Obregon may

[42] Many documents in both the ADN and the NA indicate this intensified recruiting. For example, Consul Blocker at Piedras Negras reported on September 26 that intensive recruiting had been going on for "the last week or more"; he also reported that about half those Mexicans who had earlier been interned in the United States, but were being returned to Mexico, were signing with the Carranza army (see Blocker to SecState, September 26, 1914, file 812.00/13360, NA, RG 59, particularly).

[43] Between September 22 and October 1 there were frequent interchanges between Carranza and Eulalio Gutiérrez discussing the break with Villa and planning how best to use Natera, the Arrietas, and Cesáreo Castro in halting Villa (these documents are in ADN-DF 1914 and ADN-Nuevo León 1914).

[44] The Arrietas had great fear of Villa, justifiably so. At the moment that all these negotiations were going on, in fact, Villa was sending his troops into Durango to occupy the capital city even though the state was the recognized command zone of the Arrietas.

[45] In spite of an attempt to convince Natera to give support to Carranza (shown by documents in ADN-DF 1914), Natera inadvertently confessed to Obregón on September 25 that he was in entire sympathy with Villa's position (Obregón, *Ocho mil kilómetros*, p. 215).

[46] Carranza to Eulalio Gutiérrez, September 28, 1914, ADN-DF 1914.

change [the] entire situation. Friends of Carranza have told me today that they expect nothing in the convention except dissension and disagreement.[47]

But even under these circumstances Carranza was willing to make one more effort at placating Villa and his generals prior to the meeting of the convention scheduled for October 1. When Obregón returned from Chihuahua on September 26 with the word that he believed he could wean some of Villa's generals away from their chief, Carranza gave his blessing to another Obregón trip—this time to Zacatecas—in company with eight other officers to attempt to work out an understanding with the generals of the Division of the North, particularly with respect to the conditions under which they would attend the convention already called by Carranza.[48] He also authorized Eulalio Gutiérrez, then in San Luis Potosí, to attend the meeting.[49] And in the meantime Villa's troops poured into Zacatecas.

In the conference at Zacatecas, Obregón and his group[50] drew up an agreement with Villa and a number of his officers, including Robles and Aguirre Benavides, to the effect that the convention, instead of meeting in Mexico City, would convene on the neutral ground of Aguascalientes on October 10 and would consist of "the greatest possible number of Constitutionalist generals." In the meantime all troop movements by both groups were to be stopped and there was to be a "suspension of hostile attitude by both parties."[51] The following day Obregón and his companions returned to Mexico City just in time to attend the first session of the junta, or convention, called by Carranza for October 1. Their function was to convince those who had come to Mexico City, none of whom represented either Villa or Zapata, not only to transfer the convention to Aguascalientes but also to limit that meeting to military men; technically, this decision eliminated Carranza from attendance, but this ap-

[47] Silliman to SecState, September 22, 1914, file 812.00/13268, NA, RG 59.

[48] Obregón, *Ocho mil kilómetros*, pp. 215–216.

[49] Carranza to E. Gutiérrez, September 28, 1914, ADN-DF 1914.

[50] When Villa arrived in Zacatecas at the head of a heavy troop contingent, Obregón himself left for Aguascalientes; he had no desire to repeat the Chihuahua nightmare.

[51] As reproduced in Obregón, *Ocho mil kilómetros*, p. 217.

parently did not occur to any of those involved in drafting th
agreement.

But even as Villa and his officers were in the act of signing i Zacatecas the agreement to suspend hostilities and to attend a con vention to make major political decisions, in Chihuahua a Vill manifesto, drafted some days before,[52] began circulating.[53] The an nouncement called on all Mexicans to "unite with the Division of th North, contributing in the most effective possible way towar effecting the removal of Venustiano Carranza" in order to allow fo the "reestablishment of constitutional order through proper elec tions" and for "the solution of the problem of agricultural lands."[5 The manifesto was a rehash and a broadening of all the charges th Villistas had been making against Carranza for some time past. A few days earlier Villa's advisors had apprised Leon Canova of " portion of their criticism." Carranza, they said, had assumed "th role of Dictator," and "from one abuse of position he serenely ad vanced to another." He did not depend upon "a cabinet or board o advisors," but "dispensed with all counsel." He had "throttled th courts," and he did not "appreciate the importance of considerin some means of meeting the interest on the National Debt and on th National Railway bonds." But apparently more important than these in the eyes of Villa and his advisors, was Carranza's treatment o them; they cited "the many insults and slights which have been pu upon the Division of the North, which they claim has done more fo the success of the revolution than all the balance put together."[5 Because of all these acts of commission and omission, Carranza con stituted a threat to the "broad principles of the revolution" and ha to be eliminated.

Now these criticisms, which were presumably to serve as a justifi cation for a new armed conflict if necessary, are of more than passin

[52] Canova reported (Canova to SecState, September 25, 1914, file 812.00 13326, NA, RG 59) that he had been given a rough draft of the manifesto o September 25.

[53] Letcher to SecState, September 30, 1914, file 812.00/13430, NA, RG 59 including a translation of the manifesto.

[54] Villa manifesto, undated, included as translation in ibid.

[55] Canova to SecState, September 22, 1914, file 812.00/13323, NA, RG 59.

interest; their acceptance as gospel by the Villistas cost Mexico over 100 million dollars and probably 200,000 lives. And they have about them the savor of a fraud, if either earlier or later actions may be used as a basis for objective judgment. It must be remembered that Carranza entered Mexico City on August 20, and that on September 3—exactly two weeks later—Villa was demanding an immediate election at the municipal level and a reestablishment of the civil courts. And yet in Chihuahua, over which Villa exercised supreme sway after the middle of May when Carranza left the state, no elections were held and no civil courts operated even though the state was completely free from any significant military action. Furthermore, in the months during which the so-called Convention government guided the destinies of most of the country, no elections were held and few civil courts opened; had Villa really been committed to the "reestablishment of constitutional order" he certainly had both the time and the opportunity to make a move in that direction. He was certainly no paragon of constitutionalism, and his frequent orders for executions without any hearing, military or otherwise, do not indicate deep concern for courts and legality. The "problem of agricultural lands" may well have been dear to the Villa heart, but the convention did nothing to solve it on a national base even though the Zapatistas urged it. Exactly why Villa and his advisors thought it so important to make provision for the settlement of the debt within a matter of days after Carranza entered Mexico City remains in some doubt, but certainly Villa's habit of seizing property, and his sale of unbranded cattle for half a million dollars in July, made his protestations over debt payment appear to be hollow propaganda for foreign consumption. The charge that Carranza had no advisors is patently false; he was surrounded by them, the most important being Gerzayn Ugarte, Rafael Zubarán Capmany, Isidro Fabela, José N. Macías, Alberto Pani, and Luis Cabrera. Whether he listened is moot, but the scant evidence suggests that any advice they may have given Carranza regarding Villa would scarcely have aided the latter's cause. Carranza *was* dictatorial during the conflict with Huerta, and by the time the convention met on October 1 he had changed his way but little if at all. But he had called the convention within about two weeks of his entrance into the capital, and in numerous statements he had said that he would surrender all authority as soon as provisions had been made for an established government. But the Villistas insisted that Carranza had a plan that "contemplated his holding the Executive Power for about two years as First Chief,"[56] and nothing Carranza could say would alter that conviction. The sad fact seems to be that the last of the criticisms—the "insults and slights"—was the greatest and the key to the Villa attitude. On one occasion Villa complained to Canova that "everyone knew that Carranza had a head, for they could see it, but what he had it for no one could understand as he never used it to advantage. He [Villa] said that it might as well be an empty shell or a solid block, so far as usefulness was concerned. He expressed regret that he had not gone right on down to Mexico City from Zacatecas, arriving there first."[57] Villa's suspicions and resentments and contempt for Carranza knew no bounds, and all the rest was window dressing. But Villa's attitude toward Carranza spilled over to the First Chief's advisors and supporters; since Carranza could not be trusted, neither could Pablo González, nor Obregón, nor any others who had been closely affiliated with Carranza after April.

Whether Carranza was in fact prepared to step aside meekly after the collapse of the Huerta government and its successor will never be known. The likelihood is strongly against it, given Carranza's own sense of importance of mission. He had, after all, been the recognized leader of the revolutionary forces that had destroyed the usurping government, he had forced the United States to recognize certain attributes of Mexican sovereignty, and he had endured as many physical discomforts as had his generals in the field. He had become the internationally recognized leader, and history gives few examples of men in his position quietly fading away into voluntary obscurity. There is a possibility that he would have done so, but it is unthinkable that he would have surrendered his power at the demand of a few rebellious generals—and to Carranza those who

[56] As reported by Canova to SecState, September 25, 1914, file 812.00/13326, NA, RG 59. Nothing that Carranza ever said or did justified the assertion.

[57] Canova to SecState, September 22, 1914, file 812.00/13323, NA, RG 59.

were demanding his immediate surrender of power to Fernando Iglesias Calderón were insubordinate and not worthy of consideration.[58]

In view of the conditions that existed, the convention that met in the afternoon of October 1 had one major and some minor decisions to make. The roughly eighty men who attended meetings during the five days the convention remained in session in Mexico City represented almost every shade on the political spectrum and differed widely in their loyalty to Carranza. Villa in his manifesto a few days earlier had stated that "if the Division of the North had lost confidence in the First Chief it would naturally have none in any council whose members were chosen by him,"[59] and all violent anti-Carrancistas had assumed that the convention would be nothing more than a Carranza creature, ready to do his will blindly. The evidence shows otherwise. Even in this bobtail convention to which Zapatistas were not invited,[60] and to which the officers of the Division of the North would not come, Carranza did not have his way. Not only did the group refuse to do his bidding, but also when the active military campaigns began a few weeks later about half the generals who took an active part in the debates stayed with Carranza and the other half abandoned him.[61] By and large it was a meeting of independent men, not sycophants.

The major decision facing the group was whether to go to Aguas-

[58] The Torreón agreement had suggested a number of names from which Carranza might choose to constitute his cabinet after the victory; Iglesias Calderón was listed. On September 26 Villa demanded that Carranza deliver the government to Iglesias Calderón immediately, and two days later he notified E. Gutiérrez "that only Iglesias Calderón will receive the First Magistracy of the Nation" (E. Gutiérrez to Carranza, [September 28], 1914, in ADN-Nuevo León 1914).

[59] Villa manifesto, translated and submitted by Letcher to SecState, September 30, 1914, file 812.00/13430, NA, RG 59.

[60] A number of attempts were made to reconcile Carranza and Zapata, who had steadfastly refused to consider himself a Constitutionalist, but to no avail. The only condition under which Zapata would agree to cooperate was Carranza's recognition of the Plan de Ayala.

[61] The group selected Eulalio Gutiérrez as president, with Francisco Murguía and Francisco de P. Mariel as vice-presidents; Gutiérrez abandoned Carranza, and the other two remained loyal to him. Among the most persistent debaters in the meetings, Obregón, Eduardo Hay, and Francisco Coss remained with Ca-

calientes; Carranza was dubious and would have preferred that the meetings continue in Mexico City,[62] but after sometimes acrimonious debate the decision to go north was supported by an overwhelming majority of the military men. The next item of real import concerned the nature of the Aguascalientes meeting itself: whether it was to be purely military or to include civilians. In the Mexico City meetings the most ardent Carranza supporters were civilians either representing or purporting to represent military men who preferred not to come, and it is clear that Carranza hoped to foster a convention representing both the civilian and the military point of view. But again he lost. And finally, when Carranza with a great gesture submitted his resignation to the convention in the firm conviction that it would be rejected, the group indeed rejected the surrender of power, but did so in a manner that suggested temporary prolongation of that power rather than absolute confirmation.[63]

Even before the Convention of Aguascalientes began its formal sessions on October 10, the military men who had arrived early formed a "neutral military government to give guarantees to all and to govern the state during the convention,"[64] and in the process indicated clearly that they considered themselves to have authority to take any action they saw fit in order to reestablish peace. In spite of this decision to guarantee to all participants complete freedom from pressure, the conditions were ominous long before the first session. The Zacatecas agreement ordering the suspension of all troop movements had been completely ignored by all groups: Maclovio Herrera and the Arrieta brothers fought Villa supporters in Durango,[65] Anto-

---

rranza, while Lucio Blanco, Julián Medina, and Rafael Buelna fought against him.

[62] On October 5 Carranza wired Antonio I. Villarreal: "I have no hope of good results from the conference in Aguascalientes" (Carranza to Villarreal, October 5, 1914, ADN-Nuevo León 1914).

[63] The resolution, introduced by Obregón and passed overwhelmingly, provided that Carranza would remain in power until some action was taken at Aguascalientes.

[64] Guillermo García Aragón and others to Carranza, October 8, 1914, ADN-Aguascalientes 1914.

[65] Maclovio Herrera to Domingo and Mariano Arrieta, October 2, 1914, ADN-Sinaloa 1914; Mariano Arrieta to Carranza, October 12, 1914, ibid.

nio Villarreal in Coahuila busied himself in destroying the railroad leading from Saltillo to Torreón,[66] Carranza in Mexico City was "continuing recruitment everywhere, and getting arms and munitions,"[67] and thousands of troops from the Puebla region poured into Mexico City.[68] But Villa, too, prepared by buying "practically all the output of the Remington gun factory" and recruiting as fast as he could.[69] He also placed "approximately 40,000 well armed, fully equipped and fairly enthusiastic men, within a day's striking distance of the town of Aguascalientes," with fifteen thousand within two hours' distance.[70] Furthermore, the renegade forces of Benjamín Argumedo and Higinio Aguilar caused so much havoc and a reported fifteen thousand menacing Zapatistas so worried the Constitutionalists near Matamoros Izúcar and Huejotzingo that Pablo González was doubtful whether he could attend the convention.[71]

The Zapatistas were still uncommitted in the Carranza-Villa fight, although everything indicated that Zapata was through with Carranza forever. The arrangements for the surrender of Mexico City in August, which carefully excluded Zapatistas from the occupation, were taken as a deliberate act of hostility by the southern chiefs,[72] but total rupture did not come at once. Throughout August, Carranza representatives labored, at first more or less behind the First Chief's back, to reach some kind of understanding with Zapata that would keep him out of Villa's arms. Lucio Blanco, Dr. Atl (Gerardo Murillo), and others approached the Zapatistas, and Carranza himself, after entering Mexico City, swallowed his pride enough to offer to meet Zapata personally.[73] He even angled for U.S. help to try to

66 Villarreal to Carranza, October 5, 1914, ADN-Nuevo León 1914.

67 Carranza to Antonio I. Villarreal, October 5, 1914, ibid.

68 Belt to SecState, October 2, 1914, file 812.00/13361, NA, RG 59.

69 According to a report passed on by Blocker to SecState, October 10, 1914, file 812.00/13487, NA, RG 59.

70 Canova to SecState, October 2, 1914, file 812.00/13518, NA, RG 59.

71 Pablo González to Carranza, October 1, 1914, ADN-Puebla 1914.

72 Gildardo Magaña and Carlos Pérez Guerrero, *Emiliano Zapata y el agrarismo en México*, IV, 240–241.

73 John Womack, *Zapata and the Mexican Revolution*, p. 198. Gerardo Murillo, a painter who took the name of Dr. Atl for his professional work, happened to be in France at the time of the Huerta coup and early joined other Mexicans

persuade Zapata to go to Mexico City to talk.[74] But it was all quite futile. The southerners had never liked Carranza and his pretensions, and Carranza despised the Zapatistas as ignorant, narrow-minded troublemakers. Nevertheless, a Carranza delegation went to Cuernavaca the last week of August. Zapata—shy, suspicious, and afraid he might be tricked into compromising his principles—kept the envoys waiting for two days, then bluntly told them that, before he would treat at all, Carranza would have to sign the Plan de Ayala and either step down or agree to make executive decisions only with Zapata's approval.[75] Carranza of course rejected this ultimatum.[76] On September 8 the Morelos chief decreed enforcement of Article 8 of the Plan de Ayala, which provided for confiscation of properties belonging to anyone who in any way opposed the Ayala revolution; the holdings seized would be used to augment village lands, establish agricultural banking institutions, and provide pensions for widows and orphans of men who had died in the struggle.[77] It seemed like the final break, and yet, despite some skirmishes between his forces and the Carrancistas, Zapata held back from headlong war. He knew that militarily he could not prevail alone, that somehow he would have to have wider leverage if he was to influence matters decisively. He waited for an opening. He even kept a line out to the Carranza leaders[78]—but also stepped up contacts with Villa.

Zapata had been in communication with Villa since late in 1913, when his aide Gildardo Magaña went to Villa's headquarters.[79] Judging from Magaña's reports and other sources of information, Villa

---

there in efforts to raise money for the Constitutionalists. He returned to Mexico in July, 1914, undertaking a number of special assignments at Carranza's request. He had no sympathy for Zapata, but he firmly believed that the strength of society lay in the "proletarians," and he generally supported the anarcho-syndicalist approach.

[74] Ibid., p. 201.

[75] Magaña and Pérez Guerrero, *Zapata*, V, 82–90.

[76] Ibid., p. 95.

[77] Ibid., pp. 102–103.

[78] Womack, *Zapata*, p. 213.

[79] Magaña and Pérez Guerrero, *Zapata*, III, 285–286. Magaña had met Villa when both were in prison in Mexico City in 1912; he had tutored the northern

seemed to be sound on agrarian reform, and Zapata's relations with him slowly warmed. After September, 1914, they became closer, and the two would become partners of a sort at Aguascalientes.

The upcoming convention, Zapata hoped, might be the break he had been searching for, and now he had men able and eager to represent him in the slippery game of national politics. The Morelos movement had acquired a veneer of sophistication it never had before due to the addition of a group of urban intellectuals, members of the radical Casa del Obrero Mundial who had fled the capital when Huerta closed their establishment in May. Those who went to Zapata (some moved to the Constitutionalist cause) included Antonio Díaz Soto y Gama, Rafael Pérez Taylor, Octavio Jahn, and others, who proceeded enthusiastically to elaborate Zapata agrarianism into rigid and very articulate doctrine.[80] They soon became loquacious proponents of it in a national forum.

Every circumstance indicated a colossal failure for the meeting of military men—more prone to act than to debate—but many of them made a valiant effort. Antonio I. Villarreal, whom some accused of presidential aspirations of his own, urgently requested from Carranza permission to attend the Aguascalientes meeting in person, since "there is no reason to lose all hope of arriving at a patriotic arrangement, and whatever effort can be made in this direction is meritorious because it is nothing less than for national life itself."[81] The Arrietas, holed up in western Durango and eastern Sinaloa fending off the Villistas and completely convinced that only the eradication of Villa would bring peace, sent delegates,[82] as did Maclovio Herrera, who insisted that Villa's only justification for his "rebellion" was "his ambition to rule and his thirst for gold like all

rebel in reading and writing and also had told him about the Plan de Ayala (ibid., II, 145–154).

[80] Womack, *Zapata*, pp. 193–194.

[81] Villarreal to Carranza, October 5, 1914, ADN-Nuevo León 1914.

[82] Various instructions from M. Arrieta to Manuel Manzanera and from D. Arrieta to Salvador Castaños, the respective delegates, may be found in ADN-Sinaloa 1914. Most of the instructions urged the necessity to support Carranza and to curb Villa.

other bandits."[83] Troop commanders or their delegates came from all over the country determined to find a formula for peace; their sincerity so impressed Canova that he told Bryan "it is doubtful if there are more than a half a dozen of the delegates who are not imbued" with the hope for a peaceful solution.[84]

And when the Revolutionary Convention of Aguascalientes met on October 10 the enthusiasm for peace seemed infectious. One over-sanguine correspondent wired his office in Mexico City: "The country is saved," pointing out that the delegates had constituted themselves a sovereign convention, rather than a mere consultative or advisory body, and that each agreed to swear a solemn oath—and to dramatize that oath by signing the flag—to respect the decisions there made.[85] Amid great joy and with great spontaneity the more than 150 delegates selected Antonio Villarreal as president of the Convention and shortly thereafter ordered a complete suspension of hostilities everywhere, particularly in Sonora—without effect, as it turned out.[86] They also concluded that Zapata should be represented and invited him to send delegates; until the southern delegation arrived, the Convention decided, no real work could be done. From about October 14 to October 26 when the Zapatistas finally arrived,

[83] Maclovio Herrera to D. and M. Arrieta, October 2, 1914, ADN-Sinaloa 1914.

[84] Canova to SecState, October 21, 1914, file 812.00/13633, NA, RG 59.

[85] R. Martínez to Oficina Información, October 14, 1914, ADN-Aguascalientes 1914.

[86] The orders to suspend hostilities were sent from Aguascalientes on October 14, 15, and 16, going to Carranza, the Zapatistas, the Arrietas, Maytorena, and Hill, and possibly others; documents relative to these orders were found in ADN-Sinaloa, Sonora, Aguascalientes, and Distrito Federal. Maytorena, claiming that he had received no such order (even though General Bliss was able to send a copy of the order to the War Department on October 17), mounted a heavy attack on Hill at Naco. He was repulsed, but intermittent fighting continued in the area. Maytorena informed Consul Charles L. Montague in Cananea that "he considered Hill a bandit and [would] drive him from Sonora regardless" of orders or armistice. These documents may be found in the War Department section of the National Archives as a part of the Adjutant General's Office Records; the specific documents referred to here are attachments to a base document carrying the file designation 2216704, NA, RG 94.

the Convention did little but mark time; for some reason Villa and his adherents seemed to have lost their appetite for an immediate restoration of the courts and for municipal elections.

When the Zapata delegates arrived—all sporting military titles but most of them in fact civilians who had never led troops in any form—the Convention got down to the serious business of trying to establish a government and institute reforms. But Carranza's position was not clear, except in one particular: he refused to accept the Convention as sovereign, a point he made clear a number of times. On one occasion he instructed one of his officials: "You may tell the press that the Convention has neither the character nor the attributes which some have supposed. Beyond the pacification arrangements, for which it was constituted with my acquiescence, the Convention has no faculties for action except those taken in agreement with the First Chieftainship."[87] But at the same time he was leaving nothing to chance. He sent messages to most of his absolutely loyal generals, instructing them to ignore any orders emanating from the Convention,[88] he continued recruiting regardless of a Convention prohibition,[89] he deployed troops despite a Convention decision against troop movement of any kind without express Convention approval,[90] he continued to import munitions,[91] and he ignored a Convention demand that all generals come to the meeting in person rather than depend on delegates.[92] In these activities he differed not one whit from his opponents, for the Villa supporters were on the move as well, particularly in Sonora, Durango, Sinaloa, and Zacatecas. But in one particular they differed: Carranza steadfastly re-

[87] Carranza to Zubarán Capmany, October 27, 1914, ADN-DF 1914.

[88] Among the generals to whom he sent such instructions, and from whom he received favorable replies, were Luis Caballero, Emiliano Nafarrate, Francisco Coss, Pablo González, A. Millán, and Saturino Cedillo. He did not overlook the navy, and he received a favorable reply from Admiral G. A. Carvalla.

[89] V. Alessio Robles to Carranza, October 21, 1914, ADN-Aguascalientes 1914.

[90] V. Alessio Robles to Carranza, October 20, 1914, ibid.

[91] Within a space of three days in late October he received three carloads through Matamoros (L. Uribe to Carranza, October 23, 1914, ADN-Tamaulipas 1914).

[92] V. Alessio Robles to Carranza, October 23, 1914, ADN-Aguascalientes 1914.

fused to attend in person or to send a personal representative, while Villa at one time or another did both.[93]

Despite the First Chief's cold attitude, the Convention continued to act as a sovereign body. A special commission to Carranza virtually forced him to take a stand; his most important point was that he would surrender his position only if both Villa and Zapata were to retire to private life.[94] When the commission returned to Aguascalientes with the report, a Convention committee accepted the resignation of Carranza and the elimination of Villa but temporized on the Zapata question because of a legal technicality.[95] But the committee also went a step farther in attempting to resolve the pressing issues: it recommended the abolition of all army corps and divisions, with the various generals then becoming directly subject to the orders of the war department to be established by the new government.[96] Since the tendency up to that time had been to think and act in terms of individual armies or forces (such as Villa's, Obregón's, González's, Natera's, Arrieta's, Maytorena's, Herrera's) rather than a centralized military force subject to the command of a central agency, the recommendation was excellently conceived—but impossible of application under the circumstances. The loyalties were to individuals rather than to abstractions. On November 1 the Convention selected Eulalio Gutiérrez as temporary president for a period of twenty days, at the expiration of which his tenure was to be either "ratified or rectified." Obregón saw in these developments great hopes for the future. He believed that the anti-Villa generals held the majority, that ultimately both Villa and Zapata would be forced into retirement, and that Villarreal would be selected as pro-

[93] Villa visited the Convention on October 17, gave a short speech, and then retired to Guadalupe, not far from Zacatecas.

[94] Canova to SecState, October 29, 1914, file 812.00/13638, NA, RG 59.

[95] The Zapata delegates, though they arrived with great fanfare, refused to present credentials or to sign an oath of support; they insisted they were a "commission" to determine whether Zapata's generals should take part, but nonetheless they demanded the right to speak and vote. They were allowed to speak but not to vote. Since Zapata was not officially represented, the Convention took the position that it would not be just to make any decision on Zapata until he had official representation, promised for November 20.

[96] Canova to SecState, October 30, 1914, file 812.00/13658, NA, RG 59.

visional president on November 20.[97] But the "ratification or rectification" scheduled for November 20 never took place; by that time conditions had changed drastically.

For reasons never made completely clear but that can be interpreted only as a threat to the independence of the Convention, on November 2 Villa arrived in Aguascalientes with six thousand troops and five trains of artillery. Gutiérrez tried to explain away the action by saying that the troops had come with his permission to obtain provisions—why the five trains of artillery were necessary on a provisioning trip was not made clear—and that they would soon leave. Regardless of the reasons or the intent, the action threw the delicately balanced negotiations into complete ruin. Pablo González from Querétaro insisted that the troop movement nullified all the acts of the Convention, and Francisco Coss from Puebla instructed his delegate to withdraw immediately.[98] Ignacio Pesqueira, in charge of Carranza's war department, did likewise,[99] and troop commanders from many parts of the nation protested either by making threats or by demanding explanation. Whatever meager chances for peace might have existed previously had all but disappeared.

And yet some of the more steady minds labored to prevent war. Immediately after the Convention decided to accept Carranza's "resignation," a commission composed of Eduardo Hay, Eugenio Aguirre Benavides, Antonio Villarreal, and Obregón was dispatched to Mexico to deliver the resolution to the First Chief[100]—but by that

[97] Obregón was in constant communication with Carranza. He, along with G. Osuna and C. M. Santos, made a long report to him on November 1; the document is in ADN-Aguascalientes 1914.

[98] Cobb to SecState, November 4, 1914, transmitting a message from Canova of November 3, 1914, file 812.00/13684, NA, RG 59. In this long and hurried message Canova gave all the information used in the preceding sentences.

[99] Pesqueira to Carranza, November 2, 1914, ADN-DF 1914. The Convention refused to allow him to leave, however.

[100] Obregón, *Ocho mil kilómetros*, p. 220. There seems to be some confusion regarding the personnel of the commission. Canova mentioned a "committee of six" (Canova to SecState, November 2, 1914, file 812.00/13666, NA, RG 59), while Robert E. Quirk (*The Mexican Revolution, 1914–1915*, p. 119) includes the name of Eduardo Ruiz but does not include Villarreal or Hay; and Obregón (see note 101) omitted Hay. Later dispatches by Canova and Carothers, however, make it clear that the four listed did indeed constitute the commission.

time Carranza was no longer in Mexico City. Not completely convinced of the loyalty of the troops in the capital, but reposing absolute confidence in his brother Jesús and in Francisco Coss, whose troops occupied the Puebla-Córdoba area, on November 1 Carranza quietly slipped out of the capital for a trek to the east. The commission, arriving in Mexico City on November 3, wired Carranza, then in Puebla, requesting a hearing;[101] Obregón and the others ultimately consulted with Carranza in Orizaba,[102] where the First Chief had established himself. In the meantime Carranza had received telegraphic notification of the action taken on November 1; on November 3 he replied:

> I have received your message of yesterday in which you informed me of the naming of General Eulalio Gutiérrez as Constitutionalist President. I am waiting for the document [so that I may] study the approved resolutions carefully, and I will answer in time, giving my decision, looking always to the good of the country and the Revolution which conferred the First Chieftainship on me. In the meantime I must insist again and for the third time that I be told whether Villa has surrendered the command of his troops . . . It seems strange to me that while treating the conditions I laid down [as a basis of retirement] I have not been told what has been done to acquire the retirement of . . . Villa and Zapata, because I cannot believe that you are preoccupied only with my retirement without first assuring yourselves that Villa and Zapata will also retire.[103]

With Villa troops in Aguascalientes and more pouring in every day —by November 7 there were thirty thousand in the city and its environs, and another seven thousand between Aguascalientes and Querétaro[104]—and with the Zapata delegates in an uproar at the very thought of their chief being asked to retire,[105] Carranza had

[101] Obregón, Villarreal, and E. Aguirre Benavides to Carranza, November 3, 1914, ADN-Puebla 1914.

[102] Obregón, *Ocho mil kilómetros*, pp. 220–221.

[103] Carranza to The Junta of Military Chiefs and Governors meeting in Aguascalientes, November 3, 1914, ADN-Puebla 1914.

[104] Canova to SecState, November 7, 1914, file 812.00/13789, NA, RG 59. He said that Chao "told me a few days since" that the seven thousand were south of León.

[105] As one observer reported to Carranza, the "retirement of Zapata [is] im-

considerable justification for wondering whether the Convention actually was as free as it was presumed to be. His answer to the commission was predictable: he refused to surrender his position until Villa was out of the way.

But the Villa issue was only part of the problem as Carranza and some of his most trusted friends saw it. To them, the designation of a provisional president for a term of twenty days was absolute nonsense, a truckling to the whims of the intransigent Zapatistas, who had refused to cooperate in any constructive endeavor since 1910 and who now made impossible demands on the Convention itself. And, as Canova pointed out in one of his lengthy and semiliterate dispatches, "they won every point they contended for."[106] Gutiérrez, a stolid, honest, and slow-thinking man, "more adept at dynamiting a train than in turnin[g] the simplest political trick,"[107] could not possibly be the man of the hour to harness Villa and placate Zapata. The designation of Gutiérrez, said Francisco Murguía, "far from settling the issue, will only contribute to complicating it more . . . [and, as] long as the Convention does not arrive at a reasonable and satisfactory agreement for bringing peace to the Republic,"[108] Carranza was duty bound to maintain his post.

But in the public mind the Convention and Villa seemed to have the upper hand on the question of ethics. Villa, who earlier had stated that he would "support any provisional president that may be selected by the Convention except Carranza,"[109] now notified the Convention that he accepted the Convention's action "as an expression of the national will," which, in the words of a Carranza inform-

possible since he has no delegation here" (Gutiérrez de Lara to Carranza, November 5, 1914, ADN-Aguascalientes 1914). The Zapatistas had the best of both worlds—they could demand Carranza's retirement but at the same time refuse to consider a like act for Zapata.

106 Canova to SecState, November 10, 1914, file 812.00/13924, NA, RG 59.

107 Ibid.

108 Murguía to Carranza, November 4, 1914, ADN-México 1914.

109 Carothers to SecState, October 18, 1914, file 812.00/13531, NA, RG 59. The Villa supporters, who demanded Carranza's unconditional retirement, apparently never saw the inconsistency of Villa's stated limitation on the sovereignty of the Convention.

ant at Aguascalientes, gave him "enormous prestige."[110] Canova in his dispatches consistently portrayed Carranza in uncomplimentary terms (in one he referred to the "Dog in the Manger")[111] and probably made his point of view quite clear to the militant Conventionists. At any rate the Convention, in a wave of righteous enthusiasm on November 5, decreed that Carranza be sent an ultimatum to surrender the government to Gutiérrez by 6:00 P.M. on November 10;[112] the Obregón commission that had been sent to confer with Carranza had not yet returned. Following this intemperate action (Gutiérrez had not yet taken the oath of office), the situation quickly deteriorated. Some sterile exchanges between Carranza and the Convention served merely to harden lines, and on November 10 at 6:00 P.M. the "Convention declared Carranza in rebellion."[113] Later that evening Aguirre Benavides returned to Aguascalientes, but the other three members of the commission—Villarreal, Hay, and Obregón—remained well out of range of Villa's men. That same day Villa's troops began a slow move to the south.[114] Even though war had not yet been declared, the fight was on.

During the five days intervening between the ultimatum and the declaration of rebellion against Carranza, a number of interesting and somewhat curious events occurred. On November 6 Villa, who had been in daily concourse with Gutiérrez and whose troops had certainly not abandoned the state after "provisioning," with great fanfare surrendered command of his troops to Gutiérrez and put himself at the disposition of the new minister of war[115]—but Gutiérrez had only shortly before appointed to that post José Isabel Robles, one of Villa's generals. What possessed Gutiérrez to make

[110] Gutiérrez de Lara to Carranza, November 5, 1914, ADN-Aguascalientes 1914.

[111] Canova to SecState, November 10, 1914, file 812.00/13924, NA, RG 59. Canova, whose reports admittedly had a piquancy, was consistently wrong in both his reading of the past and his foretelling of the future.

[112] Canova to SecState, November 5, 1914, file 812.00/13704, NA, RG 59.

[113] Cobb to SecState, November 11, 1914, transmitting three Canova telegrams of November 10, file 812.00/13471, NA, RG 59.

[114] Ibid. Also, documents to Carranza from Pablo González after November 10 indicate the Constitutionalist withdrawal in view of the Villa advance.

[115] I. Pesqueira to Carranza, November 12, 1914, ADN-DF 1914.

such an appointment is not clear. Certainly Robles was able and popular, and Obregón had great respect for his integrity;[116] but he was strongly attached to Villa in spite of his disapproval of some of his chief's violent actions—and he was only twenty-three years old. With some ninety-five generals there from whom to choose, the designation of Robles was at best a political mistake and at worst a fraud, confirming the Carrancistas' worst suspicions that the Convention was Villa's creature and that Gutiérrez had "been bought by Villa's mounted police."[117] But much more significant than Robles's appointment was Gutiérrez's decision to select Villa as his "*jefe de operaciones*," in command of all forces in the field combatting the Carranza "insurrection." Exactly when this high honor and supreme authority fell on Villa is in doubt. Ignacio Pesqueira reported to Carranza that Gutiérrez made the appointment at about 6:00 P.M. on November 12,[118] and Gutiérrez in a message to Obregón stated that Villa was named "chief of his former forces" after the declaration of insurrection;[119] but on November 8, in a message to Luis Caballero, Villa signed himself as "The General in Chief,"[120] a title he had never before used. The conclusion seems to be clear that Gutiérrez and Villa had an understanding, at the very least, that Villa would not be divested of a military command, and it further seems clear, in view of Villa's entire career up to 1920,[121] that anyone who expected the northern revolutionary to surrender the command of his troops did not really understand him.

116 It will be remembered that Robles was instrumental in saving Obregón's life on his second Chihuahua trip in late September.

117 In a telegraphic conference with Gutiérrez on November 10, Carranza made the accusation (Cobb to SecState, November 11, 1914, transmitting three messages from Canova, September 10, file 812.00/13571, NA, RG 59).

118 I. Pesqueira to Carranza, November 12, 1914, ADN-DF 1914.

119 Gutiérrez to Obregón, November 11, 1914, as transmitted in incomplete and muddled form from Cobb to SecState, November 13, 1914, transmitting two Canova telegrams (of November 11 and 12), file 812.00/13769, NA, RG 59.

120 Villa to Luis Caballero, November 8, 1914, ADN-Aguascalientes 1914. There seems to be no reason to doubt the authenticity of the document

121 After Carranza's fall in 1920 Villa "retired" after an understanding with the new government. But he had at that time no more than a ragtag force at his command, not the forty thousand men he reputedly had in 1914.

Obregón and others made a few more puerile efforts to prevent an all-out war, but the moves were probably more for propaganda effect than anything else; everyone apparently knew that the issues would be settled by a contest of arms. On November 11 a group of generals, including Pablo González, Antonio Villarreal, Lucio Blanco, Eduardo Hay, and Andrés Saucedo, sent messages to both Carranza and Gutiérrez. To Carranza they said, in part: "In view of the painful circumstances confronting the country, of which we have perfect knowledge, and in the prescience of their becoming worse, we consider it of imperious and patriotic necessity that you become separated, at once, from the posts you now hold. At the same time we are directing ourselves to the Convention and to General Eulalio Gutiérrez, demanding that they require General Villa to retire completely from all political and military affairs of the country."[122] The same group, with a few added for good measure, suggested to Gutiérrez that he send Villa out of the country on some appropriate commission, and guaranteed in return that Carranza would be forced to retire.[123] Gutiérrez even journeyed to Lagos to discuss the situation with Pablo González, but he took the position that "as soon as Carranza turned over the government" Villa would resign his post;[124] this offer was scarcely satisfactory, but González did submit the proposition to Carranza, and Carranza in turn proposed that both he and Villa leave the country at the same time. One enthusiastic but unrealistic colonel at the Convention was so buoyed by the news that he wired his general: "Military operations suspended. Villa and Carranza going into exile. Eulalio Gutiérrez receives Provisional Presidency. Pacification satisfactorily defined."[125] But with Villa troops moving down the line toward Querétaro and to the east toward San

[122] Obregón, *Ocho mil kilómetros*, p. 225. The same document appears in English, but in incomplete form and in poor translation, in Cobb to SecState, November 13, 1914, file 812.00/13769, NA, RG 59. I have preferred to use Obregón's published version for its greater clarity of words.

[123] Obregón, *Ocho mil kilómetros*, p. 226, prints the document.

[124] *La Convención*, November 14, 1914. This was the newspaper for the Convention government; it followed the government wherever it went.

[125] Miguel M. Ramos to Gertrudis G. Sánchez, November 15, 1914, ADN-Aguascalientes 1914.

Luis Potosí, Carranza had no illusions; he gave the order for the complete evacuation of Mexico City and the concentration of troops along the road to Veracruz.[126]

Obregón, now back in the capital, would have preferred to make a stand there at least temporarily, if for no other reason than to divert Villa's energies from attacking Saltillo and Monterrey and the border points beyond; his own plan at that time was to take his forces to Salina Cruz, embark for Manzanillo, and from that point move against Villa's flank.[127] But Carranza gave the orders, and Obregón obeyed; on November 18 the troop trains began leaving.[128] By that time Carranza's condition might have been described as desperate. The Convention could count on all of Villa's troops with the exception of the small Herrera force that had long since abandoned the northern *caudillo*. Pánfilo Natera remained with the Convention, as did dozens of others throughout central Mexico. Manuel Diéguez supported Carranza in Jalisco, but he doubted the loyalty of some of his subordinates and at best he commanded insufficient forces to undertake any offensive action. Villarreal had thrown in his lot with Carranza, but only a minority of his officers manifested any intention of staying with him; besides, said one Carrancista, "Nuevo León distrusts Coahuila and Coahuila distrusts Nuevo León."[129] In spite of rail destruction west of Saltillo, the Carrancistas generally assumed that Villa could take Saltillo if he wished. Luis Caballero in Tamaulipas denounced the Convention, but the state had many Villa sympathizers. In the northwest Maytorena controlled Sonora almost completely, and in Sinaloa the Conventionists controlled the capital. The Michoacán forces under Gertrudis Sánchez decided to remain completely neutral, but General Murguía in Toluca with ten thousand men rejected the Convention to support Carranza. In sum, when Obregón began evacuating Mexico City the Constitutionalist

[126] Obregón to Carranza, November 16, 1914, ADN-Veracruz 1914. Obregón indicated that he had received the order to evacuate.

[127] Ibid.

[128] Obregón, *Ocho mil kilómetros*, p. 227.

[129] G. Espinosa Mireles to Carranza, November 11, 1914, ADN-Tamaulipas 1914.

forces consisted of some sixty to seventy thousand widely scattered men, with the major portion of them in the states of Puebla and Veracruz cut off from the sea by the U.S. forces in Veracruz and from the capital by Zapata. In contrast, Villa himself had some forty thousand men, Zapata some twenty-five thousand,[130] and the other Conventionist generals combined some twenty to thirty thousand. More importantly, perhaps, the Conventionist troops had excellent lines of communication and transport and access to major ports of entry. But there was also another element; Lucio Blanco and his troops, then in Mexico City and included in the above calculations as Constitutionalists, were even then in the process of defecting to the Convention.[131] Suspicion concerning Blanco's intentions played a major role in Carranza's decision to evacuate the capital.[132]

But the Constitutionalists enjoyed three major advantages. Perhaps the greatest of these was Obregón's loyalty. During those tempestuous days of October and early November when it appeared that peace was a possibility, Obregón acted with great moderation and neutrality; as a result of his attempts to convince Carranza to retire, in fact, the First Chief characterized him as an "ingrate."[133] But once the split became irreparable and he had to make the choice between Carranza and Villa, he did not deviate for a moment; on November 17 he issued a bitter denunciation of the "cursed trinity, made up of Angeles, Villa and Maytorena,"[134] and he set himself the task of de-

[130] The Zapata "commission" in Aguascalientes claimed that there were sixty thousand men under arms, which would have given them the right to sixty delegates under the terms set down by the credentials committee. After long consideration the Zapatistas were allowed "not more than thirty" delegates. Colonel Harry C. Hale of the U.S. Army reported (Hale to the Commanding General, Southern Department, October 30, 1914, file 2225544, NA, RG 94) that Zapata had twenty-five thousand, Villa forty, Obregón twenty-two, and Jesús Carranza eighteen.

[131] Blanco's position was curious, with both sides believing him to be loyal but not completely trusting him. He definitely joined the Convention on November 24.

[132] In early November, Carranza had requested Blanco to come to his headquarters for discussions, but the general found excuses and did not appear.

[133] Canova to SecState, November 7, 1914, file 812.00/13789, NA, RG 59.

[134] Obregón Manifesto, as reproduced in Obregón, *Ocho mil kilómetros*, pp. 226–227. The manifesto was published in various forms, with slight word

stroying Villa's power. But Obregón brought more than mere loyalty to Carranza—certainly none could have been more loyal than Coss, Murguía, and González; he brought a kind of military genius that no other field commander at the time could even approach. Without Obregón it is doubtful that Carranza could have lasted more than a few months; with him he rode to victory.

The second major advantage of the Constitutionalists was control over Veracruz, occupied by the United States since April. As early as mid-September the evacuation had been promised,[135] and at that time Carranza was ready to occupy the city as the United States withdrew; but a number of differences developed that held up the move for over two months. With the quarrel between Carranza and the Convention developing, the Department of State was put in the uncomfortable position of having to choose either of three unattractive alternatives: remain in the city until peace had definitely come to Mexico, move out at once leaving the port in the hands of a Carranza-designated official, "or whether there should be [a] delay until some other officer is designated by [the] convention [*sic*] to receive the surrender of the city."[136] The first alternative was unthinkable because of the probably disastrous consequences, and the third became untenable when the Constitutionalist forces began concentrating in Puebla and Veracruz states.

On November 13 Bryan announced that the occupation would be terminated on November 23.[137] While the secretary of state made no mention of the recipient and carefully sent the announcement to Carranza, Villa, and Gutiérrez, the conditions of the moment made it perfectly clear that Carranza would be the beneficiary. At 2:00 P.M. on November 23 the last of the transports cast off its lines, leav-

---

changes and under different dates, in the following weeks. One version, under date of November 28, was found in ADN-Veracruz 1914.

[135] For a full discussion of the problems involved in the evacuation, and the evacuation itself, see Robert E. Quirk, *An Affair of Honor*, pp. 156–171.

[136] Lansing to Cobb, November 6, 1914, file 812.00/13744a, NA, RG 59. Cobb was instructed to forward the message to Carothers, who at Villa's headquarters was to obtain Villa's opinion "unofficially and confidentially."

[137] Bryan to Cardoso de Oliveira, November 13, 1914, file 812.00/13766a, NA, RG 59.

ing the Veracruzanos "deliriously happy."[138] The Constitutionalists now had easy access to the outside world—and munitions.

The final advantage held by Carranza was the nature of the Convention government. In spite of the façade of a government that as early as November 23 was planning for a vast educational program,[139] the Convention was an agglomeration of conflicting aims and personalities. The Zapatistas, led by the brilliant but erratic Antonio Díaz Soto y Gama, tended to be suspicious, arrogant, and demanding but they were tightly knit and selfish; they knew what they wanted and they were determined to have it. The Villistas represented the widest possible variations in personalities and ethical standards. On the one extreme were Rodolfo Fierro, Tomás Urbina, and Villa himself, untutored men who lived by the law of the jungle,[140] whose solution to any problem was the gun; on the other were Raúl Madero and Robles, gentle and sensitive men with a keen sense of ethics who had been drawn into the maelstrom of revolution by conviction, not delight in fighting. Somewhere in between were Felipe Angeles and others of his ilk—educated, crafty, ambitious, and conniving. Outside the Villa camp, but a part of the Convention, were such men as Eulalio Gutiérrez and Pánfilo Natera, honest and honorable and somewhat dim-witted men who could not stomach Villa's intemperance but who for a time were dominated by him. And, as of late November, Villa dominated them all through the exercise of sheer brute power. The Convention government might concern itself with justice and law, but it was Villa who ordered or allowed the capricious execution of anyone who crossed him or his friends. The best example of the utter insanity of the entire situation was Villa's *ordering* José Isabel Robles, his superior as minister of war, to execute Eulalio Gutiérrez, his president, in January. The Convention government, in fact, was never a government at all. It appeared to be one, and it had interminable debates over abstrac-

[138] As reported by Emilio Balboa, an observer of the event, to Carranza, November 23, 1914, ADN-Veracruz 1914.

[139] Canova to Bryan, November 23, 1914, file 812.00/13951, NA, RG 59.

[140] One of the things that Villa held against Carranza was that, during their meeting in Chihuahua, Carranza lectured him on law.

tions of law and the necessity for reform, but it had no power to enforce its policies. The Convention government was whatever Villa or Zapata, going their separate ways, did. Obregón was perspicacious enough in mid-November to see the inevitable stresses and strains, and he developed much of his military strategy on the assumption of the eventual parting. To Carranza he predicted the split between the two camps, and he foretold defection on the part of many of the Conventionists; but he believed that Villa and Zapata would work together, while Angeles would go his own way.[141]

But these advantages could best be seen in retrospect;[142] at the moment the Convention forces held the upper hand and the first few weeks of military activity appeared to be one long parade. Coming down the main line through the Bajío, the Convention forces by November 18 had occupied Guanajuato, Irapuato, Celaya, and Querétaro successively without fighting;[143] San Luis Potosí was soon added to the list, and here the Convention government established itself momentarily.[144] Obregón completed his withdrawal from Mexico City on November 24, barely eluding an attempt on Blanco's part to take him prisoner,[145] and two days later the first of the Zapatistas entered the city.[146] On November 27 Zapata himself entered the suburbs but refused to come to the center, the following day Angeles led the advance guard from the north into the capital,[147] and on November 30 Villa occupied Tacuba in the suburbs.[148] With the aid of George C. Carothers, Villa and Zapata held a long meeting at Xochi-

[141] Obregón to Carranza, November 16, 1914, ADN-Veracruz 1914. Obregón also predicted that Villa would lose "his false prestige as an astute politician and a man of honor."

[142] Canova first predicted a short struggle, with the Convention winning easily, and then modified his position somewhat but never doubted an ultimate Convention victory.

[143] *La Convención*, November 18 and 19, 1914.

[144] Canova to SecState, November 23, 1914, file 812.00/13951, NA, RG 59. Canova accompanied the Convention government, while Carothers stayed with Villa.

[145] Obregón, *Ocho mil kilómetros*, pp. 227–230, discusses Blanco's defection.

[146] P. González to Carranza, November 26, 1914, ADN-Hidalgo 1914.

[147] Cardoso de Oliveira to SecState, November 29, 1914, file 812.00/13940, NA, RG 59.

[148] Carothers to SecState, December 16, 1914, file 812.00/14061, NA, RG 59.

milco on December 4, agreeing that they would enter the city in a triumphal march on December 6. While the Zapatistas and Villistas planned for these arrangements, Gutiérrez, the president selected by the Convention, "arrived in the city on the 5th [3rd?] and it was deemed wise by General Villa and himself that he enter and take possession of his office immediately and not wait for the triumphal entry."[149] If Gutiérrez had any lingering hopes that his position of provisional president had any meaning, this interposition of the northern chieftain should have dispelled them; Villa and Zapata were the men of the hour, their glory not to be shared by a mere president selected by an assembly that "declared itself to be the sovereign power of the Republic, as being the representative of the people in arms who had fought to reconstitute the nation."[150] Gutiérrez's exclusion from the limelight was the first public sign of an internal fracturing that would make the Convention government a sham within a matter of weeks.

On December 6, as scheduled, Villa and Zapata led some fifty thousand troops into the city and in review before President Gutiérrez.[151] The two men remained in the capital only long enough to pay perfunctory calls on the president, make a few plans, and see the highlights; Zapata left on December 9 to make ready a final assault on Puebla, and Villa left the next day for a hurried trip to the north in order to set his forces in motion against Jalisco to the west and Coahuila–Nuevo León to the east of the main line.[152]

In the disorganized state of the Constitutionalist forces at the mo-

[149] Ibid. By that time Carothers was in El Paso and had been seriously ill; his recollection of the date must have been faulty, since it is clear that Gutiérrez entered on December 3, escorted by Villa and a small force.

[150] Gutiérrez thus classified the Convention in a letter to Canova on November 13 (see Canova to SecState, November 13, 1914, file 812.00/13774, NA, RG 59).

[151] The number is in doubt. Carothers (Carothers to SecState, December 16, 1914, file 812.00/14061, NA, RG 59) said there were sixty thousand who actually paraded and thousands more who did not for lack of time; Canova (Canova to SecState, December 8, 1914, file 812.00/14048, NA, RG 59) gave the number as thirty thousand.

[152] Carothers to SecState, December 16, 1914, file 812.00/14061, NA, RG 59. Carothers accompanied Villa to the north, and discussed his plans with him.

ment, a combined Villa-Zapata movement on Veracruz might have been successful; plans for such an attack were made, but Villa feared that the Constitutionalist forces to the north would cut his line of supply at Celaya or some other northern point, and he wished to eliminate them first. It was a critical and probably an erroneous decision, for it gave the Constitutionalists time to organize. But there may have been another reason for Villa's hasty departure; as soon as he left, a minor reign of terror began in the capital, and in his absence he could disclaim responsibility. Villa and Zapata had agreed at their Xochimilco meeting to the summary execution of a number of men one or the other considered as personal or political enemies,[153] but the executions went far beyond any list prepared by the two men. How many disappeared into shallow graves with the connivance of the man who had made such a point of Carranza's failure to reestablish civil courts will always be unknown, but there may have been as many as two hundred such executions. And the executioners had catholic tastes. Among those subjected to "justice" were three prominent Conventionists (Guillermo García Aragón, David Berlanga, and Paulino Martínez) and three elderly ex-federal generals (Eutiquio Munguía, Pedro Ojeda, and Víctor Preciado),[154] whose inefficiency had aided the Constitutionalist cause. Gutiérrez was appalled by the savagery, but the most he could do was issue a pusillanimous "decree" on Christmas Eve in which he spoke of the necessity for law and order and ended by saying: "In view of the above I exhort you generals to whom this [is] addressed to join your patriotism and honesty to that of [the] government and prevent your subordinates from continuing the perpetration of acts referred to in this note, admonishing you that the executive is resolved to afford guarantees to all inhabitants of the Republic."[155]

A president who is forced to "exhort" and "admonish" his subordinates, rather than order them, is indeed devoid of power. By this

[153] Quirk, *Mexican Revolution*, pp. 139–145, discusses the executions.

[154] Canova to SecState, December 16, 1914, file 812.00/14061, NA, RG 59, gives the names of the most prominent individuals executed to that date.

[155] As given in somewhat abbreviated form by Silliman to SecState, December 29, 1914, file 812.00/14106, NA, RG 59.

time Gutiérrez had come to realize that Villa could not be tamed; his only hope was to induce the northerner to "retire," and Robles journeyed to Guadalajara to make the suggestion.[156] Far from announcing his plans to retire, Villa returned to the capital, virtually put Gutiérrez under house arrest after accusing him of getting ready to defect, and so frightened members of the "government" that about half the permanent commission quietly slipped out of the city to go to San Luis Potosí—and they took with them the flag bearing the signatures of the participants in the Aguascalientes Convention.[157] As Silliman reported it from Mexico City, "The rupture heretofore intimated as possible appears to be beginning."[158] It was not beginning; it was nearly complete.

But as the year came to an end the split among the Conventionists was the only good news coming to the Constitutionalists. When Obregón abandoned Mexico City he left a garrison in Puebla but continued himself to Veracruz, where he arrived on November 26. Fearful of an immediate attack from a combined Zapata-Villa army, he spent a few days making a personal survey of the terrain over which the fighting would probably occur in the state of Veracruz, and made a disposition of his troops.[159] But he recognized the likelihood of a defeat at the hands of vastly superior forces, and in order to secure a line of retreat he made a week's jaunt to Salina Cruz, observing the nature of the land and picking spots for rearguard action if it became necessary; he returned to Veracruz on December 11,[160] just in time to get news that the Constitutionalist forces in Sonora were "in desperate condition,"[161] that the Conventionist forces were mounting a heavy attack in the direction of Tampico with its valuable oil

[156] Canova to SecState, December 18, 1914, file 812.00/14043, NA, RG 59.

[157] *La Convención*, December 28, 1914; Silliman to SecState, December 29, 1914, file 812.00/14104, NA, RG 59.

[158] Silliman to SecState, December 29, 1914, file 812.00/14104, NA, RG 59.

[159] Obregón, *Ocho mil kilómetros*, pp. 231–232.

[160] Ibid., p. 232. These activities on the part of Obregón indicate a great difference between him and Villa as military men. Obregón left nothing to chance and planned his campaigns in minute detail. The knowledge he gained on this survey stood him in good stead in 1923–1924 during the de la Huerta rebellion.

[161] Calles to Carranza, December 12, 1914, ADN-DF 1914.

resources,[162] that the situation in Sinaloa and Tepic was critical,[163] and that Puebla was under attack.[164] When Puebla fell to an estimated fifteen thousand Zapatistas on December 15,[165] the absolute nadir in Constitutionalist fortunes was reached. Had the Conventionist forces made a concerted attack at that point, Carranza would almost certainly have been forced to abandon the port city; but Villa was now busy in the north and Zapata had reached the outer limits of his own world. Neither he nor his generals had the imagination or the daring—nor did they have the ammunition—to move into unknown terrain in pursuit of total victory.

Obregón's original plan of campaign had been to move his force through Salina Cruz to the west coast, where he could make contact with Diéguez and other loyal forces in Jalisco; he had even ordered ships to be readied at Salina Cruz to transport his army of eight thousand.[166] But with the critical situation in Veracruz, Carranza decided to appoint Obregón as *jefe de operaciones* and to make him responsible for directing all the available troops in the central region. The two then decided to make the attack in the direction of Mexico City and the center directly, rather than by way of the west coast; from that point forward Obregón's fortunes and the Constitutionalist fortunes would be one.

In late December, Obregón went on the offensive; by January 1 Tlaxcala, which had been occupied by the Zapatistas since early December, fell to the Constitutionalists,[167] and four days later Puebla suffered the same fate.[168] By easy stages over the next three weeks Obregón's forces reduced one Zapata bastion after another,[169] and

[162] Heriberto Jara to Carranza, December 16, 1914, ADN-Veracruz 1914.

[163] J. Carranza to V. Carranza, December 17, 1914, ADN-Colima 1914.

[164] Coss to Carranza, December 13, 1914, ADN-Veracruz 1914.

[165] *La Convención*, December 18, 1914; Obregón, *Ocho mil kilómetros*, pp. 245–246.

[166] Obregón to Carranza, November 21, 1914, ADN-DF 1914.

[167] Obregón to Carranza, January 1, 1915, ADN-Veracruz 1915.

[168] Obregón, *Ocho mil kilómetros*, pp. 249–253.

[169] The inability of the Zapata forces to operate outside their immediate reserve is clearly indicated by Obregón's capture of Apam, about fifty miles northeast of the capital on the Pachuca-Veracruz rail line. In spite of the fact that Apam was an important rail point and that it was "the centre [*sic*] of an exten-

finally they entered Mexico City, unopposed, on January 28.[170] In the meantime, Saltillo and Monterrey had fallen to Felipe Angeles and the Conventionists,[171] opening the entire northeast to Villa conquest; but this Villa gain was counterbalanced by Diéguez's capture of Guadalajara on January 18,[172] exposing Villa to a flank attack. From the Constitutionalist point of view the military situation, though still far from encouraging, had lost its desperate character.

But for a moment, at least, the political situation was even more encouraging. The earlier widely circulated rumors that Pablo González had declared himself president had been effectively scotched by that general's actions in defending the Tampico region and in publicly extolling Carranza's virtues,[173] and the viability of Carranza's government was every day more evident by the enforcement of his decrees and by his collection of taxes. A series of decrees beginning on January 7 ordered all foreign oil companies to cease operations unless they received explicit permission from the Carranza government,[174] and in spite of vigorous protests by the United States and other nations, Carranza enforced his dicta in modified terms.

---

sive agricultural district from which a large amount of supplies can be obtained," it was defended by only 150 men, who withdrew on Obregón's approach—and this even though Obregón had displaced 15,000 men from Puebla only a few days before (Silliman to SecState, January 19, 1915, file 812.00/14240, NA, RG 59, for the defense of Apam).

170 For the campaign, see Obregón, *Ocho mil kilómetros*, pp. 262–264.

171 The campaign began with a major battle at Marte on January 5 and ended when Angeles along with Emilio and Raúl Madero entered Monterrey on January 15. The documentation on the campaign is extensive in ADN-Coahuila, Tamaulipas, and Zacatecas, 1914 and 1915, and in the dispatches to the secretary of state. Among the last, see particularly Hanna to SecState, January 16, 1915, file 812.00/14228, NA, RG 59, which includes an impressive speech made by Angeles.

172 For the details of the Guadalajara campaign, see Obregón, *Ocho mil kilómetros*, pp. 259–262, which includes Diéguez's official report.

173 In early December this rumor circulated throughout Mexico and the United States; it seriously upset Zubarán Capmany, then in Washington (Zubarán to Carranza, December 1, 1914, ADN-Veracruz 1914). Who started the tale, and for what purpose, is unknown.

174 For the text of the decrees, and the questions raised by them, see the correspondence between Canada and Bevan on the one hand, and the Department of State on the other, in the 812.512 and 812.6363 series, NA, RG 59. Bevan to

Furthermore, by the end of January the Constitutionalist government reaped a harvest of well over half a million dollars a month, in gold, from import and export duties; the Veracruz custom house collected about two-thirds of the total.[175] Furthermore, Carranza was insisting, as he had done earlier in the fight against Huerta, that field commanders refer all questions of international relations to him,[176] and in this, too, he had his way. The Constitutionalist government functioned, and with moderate efficiency with large numbers of civilians occupying administrative posts, in those areas controlled by that government.

In contrast, the Conventionist agglomerate was coming apart. Gutiérrez struggled mightily to head a government composed of a heterogeneous group of Villistas, Zapatistas, and independents,[177] but by the first week in January he decided that the situation was hopeless as long as Villa held sway, and he determined to eliminate him by military action if possible. He then began a series of tortuous negotiations that he hoped would bring an end to the disastrous revolution then in process.[178] His first step was to feel out the Constitutionalist commanders with a view toward cooperating in eliminating Villa; with considerable ingenuousness he almost made a public pronouncement of his intentions: "The problem of pacification may be considered as practically solved. All of the armed groups have been

---

SecState, January 14, 1915, file 812.6363/161, contains the complete text of the original decree.

175 *Boletín de Estadística Fiscal*, January, 1915, pp. 57–59. The *Boletín* was actually published in 1917.

176 For the complete text of Carranza's directive to his field commanders restricting their actions in international matters, see Eliseo Arredondo to President Wilson, February 15, 1915, file 812.00/14397, NA, RG 59, enclosing a translated copy.

177 The cabinet consisted of Villistas José Isabel Robles and Eugenio Aguirre Benavides, Zapatistas Manuel Palafox and Rodrigo Gómez, and independents Lucio Blanco, Felicitás Villarreal, and José Vasconcelos, among others. The complete list (but not their affiliations) is given in *La Convención*, January 1, 1915, and *La Opinión*, January 1, 1915, on which date the most recent additions (Blanco, Palafox, and Gómez) took the oath of office. Chao was governor of the Federal District, until relieved by Vito Alessio Robles.

178 Gutiérrez had been sounding out some of his cabinet members long before the end of the year, but he hoped that Villa could be peaceably removed.

in touch with the government over which I preside and some of them have sent special commissioners, among them the forces of Coahuila, whose delegates are to return north today. These groups have reduced their demands to two propositions which will probably be satisfied and be made public in due time."[179] The kernel of his plan of action he expressed to Obregón on January 7: "In an agreement undertaken among General J. Isabel Robles, Minister of War; Lucio Blanco, Minister of Gobernación; Eugenio Aguirre Benavides, Sub-Secretary of War; and me, we have deemed it patriotic and honorable to direct ourselves to you, to indicate to you the wisdom of suspending your advance on this capital, while we continue giving final form to the plan of campaign which we intend to direct against General Francisco Villa, whom we have always had the intention of absolutely separating from the Constitutionalist Army, and from every class of political affairs in our nation."[180] Two days later the president asked U.S. Consul Silliman to call, and then confessed that "the conduct of both Villa and the Zapatistas was becoming unbearable and that something very important would happen in a very few days."[181] But too many men knew of the contemplated plan of action; by January 13 Gutiérrez admitted to Silliman the truth of the rumored plan, blasted the convention government as "entirely without authority and perfunctory," branded the Zapatistas as "impossible," but left the impression of having every hope that he would succeed.[182]

But two unrelated events killed all hope. Obregón, when he finally received Gutiérrez's letter on January 12, simply arrested the messengers and sent them to Carranza in Veracruz, even while he refused absolutely to cooperate with the provisional president unless Gutiérrez immediately declared war on Villa.[183] At about the same time Villa, who had gone to El Paso to confer with General Hugh L.

[179] As transmitted in Silliman to SecState, January 8, 1915, file 812.00/14168, NA, RG 59.

[180] As reproduced in Obregón, *Ocho mil kilómetros*, pp. 254–255.

[181] Silliman to SecState, January 9, 1915, file 812.00/14173, NA, RG 59.

[182] Silliman to SecState, January 13, 1915, file 812.00/14195, NA, RG 59.

[183] Obregón to Gutiérrez, January 12, 1915, Obregón, *Ocho mil kilómetros*, pp. 255–256.

Scott concerning a border problem,[184] began his return journey but, at Angeles's insistence, stopped in Monterrey. There the famed artillery officer showed Villa incriminating documents that he had captured from Villarreal a few days earlier, and Villa, in predictable fashion, on the night of January 15 acted without thinking. By coded message he ordered Robles to execute Gutiérrez at once and to execute any member of the government who tried to leave the city. During the same evening Gutiérrez called a meeting of the cabinet members whom he felt he could trust; José Vasconcelos, Valentín Gama, Felicitás Villarreal, Robles, Blanco, and the president decided, after long consideration, that remaining in the city at the mercy of Villistas and Zapatistas was an impossibility and that therefore they should leave at once. Gama and Villarreal, on the plea that their families were in Mexico City, at the last moment reneged, but the others, along with Eugenio Aguirre Benavides and Mateo Almanza, left at about 3:00 A.M., January 16, at the head of some three thousand troops.[185] Gutiérrez did not resign; in his view he was still president, and had merely changed the seat of government. He had almost half the cabinet with him, over half the members of the permanent commission were in San Luis Potosí calling for a Convention meeting there, and probably less than half the members of the Convention then meeting in Mexico City had been members of the original Aguascalientes Convention. The president therefore considered it to be perfectly proper for him to extract over ten million pesos—roughly half the amount in the treasury—to take along with him.[186] He hoped to establish his government in San Luis Potosí, and during his trek to the north—continuously harried by

[184] With Maytorena attacking Hill, then bottled up in Naco, bullets falling into U.S. territory caused a number of fatalities and many injuries, and the situation became internationally critical. Villa and Scott worked out a neutralizing agreement.

[185] José Vasconcelos to William Jennings Bryan, March 24, 1915, file 812.00/15106, NA, RG 59; *La Convención* (extra edition), January 16, 1915.

[186] The exact amount seems to be in doubt. Quirk, *Mexican Revolution*, p. 167, following *El Monitor*, gives the sum as 13 million. Villa, in a January 31 manifesto (enclosure to Enrique Llorente to SecState, March 9 [?], 1915, file 812.00/14535, NA, RG 59), stated that the amount was 10.5 million.

Villa troops sent in pursuit—he continued to issue orders in the presidential name.

Gutiérrez's flight threw the government in Mexico City into an uproar, but Roque González Garza as president of the Convention took command and within a few days had the government there functioning more or less normally. But within less than two weeks Obregón occupied the capital, causing the Convention government to flee to Cuernavaca, and interrupting all direct communication between the government there and the Villa headquarters to the north. In the face of this situation Villa by decree established a government of his own, "temporary" of course, with headquarters in Chihuahua.[187] This series of events created a most interesting problem of determining who and what the government of Mexico was. The Convention, now absolutely dominated by the Zapatistas in Cuernavaca, claimed de facto jurisdiction over the entire nation. Gutiérrez, blocked out of San Luis Potosí by a Villa seizure of that city, finally established his "government" in Doctor Arroyo—a tiny little town of no import in the extreme southern part of Nuevo León—and from that point issued orders to which no one listened, and sent to the United States agents whom no one heeded;[188] but he was the legal president of Mexico as he perceived it, and he claimed titular jurisdiction over all. Villa in Chihuahua, with a government consisting of three cabinet members,[189] claimed de facto jurisdiction over all the region in which his troops ranged—some fourteen states. And then Carranza, as the First Chief of the Constitutionalist Army in Charge of the Executive Power—an imposing title that implied purely emergency powers—claimed the right to speak for all Mexico and enforced the right to speak for those portions controlled by his armies. In this

[187] This decree, dated February 2, is an enclosure in the Llorente letter cited in note 186.

[188] José Vasconcelos was designated by Gutiérrez as "general representative of the Government of Mexico before the Government of the United States of America," with special and extraordinary powers (Vasconcelos to Bryan, March 24, 1915, file 812.00/15106 (enclosure), NA, RG 59).

[189] Miguel Díaz Lombardo for Foreign Relations and Justice, Luis de la Garza for Communications and Gobernación, and Francisco Escudero for Finance and Industry.

welter of competing claims it was Carranza who gained. Gutiérrez's flight, which triggered the fragmentation among the Conventionists, was indeed "stupendous news," as one avid Constitutionalist phrased it.[190]

For the Constitutionalists, capturing Mexico City proved infinitely easier than retaining it. For defending the city, Obregón had fewer than six thousand men, the others of his command being occupied in protecting Puebla and the rail connections with Veracruz, while the combined Zapata-Villa forces in the immediate vicinity,[191] not counting those in Pachuca and to the east, probably numbered ten to fifteen thousand. The Zapatistas seldom proved themselves competent in formal battle, probably because of lack of imaginative leadership and the total absence of military discipline, but they proved formidable in guerrilla warfare. Their attacks on the capital were completely uncoordinated,[192] but they were constant, and the Constitutionalists found themselves in an impossible position. The sheer problem of fending off attacks exhausted men and munitions to such an extent that no offensive campaign could be undertaken against either the Zapata hordes in the vicinity or the Villa armies to the north. As a military point, the capital was a complete white elephant.[193]

But politically the Constitutionalist occupation of the capital was a near-disaster. Under the best of circumstances the occupation would have posed serious difficulties. By virtue of the long revolutionary struggle prior to the Carranza-Villa break, the economy in Mexico City revolved around paper money, and until the Convention forces occupied the city in November, the Constitutionalist bills circulated at reduced value but as legal tender for most items. When

[190] J. N. Amador to Gustavo Espinosa Mireles, January 17, 1915, ADN-DF 1915.

[191] Villa withdrew most of his troops from the capital immediately after Gutiérrez's flight, but a few did remain as escorts to the small number of northern delegates to the Convention.

[192] Obregón, *Ocho mil kilómetros*, p. 269, demonstrates this lack of coordination by pointing out that frequently an attack on one side of the city would begin just at the moment that another on the opposite side was withdrawing.

[193] In odd paragraphs here and there, Obregón discusses the problem in ibid., pp. 264–293.

Villa entered he brought with him paper of his own earlier printing, and for the period prior to Obregón's occupation all the bills—Constitutionalist and Villista—were acceptable except those Constitutionalist bills which slipped into the city *after* December 1; they could be identified only by number,[194] but the government imposed harsh punishment, even execution, for those trafficking in them. And then when Obregón entered the city on January 28, one of his first actions was to outlaw all bills save those which had been issued after December 1 by the Constitutionalist government; the result was chaos. Merchants with valuable goods on their shelves hardly knew which way to turn, for bills then good would be worthless if the Convention government returned to the city, and bills then in their possession would be worthless as long as Obregón occupied the city; even having them in a safe would be dangerous. Predictably, some merchants closed their doors and others, willing to gamble, raised prices. Added to this natural circumstance, "painful but unavoidable" as Carranza later phrased it,[195] were the constant interruption of rail traffic as a result of Zapatista attacks and the critical shortage of food in those areas controlled by the Constitutionalist forces. The consequences were food shortages, high prices, and general misery, exaggerated to an almost unbearable degree when the Zapatistas destroyed the pumping plant at Xochimilco and left the city dependent for its water on the tiny supply that could come in by way of the colonial aqueduct from Chapultepec.[196]

Some of the decisions deliberately made by Carranza and Obregón—not to punish the city but to prosecute the war both politically and militarily—added to the misery. As a means of forcing other nations to accept him as spokesman for Mexico, Carranza ordered all national government offices in Mexico City closed and a transfer of these offices to Veracruz; even though some of the lesser bureaucrats

[194] Decree dated December 17, 1914, in *La Convención*, December 22, 1914.

[195] As transmitted by Silliman to SecState, March 10, 1915, file 812.00/14550, NA, RG 59.

[196] The correspondence in the 812.00 series for February and March, NA, RG 59, is filled with horrible descriptions of conditions in the city. Much of this correspondence may be found in *Foreign Relations, 1915*.

accompanied those offices, the major portion of the work force remained in the city without employment. Furthermore, some fabricating plants—notably the munitions factory—were dismantled and shipped to Veracruz, there to be reassembled and put in operation, resulting in more unemployment. Obregón then demanded contributions from the "monopolists" of prime necessities, a special tax contribution from all businesses, and a contribution of half a million pesos from the clergy, all for the purpose of relieving the distress of the poor, he said. Whatever the motivations on both parts, the businessmen in general refused to pay, the clergy insisted they could not pay, and Obregón arrested hundreds of clergymen and businessmen. Obregón himself insisted that the "privileged castes" were responsible for the difficult times, the food shortages, and all the attendant problems; they all, he said,

> converged on me. . . . And General Obregón appeared, to these men, monstrously evil, monstrously heretical and monstrously intractable and brutal.
>
> The moment had arrived, then, when I was confronted with the following disjunctive: confront all the enemies of the Revolution or, giving in to the pressure of their perverse influences, declare myself conquered.
>
> A thousand times the first! that was my resolution. And in my innermost soul I swore, on my honor as a man, to throw down the gauntlet to them and treat them as their attitude demanded.[197]

But a major portion of the merchant class and clergy, and practically all the foreigners, including the diplomats, conceived the miseries to have been a deliberate plot on Obregón's part to punish the city for having been host to both Huerta and Villa, and to have consciously created a food shortage as a means of recruiting desperately hungry men. This view was forcefully, and undiplomatically, expressed in a note that Bryan asked Cardozo de Oliveira to deliver to Obregón on March 7:

> The government of the United States is led to believe that a deplorable situation has been willfully brought about by the Constitutionalist leaders to force upon the populace submission to their incredible demands and to punish the city on account of refusal to comply with them. When a fac-

[197] Obregón, *Ocho mil kilómetros*, p. 270.

tional leader preys upon a starving city to compel obedience to his decrees by inciting outrages and at the same time uses means to prevent the city from being supplied with food, a situation is created which is impossible for the United States to contemplate longer with patience. Conditions have become intolerable and can no longer be endured.[198]

Mr. Bryan failed to specify the rule of international understanding that gave him the authority to condemn the Constitutionalist general for his conduct, but Obregón—internally steaming no doubt—merely accepted the message and sent it on to Carranza without comment. But by this time Carranza and Obregón had agreed that continued occupation of the city was ruinous and had laid plans for evacuation.

The occupation of Mexico City by the Constitutionalists was not absolutely devoid of advantages, and one of the successes of Carranza's agents in the capital laid the base for accusations already presented: Alberto Pani and Dr. Atl were able to generate considerable enthusiasm for the Constitutionalist cause among the poorer classes in the city. Both men were members of Obregón's Revolutionary Junta for Aid to the Public, which he had created to mitigate some of the worst conditions of hunger, and in their work they came in daily contact—often with food and money—with thousands of the destitute.[199] From this ideal position they recruited over nine thousand men for Obregón's army, four thousand being issued arms immediately and the other five thousand being sent to Veracruz to await the arrival of arms from abroad. This extra nine thousand men, even though they might be classified as cannon fodder, not only gave Obregón the necessary military personnel to undertake his campaign to the north, but also gave the Constitutionalist government an anchor in the urban proletariat,[200] which had been lacking previously.

[198] The quotation here is taken from the note as transmitted, in the original English, by Obregón to Carranza, March 7, 1915, ADN-DF 1919 [*sic*]. It may also be found, with minute deviations as a result of transmission difficulties, in Bryan to Cardoso de Oliveira, March 6, 1915, file 812.00/14500, NA, RG 59.

[199] See Alberto J. Pani, *Apuntes autobiográficos*, I, 224–231, for the conditions in the city and his work there.

[200] Dr. Atl to Carranza, March 1, 1915, ADN-Veracruz 1915. Atl did great

Once the decision had been reached to evacuate the city, Carranza ordered Obregón to destroy the rail lines to the north and to withdraw to Ometusco on the way to Veracruz. But Obregón, backed by the new recruits and by great shipments of arms and ammunition, felt that the time had arrived for an assault on Villa's territory; he requested, and received, permission from Carranza in early March to undertake an offensive campaign. On March 3 the Constitutionalist government ordered the suspension of all railway traffic between Mexico City and Veracruz, except for military trains,[201] and a few days later the final evacuation of loyal civilian personnel from Mexico City began. By March 10 all the civilians had left; that night the troops withdrew from their positions and abandoned the city, most of them moving out by the northern Tacuba route. Obregón, bitter over the failure of the clergy to give him the support he thought he needed and deserved, took along with him as prisoners all those clergy who remained in his custody and who were adjudged physically able to travel;[202] his intention, apparently, was to force them to see life in the raw, to witness and experience the hardships to which the Mexican poor were being exposed in struggling for liberty and decency.

During the six weeks in which he occupied the capital, Obregón

---

service to the Constitutionalists among the laboring class and later bitterly resented Carranza's failure to give organized labor sufficient support.

201 Silliman to SecState, March 3, 1915, file 812.00/14494, NA, RG 59.

202 Just prior to his leaving, Obregón ordered a physical examination of all the clergy to determine whether they could travel; the result of that physical examination is still a matter of dispute, for Dr. Gilberto de la Fuente certified that 49 of the 180 suffered venereal disease (see the photographic reproduction of the certification, Obregón, *Ocho mil kilómetros*, opposite p. 257). For a variety of reasons there are serious doubts concerning the authenticity of the findings, but not the report. Obregón decided not to take along those who were ill or were over 60, but he did take a number with him. The exact number is in doubt: Quirk (*Mexican Revolution*, p. 198), gives the number at 26; Obregón mentions no number, but when he sent the clergymen to Veracruz a week later under special escort, the officer in charge reported to Carranza that he was bringing 17 (Luis P. Guevara to Carranza, March 18, 1915, ADN-Veracruz 1915), and Silliman (Silliman to SecState, March 19, 1915, file 812.404/80, NA, RG 59) reported that "Vicar General Paremes [Paredes] accompanied by Canon Herrera and fifteen other priests" had arrived that day.

had disposed his troops in the area so that when he decided to move out he could do so with safety and with a line of communication to Veracruz. By the time he evacuated the city on March 11, his troops controlled, and were able to keep in decent repair, the railroad running from Veracruz through Jalapa, Apizaco, Apam, Pachuca, and Tula to San Juan del Río, just within the confines of the state of Querétaro.[203] It was along this line that he hoped to convey the munitions and other supplies necessary to carry out his great campaign against Villa, for now, even though he still functioned as the commanding general for all field operations, his one concern was the northern chieftain. He was vitally concerned, of course, with the fortunes of the Constitutionalist forces operating in Tamaulipas, Nuevo León, Coahuila, Sonora, Sinaloa, and Jalisco, but these regions, he correctly estimated, were peripheral and relatively unimportant. Reducing all those regions to Constitutionalist control would not eliminate the great threat posed by Villa, but eliminating Villa would leave Maytorena and others like him without support; they could be gobbled up easily one by one. Conditions in the outlying areas were indeed critical, with all border points save Matamoros, Nuevo Laredo,[204] and Agua Prieta in enemy hands, with Guadalajara again secured by Villa,[205] and with Tampico under constant and dangerous threat.[206] He would have preferred to tarry just a little longer, building up his force and his supplies, before risking his much smaller army in a confrontation with Villa, had it not been for the imperious necessity for relieving pressure on Tampico and the remaining bor-

[203] San Juan del Río had been occupied some days earlier by a small Obregón force as the advance guard. On March 6–7 a Villista force attempted to dislodge them without success and withdrew to Querétaro (Obregón, *Ocho mil kilómetros*, pp. 279–287).

[204] After the capture of Monterrey in mid-January, Villa's troops flooded the populated places of the northern states but had not captured these two points even though they were then moving toward an unsuccessful attack on Matamoros. The progress of the campaign there may be followed in the dispatches from Johnson and Blocker to SecState, in the 812.00 series, NA, RG 59.

[205] In late February, Villa recaptured Guadalajara (Obregón, *Ocho mil kilómetros*, p. 280).

[206] Numerous documents in the ADN-Veracruz 1915 file concern the threats to Tampico, but González had been successful in defending the region.

der points.[207] And in spite of the twenty-odd thousand men still operating under Zapata's general banner, Obregón never seriously considered that group as an army posing a threat to his line of communication. He had to have troops guarding the rail line, of course, but the limitations already so obvious in the make-up of Zapata and his followers convinced Obregón that the southerner and his Liberating Army of the South would remain within the confines of their familiar bailiwick rather than undertake a formal offensive campaign. They could have Mexico City—it was useless to the Constitutionalists—and there they could go through their charade of constructing a government that would inevitably come to an end when Villa came to an end. Villa and Zapata could no longer cooperate, because of distance and interrupted communication, but Villa's very existence kept the Zapata-Convention government alive.[208]

Using extreme caution and slowed by the conditions of the track, which had to be repaired at frequent spots, Obregón began his movement to the northwest in quest of the victory over Villa; by April 1 he was in Querétaro and his advance guard south of Guanajuato. In the meantime, Villa gave no indication of any concern, even though some of his generals suffered setbacks. Chao and Urbina, in an attempt to move on Tampico, on March 23 met such a stinging defeat at El Ebano, thirty miles from the port, that they withdrew to San Luis Potosí. On the same day Constitutionalist forces in Jalisco drubbed Rodolfo Fierro. But Villa found time to attend a dinner at the U.S. consulate in Monterrey on March 26, where he "conversed with the foreigners in a most friendly manner,"[209] and three days later he was taking it easy in Torreón.[210] Since his general mode of attack put heavy emphasis on cavalry

[207] Obregón, *Ocho mil kilómetros*, pp. 294–295.

[208] Before the great first battle of Celaya in early April, Villa did have a communication line into Mexico City by way of the Acámbaro–Toluca–Mexico City route and did occasionally send munitions. Even though Celaya closed that route, as long as Villa had an imposing army in the field the Constitutionalists could make no concerted offensive effort against Zapata.

[209] Hanna to SecState, March 27, file 812.00/14719, NA, RG 59.

[210] Carothers (via Cobb) to SecState, March 29, 1915, file 812.00/14731, Hanna to SecState, April 1, 1915, file 812.00/14765, NA, RG 59.

charges, he was probably waiting for Obregón to move into the flat country of the Bajío before attacking, and since his available troops outnumbered the Constitutionalists by about two to one, he had every reason to hope for a crushing victory.[211]

The first major battle took place on April 6–7 at Celaya, where Obregón had arrived two days earlier and entrenched himself after having sent some four thousand of his eleven-thousand-man army on forays to Acámbaro and Dolores Hidalgo. Here his army, outnumbered three to one, repulsed the Villa charge with heavy losses while losing about 15 percent of its own effectives through death or wounds.[212] He won the battle, Obregón reported, because "Villa, personally, directed the battle, fortunately."[213]

The defeat stung the northern *caudillo.* His string of victories had been uninterrupted during the past year, and he planned to erase this one blemish from his record as quickly as possible. In a defiant and boastful mood on April 9 he challenged Obregón. Within three days, he said, he would renew the attack, and he warned the Constitutionalist general to make provision for the safety of civilians from "the projéctiles of the People's Army, and from the sixty mouths of flame [artillery] which will rain fire and sow ruin and desolation in your trenches."[214] But the second battle of Celaya, beginning late in the afternoon of April 13 and ending two days later, was not merely a defeat for the Villistas; it was disaster. Obregón, who knew his enemy well, planned carefully. His army now swelled to fifteen thousand, he sent seven thousand cavalrymen under Cesáreo Castro to the rear as a reserve and counterattacking force while he positioned the remaining eight thousand in a complete ring around the city,

[211] The number of troops involved in any battle is at best an intelligent guess. Obregón said (*Ocho mil kilómetros,* p. 319) that his total force at that time was eleven thousand; Villa probably had a total force of some twenty thousand.

[212] Obregón (ibid., pp. 302–305) gave Villa's losses as 1,800 killed, 3,000 wounded, and 500 captured; his own losses he reported as 557 killed and 365 wounded—an extraordinary ratio. Villa reported to Carothers, on the other hand (Carothers to SecState, April 20, 1915, file 812.00/14897, NA, RG 59) that he had lost 300 killed and 700 wounded.

[213] Obregón to Carranza, April 7, 1915, ADN-Guanajuato 1915.

[214] As given in Obregón, *Ocho mil kilómetros,* pp. 305–306.

protecting it from all sides. Knowing that Villa followed only one military tactic—charge!—Obregón hoped to fend off the attackers until they had exhausted both their ammunition and their energies, and then to order a counterattack by Castro on the flanks. His plan worked to absolute perfection. By the early morning of April 15 Villa had committed all his thirty thousand men to the attack, ordering charge after charge, suffering mammoth losses. At the opportune time, Castro began his enveloping movement and by early afternoon the Villistas started to flee; by nightfall the battle was over. Obregón, who probably exaggerated, estimated Villa's losses at over ten thousand dead and captured and another five thousand wounded; Villa admitted a loss of two and a half thousand.[215]

The second battle of Celaya characterized the differences between Villa and Obregón both as individuals and as military men and was an augury of things to come. Obregón planned, Villa charged; Obregón thought, Villa felt. Even after the battle was over, Villa did not recognize that he had been trapped; he thought the defeat was an accident brought on by a shortage of ammunition. The men making the charges were indeed short of ammunition, but Villa had millions of rounds only a few miles away; the shortage came because Villa had not taken the necessary steps to reprovision the men at regular intervals. In reporting Villa's account of the battle, Carothers wrote:

> Villa was again compelled to withdraw yesterday owing to shortage of ammunition. He had the city completely surrounded and with every probability of success when Carrancistas made cavalry sally flanking the infantry[216] causing a retreat which soon became a rout, having abandoned nearly all the artillery after removing breech locks. Large number infantry taken prisoner by Carrancistas. Villa says that they beat him this time but that he will try again and that the next attack will be successful. Has al-

[215] The most convenient source for the battle is ibid., pp. 305–329, which includes Obregón's telegraphic reports to Carranza during the battle. Most of these reports may be found in ADN-Guanajuato 1915. Additional information may be found in dispatches from Carothers to SecState in the 812.00 series, NA, RG 59, particularly two of April 20, 1915, numbered 14897 and 14898. A few documents are also in ADN-Veracruz 1915.

[216] The document has the word *fumigator*, which the code clerk for some reason did not decipher, but which in context clearly means infantry.

ready commenced reorganizing his army here and has ordered ten thousand veterans from the north and five thousand from Guadalajara and Michoacan.[217]

The two battles of Celaya did not bring the warring to an end, but they foretold Villa's ultimate defeat.[218] By April 20 Villa had lost thousands of men through death, wounds, capture, and defection; Obregón had come through with a net gain, since his losses in battle were far overbalanced by new recruits coming to his ranks as a result of a general amnesty proclaimed on April 20.[219] Success brought to Obregón many officers, and their men, who abandoned the losing Villa to join the winning Constitutionalists.[220] Celaya proved, beyond a shadow of a doubt, that Villa was not invincible in the field. Obregón still had great respect for Villa's ability to raise armies and undertake audacious attacks, but the Villa myth had died. After Celaya the Constitutionalists had the momentum, and Villa's empire gradually collapsed.

Giving the details of the long series of battles over the next year, during which Obregón forced Villa farther and farther to the north and reduced him to the status of a wandering bandit, would be of some interest but would be a repetition, with variations, of Celaya. Tarrying in Celaya only long enough to bury or burn the dead, Obregón began to advance on April 19; three days later Irapuato fell

217 Carothers to SecState, April 20, 1915, file 812.00/14898, NA, RG 59, a repeat of an undelivered message of April 16.

218 Obregón's basic tactic against Villa, which the latter apparently could never fathom, was simple. He selected the battle site, formed his infantry in a strongly entrenched square not differing greatly from the wagon-train form against the Plains Indians, sent the cavalry out on flanking forays, and invited Villa to attack. Even on the offensive Obregón always, except for the battle of Aguascalientes, enticed Villa to make headlong charges against his fortified positions. Villa's charges were incredibly expensive in manpower, and he was always repulsed; he then withdrew, waited for Obregón to advance and select another site, and then charged again. These blind charges in the months between March and August probably cost Villa as many as fifty thousand men in dead and captured.

219 Obregón to Carranza, June 21, 1915, ADN-Jalisco 1915, giving the text of an amnesty he had proclaimed on April 20.

220 Carranza to Obregón, April 16, 1915, ADN-Veracruz 1915, instructed Obregón regarding policy with respect to such officers.

without a battle, and the offensive continued to the north. After a long series of minor engagements, a major battle developed in late May and early June in the vicinity of León; in the latter phases of the battle, at Trinidad, Obregón lost his right arm on June 3, but the victory was his three days later when the Villistas fled farther to the north with Obregón in slow pursuit. By late June, after Woodrow Wilson had called "upon the leaders of factions in Mexico to act together, and to act promptly for the relief and redemption of their prostrate country,"[221] Villa proposed that the three groups—Villistas, Zapatistas, Constitutionalists—join to prevent the U.S. intervention that he feigned to see in the offing. The Constitutionalists wanted no part of such a bargain; according to Obregón, "No sensible Mexican fails to understand that Villa is defeated as a general and is a nullity as a politician."[222]

In spite of some ticklish military situations in which he found himself,[223] Obregón on July 10 occupied Aguascalientes after a bitter battle;[224] from that time forward "the struggle against *villismo* took on a fragmentary aspect over a great part of the national territory and even though there were some encounters of some importance, none reached the proportions of a true battle."[225] Villa continued to be a thorn as long as Carranza lived, but as a national figure to be considered as the leader of a country, Villa died at Aguascalientes even though some men in Washington refused to recognize it.[226]

[221] As given in *Foreign Relations, 1915*, pp. 694–695.

[222] Obregón to Generals Joaquín Amaro, Plutarco Elías Calles, and others, June 21, 1915, ADN-Expedición Punitiva. The filing of this document with the material concerning the Punitive Expedition is odd.

[223] Just before the Aguascalientes battle, Rodolfo Fierro slipped behind Obregón and destroyed the Constitutionalist army's communication with Veracruz.

[224] Obregón, desperately short of food and ammunition, was forced to attack Aguascalientes rather than wait for Villa to come to him. But Villa, expecting the attack to come from the south, had put all his strength in that sector and had left the northern approaches undefended. In a flanking movement, Obregón slipped around to the north and came on Villa's rear.

[225] Francisco J. Grajales in Obregón, *Ocho mil kilómetros*, pp. cxxvii–cxxviii.

[226] The 812.00 series, NA, RG 59, shows clearly that many of the members of the Department of State still considered Villa to be a major political figure, though on the decline.

In the meantime the Convention government, which had moved back to Mexico City from Cuernavaca, oscillated between futility and sterility. Day after dreary day the Convention debated a proposed plan of government authored principally by Antonio Díaz Soto y Gama, and day after weary day Roque González Garza—who deserved better—attempted to head an administration that had neither power nor authority. In an effusion of theoretical abstractions, the dominant leaders of the Convention insisted that González Garza, who had stepped into the breach when Gutiérrez fled, continue as president of the Convention and exercise the national executive function in that capacity, but not as provisional president and only as directed by the Convention itself. The result was a strangely aberrant "parliamentary" form of government that had no real executive and that hamstrung any kind of intelligent administrative action. At the center of the stage was the Zapatista Díaz Soto y Gama, who perceived his role to be that of the great intellectual leader; he steadfastly refused to accept the responsibility of a cabinet position, since that would have limited his stage. He preferred to carp, to criticize, to bait; the scope of his invective knew no bounds. At best, given the nature of the interests and the character of the men, the Convention would have been a difficult body from which to extract a viable system of government, but Díaz Soto y Gama turned it into a snarling and quarrelling mass of humanity, which at times lost all semblance of a deliberative body. This sovereign convention, which it called itself, was in continuous legal session from January 1 until late in August, but it produced no effective government, it failed to solve the pressing problems of food for the city, it undertook no strong offensive campaign; it did nothing, in short, but debate and haggle. Even in the precious area of land reform, so dear to the heart of the Zapatistas, no firm legal base was established upon which a program could be instituted. Zapatista Minister of Agriculture Manuel Palafox did indeed undertake to distribute some lands in Morelos on an ad hoc basis—and rumor had it that he took more than his share—but he made no attempt to institute a program in the other areas then under the military control of the Liberating Army of the South or of the Convention. And even when the Constitutionalist forces in the north, particularly those directly under Obregón's command, went from victory to victory, the Convention made no serious attempt to interrupt Obregón's line of communication with Veracruz. An occasional foray against a garrison point or an infrequent raid on the rail line itself (these in fact undertaken by inept commanders in the field and not as the result of any superior orders or aid from Mexico City) sometimes severed communications for a short period but never for long. When the communications were cut between Obregón and Veracruz in late June, putting the Constitutionalist force in serious jeopardy, the action came from Rodolfo Fierro in the Bajío, not from the Conventionists near Mexico City.

Like Villa, the Conventionists saw in President Wilson's demand for peace an opportunity to salvage something from a lost cause. Their proposals of June 15 indicate their complete lack of realism. They demanded the cessation of all hostilities for one month, during which time a reconstituted Convention would select a new civilian provisional president and establish a government composed of nine cabinet members, three from each of the three groups. Furthermore, they demanded that every military commander be allowed to retain control, unmolested, over the region he then held, and that a general amnesty be proclaimed to apply to all save "reactionaries," whatever that meant. Pablo González, then at Ometusco and to whom the proposal was sent, rejected the suggestions out of hand as being completely unacceptable at every point.[227] Having fought bitterly for nearly seven months in behalf of a victory of what they conceived to be their principles, Carranza and his chieftains were scarcely in the mood to make these concessions when victory was a certainty and U.S. intervention a strong improbability.

In the meantime another element was injected into the already messy situation. Victoriano Huerta in Spain thought he saw, in the

[227] *La Convención*, June 7, 1915, printed the full text of the proposals and González's answer; also, Cardoso de Oliveira to SecState, June 15, 1915, file 812.00/15229, NA, RG 59. González Garza made a similar proposal to Carranza on June 2 and another on June 8 (Cardoso de Oliveira to SecState, June 8, 1915, file 812.00/15179). The *ayuntamiento* on June 5 requested Carranza to come to some agreement with Villa (Municipal President Juan Vanegas to A. I. León, June 5, 1915, ADN-Veracruz 1915).

vast split in the Mexican political situation, an opportunity for his own return. On March 28 he traveled to Seville, conferred with Enrique Creel and others,[228] and four days later sailed for New York along with a large group of exiles.[229] After a slow trip across the Atlantic he appeared to establish himself in New York, even while a group of his ex-generals, including Caraveo, Orozco, Bravo, and Téllez, gathered in El Paso.[230] Orozco made a special trip to New York to see him, returning to El Paso on June 23;[231] four days later Huerta appeared on the scene, to be arrested by U.S. authorities and then released on bail.[232] While these events transpired, Mexican exiles in the United States of almost every hue bombarded President Wilson and the Department of State with requests for aid, with plans for bringing the revolution to an end, and with suggestions as to the role to be played by the United States.[233] During the May–July period, juntas of one kind or another met in Los Angeles, El Paso, San Antonio, New Orleans, Washington, and New York, all perfectly willing to solve the Mexican situation by starting a new revolution to which all Mexicans could adhere.[234] Everybody had the answer: Félix Díaz, Nemesio García Naranjo, Medina Barrón, Huerta, Moheno, and a multitude of others. Even Felipe Angeles got in on the act; after the devastating defeat at León, Angeles decided to go "to Boston to see

[228] Gracey (Seville) to SecState, undated but received March 31, 1915, file 812.00/14751, NA, RG 59.

[229] Gracey to SecState, April 1, 1915, file 812.00/14753, NA, RG 59.

[230] Cobb to SecState, May 12, 1915, file 812.00/15008, NA, RG 59.

[231] Cobb to SecState, June 25, 1915, file 812.00/15308, NA, RG 59.

[232] Weekly report No. 120, Commanding General Southern Department to War Department, July 8, 1915, NA, RG 94; Juan N. Amador to Carranza, June 27, 1915, ADN-DF 1915.

[233] The most interesting of these proposals came from General Salvador Domínguez in San Antonio, who outlined his plan to form and equip an expeditionary force in Texas, and asked only that the United States not interfere (Domínguez to President Wilson, April 21, 1915, file 812.00/14937, NA, RG 59). One is inclined to agree with the query posed by Mr. Tanis in the State Department: "Do you think we should take him seriously?"

[234] The 812.00 series, NA, RG 59, is filled with reports, rumors, and requests. A sedulous examination of the documents will indicate that at least seventeen groups were claiming some kind of priority in ability to settle the revolution then in process.

his family," and incidentally to tell President Wilson how to settle the Mexican problem.[235] The result of all this maneuvering was an extraordinary proposal that Leon Canova, who at Villa's "invitation" had ended his career as a special Department of State representative in Mexico but who had returned to Washington as an officer in the Division of Latin American Affairs, made to the secretary of state in mid-July. According to Canova's statement, he had consulted with special representatives from Zapata and Villa, with Gutiérrez's representative,[236] with Blanquet, with Mondragón representing Félix Díaz, with Gamboa and Esquivel Obregón "representing a large part of the Catholic party, and others." On the assumption that "no man in Mexico could establish order without the approval of President Wilson," these representatives of every faction save that of Carranza "would unite under the standard of any man or group of men who would be countenanced by President Wilson." The nub of Canova's proposal, then, was:

If you will authorize me, I feel quite confident that within ten days . . . I can submit to you the names of a group of men who will be worthy of confidence and who will, by that time, have the endorsement of all the Mexican element except Carranza himself and some of his immediate advisors. I am assured that 5,000 officers and men can be assembled by this group just across the Río Grande, as soon as the encouraging word is spoken; that 20,000 men, mostly the trained soldiers of the old Federal army, coming largely from Villa's ranks, will rally to it; that, in all probability, Villa's entire army will join the movement . . . ; that other forces will be started from Oaxaca and the Yucatán coast to move northward; that, as soon as President Wilson indicates his willingness to this proposal, these people can raise the money needed for their campaign. As the movement progresses, order will be restored, municipal and State governments set up, courts opened, guarantees given, the Constitution reinstated, and general elections held as soon as practicable. The Carrancista element will, in large part, come over to this new movement, for it will enter Mexico with gold

[235] Carothers to SecState, June 18, 1915, file 812.00/15263, NA, RG 59. By implication, Carothers urged that President Wilson consult with Angeles.

[236] Canova did not identify the individual, but presumably it was Vasconcelos.

or its equivalent to pay its soldiers, and with ample supplies of food, and probably the Red Cross will follow with supplies for the non-combatants.

In order to assure the success of this magnificent "new movement" the United States need only "close its eyes to the operations" and "restrict, or place an embargo on, the shipment of arms and ammunition to Carranza." This would all be followed, in due course, by the selection of a provisional president designated by Wilson, the appointment of "an unofficial administrative adviser" to oversee the necessary reforms (Canova certainly saw himself in that role), the extension of a great loan and "American supervision of the customs collections . . . [to] serve as a guarantee for such a loan."[237]

While Secretary of State Robert Lansing had the "Mexican situation . . . much in . . . mind," and was not above applying any pressure available for a settlement of the fighting, he operated under the assumption that a "condition precedent to any plan is, of course, that the old aristocratic party must not be recognized in a settlement of the present situation."[238] And Wilson, even though he found some of Carranza's policies "not only disappointing . . . [but also] disgusting" and had "never known of a man more impossible to deal with on human principles that [*sic*] this man Carranza,"[239] wanted to have nothing to do "with the scoundrel, Huerta."[240] These considerations, along with the march of events, prevented any serious consideration of Canova's plan; fortunately it died aborning. How Canova, who lost no opportunity to impress upon his colleagues his vast knowledge and understanding of the Mexicans, could possibly have envisioned an acceptable working arrangement between men of the integrity of a Roque González Garza, the radicalism of a Díaz Soto y Gama, and the progressivism of a Villarreal, on the one hand, and Mondragón, Blanquet, Félix Díaz, and Gamboa, on the other, is beyond comprehension.

[237] Canova memorandum to the Secretary of State, July 17, 1915, file 812.00/15531 1/2, NA, RG 59.

[238] Lansing to President Wilson, July 5, 1915, file 812.00/15410 1/2a, NA, RG 59.

[239] Wilson to Lansing, July 2, 1915, file 812.00/15409 1/2, NA, RG 59.

[240] Wilson to Lansing, July 8, 1915, file 812.00/15412 1/2, NA, RG 59.

The Constitutionalists' opponents did not come to a sudden end; they simply faded away over a long period of time, in part from repeated defeats and in part from disgust. Despite urgings from Washington that the various factions join together, and in spite of demands from the same source that Carranza be eliminated, the Constitutionalists pressed steadily forward against their foes. On August 2 Pablo González occupied Mexico City;[241] the Convention government there came to an end, though it continued to sit in Toluca until October 10. During August and September, Obregón's army pushed Villa farther and farther to the north, and González's army confined the Zapatistas more and more to their small anarchic realm of Morelos. Even Wilson by late September had concluded that Carranza could not be eliminated and that it would be feckless longer to pretend that the factions could be joined; on October 19, 1915, the United States extended de facto recognition to Carranza and the Constitutionalists. The Convention aberration had come to an end, even though thousands of lives would still be lost before final pacification.

When the Aguascalientes Convention failed, the result of a compound of Zapata intransigency, Villa intemperance, and Carranza obstinacy, the Mexican nation was saddled with a double tragedy. The costs of that failure are incalculable. The loss of life alone during the year-long period from the first meeting of the Convention on October 10, 1914, to its final dismal march from Toluca into oblivion on October 10, 1915, may have run as high as 200,000 and was certainly more than 100,000. González Garza calculated in mid-July that death from military action in the northern zone alone passed 70,000. But the end of the Convention did not mean the end of military action; not for one single day until after Carranza's demise in 1920 was the country at peace within itself, and that five-year span witnessed additional tens of thousands of deaths. Furthermore, for every man who died in battle probably two persons or more died as an indirect result of the conflagration. Food shortages were endemic throughout the nation all during 1915, with the situa-

[241] González had occupied and abandoned the city on some earlier occasions, but after this date the Constitutionalists remained.

tion critical in Mexico City, Monterrey, Guadalajara, Chihua
Hermosillo, and many other centers of population. Probably
"starved" in a technical sense, but malnutrition left hundred
thousands prey to all manner of disease; death was everywhere.

In addition, the destruction to mines, factories, buildings o
sorts, and particularly railroads, reached astronomical figures.
the success of military movements depending upon the availab
of supplies coming from distant points, all rail lines became im
tant military targets. When Rodolfo Fierro made his foray f
León to Tula in June–July he destroyed over a hundred mile
track, according to Obregón's estimates, and this was only a m
incident of destruction. This fantastic destruction of physical f
ities in a nation already poorly endowed in such assets left
country in an impossible economic position when the Constitutio
ist government finally returned to Mexico City.

Physical and economic losses were staggering, but the intellec
losses were probably greater as far as the well-being of the na
was concerned. The ugly animosities engendered by this most b
of wars demanded the elimination from public affairs of all t
who had been on the losing side. Many Mexicans and some
scholars have been overly impressed with the idealism and
intelligence of those who were involved in the debates of the C
vention, and as a consequence they have taken the position that
later progress of the Mexican revolution and its social reform
direct outgrowths of Conventionist activity.[242] The evidence sh
otherwise. Though many of the men who followed the Conven
or Zapata, or Villa were able and conscientious, that they had
real influence on later developments is highly problematical. Th
the real tragedy of the Conventionist-Constitutionalist war. Me
the intellectual caliber and moral fiber of Roque González G
Miguel Díaz Lombardo, Raúl Madero, Francisco Escudero,
many others of that stamp are never plentiful in any society,
during the critical times after 1915 when Mexico was attemptin
create a new society the nation could ill afford to dispense with

[242] For example, see Quirk, *Mexican Revolution*, Chapter II, entitled "Vi
in Defeat."

benefits of their thinking and their example. But for many years they were denied any voice in public affairs. Nor did the work of the Convention itself, during those long and bitter days of debate in the first six months of the year, affect in any ascertainable fashion the future pattern of government or institutional development; the Constitutionalists themselves developed programs and ideas that ultimately determined the course of events, quite independently of Convention actions. The Convention was, to borrow and paraphrase Obregón's characterization of Villa, a political nullity.

7. THE PROCESS OF CHANGE IN THE PRECONSTITUTIONAL PERIOD

Woodrow Wilson's reluctant recognition of the Carranza government on October 19, 1915, put no stamp of approval on Carranza policies but did aver that the Constitutionalists effectively controlled the nation. "Effective" is of course not an absolute, and the battle was far from over. Thousands of men continued to peck away futilely at the base of the Constitutionalist government, and Carranza expended an enormous sum of money in maintaining an oversized military establishment to defeat those bandit-revolutionaries active in most states. In early 1917, twenty-one months after González had occupied Mexico City, the army consisted of 150,000 men;[1] the economically prostrate nation could ill-afford such a burden, but war had become a way of life. During the period between Huerta's destruction of constitutional government in February, 1913, and the reinstitution of constitutional government in May, 1917, the

[1] Venustiano Carranza, *Informe . . . encargado del poder ejecutivo de la República*, p. 205. The size of the army was roughly equivalent to that of the United States on the eve of U.S. entrance into World War I.

political process was a shambles. Any semblance of representative government disappeared. All contestants to power governed by decree; even the Convention, which claimed to represent the national interests, was a self-designated body, nonrepresentative in its form and nondemocratic in its actions. Villa from his Chihuahua aeyrie governed by decree, and Zapata from his Morelos lair imposed law by fiat. And Carranza frankly exercised dictatorial power "in use of the extraordinary faculties with which" the revolution invested him.[2]

Despite this chaotic situation, which seemed to have neither plan nor direction, a real revolution was in the making. By 1917 the accepted values under which Mexico operated had changed enormously since 1910, and even the most "conservative" of those in administrative positions were "radical" in comparison to their counterparts of a few years earlier. The changes came slowly, and they came primarily because war eliminated the porfirian governmental and social plutocracy as a focus of power. Those constitutional precepts which distinguish the Constitution of 1917 from its predecessor came from no one man or small group of men consciously composing a reformation program; they were an accretion of many acts and pragmatic decisions over a four-year span. Carranza occupied center stage in the process. He governed dictatorially and he doubted the efficacy of social change by fiat, but he was forced by circumstance and clamoring voices to accept a revolutionary philosophy that became the hallmark of the new constitution.

During those four preconstitutional years, particularly the last two, six areas of domestic practice and policy came under serious revision. Three of the six brought bitterness in and out of Mexico: the relationship between Church and State, the nature of land tenure, and the ownership of subsoil deposits. The other three areas of policy revision—concerning labor, education, and politics—brought little international tension but nevertheless had enormous import for the nation's future.

[2] All Carranza decrees began with some such formula. The normal form was the following: "VENUSTIANO CARRANZA, First Chief of the Constitutional Army, in Charge of the Executive Power of the Nation, in use of the extraordinary faculties with which I find myself invested, has seen fit to decree . . ."

Violent anticlericalism, for want of a better term, had been Mexican characteristic for four generations when Huerta destroy Madero's government. An entire body of law, constitutional a statutory, imposed severe limitations on the Church as an insti tion and on clerics as individuals, despite the country's overwhel ingly Catholic population. Law banned monastic vows, stipulated conditions under which church bells could toll, prohibited cleri garb on the streets, and forbade public officials from participating Church functions save as communicants. Law defined marriage a civil contract rather than a religious rite, prevented clerical teachi in public schools, forced clerics to perform certain rites for t poverty-stricken without compensation, and opened all cemeter to public burials regardless of religious affiliation. And finally, t legal code prohibited Church ownership of any real property. The were the most important laws, and in general they were unenforce

Emotion plays a dominant role in any question concerning ligion, and emotion engenders a belief in rumors. In the welter claims, charges, and accusations, which began in muted form 1913 and swelled to a roar in 1915, it becomes almost impossible separate truth from fiction or fact from fancy. The enormous doc mentation extant on the question of religion and the Church duri the revolutionary years is a morass. In that documentation one c find "proof" that the members of the clergy made enormous cont butions to Huerta, that priests carried arms and directed troops, th the clergy constantly and openly preached insurrection against t Constitutionalists, that Catholic schools served as centers for espi nage and intrigue, that churches served as arsenals, and that t

[3] There are no satisfactory comprehensive studies of anticlericalism as a nin teenth-century Mexican phenomenon in either Spanish or English. Except that portion of Daniel Cosío Villegas, *Historia moderna de México, El Porfiria La vida social*, dealing with the question, the Mexican accounts of the Churc State contest are so polemical as to be almost worthless. John Lloyd Mecha *Church and State in Latin America*, has the best general account in English, b it is far from complete. Charles A. Hale, *Mexican Liberalism in the Age of Mo 1821–1853*, carefully examines the enmity between liberals and the Church the thirty years following independence. With respect to the legal situation, t question of whether the Church owned the temples will be examined later.

Church-clergy fought bitterly and persistently against any alleviation of the miserable conditions in which the mass of the people wallowed. One can also find "proof" that revolutionaries raped hundreds—perhaps thousands—of nuns, executed innumerable priests merely because they were priests, persecuted all who professed to be devout Catholics, defiled and desecrated churches and sacred objects, and, in short, made every effort to stamp out religion in any form.

Few of these "proofs" would be admissible in a court of law. Most of the accounts fail to give the names of those allegedly suffering, and most depend upon fourth-hand evidence. A sixteen-page report submitted to Secretary of State Bryan by R. H. Tierney in his capacity as chairman of the Committee of the Federation of Catholic Societies exemplifies the situation. A memorandum on religious persecution in Guadalajara after Obregón captured the city, the paper is a long disquisition filled with errors of fact and little concrete information; even the author is unidentified, but the text labeled him as a Spanish priest.[4] The analyst picking his way through these materials is confronted with a most difficult task in arriving at a clear picture of clerical responsibility or religious persecution. But one phenomenon does stand out. By mid-1914 both anticlericals and proclericals believed every derogatory tale told about those in the other camp. The anticlerical Constitutionalist readers of *El Demócrata* in Veracruz,[5] for example, were outraged but not surprised to learn from its pages that an armed band including some "friars" (*frailes*) attacked and wounded Constitutionalist General Flores in the vicinity of Puebla; the readers assumed, as a matter of undeniable truth, that clerics engaged in espionage and armed combat against the Constitutionalist cause. But, as Flores's aide later stated,[6] the newspaper story erred in a monumental fashion. Flores was wounded at Los Frailes, a way station between Cholula and Atlixco, by a Zapata patrol; neither Flores nor any of his staff saw any clerics of any

[4] "Religious Persecution in Guadalajara," submitted as Document B by R. H. Tierney to Bryan, October 17, 1914, file 812.404/22, NA, RG 59.

[5] *El Demócrata*, July 20, 1915.

[6] Fernández Dávila to Barragán, July 22, 1915, ADN-Veracruz 1915.

kind. When *El Demócrata* received the story, *at* Frailes had been garbled into *by frailes*, and another myth was created.

Many Constitutionalists, both before and after the split into warring groups, viewed both Church and clergy as maleficent influences. Antonio I. Villarreal, as governor of Nuevo León in mid-1914 before the final victory over Huerta, probably most forcefully—even crudely—expressed this belief: "Clerical corruption has come to be a threat against morality in Mexico. The Confessional and the Sacristy are to be feared as anterooms of prostitution. To suppress them is a holy and regenerative work."[7] However unjust such charges may have been, it cannot be seriously contended that all clergy remained aloof from politics, or that all presumed spokesmen for Church and clergy took a progressive view. *El País*, which proclaimed itself to be a Catholic daily until four days after Huerta's flight, fought Madero bitterly during his short term in office, openly advocated his ouster, and generally supported Huerta.[8] Members of the episcopate gave official approval and encouragement to the creation of a Catholic party and equally discouraged members of the Church from taking part in the Constitutionalist revolution.[9] Repeated condemnations of the Constitutionalist movement by priests from the pulpit and by lay Catholic leaders in the newspapers did much to convince Constitutionalist leaders that the Church was in league with Huerta.

At the root of the matter lay three circumstances. In the first instance, a major portion of the clergy in Mexico came from abroad. Many Mexicans viewed all foreigners as rapacious or contemptuous or both, and they saw no reason to differentiate between foreign clergymen and foreign businessmen. As a consequence, Mexican

[7] Silliman to SecState, July 27, 1914, file 812.404/3, NA, RG 59, enclosing a translation of a Villarreal decree of July 14, 1915.

[8] When Huerta became an open dictator in late 1913, and as such eliminated the Catholic party as a political force, *El País* lost its enthusiasm for him. Beginning in December, 1913, Huerta continually harassed the paper, frequently closing it.

[9] "The Catholic Church and the Mexican Revolution," submitted as Document A in R. H. Tierney to Bryan, October 17, 1914, file 812.404/22, NA, RG 59. Tierney apparently wrote the paper.

nationalism, or even xenophobia, became inextricably intertwined with the Church question. To Villa all Spaniards were pernicious, be they merchants, *hacendados*, teachers, or priests, and they had to go; this he clearly demonstrated in both Chihuahua and Torreón.

Second, and perhaps of greater import, was an assumption that most clerics accepted and most revolutionaries rejected: that, given the situation in Mexico, law could do little to assuage the miserable conditions. One Catholic writer put it succinctly—referring to the Indians, he said: "They are innocent and poor, but Christians. There is no other force capable of restraining them, no other consolation in their present misery, and no other hope of uplifting them except the Catholic religion."[10] Firm in this belief and fearful of the corrupting influence of lay education, which emphasized the material rather than the spiritual, many clerics objected violently not only to public education but also to any secular tampering with the existing order. Consequently, they frequently lumped labor leaders, socialists, revolutionaries, anarchists, and bandits together as being fundamentally the same, and evil. The unidentified priest whom Tierney depended upon for his description of religious persecution in Guadalajara dismissed Colonel Esteban Baca Calderón as a "one time school master and afterwards an inmate of San Juan de Ulúa prison and now a shining light in the Constitutionalist army, although without any education and evidently without principle,"[11] overlooking the fact that Baca Calderón spent his years in prison for the crime of leading a strike in Cananea in 1906. He showed the same ignorance and contempt for General Diéguez, Calderón's companion in both strike and prison, as "once a miner at Cananea and a resident for several years in San Juan de Ulúa prison on account of a mine theft committed by him at Cananea." Given these circum-

[10] Ibid. The author, probably Tierney, stated that the "native Indian tribes number about ten million," a figure about double that given in the 1910 census. Since Tierney had interviewed a number of exiled clerics, his views probably represented theirs. It should be pointed out, however, that many clerics and laymen accepted the responsibilities implicit in Leo XIII's *Rerum Novarum* and dedicated themselves to social uplift and economic improvement within Christian principles.

[11] "Religious Persecution in Guadalajara," Document B, ibid.

stances, it is perhaps understandable, even if not justifiable, that th Constitutionalists assumed clerical ill-will unless they had evidenc to the contrary.

The third circumstance concerned Church wealth. Most Mexica assumed that the Church enjoyed enormous riches, and all co tenders hoped to tap that source. In view of the often despera financial conditions of those under arms at any time after the begi ing of the Constitutionalist movement, the leaders at all times- Huertista, Constitutionalist, Conventionist, Zapatista—used extr ordinary means to obtain funds. All groups, irrespective of affili tion,[12] seized property, confiscated goods, forced loans or donation and practiced every form of fund raising that the mind of man coul devise. Finance officers expected the clergy, as prominent citizen and the Church, as a wealthy institution, to contribute in the san manner as the bankers and banks, the mine managers and minin companies, the business leaders and business firms, or others wit liquid assets. Military commanders with men to feed and pay fr quently overlooked the fact that a parish priest or a Catholic scho had no ready cash; a cleric's failure to produce thousands of dolla at a moment's notice constituted prima facie evidence of enmit Villa simply followed the accepted practice when, after occupyin Chihuahua in December, 1913, he demanded contributions fro every citizen he thought could raise cash. From each priest h required a thousand pesos, and from the vicar general of the dioce five thousand. They all pled poverty, but they all raised most of th money when threatened with death.[13] To Villa this action prove dishonesty, not poverty.

For whatever reason, clerical persecution emerged early and gre constantly, the nature and the intensity of the acts depending upo the disposition of the military leader in command at the momen

[12] Records in AGN, ADN, NA, as well as newspaper accounts, attest to th almost universal practice here mentioned. The records show no real distincti among the contending groups as to methods, save that the Huerta governme tended to exempt parish priests and schools.

[13] Letcher to SecState, January 26, 1915, file 812.404/52, NA, RG 59. Frigh ened parishioners donated the money to the priests, who in turn surrendered to Villa.

In the early stages the actions tended to be either fiscal or xenophobic. As the revolutionaries occupied town after town their officers demanded money from the clergy, confiscated properties thought to be Church owned, and exiled foreign clerics.[14] Fleeing clerics—priests, brothers, nuns—left the schools untended and other properties unguarded, whereupon the revolutionaries seized these properties, as well. And when the revolutionists mistreated the foreign religious, often in near-barbarous forms, the national clerics took flight, leaving more schools closed and more churches unguarded. In early 1914 the national clergy began to take the brunt of the offensive. Antonio Villarreal locked all the churches in Monterrey soon after capturing that city in April, 1914.[15] When Obregón captured Tepic the following month he sentenced Bishop Andrés Segura to a prison term of eight years and exiled a number of national clergymen for the alleged offense of attacking the Constitutionalists through newspapers.[16] In Guadalajara a few weeks later, he exiled all foreign clerics, jailed all nationals, imposed on them a ransom of 100,000 pesos, closed all the churches, and converted the bishop's palace into a barracks.[17] By early June, 1914, occurrences of this nature had become commonplace throughout the regions dominated by the Constitutionalists; some priests continued their work without molestation, but they were the exceptions.

By mid-1914 the tempo increased and the direction changed. After Villa captured Zacatecas in late June, the victors executed five priests accused of various crimes against the Constitutionalists,[18] and

[14] This pattern may be followed through the 1913 documents in the 812.00 series and the 1914 documents in the 812.404 series, NA, RG 59. This account comes principally from these sources, since others are of doubtful validity.

[15] Hanna to SecState, June 1, 1914, file 812.00/12197, and July 11, 1914, file 812.404/4, NA, RG 59. Villarreal soon thereafter reopened the churches, but his activities went to the petty extreme of destroying the colonial religious statues.

[16] Alvaro Obregón, *Ocho mil kilómetros en campaña*, p. 123. The evidence that the clerics involved had been responsible for the newspaper attacks is thin indeed, but it convinced Obregón.

[17] Richard M. Stadden to SecState, January 18, 1915, file 812.404/49, NA, RG 59. Most of the churches were soon allowed to reopen. Diéguez was apparently more hostile than Obregón to the clergy.

[18] Canova to SecState, August 17, 1914, file 812.404/6, and Canova to Sec-

in August the Constitutionalist commander executed a religious at Toluca on the charge of looting.[19] By this time many clerics feared for their lives. The archbishops of Monterrey and of Guadalajara in late June requested political asylum of the Brazilian minister in Mexico City;[20] soon after Huerta fled, the archbishop of Guadalajara sought the haven of Havana, taking the archdiocesan jewels with him for safekeeping.[21] Not content with mere harassment of clergy—deadly though it might be—the revolutionists undertook a more direct assault. Villarreal in Monterrey set an example when he hauled the confessionals from the churches and made a huge bonfire of them in the principal plaza;[22] other local commanders or governors permitted masses only on Sunday and then under closely circumscribed conditions. In September the governor of Veracruz added a fillip later followed by others: he not only expelled all foreign priests, but also limited the number of priests who could officiate at religious rites. By the decree, towns with a population of up to ten thousand could have one priest and no city could have more than four.[23]

With the fighting over temporarily and the Constitutionalists ensconced in Mexico City in late 1914, Church and clergy gained a short respite. But with the renewed bitter war between Constitutionalists and Conventionists, the Constitutionalists again hounded the clergy at every turn by demanding money, arresting priests, and closing churches. Much more importantly, Constitutionalist field

State, August 10, 1914, file 812.00/12888, NA, RG 59. One of the accusations was that the priests had donated a "large sum" of money to Medina Barrón for the defense of the city. The priests undoubtedly had little choice in the matter.

[19] Father Francis C. Kelley to Bryan, April 17, 1914, file 812.404/112, NA, RG 59, includes three notarized accounts by priests who were jailed at the same time and who saw the victim's body suspended for public view. None of the three identified the victim, or even whether he was priest or friar. The "looting" charge came because he carried some sacred vessels from a church.

[20] Cardoso de Oliveira to SecState, June 26, 1914, file 312.12/20, NA, RG 59.

[21] Davis to SecState, July 21, 1915, file 812.404/96, NA, RG 59.

[22] After this first burning in late June, 1914, such acts became commonplace.

[23] W. W. Canada to SecState, September 25, 1914, file 812.404/16, NA, RG 59, transmitting a copy of the decree as it appeared in the *Periódico Oficial* of September 19, 1914.

commanders and governors added an interpretation to existing law with respect to Church ownership of real property. Since the beginning of the revolution some commanders had habitually seized convents and schools to use as barracks, stables, and warehouses, and occasionally revolutionary groups confiscated the contents of churches, as well; sacred vessels and *objets d'art* could be converted into hard cash. Until mid-1915 such actions seemed to be dictated by caprice, with no authority other than a vague concept of "enemy goods," but from that point forward the Constitutionalists developed a systematic legal justification for their acts under decrees of 1859 and 1874.

The Constitution of 1857, which so severely limited clerical and Church activities, divested the Church of most real property, but clearly left the Church with ownership of the church buildings, the "temples"; throughout the Díaz period both clericals and anticlericals assumed that the Church continued to hold the churches as a matter of legal right. Legal dominion over the churches nevertheless suffered from a degree of fuzziness as a consequence of an 1859 Juárez decree as supplemented by an 1874 Lerdo decree. The first, issued from Veracruz during the bitterest days of the War of the Reform, provided that "all the properties [*bienes*] that the secular and regular clergy have been administering, whatever the kind of property such might be," belonged to the nation. The 1874 law stated that "direct dominion over the temples, which in conformity with the law of July 12, 1859, were nationalized . . . continue belonging to the nation; but their exclusive use, conservation and improvement" would be in the hands of the "religious institutions" to which they had been assigned.[24] Despite these provisions, no one seriously contended that the churches and their contents belonged to the nation;[25] the revolu-

[24] The legislation concerning Church and clergy may be found in a number of works, the most convenient being J. Pérez Lugo, *La cuestión religiosa en México*, which is a compilation of legislation from the colonial period to the date of publication (1926).

[25] Tierney, in his long essay concerning the unjustified attacks on the Church ("The Catholic Church and the Mexican Revolution," Document A in Tierney to Bryan, October 17, 1914, file 812.404/22, NA, RG 59) did point out that during the Díaz period the Church did not in fact own the churches. This inter-

tionaries, according to their own terminology, "confiscated" churches, which would not have been necessary had the buildings and their contents already been national property.

In June, 1915, the Constitutionalists began to claim ownership of the churches as a matter of law, and Carranza began the first tentative steps to centralize authority over the property. When General Salvador Alvarado in Yucatán seized the archbishop's palace and converted it into a normal school, Carranza informed his general that, "since all properties attached to the Church are national property, the authorization to use one of them should be requested from this First Chieftainship."[26] But the general policy had not yet been solidified and accepted, and Alvarado did establish his normal school in the archbishop's palace later in the year. It will be noted that Carranza made no mention of existing law in his admonition to Alvarado. But the concept of national ownership based on the 1859 and 1874 decrees took hold with the field commanders and governors. Martín Triana in Aguascalientes in late 1915 instructed municipal presidents to make inventories of all churches, inasmuch as the temples were "the property of the Nation [and] the Government should be attentive of the conservation" of its property,[27] while Alfredo Elizondo in Michoacán claimed national jurisdiction over all "the real property either urban or rural, belonging to the Clergy, both regular and secular,"[28] on the basis of the two decrees. According to these precepts, then, the "nation" owned all the buildings, artifacts, decorations, or other appurtenances that the clergy had been using for any purpose. The occupation of a temple, or a seminary, or a school, or a bishop's palace and the use—even destruction—of all the contents of such a building were not confiscation at all;

---

pretation admirably fitted his thesis (that the Church suffered under Díaz and therefore was not averse to seeing him go), and therefore he made the point; but in other contexts he railed against the "confiscations."

[26] Carranza to Alvarado, June 29, 1915, ADN-Veracruz 1915.

[27] Decree of General Martín Triana, December 22, 1915, in *Periódico Oficial* (Aguascalientes), December 26, 1915.

[28] Decree of Alfredo Elizondo, undated [December, 1915], as translated and submitted in Francis C. Kelley to Lansing, December 13, 1915, file 812.404/110, NA, RG 59.

these actions were simply using a public facility in a manner different from its use in the past. And since the "nation" owned these facilities, any official of that nation's government could decide how to use them within the existing legal structure; until June, 1916, no general law governing the use of occupied Church property existed. Therefore when Carranza decreed that the central government had jurisdiction over all the buildings that the clergy had been accustomed to using,[29] he solidified the control at the national level rather than leaving it divided. The decree tended to bring some order to a chaotic situation and benefitted rather than harmed the Church as an institution. It provided that the Ministry of Finance had the responsibility for overseeing "the use, conservation, and improvement" of the buildings dedicated to worship and that the central government was the "only authority which can order the closing of temples or withdraw them from religious services." Henceforward no governor or local official could capriciously and on his own initiative even close the doors of a church, as had Villarreal in Monterrey two years before, much less convert a church into a barracks. Thus by the end of the preconstitutional period the political leaders accepted as a matter of practice and of law the national ownership and supervision over all goods and properties of whatever nature that might be used for religious purposes.

Law was silent on the question of the nationality of ministers of religion at the beginning of the preconstitutional period. Article 3 of the Constitution of 1857 gave the president power to exile "pernicious foreigners" without hearing or trial, but in those rare cases in which the president exiled foreign clergymen the action had always been accompanied by an explanation that the question at issue was "pernicious foreigner" and not "foreign clergyman." Even during the early days of the revolution this concept held sway. When Villa exiled the Spanish priests from Chihuahua in late 1913, or when Huerta General Ignacio Bravo exiled the parish priest of Chapantongo in May, 1914, he acted against a "pernicious foreigner" who

[29] Carranza decree, August 22, 1916, in Jesús Acuña, *Memoria de la Secretaría de Gobernación*, pp. 354–355.

merely happened to be a member of the clergy.[30] But under the shock of war the attitudes and the actions changed. During 1914 hundreds of foreign religious, male and female, found themselves brusquely exiled, not because they were pernicious but merely because they were foreign, and frequently they were accompanied by nationals also banned from the country. However, when Carranza in late 1914 "reformed" and broadened his original Plan de Guadalupe by including a number of projections for social change, his only mention of the religious question was a commitment to work for "dispositions which will guarantee strict compliance with the Laws of Reform."[31] He did not then believe that national interests demanded a national clergy. On the other hand, during 1915 and early 1916 governors and local officials in Sonora, Tamaulipas, Nuevo León, Michoacán, Jalisco, Durango, Aguascalientes, Veracruz, and Querétaro exiled foreign clerics as a matter of national interest. In the words of Governor Triana of Aguascalientes, "The Catholic priests who exercise their ministry in the State must be Mexicans of irreproachable conduct, subjecting themselves strictly to the duties of the ministry and without meddling [*mezclarse*] in any form in local or national affairs."[32]

The motivation or rationale for this hardening line regarding foreign clergy does not appear in the documents, but the frequent protests coming from other governments over the treatment of the clerics certainly had an influence. The United States, its government harried by insistent demands from Catholic organizations, took the lead in urging moderation and in protesting against the capricious exiling of innocent foreigners. The United States was not alone in this posture. Spain, Italy, France, Belgium—even Austria-Hungary—lodged formal complaints and frequently demanded, in polite terms, that the United States take decisive action to bring an end to clerical persecution in Mexico.[33] European and U.S. Catholics, vastly

[30] General Ignacio A. Bravo to SecGyM, May 20, 1914, ADN-DF 1914.

[31] Carranza decree, December 12, 1914, in Acuña, *Memoria*, pp. 323–326.

[32] Decree of Martín Triana, December 22, 1915, in *Periódico Oficial* (Aguascalientes), December 26, 1915.

[33] The 812.00 and 812.404 series, NA, RG 59, contain voluminous documentation on this subject.

overestimating the power of the White House and the Department of State, believed that a gesture from Washington would convince the Constitutionalists of their folly. At about the time Carranza entered Mexico City after Huerta's flight, Cardinal Gibbons of Baltimore insisted to Wilson that "one word" from the president would bring order.[34] Wilson was not so sanguine: "Alas, I am sorry to say that it is not true that 'one word from me to the Constitutionalist leaders would have a great effect and would relieve the sad condition of affairs' in Mexico with regard to the treatment of priests, for I have spoken that word again and again."[35] And Washington continued to speak "that word again and again" during the next two years. Confronted with the din of opposition to their actions regarding the Church and clergy, most Constitutionalists concluded that the safety of the government depended upon a purely national clergy for whom no foreign government could claim the right of protection.

Catholic participation in the educational process had long been a matter of public debate by 1913, with the issue occasionally exposing a simmering hatred for the clergy. The 1874 Reform Law forbade religious instruction in public schools financed by the national government, and a law of 1888 carried the process one step farther by banning clerics from teaching in such schools. Deputy Joaquín Casasús spoke for the most extreme anticlericals when he said in 1887 that the clergy wanted to hold the population in ignorance because if the child "read the scriptures he would lose his faith"; and if the child learned science "he could scoff at the fables in Genesis."[36] By the beginning of the preconstitutional period private and parochial schools existed side by side,[37] but the relationships were generally uneasy. Many Catholic laymen and some clerics objected strenuous-

[34] Cardinal Gibbons to President Wilson, August 18, 1914, file 812.404/8, NA, RG 59.

[35] President Wilson to Cardinal Gibbons, August 21, 1914, file 812.404/134, NA, RG 59. The president's quotation from the cardinal's letter was slightly in error.

[36] Cosío Villegas, *Historia Moderna, El Porfiriato: La Vida Social*, p. 553.

[37] Catholic schools prior to the Madero revolution constituted about 3 percent of the total number of schools and about 25 percent of the private schools.

ly to the concept of lay education as corrupting and morally destructive. On the other hand, many revolutionaries objected violently to Catholic education in any school, public or private. Antonio Villarreal in 1914 echoed in more virulent form Casasús's earlier condemnation when he charged that "in Catholic schools the truth is perverted; the pure white soul of childhood, the idealistic burning spirit of youth is deformed."[38] It was this conviction which led many military commanders to evict nuns and brothers from their schools and to place instruction in the hands of revolutionary laymen—or to leave them completely closed. By early 1915 opinion began to solidify. Francisco Coss in Puebla urged Carranza to issue a decree "prohibiting Catholic teaching and making lay teaching obligatory,"[39] and other governors and commanders effectively stifled Catholic education. On this issue, as on so many others, the Conventionist government saw eye to eye with its deadly enemies, and in the last session held in Mexico City the Convention passed by an overwhelming majority a proposal to eliminate the Church from any form of instruction save for that dealing specifically with dogma.[40] By late 1916 the Constitutionalists as a group still had not reached a consensus on the question, with the result that widely divergent patterns emerged.[41] In some communities the Catholic schools continued to operate openly and with impunity; in some they carried on surreptitiously; in some they remained closed.[42] Carranza himself made no comment on the question, but his very

[38] Villarreal decree, July 14, 1914, as transmitted by Silliman to SecState, July 27, 1914, file 812.404/3, NA, RG 59.

[39] Coss to Carranza, January 21, 1915, ADN-Puebla 1915.

[40] *La Convención*, May 10, 1915. The session was not intended to be the last, but on the following day a violent quarrel between the Villistas and the Zapatistas led to a boycott by the northerners, with the result that the Convention never again mustered a quorum in Mexico City. As a legislative body it came to an effective end.

[41] The picture is not clear from the documents, but it would appear that the majority of Catholic schools remained closed during 1915 and that some reopened the following year.

[42] An attempt in Tamaulipas to legislate the schools out of existence met with such violent opposition that the governor dropped the project. The documents are in ADN-Tamaulipas 1916.

silence indicated a lack of sympathy with those who desired to eliminate clerical teaching in private schools. The issue was resolved only when the Constitutional Convention met.

Developments during the preconstitutional period convinced most Constitutionalist leaders of the absolute necessity for some form of legal control over Church and clergy, for some legal structure that would divest the Church and its clergy of any political or economic power. These same developments also convinced most clerics and their friends that all Constitutionalists worked for the extirpation of all organized religion. R. H. Tierney best expressed this conviction to Bryan: ". . . the relentless war waged on Catholicism is not persecution of Catholicism, but a war on religion as such . . . Were the Presbyterian or the Methodist Church the dominant Church of Mexico neither would fare any better. An assault is made on God."[43] Not all men saw the situation with the eyes of Tierney. An elderly apostate Catholic in the United States informed the secretary of state that "any close student of Mexican affairs . . . will inform you that the chief element of deviltry, south of the Rio Grande, is the ecclesiocricy [*sic*], commonly called the church."[44] One U.S.-born Catholic, long resident in Mexico, expressed the view of the more moderate Mexican anticlericals: commenting on an article in which former President Roosevelt blasted Wilson's Mexican policy and reported as fact all the rumors concerning rape and execution, he said: "Being an humble member of the faith he attempts to champion I cannot be charged with bias when I say that the church here needs reform and a little castigation will do it a world of good. I have seen nothing here such as is described in the article in question and doubt that anyone else has."[45] But moderation tended to disappear during 1915, particularly among the proclericals; any questioning of the veracity of the rumors regarding clerical persecution brought a quick and angry response. When Vicar General Antonio J. Paredes in Mexico City stated that he had been unable to authen-

[43] R. H. Tierney to SecState, October 17, 1914, file 812.404/22, NA, RG 59.
[44] John Lloyd to SecState, January 22, 1915, file 812.404/50, NA, RG 59.
[45] James W. Keys to C. M. Hitch, January 20, 1915, file 812.404/1, NA, RG 59.

ticate a single case of the raping of a nun within the Archdiocese of Mexico, and that he had no evidence to support the accusations circulating in both Mexico and the United States,[46] he was immediately charged with being a Carranza henchman so beholden to the Constitutionalist leader that he was willing to hide the hard truth.[47] Two months later the same churchman, sent to Veracruz under guard by Obregón, led a group of priests to protest publicly against the activities of exiled or expatriate priests as "unpatriotic and unnecessary";[48] the reaction against him was instantaneous and vicious. The campaign of vilification grew so intense that Silliman, "with the red blue blood of many Presbyterian forefathers flowing from [his] heart," came to his defense as a fine gentleman, a loyal Mexican, and a dedicated churchman.[49] But Silliman's voice went unheard, as did those few others raised on the same note. Clerical spokesmen had concluded that all Constitutionalist leaders, and those who supported them no matter how mildly, were godless. But the actuality was quite different.

In fact the Constitutionalists, although adhering to the principle of clerical regulation, differed widely among themselves with respect to the Church question. Obregón recognized the situation; as he readied himself to begin the campaign against Villa's forces, he urged Carranza to establish a policy: "Please tell me what line of conduct I should follow with the Catholic priests, because I think we should adopt the same line of conduct throughout the country to prevent each commander from working in isolation according to his own criteria."[50] But Carranza had a firmer grasp on the realities than did Obregón. Any attempt on his part to order every military man to "follow the same line of conduct" would undoubtedly have created disastrous discord within his own ranks. Carranza himself

[46] Antonio J. Paredes to Silliman, January 22, 1915, as translated and submitted in Silliman to SecState, January 30, 1915, file 812.404/58, NA, RG 59.

[47] Bryan to Cardoso de Oliveira, February 24, 1915, file 812.404/73a, NA, RG 59.

[48] Silliman to SecState, March 26, 1915, file 812.404/86, NA, RG 59.

[49] Silliman to SecState, January 1, 1916, file 812.404/109, NA, RG 59.

[50] Obregón to Carranza, January 17, 1915, ADN-Puebla 1915.

had no great antipathy for the priesthood; he allowed Spanish priests to continue their ministries in Veracruz long after he established his capital there, he treated with deference Paredes and the other priests sent to Veracruz by Obregón, he discouraged the closing of churches, and he had no sympathy for those who wished to eliminate Catholic schools. Antonio Villarreal and Luis Caballero, on the other hand, gave strong evidence of anti-Catholicism and perhaps atheism. To them the theology, not merely the priesthood, was at fault. Between Carranza on the one hand and Villarreal on the other lay a vast gulf, but clerical spokesmen put them all together, and every atrocious act by soldier or officer, drunk or sober, was held to be expressive of the "revolution." To these spokesmen, these acts *were* the revolution and not, as Paredes held them to be, "a sad consequence of the revolution which . . . moved the very foundation of [the] country."[51] The inability of most clerical spokesmen to make a distinction between the Carranzas and the Villarreals, and their insistence on the monolithic nature of the Constitutionalist movement, drove many Constitutionalist leaders into a hardened position ill befitting their own beliefs.

Intimately related to the religious question was that of land tenure, since one of the recurring charges against the priesthood was that the clergy exercised more zeal in convincing the peons to follow the orders of the *hacendado* than they did in convincing the *hacendado* to give aid to the landless peon. Of the magnitude of land concentration at the end of the Díaz period there can be no doubt, and it need not be examined here except in broad outline.[52] Haciendas of 100,000 acres—nearly 160 square miles—were common, and estates of more than a million acres existed in well over half the

[51] Silliman to SecState, March 26, 1915, file 812.404/86, NA, RG 59.

[52] The literature on the land problem is extensive in both English and Spanish, but most of it concerns the postrevolutionary period. For the status of land tenure in 1910 the best sources are Daniel Cosío Villegas, *Historia Moderna de México, El Porfiriato: La Vida Económica*; Fernando González Roa, *El aspecto agrario de la revolución mexicana*; Andrés Molina Enríquez, *Los grandes problemas nacionales*; and Frank Tannenbaum, *The Mexican Agrarian Revolution*. For a short summary, see my *Mexican Revolution: Genesis under Madero*, pp. 19–25, and *Mexico: The Struggle for Modernity*, pp. 198–211.

states. The total holdings under the name of land baron Luis Terrazas encompassed an area larger than Connecticut, Massachusetts, and New Hampshire combined. To be sure, these mammoth estates were largely confined to the arid north; but even in the highly populated central states, where three of every four people lived in rural areas, the haciendas dominated the landscape. In the small state of Tlaxcala the average *hacendado* owned over 6,000 acres, and in the nearby state of Morelos the sad remains of peasant villages moldered in hacienda cane. Nearly 70 percent of the Mexicans depended directly upon agriculture for a livelihood, but less than 2 percent owned land.

More devastating than the mere concentration of land, perhaps, was the low level of agricultural technology. With few exceptions, the *hacendados* failed to introduce new techniques, but many of them did bring in new crops more suited for the export market than for domestic consumption. As a consequence, the production of domestically consumed foodstuffs declined during the last decade of the Díaz regime; the nation produced less corn and beans in 1910 than in 1867 despite the 60 percent increase in population. After Díaz fell, Madero's tentative steps toward land reform produced nothing tangible, and even these ineffectual efforts came to an abrupt end with the Huerta coup. But when Carranza began his constitutional movement, the great majority of those who took arms under his rubric were rural laborers who expected some land reform as a consequence of victory.

"Land reform" in 1913 was a confused and confusing term; it was not a concept, but a congeries of ill-formed ideas. To Zapata and the men of Morelos, land reform meant primarily the restoration to the communities of the land upon which the *hacendados* had encroached over a period of two generations. To Lucio Blanco and Luis Cabrera, the term meant the establishment of an independent peasantry owning plots of sufficient size to maintain a family in comfort. To Pastor Rouaix, governor of Durango and soon to become Carranza's secretary of agriculture, it meant the curbing of the economic and political power of the great land barons, and to others it meant the development of a system that would improve agricultural productivity. All those imbued with the idea of land reform, however, agreed on one thing: the hacienda was the center of the problem, and the hacienda had to be curbed. As was only natural, then, few indeed of the *hacendados* gave any encouragement to the new rebellion.

During the hectic days of the bitter battles against Huerta; neither Carranza nor any of his advisors gave any serious thought to the solution of the agrarian problem. To be sure, Lucio Blanco, by fiat and without recourse to law, seized and subdivided a hacienda near Matamoros in 1913,[53] Rouaix in Durango decreed hacienda expropriation in October, 1913[54], and Constitutionalist officials a few months later did expropriate and subdivide land near Agua Prieta,[55] but these were sporadic actions rather than thoughtful programs. The peasants of Morelos occupied and worked land owned by *hacendados* whom they drove from the state, and peasants all over the nation took over lands abandoned by those owners who fled the fire of revolution. But land reform as an internally consistent concept, as an organized approach to a significant economic and social problem, received virtually no attention from the Constitutionalists. The complete lack of any generally acceptable plan was perfectly demonstrated by the Torreón Conference a week before Huerta's hasty flight. Among the recommendations coming from this meeting of Villistas and Carrancistas was the following: "The present conflict being a fight by the disinherited against the abuses of the powerful, . . . the Divisions of the North and of the Northeast promise solemnly . . . to emancipate the peasants economically, by making an equitable distribution of lands or by other means which tend toward the RESOLUTION OF THE AGRARIAN PROBLEM."[56] All de-

[53] The land came from the Hacienda Las Borregas, belonging to Félix Díaz. For the documents, see Manuel González Ramírez, ed., *Planes políticos y otros documentos*, p. 165.

[54] Lands so expropriated were not to be free gifts; the village was required to pay for the cost of the land. For the decree, see Pastor Rouaix, *Génesis de los artículos 27 y 123 de la constitución política de 1917*, pp. 277–280.

[55] C. G. Soriano to Zubarán Capmany, April 15, 1914, and Zubarán Capmany to Soriano, April 17, 1914, ADN-Sonora 1914.

[56] "Pacto de Torreón," July 8, 1914, as given in González Ramírez, ed., *Planes políticos*, pp. 152–157. The emphasis was in the original.

voted revolutionaries accepted the need for "reform," but none knew the form it should take.

If Carranza had any fixed ideas on the subject, he failed to divulge them. During September he did agree, as a means of wooing Zapata into his camp, that land reform would be a legitimate topic of discussion at the proposed convention, but he did not elaborate on the subject.[57] When he finally did express himself on the general question of land reform in late 1914, he did it in sweeping terms; in a decree that came to be known as the Additions to the Plan de Guadalupe he included the following: "The First Chief of the Revolution in Charge of the Executive Power will issue and put into effect, during the struggle, all those laws, dispositions and means leading the way to give satisfaction to the economic, social and political necessities of the nation, putting into effect those reforms which public opinion demands as indispensable to establish a regime which guarantees the equality of Mexicans among themselves; agrarian laws which favor the formation of small holdings, dissolving the latifundia and making restitution to the towns of those lands of which they were unjustly deprived."[58] In drafting the decree Carranza obviously had neither great enthusiasm nor clarity of objectives, but he was playing to popular demand. He put the greatest emphasis on the creation of an independent peasantry, it will be noted, and quite clearly perceived the *ejido* as an indigenous institution. With respect to the *ejidos*, he wished only to rectify an injustice, not to create a new land-tenure system. Had the "restitution to the towns of those lands of which they were unjustly deprived" been executed with scrupulous regard for law and justice, only a tiny proportion of the agricultural population would have been affected. Most of the villages lost their lands through the application of the Ley Lerdo and the Consti-

[57] For a thorough discussion of the negotiations between Carranza and Zapata, see John Womack, *Zapata and the Mexican Revolution*, pp. 191–211.

[58] Carranza decree of December 12, 1914, in González Ramírez, ed., *Planes políticos*, pp. 158–164, and Isidro Fabela, ed., *Documentos históricos de la revolución mexicana*, I, 463–469. The decree is also sometimes called the Plan de Veracruz.

tution of 1857, not through the chicanery of the *hacendados*. The problem was not one of restitution; it was one of creation.

Some weeks later, on January 6, 1915, the first definitive law regarding the method for land distribution emanated from Carranza's office. Under the terms of the decree,[59] the governor or the military commander of any state then controlled or later to be conquered by the Constitutionalists was authorized to restore or to create agricultural villages through the expropriation of privately owned land if necessary. For the purposes of administration and investigation, the decree created a National Agrarian Commission, state agrarian commissions, and local committees where needed. Villages seeking the restitution of their illegally seized lands, or those who could make no legal case for restitution but nevertheless needed lands, could petition the governor who, after consultation with his state agrarian commission, had the power either to approve or to disapprove the request. In case of a favorable decision by the governor, the local committee had the responsibility for selecting the land and surrendering it to the village immediately but provisionally. The National Agrarian Commission was to act only as a board of review, either approving or disapproving the state action; in the case of approval, the national government was then to issue a definitive title to the village. The affected landowner could apply to the courts for relief, but only for the purpose of determining the amount of compensation.

This decree served as the base for all future consideration of land tenure, but it was defective in many respects and met only a portion of the problem. It applied only to existing agricultural towns without specifying what constituted such a town.[60] Land could be expropriated only from haciendas contiguous to the town requesting it, and neither state agrarian commissions nor governors were furnished with guidelines concerning the amount or the nature of the lands justifiably subject to expropriation. The towns received immediate

[59] Lucio Mendieta y Núñez, *El problema agrario de México desde su origen hasta la época actual*, pp. 178–181.

[60] Since there was some confusion on this point in the original decree, a year later a decree specified that only existing towns could obtain land.

possession of the land, presumably, but since such possession was "provisional" both villagers and *hacendados* were left in a state of suspended animation, waiting for a slow bureaucracy to take action —and in the confused state of affairs until Carranza again established his government in Mexico in 1916 little could be done.[61] No provision was made at all to satisfy the demands of a multitude of sharecroppers, cash renters, or daily agricultural workers who lived outside the confines of a "town," or towns not contiguous to a hacienda; the decree thus touched only a small proportion of the agricultural population. And, finally, the wording of the decree left the ultimate disposition of the land in doubt, since it stipulated that the citizens of the town would enjoy the land "in common" until such time as special laws determined the method of "distribution." It appeared as though Cabrera, the principal author of the decree, and Carranza viewed the re-creation of the *ejidos* as a temporary and an emergency stopgap to satisfy a political rather than an economic need, and that, as soon as conditions settled, the individual villager would become the owner of a plot of land. Even though Carranza modified the decree slightly in 1916, this perception of the land problem and its solution never changed significantly.

Even though only Constitutionalists took part in the Constitutional Convention beginning in late 1916, and the attitude of those who had opposed Carranza had little direct bearing on the agrarian provisions of the new charter, the widespread appeal of agrarian reform is clearly demonstrated by the attention given the question by other groups. Of the various proposals or public manifestoes regarding land reform in the preconstitutional period in addition to the Carranza decrees, three merit attention, since they came from widely divergent sources and differed somewhat in detail.

The first of these to be considered was a Villa decree—probably written by Francisco Escudero—of May 24, 1915. To the northern

[61] Even though Pablo González definitively occupied Mexico City in August, Carranza refused to reestablish his capital there immediately. He maintained his government in Veracruz for some time and then moved to Querétaro. The National Agrarian Commission, with Pastor Rouaix as president, began its work in March, 1916.

group the acquisitions by individuals of land in fee simple occupied the most important place, and accordingly the decree authorized the expropriation of haciendas for the purpose of establishing small private holdings. Land parcels were not to be a free gift; owners were to purchase the land on credit with low interest rates, and therefore the program was designed to be self-financing. Furthermore, the original owners were to be paid *prior* to any division or occupation of the expropriated land. In this respect the proposal differed from the December, 1911, Madero agrarian law only in authorizing expropriation.[62] Villa made no attempt to define the minimum size of the parcels other than to state that they should be sufficiently large to support a family, but he did specify that no man could obtain a plot larger than he could work effectively and efficiently himself. The principal thrust of the decree, including the provisions for expropriating the sources of water and for limiting the size of the holdings, lay in the direction of improved and intensified cultivation and was based on the assumption that the haciendas by their nature could not or would not produce to the maximum. But Villa did not forget the villages. Apparently in the belief that all nonindigenous people would take advantage of the opportunity to buy land, but that the Indians would not, the decree provided for gifts of land to indigenous towns only. In contrast to the Carranza decrees, the Villa law provided that the arable land donated to a village would be divided into plots no larger than twenty-five hectares and distributed to heads of family for cultivation. Only the pasture lands and wood lots, the original *ejidos*, would be retained for common use.[63]

From the standpoint of the ultimate system of land reform as it evolved over many years after the end of the preconstitutional pe-

[62] In 1911 the Madero government was authorized by law to purchase hacienda land for resale to individuals, but could not induce the owners to sell at reasonable prices. See my *Mexican Revolution: Genesis under Madero*, pp. 211–216.

[63] Many years later Antonio Díaz Soto y Gama, somewhat mellowed with age, published an account of the Villa program in *El Universal*, April 22 and 29, 1953. He pointed out the great difference between the northern and southern views on the question.

riod, three parts of the decree stand out. The first was the limitation on the amount of land any man could own. The maximum allowable amount of land was to be set by the state governments, and all excess could be subject to expropriation if it were needed for either villages or private holders. The second was the provision for individual plots to be held by the villagers, such lands to be inalienable, subject to neither debts nor seizure. The indigenes, then, were considered as special wards of the state. The third provision of importance was that concerning the expropriation of the sources of water, absolutely critical for agricultural activity in the region over which Villa then held sway. This decree is the only important public declaration in the preconstitutional period that recognized water as a national natural resource over which the nation must exercise jurisdiction.

About a year later, in February, 1916, one of the bitterest enemies of the entire Constitutionalist movement felt the pressure of the tide for land reform and, in a gesture completely foreign to his own dubious past, which gave no indication of concern for social reform, came out strongly for sweeping changes. Félix Díaz had started a new revolution and hoped to attract followers. Díaz, who had been intimately connected with Huerta in the 1913 coup but who had been pushed aside by the stronger man, had been playing at revolution for months in the United States. In 1915 he established himself in New Orleans, where he plotted and counterplotted with Mondragón and Blanquet—about as reactionary a team as could be found—for a return to Mexico. He had ambition but, as one ex-Villista confided to a Department of Justice agent, "anything he would undertake would probably result in failure,"[64] and, according to another source, his "group is really small, and highly exaggerated by his real followers, to such an extent that both Generals Mexicuero [*sic*] and Aguilar have sent out messages from Oaxaca disclaiming any connection with him."[65] In spite of a long history of failure, including an

[64] Report by F. C. Pendleton, January 20, 1916, as submitted by A. Bruce Bielaski to Leon Canova, January 25, 1916, file 812.00/17220, NA, RG 59. Pendleton was investigating activities that might be a breach of neutrality laws.

[65] Carothers to SecState, February 7, 1916, file 812.00/17259, NA, RG 59. Carothers was then in San Antonio, investigating the activities of exile groups

inability to attract the bulk of the Mexican exiles to his support, he slipped out of New Orleans in late February,[66] carrying with him a great revolutionary plan that, he thought, would sweep him into power. The manifesto,[67] under date of February 23 and datelined Tierra Colorado, Veracruz, received wide circulation and excited some comment,[68] but it brought him little support. His past was too well known to be cleansed by an all-embracing manifesto of liberal reform.[69]

Despite the source, or perhaps because of it, the Díaz formula for land reform has some points of interest. Since it was designed to be the intellectual spearhead for a general coalescing of the malcontents in the heavily rural areas of Oaxaca and Veracruz, it presumably reflected the aspirations of the farm folk—or at least Díaz's perception of those aspirations. It was not an expression of Díaz's view of the land situation, but an expression of what necessity imposed on him to state as his point of view, and since about one-third of the total proclamation dealt with the land problem, the would-be savior of Mexico certainly felt that necessity keenly. First, the government he hoped to establish would give special consideration to villages claiming they had been despoiled of land; all such pleas were to be

---

plotting revolution. He was particularly interested in four factions, all of whom believed in the "sure fall of Carranza." The generals referred to were Guillermo Meixueiro and the aged and irascible Higinio Aguilar.

[66] According to information received by Carothers, Díaz left New Orleans on February 24, but Luis Liceaga, Díaz's adulatory biographer, gave the date of February 18.

[67] The plan is given in full in González Ramírez, ed., *Planes políticos*, pp. 223–227.

[68] The plan was republished in El Paso on February 29 (Carothers to SecState, February 29, 1916, file 812.00/17333, NA, RG 59).

[69] Díaz did not actually land in Veracruz. Shipwrecked on the Tamaulipas coast, he and his companions were arrested and sent to Matamoros and then to Monterrey, where he managed to convince the authorities that he was a simple fisherman who had had the bad luck to lose his vessel. He was allowed to go to Mexico City in May, and from there he journeyed, still disguised, into the territory in which the rebel Juan Andreu Almazán still operated, and the two finally got to the state of Oaxaca. There he put himself at the head of rebel forces led by Meixueiro, and for the next four years caused varying degrees of trouble but posed no threat to the government.

given preference over other legal matters, and all claimants were to be exempt from the payment of legal fees. More importantly, he proposed an ejidal program not differing significantly from that already decreed by Carranza, including expropriation of hacienda lands for the purpose. Tied in with this proposal was one that prohibited the division of land in existing *ejidos* unless desired by the villagers themselves. Going well beyond the Carranza decree, but somewhat paralleling Villa's, he provided for the expropriation of hacienda lands for the purpose of "satisfying in each region the demands for lands requested by the working classes, in conformity with a special law to be enacted." Whether he included in his "working classes" (*clases trabajadores*) all laborers or only agricultural workers is not clear. Like Villa, too, he gave some attention to the water problem, but in quite a different form; he merely identified "irrigation works necessary for the lands of the agricultural towns or colonies" as being of "national interest" and promised a "prompt execution" of such works once he had established his government. But he did include two original thoughts: governmental control over the amount of rent paid by those working on shares,[70] and a general reworking of the property tax laws to give the small holder, rather than the large, an advantage.

Two months later, in April, 1916, the sad remnant of the Convention, consisting of Zapatistas only but clinging to the mirage of power as a sovereign revolutionary body,[71] in Jojutla, Morelos, enunciated its political-social reform program.[72] Since this was a Zapata document, predictably the agrarian program headed the list; but curiously only a minor portion of the total program concerned the land

[70] Traditionally two forms of rental agreements were made, "partnerships" (*aparcerías*) and "sharecroppers" (*medieros*), both of which gave the landowner a share of the crop. The renters frequently complained of the inequities of the arrangements and insisted that the owners often made demands not included in the original verbal agreements.

[71] Some members still claimed that they represented some of the northerners —Francisco A. Salinas representing Urbina, whom Villa had executed the year before, and Agustín Preciado representing Cabral, who had long since ceased military activity, for example—but this was a façade.

[72] The plan is given in González Ramírez, ed., *Planes políticos*, pp. 123–128.

question. The agrarian articles differed little in concept from those of Zapata's Plan de Ayala of 1911. The ejidal system was to be restored through either restitution or donation of expropriated land, *latifundismo* was to be destroyed, and small landholdings were to be created by furnishing "to each Mexican who asks for it the amount of land that will be enough to attend to his necessities and those of his family, with the understanding that preference will be given to the rural laborers [*campesinos*]." These provisions added nothing to the general pattern, which had already developed elsewhere, but the Zapatistas also had something original. One of the aims of the revolution, the program said, was encouragement to the development of agriculture by "founding agricultural banks which will provide funds for the small agriculturalist, and investing whatever sums might be necessary in irrigation works, reforestation, means of communication and all other kinds of agricultural improvement works so that our soil will produce the wealth of which it is capable." Tied closely to this idea was a plan for the establishment of agricultural schools and experimental stations "for the teaching and application of better methods of cultivation," an advanced concept for the time. And, finally, the plan enunciated a base upon which to compensate the landowners for the expropriated properties: the value of the land that they themselves had declared for fiscal purposes. Since the *hacendados* notoriously undervalued their properties for the tax rolls, payment on that basis would be, and later was, a heavy blow.

In a combination of the proposals enunciated in the preconstitutional years may be found every basic idea ever developed with respect to land reform in Mexico: *ejidos* for both indigenous and nonindigenous agricultural villages, ejidal lands worked in common or individually, a class of small landowners outside the *ejidos*, limitation on the size of land holdings, nationalization of water resources, indemnity on the basis of tax evaluation, establishment of special agricultural credit institutions, improvement of communication for agricultural purposes, and government aid to technological change. But the mere fact that the ideas were current did not mean that they were acceptable to all men whom the revolution had thrust into positions of power, and even the acceptance of the basic tenets did not necessarily mean an agreement on the details of administration. Francisco Múgica and Luis Manuel Rojas, for example, agreed on the principle of ejidal restoration, but they differed fundamentally on both the definition of an agricultural village and the methods to be used in restoring the institution.

But on some points all Constitutionalists agreed—and by late 1916 all public officials could be so classified in spite of the bitter quarrels then raging over membership in that exclusive club. First and foremost they agreed that Mexican agriculture was a national, not a personal, matter and that the national government had the responsibility for changing the tenure and productive systems. In this they utterly rejected the porfirian precept that no land problem existed. They insisted that land tenure had social as well as economic implications, and that Mexico could not advance unless the nation rectified the disastrous condition in which nearly three-fourths of the population lived. Second, all Constitutionalists agreed that land, as a national asset, was subject to the general principle of public utility and that as such its use could be determined by law; if the government could legally control the use of roads, or telegraph lines, or railroads, or navigable rivers, it could also control the use of land. Water, as an absolute necessity for irrigation in most parts of Mexico, was so intimately related to the land that it too was a subject of public interest. And furthermore, all agreed that expropriation, in contradistinction to confiscation, must be used. In view of the many accusations current, both in and out of Mexico,[73] that the revolutionaries were communistic, socialistic, anarchistic, or what-have-you, with no respect for law or property, the consistency of this respect for property rights is striking. Even Zapata, who hated the *hacendados* with an intensity of passion that was almost pathological, steadfastly stood by the principle of indemnity for properties taken.[74] He and his men occupied the land and worked it on an ad hoc basis, but

[73] For example, see Jorge Vera Estañol, *Carranza and His Bolshevik Regime.*

[74] He did advocate the confiscation of land belonging to men who "directly or indirectly" opposed the Plan de Ayala and of course did not consider compensation for the return of illegally acquired lands.

he never for a moment advocated permanent occupation without payment.

Even though all revolutionaries, whether following the Constitutionalist banner or another, agreed on the necessity for land reform, their precepts were not universally hailed. There were still great numbers of affluent men, nationals and foreigners alike, who damned and condemned any change in the tenure system as impolitic, unnecessary, and dangerous to the society and the economy. Toribio Esquivel Obregón in 1919 insisted that there was not and never had been an agrarian problem,[75] and a year later Emilio Rabasa held to the view that peon cupidity was responsible for the furor over the matter.[76] In the United States, Eder Cole Byam testified to the Fall Committee that he had "never heard of a land question" in Mexico.[77] But these represented the views of a tiny majority. All evidence suggests that Lucio Mendieta y Núñez correctly assessed the situation when, after analyzing the various demands for land reform over a thirty-year period, he wrote: "Consequently the agrarian question has not been, as [Esquivel Obregón and Rabasa] would want, a banner invented by politicians, but [it has] been a sad social reality."[78]

Whether the need for agrarian reform was "a banner invented by politicians" or a "sad social reality" did not particularly concern the peasantry. As the Constitutionalists effectively controlled more and more of the country in 1915 and 1916, and as word filtered out that the government had devised a system whereby land could be had for the asking, agricultural laborers in all parts of the nation began requesting their share. The request or demand for land was no mass movement; it depended too much on the proclivity or the imagination or the energy of the individual public administrator. Since the

[75] Toribio Esquivel Obregón, *La influencia de España y los Estados Unidos sobre México.*

[76] Emilio Rabasa, *La evolución histórica de México.*

[77] He so testified on May 1, 1920. His remarks may be found in U.S. Senate, *Investigation of Mexican Affairs*, II, 2688. Byam was noted for his animosity toward the Constitutionalists, having published a number of bitter attacks on the revolutionists. The Fall committee was attempting to drum up enthusiasm for U.S. intervention in Mexico.

[78] Mendieta y Núñez, *El programa agrario de México*, p. 176.

vast majority of agricultural workers neither read nor wrote, information dissemination about the 1915 decree depended upon oral communication, which was always spotty and often confused. The governor of Chiapas decreed that all ancient *ejidos* be restored, that each head of family in the rural areas receive five hectares, and that each existing landowner be allowed to retain only five hectares,[79] an order that not only distorted the Carranza decree but also proved to be a mathematical impossibility. Peasants in many areas of Hidalgo simply occupied the land without benefit of legal prescription.[80] Military authorities in Sonora gave land to individual Yaqui soldiers,[81] even though the Carranza decree did not encompass such gifts. In Puebla the indigenous agrarians felt they had a greater claim than the nonindigenous peasants and supported their claim with force.[82] In Aguascalientes lands unplanted in the spring of 1916 were distributed among rural workers for the annual planting only.[83] And so it went from state to state and district to district, without cohesion and without plan. But when the Constitutional Congress met in December, 1916, an idea of agrarian reform dependent upon land redistribution had become a firmly fixed phenomenon.

Land reform was a part of the public domain. The agricultural situation touched so many people in such sensitive spots that the vast majority of the revolutionary officers, and most of the men, knew a problem existed even if they had no solution to it. But in another area much less a question of popular concern, the revolutionary leaders began to develop policies that brought profound changes as they became a part of the Constitution of 1917. The relation of the society to the subsoil became an issue of the utmost importance.

Traditionally, Mexican and Spanish law assumed subsoil deposits to belong to the nation rather than to the owner of the land. The minerals in the subsoil were a public utility, to be regulated and

[79] Luis Sánchez Pontón to Carranza, April 3, 1916, ADN-DF 1916.

[80] Juan G. Bodillo et al. to Carranza, May 1, 1916, ADN-Hidalgo 1916.

[81] Colonel N. Fierros to Captain Gerónimo López, August 25, 1916, ADN-Sonora 1916.

[82] A. Medina to Carranza, May 9, 1916, ADN-Puebla 1916.

[83] M. Triana to Carranza, May 22, 1916, ADN-Aguascalientes 1916.

controlled by the government for the benefit of the society at large rather than merely for the profit of the extractor or the concessionaire. On that assumption the colonial mining code had been drafted, and with that knowledge those who wished to develop mines both before and after independence began their work. But the Díaz mining code of 1884 violated the principle in that it specifically granted to the owner of the land all ownership of mineral fuels in the subsoil,[84] and therefore the oilmen who came after the turn of the century to exploit the oil fields did so with the explicit understanding that the landowner could do what he wished with any oil beneath his surface, and with the implicit understanding that oil exploitation would not be subject to regulations other than those dictated by fiscal necessity.[85] At the beginning of the preconstitution period, then, by law the government could grant mining concessions, establish all manner of regulations under which the ores could be extracted, cancel concessions if the miner failed to fulfill the conditions of the concession, and impose a variety of taxes on both the land and the product. But by law the government could impose no regulations on the oil industry; it could collect taxes only.

By the end of the Díaz period all the old and profitable precious-mineral mines, which had been exploited previously with antiquated equipment, had yielded their rich bounty. Improved technology and new transportation systems—nearly twelve thousand miles of railroad between 1880 and 1910—had made new deposits of precious metal amenable to exploitation, however, and had put within reach of world markets the enormous deposits of base metals, particularly copper, lead, and zinc. But the new technology demanded heavy investments from which a profit could be expected only over a long period of time, and the Mexican financier had neither the funds nor the temperament to become a modern mining entrepreneur; the nat-

[84] Nonmetallic minerals—sulphur, for example—were also included as belonging to the surface proprietor; coal, as a mineral fuel, fell into the same category. Laws of 1892 and 1901 modified this position slightly, but a law of 1909 definitely gave complete ownership of mineral fuels to the surface owner.

[85] The law of 1901 exempted oil captured on national lands from any tax other than the stamp tax. Even though no oil was ever found on such lands by the oil companies, oilmen frequently claimed exemptions under this law.

ural result was an overwhelming control by foreign concessionaires over Mexican mining, with U.S. concerns leading the pack.[86] Exactly what that investment was, and what share of the total in mining it represented, remains in some doubt, but one of the most often cited sources estimated that U.S. citizens had invested over a quarter of a billion dollars in Mexican mining and as a consequence controlled about 80 percent of the industry. In contrast, Mexican investment in mining reached only fourteen million, or about 4 percent of the total.[87] Clearly, any policy affecting the mining industry was of international import.

Foreigners even more clearly dominated the oil industry. Again, the amount of the investment is in doubt, but the pattern is not. The Mexican Oil Association, composed of forty-two foreign concerns involved in Mexican oil exploitation, estimated in late 1913 that the total investment in Mexican oil was about a third of a billion dollars; Mexican sources gave the total as about half that claimed by the foreigners. In either case, the sources agreed that U.S. interests represented well over half the total and Mexican investments less than 1 percent.[88] And during the preconstitutional period the industry boomed, going from about seventeen to fifty million barrels annually.

Even before the beginning of the preconstitutional period many thoughtful Mexicans, some of decidedly conservative bent, had begun to worry about the foreign domination of the extractive industries; they had begun to take tentative steps to curtail the tremen-

[86] An excellent summary of the technological and financial problems may be found in Marvin D. Bernstein, *The Mexican Mining Industry, 1890–1950*, Part II.

[87] The Letcher Report, in *Daily Consular and Trade Reports, 1912*. Consul Marion Letcher in Chihuahua submitted the report, as compiled by William H. Seamon.

[88] See Mexican Oil Association, *Boletín de valores petroleros*, 1, no. 2 (1913): 1. The report claimed that the oilmen exaggerated the investment in order to make the profit appear smaller than it actually was. In 1914 the U.S. War Department attempted to determine the kinds and value of all investments in Mexico, including foreign and domestic. The report agreed with the Letcher Report on mining, but gave a total investment in oil of slightly more than 25 million, of which the U.S. held 15 million (see "American and Foreign Investment in Mexico," March 14, 1914, file 812.503/19, NA, RG 59).

dous advantages those groups enjoyed under Mexican law. Heated debates over a new mining law in 1910, the terminology of a mining-safety law in 1911, and the "Mexicanization"[89] of the railways in that same year all demonstrated a growing nationalism that bordered on xenophobia. With the foreigners owning about 70 percent of the total value of *all* money invested in Mexico in any form,[90] the Mexicans had cause for worry; foreigners literally owned the country, and in their enterprises they reserved for their own nationals the most attractive positions while they relegated the Mexicans to jobs of inferior responsibility and compensation. Even had there been no violent revolution, the probabilities are great that the government in time would have begun to impose a greater degree of control over the extractive industries. The enterprises were too profitable and their contributions to the treasury too small, the concessionaires had been granted too many advantages and had not been held to enough responsibilities. The revolution destroyed so much wealth and at the same time created such huge demands for money to purchase arms and ammunition that it made new controls and taxes inevitable. By the middle of the preconstitutional period, then, the revolutionary leaders demanded some form of solution to three major problems regarding the extractive industries. The first of these was to tighten up the terms of the concessions that had been granted by Díaz to mining companies so that both Mexican labor and the Mexican government could profit. The second was to regain control over the subsoil with respect to mineral fuels, and the third was to revise the tax structure to bring greater income to the government.

Of the three problems, the most difficult by far was that of regaining control over the subsoil. By 1913 the two greatest oil producers, Lord Cowdray of England and Edward Doheny of the United States, controlled millions of acres of oil land through purchase and lease.

[89] A Madero-sponsored law that was designed to displace foreign personnel from the operation of the lines.

[90] The various estimates agreed that the United States owned about one-half the total investment, the Mexicans between a quarter and a third, and the British about one-sixth. A number of other nations, headed by France, controlled the remainder. Peter Calvert (*The Mexican Revolution, 1910–1914*, pp. 19–21) concludes, however, that British and U.S. investments were about equal.

Each had brought in gushers that produced at a fabulous rate: Doheny's Casiano No. 7 spewed out about nine million barrels, one-third of the total Mexican production, in 1913. Furthermore, other foreigners had moved into the potentially productive regions and along with Doheny and Cowdray had expended enormous sums in building pipelines,[91] railroads, refineries, loading facilities, and tanker fleets. From the Doheny fields north and west of Tampico to the Cowdray fields almost two hundred miles south near Papantla and Poza Rica, the foreigners owned or controlled virtually every acre of potentially productive oil land. Only a minute portion of the land had been exploited, but under existing law the companies owned the oil under the surface. The question arises: How had Mexico, with its long tradition of maintaining public control over subsoil deposits, allowed itself to get in a position that prevented either public control or public profit? The answer seems to be a compound of economic philosophy and of ignorance, with no touch of illegality or lack of ethics on the part of the government.[92]

The existence of oil seepage in the Gulf coastal region had been known for centuries; both the pre-Hispanic native population and the colonial Spaniards used the thick viscous exudate for a variety of purposes, but in general both indigene and Spaniard considered the pools to be dangers rather than assets. The first attempt to drill for oil there, only ten years after Drake's successful well in Pennsylvania, proved to be a failure, as did others in the following years. These failures had completely convinced the Mexican geologists that the region had no exploitable oil deposits, and even after the first productive wells were completed the national Geological Institute continued to insist that the area was barren of any real wealth. The

[91] In constructing the first pipeline, Doheny was unable to obtain easement rights to complete the way until the Díaz government forced a reluctant landowner to allow the line to be laid (see Pan American Petroleum and Transport Company, *Mexican Petroleum*, pp. 31–33).

[92] Even the Cárdenas government, which was looking for some reason to condemn the oil companies for their illegal activities, exculpated the Díaz government from any ill intent or illegal act (Government of Mexico, *Mexico's Oil*, pp. 11–12).

Mexican geologists were not alone in their assessment. A number of British and U.S. experts gave adverse reports, and as late as 1911 a U.S. geologist insisted that the region had only limited oil deposits.[93] By the time the Mexican government awakened to the fact that the zone did indeed contain incredibly rich deposits, foreigners had acquired almost all the potentially productive lands. Added to this ignorance concerning the area's true potential, the Díaz government operated under an economic theory that held that fierce competition among private groups would inevitably bring economic growth. With Doheny and Cowdray vying for the riches, the theory held, wealth and welfare would come to the Mexican nation.

The first step of any consequence in establishing control over the industry came from the Constitutionalists even before the final victory over the "usurpation." Cándido Aguilar, whose military victories in northern Veracruz induced Carranza to appoint him governor, in early August, 1914, issued a decree from Tuxpan that was an augury of things to come, although its application at the moment caused little concern, since it merely stipulated that any transfer of property, through sale, rent, or mortgage, in the oil zone must first have the approval of the government.[94] But the rationale for the decree was a bit more impressive than the principal terms. Almost all the oil land, Aguilar said, had been alienated "in a form disastrous for the [original] owners" and was giving "fabulous fortunes" to "foreign companies who are not resigned to allow their interests to suffer even when the Mexican Fatherland is passing through dolorous times." The revolution to that time had clarified, he charged, "the threat for the Mexican nation which the domination by foreign capital in the zone has come to constitute," and since "all national progress should have the imprescriptible condition of being beneficial for the natives and never dangerous for [Mexican] integrity," some control had become a necessity. Two assumptions are clearly

[93] Pan American Petroleum and Transport Company, *Mexican Petroleum*, pp. 26–36.

[94] Decree of August 3, 1914, in González Ramírez, ed., *Planes políticos*, pp. 166–167.

manifest in the decree: the oil companies were antagonistic to the Constitutionalist movement and considered themselves to have special rights, and the companies engaged in all kinds of chicanery to cheat the unsuspecting nationals out of their rightful share in the bonanza.

The first assumption had a basis in fact, since the companies had protested bitterly and frequently whenever any military action of any kind was either contemplated or in progress in any region in which the oilmen were working. Aguilar had heard frequent rumors to the effect that the companies urged Great Britain or the United States or both to take over the region to assure continued oil production. Before they attacked Tampico in May of that year, the Constitutionalists had been threatened implicitly with intervention if the military action threatened the city's oil installations. To Aguilar the most irritating aspect of the entire situation was that the oil companies had contributed nothing to the Constitutionalist treasury but had persistently interfered with military operations.

The validity of the second assumption rests on an interpretation. Some landowners who sold their properties at the going rate for unproductive ranch land later felt themselves victimized when the land supplied extraordinarily productive wells. The Potrero del Llano property, for example, had at one time been offered for sale for a thousand dollars. What Cowdray paid for it is not publicly recorded, but one of its wells gave his company more than a hundred million barrels of oil and is reputed to be the most productive single well in the history of petroleum exploitation.[95] Since Mexican oil exploration was a gamble and necessitated the expenditure of enormous sums prior to realizing any returns—Cowdray had drilled a hundred dry wells in the Isthmus of Tehuántepec before he found a producer in Veracruz[96]—the oilmen bought lands and leases on the best possible terms. The degree to which the companies engaged in force or fraud is not clear. The companies steadfastly denied any such activities,

[95] Government of Mexico, *Mexico's Oil*, pp. 10, 14.
[96] Ibid., pp. 11–13.

but many property owners just as steadfastly contended that they were so victimized. One elderly lady from Tuxpan complained to Carranza that "since the times of Díaz, El Aguila has without right invaded lands belonging to me. I have asked for justice in vain,"[97] and hundreds of others made similar complaints. Whatever the merits of the accusations, Aguilar and Carranza believed them and acted accordingly.

The next step came from Carranza himself and, though not aimed specifically at foreign oil concerns, further stimulated animosities and distrust between the Constitutionalists and the companies. Soon after arriving in Mexico City, following the Teoloyucan Treaties, Carranza ordered the creation, in each tax district throughout the nation, of an assessment committee "the purpose of which [was] to register the real estate, and fix its value and the amount of capital invested."[98] Due to the confused political situation coincidental with the Constitutionalist-Convention war, Carranza made no attempt to enforce the decree until February, 1915. When the demand for compliance finally came, the oilmen were caught in a box; in the words of Consul Thomas H. Bevan: "The unproven oil land which was purchased years ago for insignificant amounts, on which taxes have been paid in proportion to the agricultural value up to the present time, may be valueless or worth millions of dollars. It is impossible to estimate the value of such lands until wells have been drilled. This is the question which confronts the oil men. If they place a valuation too low, they stand the chance of expropriation by the Government; on the other hand if they fix a high valuation they will have to pay taxes in proportion."[99] This was indeed a dilemma, since for the purpose of floating a loan in 1911 Doheny had been able to have his properties

[97] Virginia Casten, viuda de Newman, to Carranza, May 1, 1915, ADN-Veracruz 1915. Protests of similar import may be found in this file, in the ADN-DF file, and in the Archivo de los Presidentes for both the preconstitutional and the constitutional periods.

[98] Decree of September 19, 1914, as enclosure of Bevan to SecState, February 21, 1915, file 812.512/556, NA, RG 59.

[99] Bevan to SecState, February 21, 1915, file 812.512/556, NA, RG 59.

valued at over sixty million dollars,[100] but the value recorded for tax purposes was only a fraction of that amount.

In the meantime Carranza issued a decree that moved on the companies from another direction, limiting the rights of exploration and exploitation. Under date of January 7, 1915, he ordered all work then in progress "in connection with the exploitation of petroleum" immediately suspended. Under certain conditions work in progress could be continued under special license granted by Constitutionalist authorities, but no new work could be undertaken under any circumstances, pending the promulgation of a revised general law regarding petroleum. "The pools of petroleum encountered by virtue of operations executed in contravention of this decree will be considered the property of the nation,"[101] Carranza concluded. Some oilmen read the decree to mean that all wells would have to be shut down, and they protested vigorously, since many of the wells had such gas pressure that stopping the flow was a literal impossibility. But the last thing Carranza wanted was a suspension of oil exports; the export taxes were low but they brought a trickle of badly needed gold to Constitutionalist coffers. He quickly made it clear that the suspension concerned construction and exploration, not production.[102] He was primarily engaged in setting precedents by which the national government could ultimately bring about an effective control of, and reap profits from, the industry. This bent is clearly shown in the interpretation of the decree and in the manner by which permits were granted to terminate work already begun. When the Cortez Oil Corporation applied for a permit to complete the drilling operations on a well very near completion, Carranza's local inspector met the request on condition that the company "submit to the laws and regulations which the . . . Department will soon issue."[103] In the face of strong protests by both the oil companies and

[100] Pan American Petroleum and Transport Company, *Mexican Petroleum*, p. 36.

[101] Decree of January 7, 1915, as enclosure in Bevan to SecState, January 14, 1915, file 812.6363/161, NA, RG 59.

[102] Arredondo to SecState, January 17, 1915, file 812.6363/151, NA, RG 59.

[103] J. Cabrera to Mordelo Vincent, February 3, 1915, as enclosure in Bevan to SecState, February 6, 1915, file 812.6363/170, NA, RG 59.

the Department of State, Inspector Jesús Cabrera issued Cortez Oil a temporary permit to be valid until the revised law went into effect, at which time a new permit would be necessary.[104]

But by this time the Constitutionalists no longer had military control of the oil regions, except for the port cities. Manuel Peláez rebelled against Carranza in late 1914, ostensibly in support of Villa and the Convention, and effectively occupied most of the producing regions, which he still controlled in 1917. Under these conditions it was feckless to attempt any serious revision of the petroleum laws during the preconstitutional period or to enforce the decrees already promulgated. But the mere fact that he did not control the producing regions did not deter Carranza from making plans for the future, and in early 1915 he appointed a technical commission to study the industry "and its relations with the Government."[105] When the commission reported in April, 1916, it held that property rights were not absolute, and that both expropriation and taxes could be used as legitimate instruments of control if public utility demanded it. The report concluded by stating that it was "just to return to the nation that which is its own, the wealth of the subsoil, coal, and petroleum."[106] Thus the Constitutionalists made the final decision, long before the Constitutional Convention met, to restore national control over all subsoil deposits.

Cross-currents and bickering, as well as a fundamental ideological split during the preconstitutional period, somewhat obscured the changing thought with regard to the position of labor in the Mexican society, but here too the basic design had been completed before the

[104] Bevan to Lansing, February 11, 1915, with enclosures, file 812.6363/173, NA, RG 59. Bevan transmitted correspondence involving the inspector, the company, and his office. Bevan was particularly concerned lest agreeing to the demand would create a dangerous precedent.

[105] Decree of March 15, 1915, in Fabela, ed., *Documentos históricos de la revolución mexicana*, IV, 140. Carranza and his advisors were convinced that Peláez was a creature of the oil companies, armed and supported by them. It is certain that the companies paid Peláez regularly, but they claimed they were forced to do so in order to safeguard their wells.

[106] Lorenzo Meyer, *México y Estados Unidos en el conflicto petrolero, 1917–1942*, p. 68.

opening of the Querétaro Constitutional Congress. Until 1915 the Constitutionalist support came almost entirely from the countryside and the small towns; the common folk in the larger cities played almost no role in the movement against Huerta,[107] and as a consequence Constitutionalism had no strong urban military support until after the Carranza-Villa split. When the urban workers finally did join the struggle they did so under conditions that gave a strong impetus to the development of organized labor and established a base for a labor provision in the Constitution of 1917.

Prior to the Madero period the working man had no protection, in either law or practice.[108] Criminal syndicalist laws effectively prevented union organization, government troops ruthlessly suppressed the rare strikes, and in general the central administration devoted itself to the preservation of a docile labor force as an aid to industrial development. Díaz's fall brought an immediate change in attitude if not in law, and in the latter part of 1911 and throughout 1912 urban workers organized into unions to demand better working conditions. A rash of strikes and threatened strikes, some prevented through friendly government intercession, gave labor a sense of power and did bring some slight improvement in working conditions, but at the end of the Madero administration the urban laborer's condition was only a mite better than it had been in previous years.

But at least the beginnings of a national labor movement had sprung up. In July, 1912, a small group of foreigners and Mexicans—the most important of the latter were Antonio Díaz Soto y Gama, Manuel Sarabia, and Lázaro Gutiérrez de Lara—in Mexico City organized the Casa del Obrero Mundial, a frankly anarcho-syndicalist center dedicated to the destruction of the capitalist system through the media of the general strike and sabotage. Within a short time the Casa established branches in most of the major urban centers where,

[107] Inasmuch as Huerta controlled all the major cities during 1913 and continued to control the largest until within a month or two of his flight, the Constitutionalists had little opportunity to recruit urban workers.

[108] For a discussion of the conditions in the period prior to the preconstitutional, consult Alfonso López Aparicio, *El movimiento obrero en México*, and Marjorie Ruth Clark, *Organized Labor in Mexico*. Neither is completely satisfactory.

according to one labor historian, Casa spokesmen gave "ideological orientation to the syndicates, societies, resistance leagues, alliances, guilds, unions, and every class of professional association."[109] The Casa was not in the strictest sense a union; it was a clearing house for information and propaganda. But it attracted affiliates, particularly from the railroad, mining, and textile unions, even though the typical meeting sponsored by the Casa tended to be a forum for denouncing the capitalistic system and for expounding social theory rather than a conference for discussing the best means for bringing about an immediate improvement in working conditions. The radicalism of the Casa, with its emphasis on direct and destructive action, soon brought it into conflict with the mildly liberal Madero government, which suppressed its Mexico City newspaper, arrested a number of its Mexican leaders, and exiled the foreigners. As a consequence, the natural tendency of the anarcho-syndicalist to view government with suspicion hardened into outright opposition, and Casa leadership viewed the Huerta coup as a struggle between rival factions of the capitalistic class and, as such, of no particular interest to the true syndicalist. Organized labor, then, at least as represented by the Casa, initially stood aloof from the revolution.

Attitudes began changing slowly after Huerta consolidated his power. Madero badgered the Casa, but let it exist; Huerta suppressed it completely in May, 1914, and demonstrated no sympathy either for the laboring man or for labor organization of any stripe. As a consequence labor organization during the Huerta period stood still; it neither gained nor lost ground appreciably. The small established local unions continued as nascent but largely ineffectual groups, and as long as they posed no threat to his regime, through strikes or political activity, Huerta ignored their existence. Occasionally a union protested to the government that its members were subjected to military impressment, but since this method was normal for filling the depleted ranks of the federal army, the protests fell on deaf ears.[110] In the war-torn circumstances, of course, the unions

[109] López Aparicio, *El movimiento obrero en México*, p. 153.

[110] For example, the dock workers in Veracruz made such a protest in April, 1914, to Gobernación, which routinely sent it to the governor without comment

could do nothing about forming a new and cohesive national organization; transportation and communication difficulties forbade it.

Among the Constitutionalists, during the first year of their movement the condition of the urban laborer created not a ripple of interest. The Plan de Guadalupe made no reference to any social or economic question, and when Carranza in October established a formal governmental structure he delegated to Gobernación any question concerning "work." Not until near the end of the struggle against Huerta did anyone within the Constitutionalist ranks address himself seriously to the labor problem, and the first such action was merely a pragmatic decision in answer to a specific complaint. In early June, 1914, the cargo handlers in Tampico requested the intercession of the Constitutionalist port administrator, Francisco Múgica, in their struggle to retain a closed shop and to gain an increase in wages. After a series of meetings between company and union representatives, presided over by Múgica, the workers obtained most of their requests.[111] A few other commanders, confronted by similar situations, acted to bring a modicum of justice in special circumstances, but as yet no spokesman for the Constitutionalist cause had begun to establish a base for a general policy regarding unions or the role of labor in the society.

Shortly after Huerta fled, however, Carranza made his first direct statement with respect to the needs and rights of the laboring man. Arriving in Tampico in late July, Carranza in a flamboyant speech of victory promised to bring about social and economic amelioration even "before the establishment of constitutional order; before the necessary reform laws are transformed into interminable discussions in Congress." Among the reforms he vowed to inaugurate was an eight-hour day for all laborers throughout the republic.[112] With the Constitutional struggle against Huerta coming to an end, other lead-

or recommendation (Juan V. Martínez to SecGob, April 13, 1913, AGN-Gobernación—Varios 1913–1914, with attached documents).

[111] Armando de María y Campos, *Múgica: Crónica biográfica*, pp. 83–85.

[112] As in Fabela, ed., *Documentos históricos de la revolución mexicana*, I, 313–314.

ers began issuing generalized labor decrees. Governor Alberto Fuentes D. of Aguascalientes in mid-August established a nine-hour day for all laborers—including domestic servants—with one day of rest each week and without a reduction in wages.[113] Some three weeks later Pablo González by fiat abolished all indebtedness against agricultural workers and "artisans, servants, and all classes of employees in the cities, districts, and municipalities" within the states of Puebla and Tlaxcala. Anyone demanding the payment of past debts owed by the "needy classes" would be subject to fines ranging from one hundred to five thousand pesos; the general made no attempt either to define his terms or to establish a rationale for the decree.[114]

In San Luis Potosí, Governor Eulalio Gutiérrez in mid-September issued a sweeping decree in labor's behalf.[115] He established a minimum wage of a peso and twenty-five centavos for miners and a minimum of seventy-five centavos for all other workers, while requiring a weekly payment in legal tender "without discount." No employer then paying a wage greater than the minimum could reduce wages to conform to that minimum. The decree stipulated that the maximum number of hours of labor was to be nine, prohibited garnisheeing of wages, banned the seizure of homesteads as a result of civil suits, and guaranteed to the laborer the right to change his residence or his job if he desired. Furthermore, by the terms of the new law, Gutiérrez abolished all *tiendas de raya*[116] and required each *hacendado* or owner of an industrial establishment outside the cities to designate a plot of land to be used as a marketplace freely open to all venders and buyers. Finally, the decree established a state "Department of Labor" to supervise law enforcement, aid laborers in their search for better positions, and ultimately to force employers to "establish, in proportion to their capital and assets, a fund, the object of which will be works for the benefit of their own employees."

Whether Carranza played an active role in encouraging his offi-

[113] The decree, dated August 8, may be found in González Ramírez, ed., *Planes políticos*, pp. 168–169.

[114] The decree may be found in ibid., p. 170.

[115] The decree may be found in ibid., pp. 188–190.

[116] Company stores, reputedly selling inferior goods at high prices.

cials to take a sympathetic stance toward labor is moot, but inasmuch as both Pablo González and Eulalio Gutiérrez had been his close collaborators since the beginning of the Constitutionalist movement, it is safe to assume that their posture had the support of the Primer Jefe. In none of the cases, it will be noted, was the Constitutionalist cause in any way threatened by labor actions or demands, nor was labor organization an issue; each represented an act of justice, a gift to the laborers from Carranza's triumphant movement. But when the Constitutionalists occupied Mexico City after Teoloyucan, Obregón made a gesture in behalf of labor organization itself. He turned over to the Casa for use as its headquarters the Church of Saint Brígida and the adjacent Colegio Josefino.

The First Chief himself remained silent on the labor question for months after his Tampico speech; he took no public steps to fulfill the glowing promises of July. And when he did issue a statement, in his Additions to the Plan de Guadalupe of December 12 after the Convention forced him to evacuate Mexico City,[117] the reference to the worker was something less than monumental; he merely again promised "legislation for the improvement of the condition of the rural peon, the worker, the miner, and, in general the proletarian classes." But the military necessities imposed by the war against Villa and the Convention stirred the Carranza forces to further efforts, and it was this development that produced a commitment on the part of the Constitutionalists to place urban labor in a special category.

Carranza took two steps to woo labor into the Constitutionalist camp. First he designated Dr. Atl as his special agent to convince labor leaders that their only hope for ultimate advantage lay in committing themselves to military action in his behalf. In mid-January, Atl reported to Carranza,[118] he organized a "great meeting" in Puebla where he, Obregón, and others spoke; the enthusiasm of the la-

[117] The document in its entirety, including the long preamble justifying his actions to that date, may be found most conveniently in Fabela, ed., *Documentos históricos de la revolución mexicana*, I, 463–469, or González Ramírez, ed., *Planes políticos*, pp. 158–164.

[118] Atl to Carranza, January 18, 1915, ADN-Puebla 1915.

borers convinced him that he could persuade the "workers, students and middle class" to enlist in the Constitutionalist army. He organized similar meetings in other areas under Constitutionalist control, and when Obregón entered Mexico City in late January, Atl accompanied him to repeat his work but on a grander scale. Atl was not alone in his efforts in Mexico City; Obregón designated Alberto Pani to distribute food and money to the poverty-stricken, who had been caught between rising prices and little or no work.[119] Pani and Atl, one dispensing a dole and the other propaganda, did a magnificent job of bringing organized urban labor into the Constitutionalist camp.[120]

While Atl propagandized, Carranza began to lay the groundwork for a comprehensive labor code; whether political expediency or a search for social justice was the prime stimulus remains in question. For whatever reason, he commissioned José Natividad Macías and Luis Manuel Rojas, both of whom had been jailed by Huerta in his October 10 coup and both of whom had earned Carranza's full confidence, to draft a set of laws "in which the labor problem in its various manifestations was to be treated."[121] In January the two men presented the draft to the Primer Jefe, but Carranza and his principal advisors considered the proposals incomplete and therefore dispatched Macías to the United States to make a study of labor law and practice in that country. But the Macías-Rojas preliminary study had made one thing quite clear: if Mexico were to have anything approaching a uniform code affecting labor it would of necessity come from the national, rather than state, government. Accordingly, on January 29 Carranza decreed a change in the Constitution of 1857. That instrument, he said, assured the working man the right to a just wage and prohibited any contract tending to enslave the laborer; but

[119] Alberto Pani, *Apuntes autobiográficos*, I, 226–229.

[120] Constitutionalists in other areas also enlisted labor support. Antonio Villarreal, who commanded forces in the Monterrey area, prevailed upon Lázaro Gutiérrez de Lara, one of the originators of the Casa, to popularize the Constitutionalist cause along the border.

[121] At the Constitutional Congress on December 28, 1916, Macías outlined his role in developing the projected decrees (see *Diario de los debates del Congreso Constituyente*, 1916–1917, I, 725–734).

in spite of these provisions the laborer had become the victim of debt peonage and of exploitation by employers whose only object was to "obtain from a human being the greatest amount of useful labor and to remunerate him at the lowest price." Since these conditions needed to be corrected, and since the states had obviously failed to give due consideration to proper legislation, the new decree gave to the national government the authority to "legislate for all of the Republic on the subjects of mining, commerce, institutions of credit, and labor."[122]

In the meantime Macías had left for the United States, where he visited labor offices and industrial establishments in Chicago, Philadelphia, Baltimore, and New York. In those centers he attempted not only to gain a clear picture of labor law and practice in the United States, but also to determine what the situation was in England, France, and Belgium. Armed with this information, Macías returned to Veracruz where, after long conferences with Carranza, he drafted a labor code which, he later insisted, incorporated all the best thinking of the most modern industrial nations. The projected decree included provisions for a minimum wage, an eight-hour day with one day of rest in each seven, decent housing, the right to strike, equal pay for equal work, compensation for accidents, protection for the apprentice and sweatshop worker, and a variety of other rights designed to prevent exploitation and abuse.[123]

But long before Macías completed his work the combined efforts began to bear fruit. In early February those Casa directors who had remained in Mexico City, and who claimed to represent 52,000

[122] The decree may be found most conveniently in Fabela, ed., *Documentos históricos de la revolución mexicana*, I, 524–525.

[123] The project was never formalized into a decree because, said Macías, three conditions prevented it: (1) chaos incident to the war with Villa and the Punitive Expedition would have made enforcement impossible; (2) he and many others believed that the authority should be with the states, not the national government, and Carranza therefore decided to allow the Constitutional Congress to be the final judge; and (3) there was a lack of precise information with respect to economic conditions in the country that would allow the establishment of a minimum wage in each industry and section. The arguments are not particularly convincing. Had Carranza operated in general on these principles he would have issued no decrees at all.

workers, at a great public gathering "invited" all laborers to join Carranza in his redeeming work. After the triumph of the revolution, they said, those who had borne arms in behalf of victory would have an opportunity to establish "proletarian colonies where they will find all types of guarantees and facilities for living."[124] A few days later the Constitutionalists reached a formal accord with organized labor as represented by the Casa when on February 17 eight labor leaders signed a pact with Carranza's Secretary of Gobernación Rafael Zubarán Capmany for the purpose of "normalizing the relations" between the Constitutionalists and the workers.[125] By the terms of the agreement Carranza committed himself to issue laws for the improvement of working conditions, to give aid to laborers in cases of conflict with employers, and to either supply work or give subsistence to those laborers forced to abandon cities captured by the Conventionists. In return, labor agreed to furnish men to "garrison the towns under the control of the Constitutionalist government, or to combat the reaction," as well as to undertake an active propaganda campaign to "gain the sympathy of all workers in the Republic and of all the workers in the world for the Constitutionalist Revolution." All workers, male or female, recruited as a consequence of the understanding were to remain as units and were to be called, "whether organized in companies, battalions, regiments, brigades, or divisions, . . . 'reds.' "[126]

By the terms of the pact it would appear that Carranza received much more than he gave; but labor gained an enormous concession, which Carranza came to rue bitterly: labor was a distinct and separate element in the Mexican society, owing its loyalty to itself first

124 *La Prensa*, February 12, 1915. The newspaper was established by Obregón when he entered the city and published only during his six-weeks stay there.

125 The labor leaders were Rafael Quintero, Carlos M. Rincón, Rosendo Salazar, Juan Tudó, Salvador González García, Rodolfo Aguirre, Roberto Valdés, and Celestino Gasca, all affiliated with the Casa. Salazar and Gasca were among the original organizers of the Casa, and Gasca ultimately achieved the rank of general in the army.

126 The agreement may be found in a number of places; the copy used here is that published in Secretaría de Educación Pública, *Biblioteca enciclopédica popular: Documentos de la revolución mexicana*, pp. 83–86.

and to the nation second. The leaders of the Casa entered the fray not because a Constitutionalist victory would be beneficial to the nation, but because it would be advantageous to labor.

The labor leaders took quick steps to uphold their end of the bargain; on March 4 the first contingent of over three thousand men bound for military duty left Mexico City for Orizaba,[127] and within the next few days an additional six thousand either joined Obregón's army or went to Orizaba or Veracruz for equipping and training. From laborers recruited in Mexico City and the industrial centers to the east, six battalions were ultimately formed. Two fought under Obregón in the series of battles starting with Celaya, one joined Treviño in a bitter defense of the Tampico region in late March,[128] and three remained in the Veracruz-Orizaba sector to keep open the lines of communication, which were absolutely critical to Obregón's campaign against Villa.[129]

The extent to which the Red Battalions contributed to the final Carranza victory may be questioned,[130] but the effective use of that participation by the Casa may not. Every act of heroism or reported heroism by a member of one of the Red Battalions was made the subject of paeans of praise by Casa publications, and as town after town fell to the Constitutionalist armies Casa organizers moved in to begin their work. With the obvious sanction of the central authority —whether Carranza really approved of the pact may be questioned,

[127] *La Prensa*, March 5, 1915. Orizaba, the center of the textile industry, was selected as the training center and staging area.

[128] The battle, which reached its climax on March 23, was at El Ebano, about fifty miles to the west of Tampico on the rail line to San Luis Potosí. Had Villa's forces captured Tampico the result would have been disastrous for Carranza.

[129] López Aparicio, *El movimiento obrero en México*, p. 156, lists the service areas of the six battalions and also indicates the unions from which the men were recruited for each battalion. The First Red Battalion under Treviño, for example, was composed solely of workers from the national arms factory in Mexico City.

[130] The troops, as troops, were probably no more or less heroic or effective than others in the infantry. Those with Treviño and Obregón probably made the difference between victory and defeat or stalemate; over half of Obregón's infantry, which bore the brunt of Villa's charge in the second Battle of Celaya, were Red Battalions. But the six battalions represented only a very small proportion of the total number of men in the Constitutionalist army.

but he could scarcely denounce it while the military outcome remained in doubt—Casa representatives organized strikes and became the spokesmen for labor within the area dominated by Carranza's government. By mid-1915, when the ultimate victory of the Constitutionalists seemed to be clearly in the offing, the Casa with all its syndicalist labor philosophy was the oracle for urban labor.

In addition to the recognition that he constituted a major force in the Mexican society, the laborer benefited in other ways from the pact between Carranza and the Casa. Among all the organized laboring groups, the textile workers were the least enthusiastic about going to war; they had suffered too long and had been the victims too often of government hostility to accept at face value the promises made by the Carrancistas. Some textile leaders openly urged their men not to join the military action, but simply to take over the mills where they worked, an act in perfect consonance with anarcho-syndicalist teachings. In order to combat the trend, and to dampen hostility among the workers, on March 22 Carranza decreed a 35 percent increase in the daily wage and a 40 percent increase for piecework;[131] his public rationale was that the prices of the textiles had increased but wages had not. The decree also implicitly promised a generalized minimum wage for the textile industry at some time in the future. A short time later, immediately after the first battle of Celaya and in repayment to his Red Battalions, Obregón decreed a minimum wage for all workers in the states of Querétaro, Hidalgo, Guanajuato, and Michoacán[132]—states over which he did not, in fact, exercise effective military control. In many areas, as relative peace returned, the new Constitutionalist governors established schools for workers, intervened in behalf of labor in conflicts with management, established minimum wages, reduced the number of hours per day, decreed compensation for job-connected accidents or illnesses, and in myriad other helter-skelter ways indicated support for the laboring man and the labor movement.

Amicable relations between the Casa and Carranza were always

[131] The decree may be found in Acuña, *Memoria*, pp. 337–338.

[132] As reported in Obregón to Carranza, April 10, 1915, ADN-Guanajuato 1915. Carranza approved the decree some two weeks later.

tenuous, and even during the days of greatest peril in 1915 ma of the Casa's actions gave the First Chief grave concern. When decided in May to relieve General Francisco Coss as military co mandant of the state of Puebla in order to use his undoubted taler elsewhere, the Casa in the city of Puebla sponsored a huge prote meeting;[133] to Carranza the action appeared to be a meddling administrative-military affairs beyond the province of organized bor. A short time later the Veracruz Casa protested directly to C rranza's agent in Washington about the attitude of the U.S. gover ment;[134] the evidence of support for his position must have pleas him, but the Primer Jefe undoubtedly resented the intrusion of ganized labor into the field of international relations. The Pueb textile workers as an organization objected strenuously to the sta governor's appointments to judicial positions, saying that "the Rev lution died with these appointments";[135] in view of the governo obvious and demonstrated sympathy with labor's plight,[136] Carran and his advisors viewed the protest as churlish. These and simil evidences of political action by groups who labeled themselves laborers—not merely concerned citizens—convinced Carranza th Mexican labor had come to view itself as a special class with speci rights, to whom was owed special consideration. These provocatio may have influenced the Primer Jefe against putting the Macías pr posals into decrees.

But Carranza effectively concealed whatever irritation he ma have felt, and officialdom continued to give public support to the l bor movement for the remainder of the year. When Pablo Gonzál finally reoccupied Mexico City in August, he invited the Casa to tal up sumptuous quarters in the famous Jockey Club and also allowe many individual unions in the Federal District to establish their o

[133] F. Báez to M. Méndez, May 16, 1915, ADN-Puebla 1915.

[134] Comité Revolucionario de la Casa del Obrero Mundial to Arredondo, u dated, ADN-Veracruz 1915. The protest resulted from a June demand by Pres dent Wilson that the contending parties come to an agreement.

[135] F. Báez to M. Méndez, May 16, 1915, ADN-Puebla 1915.

[136] Many documents in the ADN-Puebla 1915 file demonstrate that Govern Luis G. Cervantes attempted to give aid to the laborers through price and wag regulation.

fices in the building. Inasmuch as the House of Tiles occupied by the Jockey Club had been the very symbol of porfirian economic and social philosophy, Casa occupation of the building implied that organized labor had arrived at a position of prestige and power.[137] Strikers in various areas continued to enjoy the support of the local Constitutionalist officials and, as the value of paper money declined, some governors required employers to pay their men either in gold or in an equivalent amount of paper money; the governor of Guanajuato decreed a 400 percent increase in paper money wages over a two-month period in late 1915.[138] But toward the end of 1915 Carranza's patience began to wear thin. The railroad workers brought the situation to a head with a series of strikes late in the year, interrupting the flow of goods and, in Carranza's view, generally disrupting an economy that was already in precarious condition. With the war against Villa still going on and with semistarvation in many blighted areas, Carranza could not let a small group of men undermine both the military effort and the economy. His answer was extremely simple, and effective; he merely incorporated all railroad workers into the army, subject to military law.[139] A short time later in Mexico City, Pablo González, mirroring Carranza's thought, expressed his concern: "Since the revolution has fought capitalist tyranny it cannot sanction the tyranny of the proletariat, and this tyranny the workers, especially those of the Casa del Obrero Mundial, are attempting to impose; not satisfied with the concessions received and the benefits gained, they multiply and exaggerate their demands to the point of violent reproofs against the constitutionalist authorities who have been their resolute ally and their firm support."[140] About two weeks later the Carranza government, this time speaking

[137] The building, a sixteenth-century residence of surpassing elegance, has for many years been the site of Sanborn's restaurant and shop.

[138] José Siurob to Carranza, April 4, 1916, ADN-Hidalgo 1916. Carranza always objected to a wage increase pegged to a decline in the value of the paper peso, since such actions further undermined confidence in the currency.

[139] This weapon was not new to him. Earlier in the year he had incorporated the printers of paper money and the employees of *El Pueblo* into the army when threatened by strikes.

[140] As published in *El Pueblo*, the government press, on January 19, 1916.

through an editorial in the sponsored press, made a more vitriolic attack: "The government emanating from the revolution has esteemed the worker and has given all its support to their [*sic*] just demands; but some cunning and vile agitators, unworthy of any respect, like venomous serpents have slithered into the working group [to which the revolution] brought prosperity and, under the laudable pretext of working for labor betterment, have created discord by fomenting strikes which destroy worker unity and prejudice the consolidation of order [in the country.]"[141]

But public statements emanating from official sources neither settled the issues nor created prosperity. Under the double shock of a drastic decline in agricultural production and a similar decline in the value of paper money, food prices skyrocketed; in some urban centers the price of staples doubled in less than a month. Numerous attempts to set prices and to stabilize the currency did nothing to assuage the suffering, and the laboring men used the only weapon available to them: a wave of strikes hit every major area of urban employment during the spring and summer of 1916.[142] A general strike in Guanajuato[143] paralyzed the mines there in April and the miners received some concessions, but by mid-summer the conditions were so critical that nearly half the population abandoned the city.[144] Carranza prevented a general strike in Mexico City in May only by a combination of a hard line and a few concessions.[145] As the summer wore on, conditions in some areas improved slightly, but not enough to bring lasting relief to the national populace.

Confronted with the double jeopardy of growing government animosity on the one hand and falling real income on the other, the representatives of the organized laboring groups attempted to consolidate their ideological stand; the result was even greater intransi-

141 *El Pueblo*, February 3, 1916.

142 The 812.504 and 812.5045 series, NA, RG 59, have much data on strikes, but are primarily concerned with those affecting U.S. enterprises.

143 J. Siurob to Carranza, April 4, 1916, ADN-Hidalgo 1916.

144 According to Nicolás Cano, a Guanajuato miner, in a speech to the Constitutional Congress on December 22, 1916 (*Diario de los debates del Congreso Constituyente*, I, 608).

145 Clark, *Organized Labor in Mexico*, p. 41.

gence. Meeting in Veracruz in February, Casa and independent union leadership created the Confederation of Labor of the Mexican Region (Confederación del Trabajo de la Región Mexicana), which laid down as a basic tenet the fact that it "accepts the class struggle as a fundamental principle of labor organization, and the socialization of the means of production as the ultimate end of the proletarian movement. As a procedure in the struggle against the capitalistic class it will employ direct action exclusively, any kind of political action being outside the syndicalist effort."[146] The pact between Carranza and the Casa had come to an end.

Carranza and his immediate circle could scarcely accept with equanimity a projected "socialization of the means of production" or the generally belligerent tone of Casa publications. Even Obregón, far to the left of Carranza and Macías in matters relating to labor, became so irritated that he ordered, in his capacity as minister of war in May, 1916, all military commanders to arrest any man attempting to induce the rail workers to strike.[147] With economic conditions degenerating during the year, with hunger widespread, with Pershing chasing Villa in Chihuahua, and with a multitude of rebel, quasi-rebel, and bandit bands roaming the countryside, Carranza and his cohorts were in no mood to submit to what they considered unreasonable demands made by radical and irresponsible labor groups. But as unemployment increased—the Guanajuato mines closed completely in the early fall, for example—and food prices rose, the laborers reached the point of desperation.[148] Under these circumstances a head-on collision could be expected, and it occurred on August 1 in Mexico City. When a general strike began there on July 31, affecting not only private businesses but public facilities as well, Carranza immediately summoned the strike leaders and demanded that they rescind the strike call. When they refused, he

[146] As given in Vicente Lombardo Toledano, *La libertad sindical en México*, p. 63.

[147] Clark, *Organized Labor in Mexico*, p. 41.

[148] Nicolás Cano reported to the Constitutional Congress that at the time when miners were making three or four pesos a week he paid nineteen pesos for a poor breakfast in Irapuato.

ordered Pablo González to close the Casa and apprehend the strike leaders. On the following day, by decree,[149] he extended the 1862 Juárez Law—which stipulated summary execution for certain enemies of the state—to "those who incite the suspension of work in factories or enterprises destined to public service, or those who extend such suspension; to those who preside over meetings in which such suspension is proposed, discussed, or approved; to those who defend and sustain it; to those who approve or subscribe to it; to those who attend such meetings without leaving immediately on knowing the object; and to those who help make it effective once it has been declared." But this was not all. Those who destroyed public or private property as a consequence of the strike, or in connection with it, also came under the law, as did those who "by threat or by force impede other persons from executing the services which had been performed by the operators of the enterprise against which the suspension of work had been declared." The decree, in effect, barred the general strike, or a strike against any establishment that could claim it rendered a "public service."

But the rationale behind the decree was in many ways even worse than the decree itself, insofar as relations between government and labor were concerned; few people really expected a rigid enforcement of the law, which called for "an investigation, a verification, and an execution."[150] In the preamble Carranza launched a bitter attack on the ungrateful "working classes" for whom, he insisted, the revolution had done so much. All these concessions to labor, he said, "have made those classes believe that on them exclusively society's existence depends, and that consequently they are the ones who are in a position to impose whatever conditions they deem good for their own interests, even when those conditions sacrifice or prejudice the entire community and even compromise the existence of the Government itself." He blasted the workers for their antipatriotic and criminal actions in closing down the electrical

[149] The decree may be found in Acuña, *Memoria*, pp. 351–352.

[150] Immediately after the publication of the decree, the government arrested hundreds of strikers; one was adjudged guilty by a military court, and the others freed (Rouaix, *Génesis de los artículos 27 y 123*, p. 132).

plant, which in turn forced suspension of work in the national arms factory during a period of great military need.[151] He interpreted the strike, not as a justified action to improve the worker's conditions, but as a deliberate attack on the government and its fiscal policy, a destruction of the public peace, an aid to the enemies of the government both in and out of Mexico, and a dangerous precedent that might spread to the rest of the country and paralyze the economy. In his rationale, Carranza made it abundantly clear that he distrusted not only the leaders of the Casa, or labor organization, but the "laboring classes" in general. Nothing in the preamble or the decree itself even suggested an attempt to mollify the working men by putting the responsibility on the shoulders of a conniving leadership; the condemnation was blanket.

Whether Carranza's vituperative attack grew out of frustration from being badgered on all sides, or from a deep-seated distrust of the working man, or from a wounded ego is not clear; but he was certainly irritated by the ingratitude of both rural and urban workers. Only a few weeks later the First Chief established the procedure for convening the constituent assembly, at a time when he and his closest circle of advisors were still smarting from labor's demands. He could scarcely be expected to propose to the forthcoming congress a series of sweeping reforms that would put into constitutional law an approval of the very actions to which he had objected so violently.

But even Carranza recognized that labor had been a submerged and exploited group, and that some rights would have to be extended to it before the nation could become an integrated and progressive society. He and all other Constitutionalists agreed that prevailing wages were pitifully low and that a minimum wage should be established by law, that the long working day common throughout the nation left time for neither recreation nor intellectual development, that the worker had a right to expect compensation for debilitating accidents or disease, and that the systems of debt peonage and the *tiendas de raya* had to be abolished. They further agreed

[151] Labor leaders later insisted that the arms factory had an auxiliary source of power and that production resumed after a two-hour delay.

that the laborer had the right to organize and to go on strike, that he had a right to move freely from one job to another, and that he had a right to wages paid in legal tender at periodic intervals. The disagreements came over the method for establishing these general precepts and over the relationship of the laboring groups to the remainder of the society. When the convention met, then, the issue was not whether labor should have rights, but what the nature of those rights would be and how they could be effectuated without endangering the interests of the rest of the population.

Precepts developed during the preconstitutional period regarding the proper relations of the Church to society, the nature of land tenure, the extent of society's control over natural resources, and the rights of labor were certainly of fundamental importance and helped create a nation enormously different from that of the porfirian period. They all tended to destroy the rigid class lines so marked in the earlier period and to give to the great mass of the population a stake in the future previously denied them. Each precept ultimately became a part of a changed constitutional and legal system. In the field of political development equally significant changes occurred, but without any important modification of law with respect to either participation or system.

The period saw almost no change in thinking with respect to the political process or form. Every man who spoke or wrote on the issue insisted on the necessity for an effective suffrage, for no reelection, and for municipal autonomy and all the other forms for which the Constitution of 1857 provided but that had never been introduced into the political system. The forms of government actually used during the 1913–1917 period could scarcely be used as a pattern for the future, since every principle of political freedom and political participation was constantly violated by every contending faction. State governors by decree changed their constitutions in the same manner that Carranza amended the national charter. Government by all the revolutionary factions was by decree; the only exception was the abortive Convention when it sat in Mexico City. The four-year span was one of dictatorial government, regardless of the faction that might control a particular area, in which the authorities of the moment sternly suppressed any expressions of opposition.[152] Despite these political realities, dictated by necessity, no revolutionist of any stature, Constitutionalist or otherwise, ever publicly denounced the political system as described in the Constitution of 1857. Many revolutionists showed considerable ingenuity and imagination in proposing items of social and economic change, but they all showed sterility with respect to the political system. They were perfectly content to accept without question the federal system, the strong executive, the bi-cameral legislature, the doctrine of separation of powers, and the other political aspects of the constitution for whose restoration they were presumably fighting. A political revolution took place nonetheless; it was the product not of thought but of action.

Politics during the *porfiriato* and even during the short Madero administration was the province of the intellectual, the sophisticate whose position in society had allowed him to benefit from an advanced education and whose economic resources had allowed him to travel widely both at home and abroad. The state governors, the members of the state and national legislature, the heads of departments at both state and national levels were all of the same stamp. Even the "renovators" of Madero's lower house came from the same background, although their ideas may have differed markedly from those of their more conservative colleagues. For men of the lower educational and economic brackets, there was no place in the political process save perhaps for casting an occasional controlled ballot or serving as municipal president in a small town. But the yearnings were there, and the Madero movement stimulated political ambitions on the part of that vast proportion of the population which had never taken part in the political process. Pascual Orozco, it will be recalled, rebelled against Madero in part because he felt that his contribution to Díaz's defeat had been sufficient to warrant an important political post—even a cabinet position.

The Constitutionalist revolution shifted the base of political participation, since it was essentially a popular movement that thrust

[152] Not until September, 1916, were any elections held, and these were for municipal posts.

into positions of leadership a vast number of men whose educational preparation would have barred them from positions of political importance in an earlier period. To be sure many of the revolutionary leaders were men of educational and economic substance: Carranza, Ugarte, Escudero, Palavicini, Rojas, Cravioto, Macías, Raúl Madero, Múgica, Villarreal, Rouaix, González Garza, Soto y Gama, and a host of others were educated and sophisticated men well versed in modern political philosophy and international affairs. But many of those who emerged as leaders of men and who contributed mightily to eventual victory came from a distinctly lower educational level. Obregón was a small farmer with little formal education. Calles prior to 1913 had engaged in a number of pursuits, none successful, that kept him constantly on the edge of poverty. Lázaro Cárdenas, a brilliant young Constitutionalist officer who a generation later became president of the revolutionary republic, attended school only through the sixth grade. Villa had no formal schooling, and learned to read only while a prisoner in Mexico City. Manuel Diéguez and Esteban Baca Calderón were both hard-rock miners before being imprisoned by Díaz's officers. Eulalio Gutiérrez was a small shopkeeper. Joaquín Amaro was an indigene with virtually no formal schooling. Nicolás Cano was a Guanajuato silver miner. Luis Morones, soon to become the chief spokesman of Mexico's industrial workers and a prime mover in national affairs, was an electrician who had risen from abject poverty. Mariano Arrieta was an illiterate rustic. And yet each of these men at one time or another served in an important political post; among them were four presidents (including Gutiérrez), four cabinet ministers, four governors, and two members of the Constitutional Congress.

The significance of these developments lay not in a new element added to the Mexican body politic, but in such a devastating destruction of the old that the entire political structure was turned topsy-turvy. The most influential figures emerging into the political limelight in late 1916 were not the suave men of affairs whose training had been in the snobbish military academy, private schools, or universities, or men who had gained their experience behind polished desks in well-appointed offices. They were men of action fresh from the military campaigns, men who had experienced personal danger, who had tested the dust of the battlegrounds and the campaign trails, men who had seen every possible facet of Mexican life, earthy men with a passion for their own particular brand of political or economic philosophy. To men of this stamp a man had to prove himself before he could be trusted, and a man who could not be trusted must be eliminated from a position of power. It was this attitude which made Obregón, Alvarado, Millán, Coss, and many others despise not only the old conservatives whom they exiled but also those "renovators" who had remained in Mexico City during the Huerta period and who later joined Carranza. The thoughtful and judicious Luis Manuel Rojas, the dedicated and hard-working José Natividad Macías, the brilliant Luis Cabrera, the caustic Félix Palavicini, and the lyrical Alfonso Cravioto became objects of suspicion not for what they said, but for what they had not done during the bitterest days of the fighting; their hands were literally unscarred from days in the saddle or hours on the battlefield. But the hard-core actionists were not antiintellectual. They accepted as their own many well-educated and thoughtful men who had not actually borne arms; they bore no animosity toward Alberto Pani, Adolfo de la Huerta, or Pastor Rouaix, none of whom ever gave a military order or fired a gun, but all three of whom had taken an active part in the forefront of the conflict.

The changed political spectrum affected the political structure profoundly. The new leaders, a large proportion of whom had come from obscure peasant or proletarian backgrounds and who had emerged in positions of leadership through skill or luck or both, may not have been enthralled with the niceties of philosophical democracy, but they knew from their own experiences that intelligence and social position were not necessarily equivalent terms. Most of them would not blink a moment at denying the right of political participation to their known enemies, but none would deny such right simply on the basis of education or economic position. In a rude form they were passionately addicted to political democracy or political egalitarianism, although they all accepted as perfectly permissible the elimination of the "reactionaries" from the political process. Carranza most succinctly summed up these two aspects of revolutionary "democracy" in his decree summoning the Constitutional Convention and in his presentation of the draft constitution to that body. In laying down the qualifications for deputies, he decreed that "those who have aided with arms or who have served as public employees of the governments hostile to the Constitutionalist Cause may not be elected [to the Constitutional Convention],"[153] and in discussing his proposed voting qualifications he stated that "the Government in my charge, as a consequence [of the nature of the revolution], would consider it impolitic and inopportune in these moments, after a great popular revolution, to restrict the suffrage."[154]

Another facet of the revolution also tended to change the nature of the body politic and of political perceptions: never before in the history of the nation had there been such physical mobility. Young men who had never been beyond the confines of their own municipalities before mid-1913 found themselves in Mexico City in 1915, and urban workers who had never traveled outside the Federal District before 1915 discovered the countryside and the cities of the northern states by 1916. Probably as many as a quarter million men —a great proportion of whom never returned, to be sure—saw vast sections of their native land that they could never have seen under previously existing circumstances. In addition to this tremendous movement of military men, thousands upon thousands of civilians fled the country for temporary residence in the United States. These great temporary migrations brought to a generation of Mexicans a greater concept of their nation; they helped destroy the concept of the *patria chica* and develop the idea of *patria*.

The men who began to gather in Querétaro in late November, 1916, then, brought with them no new ideas concerning political form or system, but they did come with reinforced concepts of political participation and nationality.

The same phenomena that worked for the creation of a new political atmosphere also aided in the development of a new atti-

[153] Electoral law of September 15, 1916, in Acuña, *Memoria*, pp. 356–359.
[154] *Diario de los debates del Congreso Constituyente*, I, 266.

tude toward education. But here again, as in the case of the political system, few new ideas grew with respect to the organization of the educational system or the content of the curriculum other than the elimination of the clergy from primary teaching.[155] Some governors did attempt to change the direction slightly by opening night schools for adults, and others tried desperately to maintain a viable system, but in general the four-year period probably enrolled fewer students than any like span after 1900.[156] Therefore the preconstitutional period gave nothing in either additional school facilities or new concepts of education. But the nature of the movement did engender new attitudes.

Despite the interminable debates about public education during the latter years of the Díaz regime, and despite Joaquín Barada and his disciples' attempt to make positivism the philosophic base of the educational system,[157] education during the Díaz period was geared to the social and economic elite. In 1910 eight of every ten people over the age of ten could neither read nor write, most of the schools were concentrated in the major population centers, and public secondary schools were rare. The lack of public school facilities was not a function of governmental poverty; it was the result of an attitude on the part of the governing class, which on the one hand feared the results of a truly universal educational system and on the other believed that the mass of the population could not be educated. The elitist concept, a sort of primitive Gospel of Wealth without Carnegie's concomitant responsibilities, held that only a very small proportion of the people could ever benefit from an education; the fact that the vast majority lived on the ragged edge of poverty was in itself evidence to support the theme. As a general-

[155] Calles, while governor of Sonora in late 1915, did request information concerning the public school system of Gary, Indiana, and apparently hoped to get technical aid from that school system, but his efforts came to nought (see the exchange of correspondence in files 812.42/5, /6, /7, NA, RG 59).

[156] Reliable data for the period are completely lacking, but the scattered data do indicate the justification for this conclusion.

[157] For a short but excellent discussion of the role of positivism, see Karl Schmitt, "The Mexican Positivists and the Church-State Question, 1876–1911," *A Journal of Church and State* 8, no. 2 (Spring, 1966): 200–213.

ization—there were exceptions, of course—the lower classes had nothing to offer except labor, and never would.

It was this assumption which the revolution upset. In the fluid revolutionary armies rank more often than not depended upon the number of men an individual could persuade to follow him into battle. Mariano Arrieta became a general not because of a superior military education—he had no education, of any kind, except that acquired as a *ranchero*—but because his personality and his quick intelligence convinced others to accept his leadership. Muleteers, miners, unskilled laborers, *rancheros*, hacienda peasants, artisans, and mechanics by the thousands, some of whom had only the barest rudiments of formal education and some none at all, proved their leadership capacities by becoming commissioned officers, and many of them rose to high rank in one or another of the contending armies. Many of these men, with no more military training than that gained on campaign, showed greater tactical and strategic skill than a goodly portion of the federal army officers, who had graduated from the military academy. One does not have to approve of all the activities of men such as Villa, Argumedo, Orozco, Fierro, Natera, the Arrieta brothers, and others of like background in order to recognize them as leaders with a high order of intelligence and considerable imagination as well as courage.[158] Yaqui General Francisco Urbalejo may not have been able to quote Plato, Aristotle, Hegel, and Comte with the practised ease of Manuel Calero, Toribio Esquivel Obregón, or Francisco Bulnes, but he had a remarkable capacity for making quick and accurate judgments on the basis of the information available to him. It was these men of limited formal education but great skill who defeated the old elite with its intellectual posturing, and who controlled the destiny of the nation after 1916. They and their representatives went to Querétaro with no new and gleaming educational theories, but they went completely convinced that universal and compulsory education could be of enormous benefit to the nation.

[158] The illiterate Mariano Arrieta, when he was governor of Durango, reputedly could recall the contents of every letter he had received or sent over a period of a year.

8. THE QUESTION OF INTERNATIONAL SOVEREIGNTY

Carranza and his cohorts at the beginning of the Constitutionalist movement recognized the incredible problem posed by foreign interests within Mexico. Inasmuch as foreigners owned nearly two-thirds of the total investment in the country, any movement of troops, any attempt to raise money, or any attack on a town inevitably impinged on the financial interest of some national of another country. This condition in itself created a delicate situation in international affairs, since by habit the world powers had come to accept the premise that their nationals resident in the less stable countries had a right to expect protection from the home governments. Furthermore, the preeminent position of the United States, both financially and geographically, had led the European nations to look upon Mexico's neighbor as the principal agent for extending such protection; the Roosevelt Corollary to the Monroe Doctrine was an expression of both European need and U.S. willingness. These conditions made Carranza recognize the absolute necessity for establishing with the United States some kind of working relationship that would allow the revolution to follow its course without undue pressure, or intervention, from the outside. It was this realization which led Carranza in April, 1913, to appeal to the U.S. public for understanding and sympathy, in the hope that U.S. nationals would "pardon [the Constitutionalists] for the prejudice done to their interests during the conflict in which [the Constitutionalists] are involved."[1] But a prior apology for damages to be done would hardly compensate for the losses involved, Carranza knew, and a month later he clarified the issue by decreeing that "all nationals and foreigners" had a right to payment for damages sustained at any time from the beginning of the movement until its satisfactory conclusion; any such claims were to be adjudicated by mixed commissions of foreigners and Mexicans.[2]

But the problem facing the revolutionists was not merely one of damages sustained as an incident to the military conflict; much more crucial was the question of damages sustained as the result of an application of law. As has been pointed out, the Constitutionalist movement from its earliest months was marked by a determination to change the basic structure of the Mexican society. Any change in the society would disturb the existing order, and among the most obvious characteristics of that order were foreign influence and interest. By its very nature—not often recognized at the time, to be sure—the revolution threatened those foreigners who lived or invested in Mexico, and events in the previous two generations had shown quite clearly that the world powers would not stand idly by while internal Mexican developments brought ruin to their nationals in that country. Carranza's dilemma, then, was that of devising a policy that would recognize international obligations but at the same

[1] Carranza, "Al pueblo americano," April 4, 1913, as published in Secretaría de Relaciones Exteriores, *Labor internacional de la revolución constitucionalista de México*, pp. 21–22. This collection of documents was published under the direction of Minister of Foreign Relations Cándido Aguilar in 1918. After Carranza fell in 1920, almost the entire edition was destroyed, but a few copies had already been distributed.

[2] Decree of May 10, 1913, as published in *Decretos y demás disposiciones del ejército constitutionalista*, pp. 52–53.

time leave the future government sufficient freedom to act on domestic matters. His solution was to insist on proper diplomatic procedures, to deny that any country had a preeminent interest in Mexico, and to work for international acceptance of Mexican sovereignty as inviolable and indivisible. Carranza's utter consistency on these points later led President Wilson to lament to Lansing: "I thing [*sic*] I have never known of a man more impossible to deal with on human principles that [*sic*] this man Carranza."[3] In maintaining his policy, the Primer Jefe was indeed often difficult or even churlish, but by the end of the preconstitutional period he had made it clear to the world, and particularly to the United States, that Mexican sovereignty was as precious and as all-inclusive as that of any country, regardless of power and position.

For many months after the beginning of his movement, Carranza made no serious attempt to develop formal diplomatic relations with other governments, other than to establish "confidential agencies" in Washington, London, and Paris to work for belligerent recognition and to propagandize in favor of Constitutionalism. Occasionally he protested against the U.S. policy that allowed Huerta to purchase arms while denying that right to the Constitutionalists,[4] but he knew he was in a precarious position and he had no desire to antagonize foreign governments. His prime concern during those months was to convince foreigners in and out of Mexico that they had nothing to fear from the revolution; he even went to the length of ordering Constitutional military commanders to exercise extreme care with respect to foreign properties, enjoining them to avoid insofar as possible any damage or seizure of such properties and instructing them to give fully authenticated receipts for materials taken or damaged.[5] By

[3] Wilson to Lansing, July 2, 1915, file 812.00/15409 1/2, NA, RG 59.

[4] On April 21, 1913, he wrote such a letter to President Wilson, but apologized for his own faux pas committed in writing directly to the president when such a communiqué should have gone through proper channels. The letter is reproduced in *Labor internacional*, p. 23.

[5] Consul Louis Hostetter to SecState, October 28, 1913, file 812.00/9559, NA, RG 59, sent a number of decrees issued by Carranza before he established his government in Sonora, including this circular dated June 17. Hostetter commented that Carranza sharply reprimanded any officer who failed to follow the

such acts he hoped to generate a friendly sympathy from foreign residents and their governments for the purpose of preventing strong foreign support for Huerta.

During those same months Carranza accepted without demur the role the United States had arrogated to itself as general protector of all foreign interests; he made no protest when the Department of State informed Villa that he would be held personally responsible for the protection of all foreign interests, U.S. or other, within the area of his military command.[6] Carranza's movement was not yet strong enough, and his own authority not yet sufficiently consolidated, to allow him to make an effective protest, even though on principle he objected both to direct communication with Villa and to the U.S. assumption of general protection. But soon after he established his government in late October he began clarifying the chain of command within his own structure, and the proper relationships between his government and those of other nations. President Wilson presented him with his first opportunity in early November.

The Washington administration, confronted almost simultaneously with the Huerta October election farce and the formation of a formal Constitutionalist government,[7] undertook to devise a new policy that would bring the fighting to an end and thereby give security to foreign interests. As an incident in the development of the new approach, the Department of State dispatched a special agent to confer with Carranza, who for the first time since the beginning of the Constitutionalist movement had an opportunity to establish some precedents in the field of foreign policy. Both Wilson and Carranza had well-defined—and mutually exclusive—objectives to achieve in the conference. Wilson wanted from the First Chief a

---

circular's directions, and that he had ordered a number of executions for flagrant and open violations.

[6] Boaz Long to SecState, October 29, 1913, file 812.00/9275, NA, RG 59. Long, chief of the Latin American Division of the Department of State, objected to the policy on the grounds that it put too much responsibility on the United States.

[7] Carranza established his government, by decree, in Sonora, on October 20; the Huerta election was held October 26.

categorical statement of the minimal conditions under which he would be willing to bring the fighting to a halt and to cooperate with a new Mexico City government, while Carranza desired nothing less than a lifting of the arms embargo, which would allow him to intensify military operations.[8]

Special agent William Bayard Hale arrived in Nogales, Arizona, on November 2, ready to begin his conference with the First Chief, who was in Nogales, Sonora, only a few blocks away and reportedly "anxious" to get belligerent recognition from the United States.[9] But it soon became clear that Carranza was in no great hurry to confer with Wilson's emissary. Using a number of excuses, he postponed the first meeting until November 12, when he arranged a conference so formal as to be almost forbidding.[10] Flanked by four members of his government,[11] plus his chief of staff and the governor of Sonora, the Primer Jefe amicably informed Hale and Consul Frederick Simpich that lifting the arms embargo would be a simple act of justice, since the Constitutionalists represented progress and decency as opposed to Huerta's reaction and degeneration. He could not, he said, cooperate with either the Mexico City government or the United States to create a new provisional government. He and the other Constitutionalists, he averred, were absolutely determined to continue the struggle until the last vestige of the old exploitative society had been eradicated. The most efficient way of bringing the struggle to a quick conclusion would be to allow him to purchase all the arms and ammunition he needed; if he had the arms he could bring the war to an end within two months.

[8] Prior to the final lifting of the arms embargo, the Constitutionalists were remarkably proficient in buying and transporting arms surreptitiously, but the process was troublesome and expensive.

[9] Hale to SecState, November 2, 1913, file 812.00/9506, NA, RG 59.

[10] The most convenient source for the conferences is Isidro Fabela, *Historia diplomática de la revolución mexicana, 1912–1917*, I, 243–255. Hale's reports may be found in the 812.00 series of November and December, NA, RG 59; some are published in *Foreign Relations, 1913*.

[11] Francisco Escudero, Foreign Relations; Rafael Zubarán Capmany, Gobernación; Adolfo de la Huerta, also of Gobernación; and Ignacio Bonillas, Communications. Bonillas, educated in the United States, acted as interpreter. Of these four, only Bonillas still supported Carranza in 1920.

But Hale was determined to present the U.S. point of view as firmly as possible and insisted upon the vital necessity of solving the problem by ballots instead of bullets; at one point he read a Bryan dispatch to the effect that the United States might be forced to intervene unless the "lives and interests of Americans and all other foreigners" were given adequate protection. Carranza met threat with threat. The Constitutionalists, he said, absolutely rejected the concept of intervention in any form for any reason, and any such attempt by the United States would "kindle a fire which has been extinguished, and carry us to an interminable struggle." On that note the first conference ended, with Carranza explicitly promising a written reply that would refine his oral statement and implicitly binding himself to further conferences in order to clarify all issues.

But Carranza never again saw Hale. He instructed Francisco Escudero to continue the talks and a few days later, through Escudero, demanded of Hale a written, rather than an oral, summary of the U.S. position. Such a document, he held, would allow him to study the question thoroughly, and to determine "the reasons why President Wilson considers it his duty to treat of subjects which [the Constitutionalists] consider to be [Mexico's] proper and exclusive competence to recognize and to decide upon." After a few more exchanges, in which Hale insisted upon the necessity of compromise and Carranza held firm to his thesis of complete victory, the conferences came to an end with no ascertainable results.

The manner of conducting the conferences and the language emanating from them were an augury of the Carranza style in international relations. Though the Department of State did not realize it at the time, Carranza's mode on this occasion was to become his norm of action. First, he was dilatory; only on rare occasions did he make an immediate response of a categorical nature. Second, he rarely conferred directly with representatives of other nations, generally insisting that all protests or requests be handled through his Foreign Relations office. Third, he consistently demanded written communications, so that he could "study" them, and in this fashion personally made all decisions with respect to international affairs. Fourth, he always insisted that his government would give ample protection to legitimate foreign interests and fully accepted the principle that his government had a responsibility to do so. And finally, he always denied the right of any country or group of countries to make any representation with respect to a domestic problem or policy. These were the rules he implicitly laid down in the Hale conferences, and these were the rules by which he played throughout the preconstitutional period.

Not long after the conclusion of the abortive Hale mission, three unrelated actions by Francisco Villa gave Carranza an opportunity to make a further delineation of his international posture and to underscore the position he had already taken. In mid-January, Villa ordered the municipal president of Guanaceví in northern Durango to confiscate a mine belonging to a group that included a number of Mexicans, some Spaniards, and one U.S. citizen; the United States made an immediate representation in behalf of all the foreign owners. On February 16 Villa ordered the execution of one William Benton, a British subject; the Department of State made representations directly to Villa without even informing Carranza of the action. In late February, Villa ordered the execution of Gustavo Bauch, a U.S. citizen; when Bauch was discovered by his friends to be missing, the department made direct representations to Carranza. The combination of cases,[12] consisting as it did of U.S. representations in behalf of its own nationals, representations in behalf of nationals of other countries, and representations made to a Carranza subordinate, forced Carranza into a direct conflict with the United States over an

[12] The exact sequence of events in the Benton and Bauch cases remains a mystery, though Benton was certainly executed and Bauch probably was. Villa claimed that Benton tried to kill him and that the execution was ordered by a properly constituted court-martial, but much evidence suggests that Villa himself ordered the execution after Benton had upbraided him in violent terms. Villa denied any knowledge of the Bauch case other than that Bauch had been in jail and that he had been released, but again the evidence suggests that Villa ordered his execution, probably on the grounds that he was a Huerta agent. The documentation for the cases may be found in *Labor internacional*, pp. 27–45; Fabela, *Historia diplomática de la revolución mexicana*, I, 257–309; and in the 812.41 and 812.50 series for January through March, 1914, NA, RG 59. Much of the Benton documentation has been published in *Foreign Relations, 1914*, but none of the Bauch material is included.

interpretation of international law and the proper relations among sovereign states, as well as over the question of the nature of his own government. In the conflict he was aided by two conditions. First, the three cases proved to be an acute embarrassment to Villa, and he was therefore willing to allow Carranza to handle them even though he was to become suspicious of the First Chief before the issues were settled. And second, the press of events in Washington and the poor communications between Carranza's peripatetic headquarters and the outside world often caused long delays in message transmission, giving the Primer Jefe a perfect excuse for dilatory tactics.

In handling the cases Carranza was able to make two points that became important in establishing Mexican sovereignty and Constitutionalist power. In the Benton case, at the request of the British Embassy, Bryan on February 19 instructed both Consul Thomas D. Edwards in Ciudad Juárez and Special Agent George C. Carothers with Villa (then in Ciudad Juárez) to "interpose their good offices" in Benton's behalf. Carothers immediately sought out Villa, who assured him—as Carothers reported to Washington—that Benton was not under arrest. Two days later the news of Benton's death became public knowledge, and Villa informed Carranza that a military court had ordered the execution, but as yet Carranza and his government had received no representation from Washington; Bryan continued to deal with Villa. On February 22 and 23 Bryan issued instructions to Edwards, Carothers, and Consul Marion Letcher in Chihuahua—Villa was then in the state capital—to demand the delivery of the body to U.S. officials, who would in turn surrender it to the family. Only in the face of Villa's refusal to deliver the body, or even to indicate where it lay, did Bryan finally on February 24 instruct Frederick Simpich in Nogales to present the case to Carranza. On February 26 Simpich, presenting the substance of the situation to Isidro Fabela, requested an interview with Carranza, and Fabela in turn gave an accounting to the First Chief. Carranza agreed to the conference for the following day—it was then late at night—but in so doing indicated verbally his displeasure at both U..S representations in behalf of a British subject and representations to Villa rather than to him; on frequent occasions in the past he had made the same objections to both Simpich and Louis Hostetter in Hermosillo.

When Simpich reported Carranza's view to Bryan, the secretary of state on February 27 replied:

If Carranza complains that we appealed to Villa, please explain to him that we have acted in this case as we have in all others whether the question arose in territory under his control or in territory under Huerta. We have made representations to the local authorities first in the hope of securing immediate action and afterwards to the highest authorities. Villa has consented to allow inspection of Benton's body and assuming that Carranza will approve of this we are arranging a trip but would like specific approval from Carranza and assurance of protection of party, which will include British Consul.[13]

When Simpich did confer with Carranza on the night of February 27, eight days had elapsed since Bryan's first representation to Villa and eleven days since Benton's death.

Now the mere fact that by habit the Department of State made representations to local commanders did not, in the First Chief's eyes, justify the method's continuation. In any event, the eight-day delay before the request was made to Carranza could be interpreted as nothing less than a gross insult to Carranza as head of the Constitutionalist government. Bryan's actions said, in essence, that no Constitutionalist government existed and that each military commander exercised complete and autonomous authority within his sphere of military operation. To this general proposition Carranza could scarcely admit; in his eyes the Constitutionalist government was a viable institution, and he as "First Chief in Charge of Executive Power" of that government had the final authority in any case of policy or practice. This was a principle to which he must adhere if the revolution were to be something more than simple nihilism, and he could approve of no action that seemed to undermine that scarce authority which in reality he exercised over Villa;[14] Carranza

[13] Bryan to Simpich, February 27, 1914, file 812.41/139, NA, RG 59.

[14] Despite Carranza's orders with respect to foreign property and foreign persons, Villa consistently and contemptuously seized foreign property and exiled

was acutely aware of it, but the implications seemed to have escaped the secretary of state.

Irritated by both Villa's intemperate action and Bryan's handling of the case, Carranza made an immediate reply after Simpich had delivered to him Bryan's message of February 27. After discussing the substance of the Benton case, the First Chief took up the question of representations to subordinate officials:

I must especially point out to you [Simpich], so that you may lay it before your government, that the representation which you made to me yesterday with respect to the Benton affair is the first I have received, since the reclamations and representations which have been made in this case have been brought before other authorities of the Constitutional government who have felt obliged to treat the case even though in conformity with the Plan de Guadalupe of March 26, 1913, I am the First Chief of the Constitutionalist Army, and it is to me, as I have pointed out to you on numerous occasions, to whom the Governments or foreign authorities should address themselves in affairs of an international character. And even though the Secretary of State points out that, if in some cases he has directed himself to local authorities, it has been done with the object of obtaining immediate action on his request, I think it wise that you impress upon your government that in all requests coming from its nationals, it must address itself to this First Chieftainship of the Constitutionalist Army, which will take up with subaltern authorities the situation which motivates the representations, in order to resolve the issue and to order that which is proper.[15]

But the Benton case had ramifications much more important than those of representations to subordinate officials. The principal point in dispute was whether the United States had a right to make any representation at all in view of Benton's British citizenship. The question had arisen frequently in the past, and in the Guanaceví case Carranza had made himself perfectly, even abruptly, clear. A

---

foreign residents. After his capture of Chihuahua he shipped out the Spaniards like so many cattle.

[15] Carranza to Simpich, February 28, 1914, in *Labor internacional*, pp. 39–40. The translation here is somewhat different from that in *Foreign Relations, 1914*, pp. 856–857. Carranza, of course, was fully aware, from other sources, that the representations were being made to Villa.

week after Simpich had demanded protection against confiscation of the mine, indicating that the request came at the instance of the Spanish minister in Washington, Carranza curtly replied that "representations or reclamations which refer to the interests of foreigners must be made to the First Chief of the Constitutionalist Army, through the Ministry of Foreign Affairs, by the diplomatic representatives of the country of which the affected foreigner is a national and who have authority from their governments to make such representations or reclamations."[16]

When Simpich transmitted the reply to Washington,[17] Bryan took sharp exception to the Constitutionalist position. He pointed out that under the circumstances foreign governments could not, with propriety, maintain two groups of diplomatic representatives in Mexico, one for the Huerta government, which they had recognized, and one for the Constitutionalists, whom they had not. Furthermore, in many sections of the country some European nations had no representatives at all. It followed therefore that if a European nation—in the Guanaceví case, Spain—were to extend any form of protection to its nationals it would have to be done through the agent of another country; since the United States had the greatest number of consuls and vice-consuls, this service had naturally fallen on the Washington government. Bryan insisted that such extraofficial representations were strictly in accord with international law and occurred "almost daily" in diplomatic practice. He then went from cajolery to threats by saying that the United States had done all it could to prevent other powers from taking "coercive measures" and implying that, unless Carranza changed his policy, intervention would probably follow.[18]

By this time both Carranza and Bryan had more to worry about than protecting a mine in Durango. The circumstances of Benton's death created a storm of criticism in both the United States and

[16] Fabela to Simpich, January 27, 1914, in *Labor internacional*, p. 27.

[17] Simpich transmitted Fabela's note, in abbreviated form, on February 19. The cause of the long delay is not explained, but probably resulted from poor communication; Fabela wrote the note in Culiacán.

[18] Bryan to Simpich, March 2, 1914, file 812.52/180, NA, RG 59.

England, and by late February, U.S. agents were demanding Benton's body and a full investigation of his death. But in spite of the major differences between the Guanaceví and Benton cases—England was much more powerful than Spain and at Guanaceví no lives had been lost—the principle was exactly the same and so was the First Chief's immediate response: the United States had no right to intercede in the behalf of a non-U.S. citizen, and any acceptable representation in the Benton case would have to come from an agent of the British government.[19] Carranza's note to Simpich gave no indication that he contemplated any further action in the case unless approached directly by the British government, but he knew full well the dangers of the situation and therefore appointed a commission of three Constitutionalists to determine the facts in the case. At further insistence from the Department of State, on March 12 Carranza justified his position in biting terms in discussing both the Guanaceví and Benton cases.[20] He accused the Spanish government of complicity in the Madero and Pino Suárez assassinations, and the British government of attempting to pressure the United States into abandoning its "just policy" of refusing to recognize Huerta; if the subjects of these two nations suffered from a lack of agents who could intercede with the Constitutionalist government, it was a consequence of the erroneous acts of which those governments had been guilty. He had always, he said, given the fullest protection to foreigners and had always been prompt in complying with requests made by U.S. agents in behalf of U.S. citizens; representations made by the United States in behalf of other foreigners he had not accepted, but he had used the "information to correct and prevent the injuries to which they referred." He then mollified his stand somewhat. In those areas in which there were no European agents, the nation in question could legitimately authorize "other persons, who might well be the consuls of the United States," to make the representations. But to the basic principle he held firm: "All representations which I have received or will receive in the future [from the United States] relative to non-American foreigners will serve only to give

[19] Carranza to Simpich, February 28, 1914, in *Labor internacional*, pp. 39–40.
[20] Carranza to Simpich, March 12, 1914, ibid, pp. 30–33.

me knowledge, if I have not previously received it from Mexican authorities, that some foreigner has suffered some injury, and to give the proper orders to preserve and to have preserved public tranquility and to give individual guarantees to all foreigners, punishing if necessary those responsible who, violating the law and failing to comply with their duties and my orders, molest in the slightest degree any foreigner." But, he said, intercession by the governments was not really necessary; any foreigner subject to any injury could come to him directly with the perfect assurance that his plaint could receive immediate attention "without the necessity of his government intervening in the affair, either officially or extraofficially."

The Bauch case, which came to Bryan's attention ten days after that U.S. citizen's disappearance in Ciudad Juárez, allowed Carranza to underscore the points he had made in the other cases. Within hours after Simpich delivered Bryan's request for an investigation, Carranza answered in the most cordial and apologetic terms.[21] He had, he said, requested a prompt investigation by the proper authorities, and he would transmit further information as soon as he had it. He also wished Simpich to transmit to Bryan the fact that he "lament[ed] sincerely this unfortunate event" and was determined to give foreigners protection under the law. Four days later, through Isidro Fabela and without further urging, Carranza supplied the information he had received. Bauch had been in jail on suspicion of being an enemy agent, but he had been released and could not be found. Nevertheless, said Fabela, "the First Chief of the Constitutionalist Army, desiring a complete and detailed investigation into the affair in order to satisfy the Secretary and ourselves and in order that your government may see the good will which animates us in attending to representations properly made [to him], has consigned the case of Mr. Gustavo Bauch to the special investigating commission which is handling the Benton case."[22] Over the following

[21] Carranza to Simpich, February 28, 1914, ibid, pp. 43–44.

[22] Fabela to Simpich, March 4, 1914, ibid., pp. 44–45. Either by accident or design, the Benton commission did not make an investigation of Bauch's death. Carranza and Fabela claimed that the order was given telegraphically, but the chairman of the commission said he never received the instructions. By the time

months the Department of State made periodic inquiries concerning Bauch, and Carranza made unfailing prompt and courteous replies, but the details of his death were never accurately ascertained.

In handling these three cases Carranza was able to establish a number of precedents for the conduct of foreign affairs, even though most nations at that time refused to accept the validity of his policy. As time wore on, foreign governments found it necessary to accept, on an ad hoc basis, Carranza's precepts in principle though not necessarily in practice. United States consuls in Carranza territory continued to approach the local leaders directly on instructions from Washington, but in most cases the Department of State made a simultaneous appeal—or demand—to Carranza.[23] The same consuls, or special agents, also continued to intercede for non-U.S. citizens, but with a note to the effect that the representation was made at the specific request of officials of the nation involved,[24] thus falling within the category of "other persons, who might well be consuls of the United States," which Carranza had legitimized in the Benton-Guanaceví cases. If we are to believe the statements made by the principal Constitutional participants at a later time, Carranza and some of his aides were determined to break U.S. hegemony—or as they called it, "tutelage"—in Mexico. The demand made by Carranza that foreign governments make representations in behalf of their own

---

this discrepancy was discovered, it was June, the break between Villa and Carranza had taken place, and it was too late to make a proper investigation.

[23] The failure of the Department of State to follow this simple precept may have cost one U.S. citizen nearly fifty thousand dollars. When Villa captured Torreón on April 5, he confiscated over seven hundred bales of cotton recently purchased by U.S. Consular Agent William O. Jenkins for his mills in Puebla. Even though Jenkins asked Bryan for aid or advice ten days later, Bryan never brought the case before Carranza, who was then in Ciudad Juárez. The exchange of documents between Jenkins and the Department of State are in the 412.11 J41 series, NA, RG 59.

[24] In a long note to the secretary of state in April, Carothers discussed the general pattern of relationships that should exist. At that time Villa and Carranza were quarrelling over Manuel Chao, and Carothers made some interesting observations on the international implications of that quarrel (Carothers to SecState, April 12, 1914, file 812.00/11755, NA, RG 59).

citizens only was deliberate, the product not of accident but of design, and aimed directly at the concept of U.S. "preeminent interest."

In addition to the specific policies laid down in these three cases, Carranza's handling of them demonstrated two other facets of his mode of diplomacy. In spite of the tensions arising, particularly with respect to the Benton case, the First Chief was careful never to address himself directly either to President Wilson or to Secretary of State Bryan, and only on rare occasions did he send out a message under his own signature. Simply by his method of operation he made it clear that all communications of an international character had to go through the proper channels, that he as the head of a government reserved the right to make the final decision but would not be bothered by routine matters. Virtually all messages transmitted, therefore, were between representatives of the U.S. government and Isidro Fabela, who acted as Carranza's minister of foreign relations. Furthermore, the First Chief seemed to be a firm adherent of the principle of administration by inaction; he frequently delayed days before answering urgent messages.[25] Many of the delays were occasioned by the nature of the situation itself, since at the moment when some of the most difficult decisions had to be made Carranza was in the process of moving from Hermosillo to Nogales to Agua Prieta to Chihuahua. Since he adamantly refused to leave Mexico, and since there were no rail connections between Sonora and Chihuahua, the First Chief was frequently far from telegraphic connections. But much of the delay, particularly with respect to the Benton case, was deliberate. It was a source of irritation to the Department of State and to a number of his own subordinates. Villa saw in Carranza's dilatoriness a calculated affront to the United States and reportedly threatened to call a council of generals to force the titular leader to change his posture or surrender his authority.[26] But Carranza did neither, and delay became a characteristic of his diplomacy.

Even before the noise of these three cases died down a much more serious question of international relations, which ultimately al-

[25] Ibid.

[26] As reported by Carothers in ibid.

lowed him to underscore his general contention that Mexican sovereignty was absolute, confronted the First Chief. On April 21, after eleven days of sterile negotiations with the Huerta government over an insult at Tampico, the United States occupied the port of Veracruz as a means, Bryan and Wilson thought, of forcing the dictator's retirement.[27] But the reaction in Mexico was the exact opposite of that expected in Washington, where both the president and the secretary of state fully expected Huerta's enemies to applaud the action or, at the worst, to remain completely neutral in the affair.

Those within the Huerta zone quite naturally responded with violent condemnations and attempted to use the incident as an instrument for whipping up enthusiasm for the dictator; volunteers flooded the recruiting offices, Huerta officials mistreated U.S. representatives,[28] and Huertista spokesmen threatened retaliatory actions.[29] The Department of State expected these reactions, and they caused no great concern. Much to Bryan's surprise, however, many Constitutionalists condemned the occupation in terms as harsh as those used by Huerta, and some local revolutionary leaders, particularly those operating along the Gulf Coast, promised to cooperate with the Huerta forces in fighting the invaders if they made any attempt to move to the interior.

Secretary of State Bryan was less concerned with the attitudes of lesser Constitutional commanders than he was with the positions to be taken by Carranza, Villa, Obregón, and Pablo González. These

[27] The occupation has been the subject of much writing. The most convenient study is Robert E. Quirk, *An Affair of Honor*; the best presentation by a Mexican is Justino Palomares, *La invasión yanqui en 1914*, but it has many inaccuracies. In brief, Huerta officers in Tampico arrested a shore party from a U.S. warship, whereupon the admiral demanded a "proper" apology, and Wilson ultimately requested power from Congress to act for a redress of grievances. The actual occupation of Veracruz on April 21 stemmed from a determination to prevent the docking of a ship loaded with German munitions for Huerta.

[28] U.S. consuls in Saltillo, San Luis Potosí, and Monterrey were treated in a particularly undiplomatic fashion, with Huerta officials arresting the personnel, seizing the consular files, and destroying office fixtures. The actions were deliberate, in the hope that they would provoke the United States into a full-scale invasion and thereby make Huerta a hero as the defender of his nation.

[29] The ADN and AGN files for April and May, 1914, are rich in documentation of events in the Huerta areas of control.

were the recognized leaders of the Constitutionalist movement, and their actions would determine the relationship that would exist between the United States and Mexico; if they agreed publicly with the occupation, the United States would be in a strong and comfortable position, but if they disagreed the affair would be at best embarrassing and at worst dangerous. Pablo González made no public statement other than that he would abide by Carranza's decision. Obregón publicly stated that if war came he would fight to the bitter end, but privately he urged Carranza to declare war on the United States because, he said, that action would not only strengthen the Constitutionalists in public opinion but would also make them the principal negotiators with the United States at the conclusion of the affair.[30] But Carranza was the key, and Bryan made a special effort to secure the Primer Jefe's friendship. Within hours after the first landings occurred shortly before noon, Bryan instructed Carothers to assure Carranza that Wilson made a distinction between "General Huerta and his supporters on the one hand and the Mexican people on the other"; the occupation was aimed at Huerta, not the Mexican people. According to press reports, said Bryan, the Constitutionalists displayed a "very proper attitude" in remaining aloof from the "controversy"; he hoped this to be the case, and that Carranza did not "misconstrue" the act.[31] The general tone of the note suggested that Carranza should know that the United States wanted to rid Mexico of Huerta, that the occupation was designed to accomplish that end, and that Carranza should have no objections. Bryan obviously looked forward to a friendly reply from the First Chief.

Because of communication difficulties,[32] Carranza received the note on April 22; he made his own concern quite clear when he addressed his reply to Bryan and to Wilson rather than to Carothers, from whom he had received the Bryan note. Far from being affable, Carranza demonstrated a startling bellicosity. He condemned Huer-

[30] Obregón to Carranza, April 21, 1914, ADN-Chihuahua 1914.

[31] Bryan to Carothers, April 21, 1914, file 812.00/11608a, NA, RG 59.

[32] Carothers was in El Paso and Carranza in Chihuahua. Carothers transmitted the message in a telegraphic conference with Carranza on the morning of April 22.

ta's action on the one hand, but on the other interpreted the military invasion as an act hostile toward Mexican sovereignty and demanded an immediate troop withdrawal; he made repeated references to war and left the strong impression he was contemplating some drastic retaliatory action.[33] At the same time he attempted to assuage the note's belligerency by privately requesting Consul Marion Letcher to point out to President Wilson the difficult situation in which the occupation put the Constitutionalists, who had to consider Mexican sensibilities.[34] The following day he asked Letcher to ascertain whether Wilson would receive a special representative with plenary powers to treat "affairs of state," or, failing that, whether it would be "convenient" for both Wilson and the Constitutionalists to designate commissioners with such powers. Bryan, obviously irritated by Carranza's note and equally obviously completely misreading the Mexican temper, replied that such a meeting of commissioners would be impossible in view of Carranza's public statements and that Carranza must publicly declare his neutrality before any constructive conferences could be held.[35]

In the meantime Villa, in Chihuahua and fresh from his capture of Torreón, became so alarmed by U.S. public reaction to Carranza's note that he made a hasty trip to Ciudad Juárez to investigate the situation personally; current rumors that the United States planned to reimpose the arms embargo especially concerned him, since he needed arms and ammunition for his planned attack on Saltillo.[36] In El Paso he assured Carothers that he had no objection to the Veracruz occupation.[37] But Villa was not content merely to make his statement to Carothers; on April 25 he addressed a note to President Wilson in which he reiterated his friendship for the United States, castigated Huerta, and characterized Carranza's note as an "entirely

[33] Carranza to SecState and Wilson (sent by Carothers), April 22, 1914, file 812.00/11618, NA, RG 59.

[34] Letcher to SecState, April 22, 1914, file 812.00/11650, NA, RG 59.

[35] Letcher to SecState, April 23, 1914, and Bryan to Letcher, April 24, 1914, file 812.00/11651, NA, RG 59.

[36] The touchy diplomatic situation did not affect Wilson's decision to lift the embargo, which he had earlier made.

[37] Carothers to SecState, April 22, 1914, file 812.00/11654, NA, RG 59.

personal" comment by a man who had "momentary authority" and therefore of no real consequence. He concluded: "I can assure you that our chief Carranza is animated by the keen desire to avoid difficulties between our respective countries and we following his patriotic impulses and as faithful servants find ourselves of the same inclination. Mr. Carranza in his note has only endeavored to defend the dignity of the Republic without intending his attitude under any condition to be considered a hostile act against the United States of America, from which country we have received such great demonstrations of consideration and sympathy."[38] Bryan, of course, chose to believe that Villa more nearly represented Constitutionalist thought than did Carranza, and he praised Villa's position as one of great statesmanship and responsibility.[39] A few days later Carothers reported that he had "authentic information" indicating that Carranza was "in accord with Villa on [the] policy toward [the] United States";[40] if it were so, the First Chief never made it public.

In view of Huerta's bellicosity and Carranza's belligerency, and with all manner of rumor along the border respecting imminent attacks by either Constitutionalists or Huertistas, the Wilson policy seemed to be leading to a war that no one really wanted. When Wilson accepted, on April 25, good offices extended by Argentina, Brazil, and Chile on the "question of [the] American government and Huerta,"[41] the tension eased; and when Carranza, on invitation by the three diplomats, also accepted the good offices "in principle" four days later,[42] the worst seemed to be over. Then a strange situation developed. After Wilson accepted the bid for good offices, he either changed his mind or did not recognize the issues, for he concluded that the basic question was internal Mexican chaos and that a viable

[38] Villa to Wilson, as transmitted by Carothers to SecState, April 25, 1914, file 812.00/11714, NA, RG 59.

[39] Bryan to Carothers, April 24, 1914, file 812.00/11654, NA, RG 59.

[40] Carothers to SecState, April 29, 1914, file 812.00/11770, NA, RG 59.

[41] As reported by Francisco Urquidi to Fabela, April 25, 1914, in *Labor internacional*, p. 49.

[42] Carranza to Ambassador Dionisio da Gama of Brazil and Ministers A. S. Naón and E. Suárez Mújica of Argentina and Chile, April 29, 1914, in ibid., p. 51.

and recognizable government in Mexico would have to be created before the United States could become a party to any negotiations. He therefore insisted that the United States was not party to the dispute and that the task of the three nations extending good offices was to mediate between the Mexican disputants. Huerta, by this time realizing that only a miracle could save his government, pinned his hopes on the outcome of the mediation and accepted all suggestions with rare good will.[43] But at the new developments Carranza balked. The day after he accepted good offices in principle, he received word from the mediating diplomats that they were calling on him and Huerta to suspend all military movements and actions until the case had been settled. In an immediate response the First Chief insisted that the quarrel between the United States and Mexico was "independent of our internal war for liberty and rights and I consider it neither just nor wise to suspend the hostilities and military movements, since from the suspension which you propose only Huerta could profit. In view of this I beg you to excuse me for not accepting the armistice which you have proposed to me, hoping that you will see in my acts only my intention to do that which is best for the interests of my country."[44]

Thus, in spite of a long exchange of notes, here the matter stood. Carranza adamantly insisted that he could send no representatives without first knowing the exact limits of the conference, and that he would under no circumstances be a party to an international conference held for the purpose of discussing internal Mexican conditions. At the same time he insisted that no conference discussing the quarrel between Mexico and the United States could make any legitimate decision unless it included representatives from the Constitutional government. From this position Carranza would not budge—though he did agree to consult his generals.[45] The mediators refused to re-

[43] The documentation in AGN and ADN makes it clear that Huerta had great faith in the conferences as a means of saving his government. He apparently thought, well into June, that the Latin American diplomats would devise a formula that would include recognition of his government; he even kept Congress in an extended session so that action could be taken immediately.

[44] Carranza to da Gama et al., May 1, 1914, in *Labor internacional*, p. 52.

[45] On June 21 the mediators invited Carranza to confer with Huerta officials

treat from their contention that their purpose was to bring peace to Mexico, and that such peace could be achieved only by conferring in an atmosphere of tranquility undisturbed by military actions in Mexico. Under the circumstances the conference, which met sporadically in May and June without the Constitutionalists in attendance, could accomplish nothing of any consequence. In late June it finally recommended a formula for establishing a provisional government through consultation between Constitutionalists and Huerta officials, and the mediators perceived their task to have been concluded; but Carranza refused to treat with the federals on any ground other than unconditional surrender. The long haggling series of meetings over a six-week period had no effect whatsoever on either the course of the revolution in Mexico or the settlement of the occupation issue, but the entire affair did allow Carranza to carry his point that no outside agency had any right to concern itself with Mexican matters.

In taking his immovable stand Carranza was immeasurably aided by events on the military front. Despite the developing quarrel between Carranza and Villa, the Constitutionalists marched from victory to victory during the two months following the Veracruz occupation; beginning on April 24 and ending on July 8, revolutionary armies captured Monterrey, Nuevo Laredo, Tampico, Zacatecas, and Guadalajara, in that order, and in the process virtually destroyed effective Huerta resistance in most of the country. With Huerta's power crumbling, the First Chief could well afford to give affront to an international group attempting to bring the fighting to an end and to resist pressures from the United States, the ABC powers, and his own subordinates;[46] he was supremely confident that his own armies could accomplish the task, and therefore he needed no help from the outside. He could boast, as he did late in June to a New York newspaper, that the Constitutionalist government had

---

concerning the formation of a provisional government; a few days later the First Chief agreed to "consult the opinion of the generals" on the question, and he apparently did so. On July 10 he reported to the mediators that the majority of the generals refused to agree to such conferences.

[46] In mid-June, Zubarán Capmany from Washington urged Carranza to alter his stand, since his position was causing unfavorable comment.

made "no compromises with that government [the United States] nor with any other; that [the Constitutionalists] have received no pecuniary aid from foreign governments or citizens and that from the beginning of the . . . struggle [the Revolution] has been sustained and will continue to be sustained with national resources only."[47]

Despite Carranza's rebuff to the well-intentioned ABC mediation, and even though the Washington government had ample evidence that the Constitutionalists would resent outside interference, Wilson and Bryan continued to meddle in Mexican politics. Within a week after Huerta fled, Wilson decided to give the First Chief a lesson in elementary political science. In establishing the new government in Mexico City, the president said, the Constitutionalists must create confidence, and the first acts would determine the success or failure of the revolution. Three areas of policy gave the president particular concern. First, "foreign lives, foreign property, foreign rights, and particularly the delicate matter of the financial obligations, the legitimate financial obligations" of the Huerta government had to be respected. Second, "a most generous amnesty" for all military and political opponents would have to be proclaimed, otherwise world public opinion would be "hopelessly alienated." And finally, the Catholic church and its ministers would have to be treated with care and circumspection; the overt anticlericalism of some Constitutionalists had already made a "most unfortunate" impression on world opinion. President Wilson informed the First Chief that these suggestions were made in a spirit of great friendship and sympathy, and then added: "We have been forced by circumstances into a position in which we must practically speak for the rest of the world. It is evident that the United States is the only first-class power that can be expected to take the initiative in recognizing the new government. It will in effect act as the representative of the other powers of the world in this matter and will unquestionably be held responsible by them for the consequences."[48] Obviously, neither Wilson

[47] Carranza to the editor of the *New York Herald*, as he reported to Zubarán, June 29, 1914, in *Labor internacional*, p. 24.

[48] Bryan to Silliman, July 23, 1914, file 812.00/14052a, NA, RG 59.

nor his secretary of state had learned anything during the previous year of dealing with Carranza; they still felt called upon to exercise the tutelage that the Primer Jefe was determined to destroy.

Carranza's answer, transmitted through Fabela three days after receiving the note, was short and to the point and should have been expected. With respect to the foreign rights and financial obligations, the Constitutionalists would continue to act as they had in the past, giving protection and respecting obligations. But, Fabela said, "as far as the other points covered by your note are concerned, I am pleased to say that the First Chief will take them into consideration for careful study. They will be decided *according to the best interests of justice and our national interests.*"[49] In this reply Carranza stuck to a consistent line of policy. He admitted that foreign governments did have certain legitimate rights, and he was perfectly willing to give assurances with respect to those rights; he therefore could comment with dignity on the first point raised by Wilson and Bryan. But foreign governments had no rights with respect to purely domestic affairs, and he would therefore not even divulge his thinking on the subjects covered in the second two points.

Bryan, obviously miffed by the curt reply, immediately responded by reemphasizing the original points and adding a twist that Carranza could well have interpreted as an attempt at either blackmail or bribery. Unless Carranza followed the advice given in the previous message, said Bryan, it "might make it morally impossible for the United States to recognize a new government. If we do not recognize it, it could obtain no loans and must speedily break down. The existence of War in Europe would clearly make it impossible to obtain assistance anywhere on the other side of the water even if such excesses as we have alluded to did not themselves make it impossible; and such excesses would be quite as certain to alienate sympathy in Europe as they would be to alienate sympathy in the United States. . . . Our advice offered, and everything stated in our telegram of the 23rd, cannot be modified nor can we recede from it in the

[49] Fabela to Silliman, July 27, 1914, as transmitted in Silliman to SecState, July 31, 1914, file 812.00/12759, NA, RG 59. Emphasis supplied.

least."[50] Silliman duly transmitted the message to Carranza, who did not bother to respond.[51]

Carranza's attitude failed to daunt the secretary of state, who continued to bombard the First Chief with advice, comment, and protest during the critical days in early August when Carbajal's caretaker government was attempting to negotiate with the Constitutionalists. He urged Carranza to accord proper treatment to Carbajal's delegates and protested when the First Chief demanded unconditional surrender as a prerequisite to any discussion. He demanded that the Primer Jefe announce a general political and military amnesty to prevent fighting near Mexico City and pressed him to come to some agreement with Carbajal in "a conciliatory spirit." And, after Carranza finally entered Mexico City and pointedly ignored the diplomatic corps, he scolded the First Chief for his lack of courtesy. The correspondence of the period reveals that Bryan thought that he, not Carranza, was making the decisions, but it also reveals that the Primer Jefe's course of action was changed not one whit by the secretary of state's importunities.[52]

During all this period neither the Department of State nor the Constitutionalist government mentioned the vexing question of the Veracruz occupation. As a matter of principle Carranza had to protest the occupation, as he did, but, as a matter of practical politics, after mid-May he preferred that the port remain in U.S. hands rather than be returned to the Huerta government. Once he had established his government in Mexico City, however, he soon called the attention of the United States to the anomalous situation. On September 8 Fabela reminded George Carothers that the object of the original occupation had been to chastise Huerta only, according to Wilson's statements.[53] Now Huerta was gone, and with him went

[50] Bryan to Silliman, July 31, 1914, file 812.00/12648a, NA, RG 59.

[51] I have not been able to locate any response from Carranza.

[52] In the 812.00 series for the last days of July and the month of August, NA, RG 59, much of which has been published in *Foreign Relations, 1914*, pp. 568–591.

[53] Fabela to Carothers, September 8, 1914, in *Labor internacional*, pp. 109–110. I have been unable to find any document by which Carothers transmitted

the causes for the occupation; as a consequence the Mexican people were "showing daily in a more positive manner their aversion to said occupation, and some military chiefs have begun to direct themselves to the First Chief requesting him to ask the United States for the evacuation of that port." Carranza then asked, in most polite terms, for immediate action on the part of the United States.

When nearly a week passed without reply from Washington, Fabela called on the Brazilian minister, who was acting for the United States, to make a similar request but with a slight tinge of a threat when he pointed out that failure to withdraw from the port immediately would "greatly increase the bad sentiment already aroused against Americans, with deplorable results."[54] At approximately the same hour that the Brazilian sent his telegram informing Bryan of Fabela's demand, Wilson in Washington announced that he had ordered the army to withdraw its troops from the Mexican port, and a few days later Carranza designated Cándido Aguilar, his governor in Veracruz, to receive the port from the U.S. authorities. But within a few days a serious complication, which in Carranza's view again impinged on Mexican sovereignty and on Mexico's right to make her own domestic decisions, arose.

In Veracruz, General Frederick Funston began to hear rumors—probably correct but never completely verified—that as soon as the Carranza forces took over they would mete punishment to all those who had cooperated with the occupying force, to all those who had sought refuge in Veracruz fleeing from the victorious Constitutionalists, and to all those who had paid taxes or customs duties to the occupying army; the last were to be required to pay the duties again. Soon after Funston reported these rumors, the Washington administration on September 22 demanded that Carranza give specific assurances that the actions would not be undertaken and then, after waiting in vain for over a week for a reply, reiterated the

---

the note to Bryan. It is not clear why the note went to Carothers instead of Silliman, who had been accompanying Carranza as a special agent since June.

[54] As reported in Cardoso de Oliveira to SecState, September 15, 1914, file 812.00/13193, NA, RG 59.

demand.[55] On October 5 Fabela, without making any reference whatsoever to either of the previous notes, informed the United States that Carranza had given "full instructions" with respect to Veracruz, that Aguilar was ready to move in to maintain order and to give "full guarantees" to the populace; the only ingredient lacking was a fixed date for the withdrawal.[56] This response scarcely met the demand, and two days later the Department of State insisted on "a clear, explicit and public statement from General Carranza"; otherwise, the note strongly implied, the troops would stay in the port city.[57] A week later (part of the delay was occasioned by poor communications) Carranza informed Washington that the message had been sent to the Convention, then organizing in Aguascalientes, for a decision; after hearing from the Convention, Carranza would answer.[58]

By this time a full month had passed since Wilson's announced evacuation order, transports were in the bay, and the troops all packed—but they still occupied Veracruz. Seeing signs of a rupture within the Convention itself, and by now convinced that a war with Villa was inevitable, Carranza again requested that the Convention give him guidance;[59] he was obviously becoming concerned lest Veracruz be surrendered to the Convention rather than to his own forces. After a lengthy secret session on October 17 the Convention

[55] Lansing to Cardoso de Oliveira, September 22, 1914, file 812.00/13384, NA, RG 59. Much of the correspondence relating to the withdrawal has been published in *Foreign Relations, 1914*, pp. 596–627, and in *Labor internacional*, pp. 109–150. For a short description of the event see Quirk, *An Affair of Honor*, pp. 156–171.

[56] Cardoso de Oliveira to SecState, October 5, 1914, file 812.00/13397, NA, RG 59.

[57] Bryan to Cardoso de Oliveira, October 7, 1914, file 812.00/13431a, NA, RG 59, transmitting a message from Silliman to Fabela of the same date. Silliman had gone to Washington a few days earlier at Carranza's behest, and, since both the First Chief and Fabela had great confidence in his integrity, he sent the message to give the contents greater impact.

[58] Cardoso de Oliveira to SecState, October 14, 1914, file 812.00/13510, NA, RG 59. Carranza received the Silliman note on October 10, transcribed it to the Convention on October 13, and notified Cardoso de Oliveira on October 14.

[59] Carranza to the president of the Constitutional Assembly, October 15, 1914, in *Labor internacional*, pp. 117–118.

rendered its judgment: meet every U.S. demand by making a public declaration, perhaps through the Foreign Office, to the effect that no new duties would be imposed, that no punitive action would be taken against those Mexicans employed by the occupation forces, and that civil courts would handle all cases involving a charge of a crime against the state.[60] The Convention, obviously, was more anxious to oust the foreigners from Mexican soil than it was to uphold an abstract principle of Mexican sovereignty.

Whether Carranza himself was merely playing for time in the hopes that Wilson would tire of the game and order an immediate evacuation, or whether he believed that the Convention would denounce the demands as improper, cannot be ascertained, but the First Chief's entire career had made it perfectly plain that he would not agree to the Convention position. He hastened to inform those gentlemen of the errors in their thinking. The members of the Convention, he said, had failed to touch upon the fundamental question involved, which was the wisdom of acceding to the demands of the United States as a condition of the withdrawal; and then he amplified the point: "I think that any exemptions from contributions [paying customs duties or other taxes again] and the amnesty of the employees who served the invader are acts pertaining to Mexican sovereignty; acts which could be spontaneously dictated by the Mexican government without affecting national dignity, but if accepted as a condition imposed by the American Government would constitute an attack on the sovereignty of the Republic. I equally fear that acceding to the desires of the Government of the United States in this respect will be considered as a precedent of fatal consequences in our future relations with the United States, with respect to the question of our autonomy."[61]

About ten days later Carranza, through Fabela and without any noticeable heed to the Convention, finally delivered his reply to the United States. Bryan's first announcement of the evacuation, he recalled, had made no mention of any condition of any kind, and there-

[60] Antonio Villarreal to Carranza, October 17, 1914, ibid., pp. 118–119.

[61] Carranza to the generals of the Constitutionalist Army and governors of the Union, October 19, 1914, ibid., pp. 119–120.

fore the Constitutionalist government had taken the necessary ste to receive the port from General Funston; furthermore, Aguilar ha issued a manifesto that promised full guarantees to all residents Veracruz. This action should have been sufficient. Then the note g to the kernel of the matter: "As a consequence [of the above], Ven stiano Carranza, in charge of the Executive Power of the Natio cannot make declarations or [issue] manifestoes by which he w comply with the conditions of the American government, since th affairs to which these conditions refer must be under the exclusi jurisdiction of [Mexican] authorities and since, as in the prese case, giving them an international character would affect the dome tic sovereignty of the Republic."[62] But the department remain firm, just at the moment that Carranza felt it expedient to lea Mexico City in the face of Villa's threatening attitude in Aguasc lientes; in a note delivered to Fabela in Mexico City on Novemb 2, the day after Carranza's quiet retreat to Córdoba, Acting Secr tary of State Lansing insisted that the First Chief accede to th demands. The United States, he said, was not disposed "to delay th evacuation of Vera Cruz [*sic*], and that as soon as General Carran gives definite assurances in accordance with the request containe in the Department's September 22, 9 P.M., the date for the evacu tion will be fixed without further delay."[63]

The First Chief was in something of a dilemma. He could n knuckle under to U.S. demands, but with the impending strugg against Villa and the Convention he desperately needed the po facilities. Furthermore, Gutiérrez announced that his first act provisional president would be to issue a proclamation acceding U.S. wishes.[64] As the direct confrontation with the department ha

[62] Fabela to Cardoso de Oliveira, October 27, 1914, ibid., pp. 123–124. Th translation here differs slightly from that submitted by Cardoso de Oliveira Bryan on October 28, 1914, file 812.00/13699, NA, RG 59.

[63] Lansing to Cardoso de Oliveira, November 1, 1914, file 812.00/13610, N RG 59.

[64] Carothers to SecState, November 3, 1914, file 812.00/13685, NA, RG 5 This commitment on Gutiérrez's part put the department in a quandary, sin such assurances from the Convention would seem to meet the demands made b the department. In a "strictly confidential" message on November 6 (file 812.0

not produced the desired results, and since time was running out, Carranza decided to give in but to do it so obliquely that he could claim that Mexican sovereignty remained unsullied. He arranged to have the Veracruz Chamber of Commerce, which included most of those who had paid import duties to the occupying force, by petition indicate its full confidence in the justice of the Constitutionalist government and its faith that the government would not demand another payment.[65] But, said the petition, "be that as it may, those of us who sign this statement, the Mexicans by reason of proper decorum and patriotism and the foreigners through sympathy with this country which we esteem as our second motherland, neither wish to nor can admit that the government of the United States [has the right] to give us any kind of protection over the point to which we have alluded, believing that it is the Government of Mexico which should, without any pressure from a foreign power, in justice resolve the question of exemptions from fiscal imposts of any kind."[66] Carranza then, with great magnanimity, issued a decree stating that when the Constitutionalists took over the city no additional taxes of any kind would be demanded.[67] A few days later a similar series of events granted a general amnesty to all those Mexicans who had worked for the occupation authorities.[68] Fabela informed the Department of State that the decrees had been issued,[69] and the impasse

13744a) Lansing asked Carothers to discuss the question with Villa, since "this Department is doubtful as to course to pursue since the duty to enforce the guarantees of the convention, if Vera Cruz is delivered to [Cándido] Aguilar, would seem to fall on a general who has not recognized the authority of the convention to give such guarantees."

[65] According to Consul William Canada in Veracruz, a Constitutionalist officer circulated the petitions, and the men had little choice but to sign.

[66] C. Aguilar to Carranza, November 6, 1914, in *Labor internacional*, pp. 126–127.

[67] Decree of November 8, 1914, ibid., pp. 131–132.

[68] The documents may be found in ibid., pp. 133–138. Quirk (*An Affair of Honor*, p. 170) says that Carranza did not honor his own decree, and that the men who had worked for the occupation, "even the teachers," were dismissed from their positions and were not allowed to work in any government office.

[69] Cardoso de Oliveira to SecState, November 10, 1914, file 812.00/13730, NA, RG 59.

came to an end; on November 13 Bryan set November 23 as the date of the definitive withdrawal, and on that date the evacuation was completed without incident. Carranza had capitulated, but in a fashion that prevented the event from being used as a precedent for interference with domestic affairs.

The military events accompanying the great struggle against Villa brought the Constitutionalists additional international pressures, some legitimate and some of dubious justification under accepted practices of international comity. Attacks on border cities by either of the contestants almost invariably brought international complications, since rifle bullets—and occasionally artillery shells—fell into U.S. territory with sometimes fatal results. When these dangerous situations were called to Carranza's attention, he was invariably polite and cooperative, though generally ineffectual, and he even overlooked representations made directly to the local officials. Raiding bands operating within presumably Constitutionalist-held territory frequently endangered foreign property and lives. Constitutionalist officers often seized foreign properties and always used paper currency for their purchases, again to the detriment of foreigners as well as Mexicans. Throughout 1915 Carranza and his staff were continuously beset by grave diplomatic problems, some extremely embarrassing; he frequently had to fend off imperious demands made by the United States and in some cases found it expedient to give way,[70] but he generally held firm to the line he had established. The furor over Mexico City in the early months of 1915 was probably Carranza's most difficult problem, but it also was one that helped him in his campaign to establish Mexican control over Mexican events, unhindered by foreign pressures.

In early 1915 Mexico City was not merely the capital of the na-

[70] One of the more peculiar diplomatic episodes concerned the shipment of sisal from Yucatán. As an incident to the control of the states of Yucatán and Campeche, Carranza ordered the port of Progreso closed just at the moment when the U.S. processers of binder twine, necessary for grain harvest, needed the material to prepare for the summer crop. Wilson was prepared to send a naval force to Progreso to reopen the port, but Silliman was able to convince Carranza to allow the traffic to pass. The correspondence on the matter is in the 612.1123 series, NA, RG 59.

tion and therefore the seat of national government with its various governmental offices and foreign legations; it was also the premier industrial city, the greatest center of population, and, as a prestige symbol, a prime military target. Within the city more than 25,000 foreigners resided in their various "colonies," with Spaniards numbering about one-half and with U.S., Chinese, Turkish,[71] French, German, and British nationals following in that order. Most foreign residents, still savoring the Díaz regime, considered themselves to be in a special category with special rights and therefore above the petty annoyances of a revolution; furthermore, they organized an International Committee with representatives from seventeen "colonies." Obviously, if the bitter struggle really came to Mexico City and the population there had to suffer the trials and tribulations that the residents of other cities—Torreón, Chihuahua, Zacatecas, and Monterrey, for example—had already suffered, foreigners would be involved; and just as obviously, the foreigners in the capital were in no frame of mind to accept inconvenience, let alone actual privation.

During December, 1914, and most of January, 1915, rail connections between the city and Veracruz were severed by the advancing Constitutionalists, but the other lines to the north, south, and west remained open; the half million people living within the confines of the Federal District therefore did not have to depend upon local food production. But when Obregón entered the city on January 28, the Zapatistas closely invested his army and effectively prevented any traffic with the surrounding countryside or more distant points, save that area served by the Mexico City–Veracruz road; food then depended upon the eastern sector, a region that had never been able to sustain itself through its own food production.

Still, Obregón had a war to fight. He needed trainloads of munitions, food, clothing, and all the other impedimenta necessary for a major campaign, and the Constitutionalists needed all their rolling stock to meet those most urgent necessities. With avenues to the outside closed, and with the crisis created by the anomalous money

[71] The classification of "Turk" included all those from the eastern Mediterranean area; most of them were apparently Lebanese or Syrians.

situation,[72] food prices skyrocketed, some merchants closed their doors, and the populace—particularly the poor—began to suffer from hunger. As the situation worsened and as Obregón demanded loans and tax payments from the city's wealthy to give relief to the poor, the International Committee protested, their charge being that the food shortage was "due to the deliberate campaign of military leaders desirous of starving the working classes into enlisting."[73] To this charge the foreigners and some nationals later added that Obregón was "punishing" the city for "harboring" the Huerta and Conventional governments. The situation came to head, diplomatically, shortly before Obregón evacuated the city to continue his campaign to the north. When the merchants in the city, foreign and national, refused to open their shops on Obregón's demand, the general responded by saying that he would make no effort to maintain order in the event that the poor rioted over the lack of food; most of the well-to-do interpreted the statement as an invitation to riot and looting.

In the face of constant complaints coming from Brazilian Minister Cardoso de Oliveira in Mexico City, from private individuals and groups in the city whose messages left by diplomatic pouch, from foreign legations and embassies in Washington, and from citizens all over the country who were reading daily accounts of the horrors of starvation in the Mexican capital, Bryan and Wilson felt constrained to act. At the president's direction, Bryan sent Obregón and Carranza almost identical messages; Cardoso de Oliveira delivered the note to Obregón, who merely informed the Brazilian that "since foreign relations are the exclusive province of the Primera Jefatura," the message would be sent to Carranza.[74] The note, as delivered to

[72] See Chapter 6 for a short discussion of the situation in the city with respect to currencies. For a longer presentation, which generally accepts the view that the situation in the city was Obregón's deliberate creation, see Robert E. Quirk, *The Mexican Revolution, 1914–1915*, Chapter 8.

[73] Cardoso de Oliveira to SecState, March 2, 1914, file 812.00/14477, NA, RG 59, transmitting a statement from the International Committee.

[74] So said Obregón when he transmitted the message, Obregón to Carranza, March 7, 1915, ADN-DF 1919. Obregón gave no indication at the time that he even read the note. The note as here transcribed differs in minute detail from

Obregón and transmitted by him to Carranza, follows; it is a remarkable bit of arrogant fanfaronade.

The Government of the United States has noted with increasing concern the reports on General Obregon's utterances to the residents of Mexico City. This government believes they tend to incite the populace to commit outrages in which innocent foreigners within Mexican territory, particularly in the City of Mexico, could be involved. This government is particularly impressed with General Obregon's suggestions that he would refuse to protect not only Mexicans but foreigners in case of violence and that his present decree is a forerunner of others more disastrous in effect. In this condition of affairs the government of the United States is informed that the City of Mexico may soon be evacuated by the Constitutionalist forces, leaving the population without protection against whatever faction may choose to occupy it, thus shirking responsibility for whatever may happen as a result of the instigation to lawlessness before and after the evacuation of the city. The Government of the United States is led to believe that a deplorable situation has been willfully brought about by the Constitutionalist leaders to force upon the populace submission to their incredible demands and to punish the city on account of refusal to comply with them. When a factional leader preys upon a starving city to compel obedience to his decrees by inciting outrages and at the same time uses means to prevent the city from being supplied with food, a situation is created which is impossible for the United States to contemplate longer with patience. Conditions have become intolerable and can no longer be endured. The Government of the United States therefore desires Generals Obregon and Carranza to know that it has, after mature consideration, determined that if, as a result of the situation for which they are responsible, Americans suffer by reason of the conduct of the Constitutionalist forces in the City of Mexico or because they fail to provide means of protection to life and property, the Government of the United States will hold General Obregon and General Carranza personally responsible therefor. Having reached this determination with greatest reluctance, the Government of the United States will take such measures as are expedient to bring to account those who are personally responsible for what may occur.

---

the copy in the National Archives. The first draft, which Wilson read, was made by Lansing. Wilson made a few suggested additions, including a threat of joint action, which went to Carranza but not to Obregón (Wilson to Bryan, March 6, 1915, file 812.00/14504 1/2, NA, RG 59).

Exactly how the president and his secretary of state planned to "bring to account" Obregón and Carranza they never said. Fifteen months earlier an official in the department had pointed out to Bryan that the threat to "hold personally responsible" any individual in Mexico was a completely empty gesture unless the government were prepared to send a military expedition into the country, and this Wilson was scarcely prepared to do even though he apparently did consider another Veracruz occupation. The note, with its generally arrogant tone and its acceptance as fact of every accusation made against Obregón, irritated Carranza beyond measure on a number of counts.[75]

The fact that Obregón himself had received a copy of the communication through a diplomatic official was in itself a renewed slap at Carranza's government. Only a short time before, Carranza had reminded all his officers that diplomatic relations were "the exclusive province of the First Chief" and had ordered them not to "receive or admit, and much less to pass any decision upon, notes involving complaints" or any other matter concerned with foreigners or international relations. Eliseo Arredondo, Carranza's agent in Washington, quite pointedly delivered a translated copy of that order to the Department of State with the comment that Carranza was "really the only person with whom diplomats and consuls can deal" and that following these proper channels would prevent "many misunderstandings and deficiencies."[76] Bryan's failure to honor Carranza's order implied a complete distrust of Carranza himself; unless Obregón were handed the note by a representative of the Department of State, Bryan's action suggested, that general would never receive the warning.

Second, Carranza resented being addressed as though he were an unruly child who had to be threatened with a spanking in order to

[75] Silliman handed the note to Carranza personally in Arredondo's company. He reported, "American attitudes are resented" (Silliman to SecState, March 8, 1915, file 812.00/14530, NA, RG 59).

[76] Arredondo to SecState, February 15, 1915, file 812.00/14397, NA, RG 59, transmitting a copy of Carranza's circular in translation; the date of the circular is not given, but its content makes it clear that it was of recent vintage.

assure proper behavior. He was, in his own eyes, a man of destiny upon whom the future of Mexico depended, the head of a viable government which was functioning with remarkable efficiency under the circumstances. And perhaps most of all he was exasperated by Bryan's continual interference in what the First Chief believed to be purely domestic affairs.

Carranza's answer was immediate, lengthy, a nice mixture of forcefulness and suavity—and addressed to the president with an apology for going outside the normal channels of diplomatic intercourse.[77] He could not overlook the general tone of the note or let it pass without comment; he therefore began by saying that "the terms in which this note is worded would afford me cause for not answering it," and in so doing reminded the president that international comity demanded a degree of mutual respect. He then took the U.S. government to task for taking "for granted that the imputations made against General Obregón by an international committee" were true even before his own government had been given the opportunity to investigate those charges. Furthermore, he firmly reminded Wilson that "the right to occupy or evacuate Mexico City or any other place in the Republic must at all times be reserved and be exercised" by Mexican military authorities whose decisions would be based upon the "furtherance of the cause of the revolution." He denied all the charges made against Obregón, insisting that his general had done "everything in his power to alleviate" the distressing conditions in the capital city, that he had facilitated importation of food, and that, during his six-week occupation, there had been no "mobs, assassinations, looting, or any other of the outrages which are apt to occur and which frequently do in time of war." He admitted that conditions in the capital were distressing and that the populace suffered from hunger but, he said, "such a situation is the consequence, painful but unavoidable, of the state of war in which we are and which for the first time has really reached the City of Mexico." Having firmly corrected the president for jumping to conclusions

[77] As transmitted by Silliman to SecState, March 10, 1915, file 812.00/14550, NA, RG 59. Silliman delivered Bryan's note on March 8, and Carranza's answer was handed to him on the evening of March 9.

and for general ill-manners, the First Chief nevertheless bent his efforts to a clarification of the principal issue, the protection of foreigners.

He insisted that it had always been his policy, and would continue so, to give the utmost protection possible to foreign lives and property. He admitted that the United States had a legitimate stake in the welfare of its nationals living in Mexico City and that the Constitutionalists had an "obligation . . . to safeguard the lives of foreigners." He vowed that when his forces evacuated Mexico City—due to take place within two days—he would make every effort to protect the foreigners and to give them every aid to leave the city for safer places if they chose. He reminded Wilson that only a few days earlier the United States had recommended that its nationals within the city leave the country until conditions became settled, and he pointed out that only if the foreigners abandoned the zones of military action could they be truly assured of complete safety. And he closed on a pleading note by saying that there had been much more difficult and embarrassing situations in the past but these had been peacefully settled and that it would "prove most unfortunate if now, when the City of Mexico is alone involved, a situation shall arise which will destroy the hopes and purposes of the Mexican people."

President Wilson answered immediately with a mollifying note, and the next day Bryan notified the International Committee that Wilson opposed the publication of the committee's accusations; some of the heat between the two governments was therefore dissipated. But Carranza apparently decided to press his advantage in another direction. During the previous weeks he had been deluged with representations made by the United States in behalf of other nationals, particularly those within Mexico City; in each case the department adhered to the earlier tacit agreement by stating that the representation was made at the specific request of another government. But in both Mexico City and Veracruz the other nations did have agents, and, even before he sent his note to Wilson, Carranza gruffly told Silliman that "he did not understand the Department's position in having representations made in the interest of other nations . . . when these nationals have their own representatives in the persons of their consular officers here in Veracruz."[78] Bryan's answer was an admission of defeat; he told Silliman that "the various representatives bring the troubles of their nationals to us and we have been anxious to do all we could to help them, but if our efforts provoke protest from Carranza it is better to have the effort made through the local representatives of their nations."[79] He so informed the other governments having nationals in Mexico; Carranza, at last, had gained his point.

Obregón's withdrawal from Mexico City did not solve the diplomatic problem the city posed for Carranza; if anything the city was in greater isolation than before as the army moved north to meet Villa. Food remained critical, the foreign population still resided there, the rail lines continued to be adjuncts to the military operations, and the city itself continued to be a military target. Carranza's government could not be expected to take any responsibility for the protection of foreigners, but the United States and other nations did expect him to do what he could to alleviate the distress, particularly by instituting regular train service from Veracruz to the capital. One way to relieve the city, many groups felt, would be to "neutralize" both it and the railroad. But when Bryan instructed Silliman to discuss the question with Carranza, that special agent warned the secretary of state that such a proposal to the First Chief would be useless, and his judgment proved to be correct. With respect to Mexico City, Carranza was "unconcerned as to the situation there, unaffected by it and indisposed . . . to commit" himself to any policy. The foreigners were there by choice, and if they remained they would have to "endure the same condition endured by" Mexican nationals.

In addition, attempts to neutralize other cities, notably Naco, had proved fruitless, and there was no evidence to suggest that a similar attempt would be more successful with the capital. Nor could the Constitutionalists give serious consideration to the neutralization of the railroad or the institution of regular train service between Mexi-

[78] Silliman to SecState, March 10, 1915, file 812.00/14552, NA, RG 59.
[79] Bryan to Silliman, March 11, 1915, file 812.00/14552, NA, RG 59.

co City and Veracruz. The use to which the Carranza forces put the railroad constituted a critical part of the military operations, Constitutionalist officials maintained military authority and discipline ("even execution if necessary") over the trainmen, and "railroad service between points which are respectively within the lines of the opposing forces is entirely without precedent." Furthermore, regular train service would make it too easy for spies to gather information on the "Constitutionalists' affairs, plans and military movements."[80] Despite additional prodding, somewhat gentler than in the past, Carranza held firm, and the question gradually faded from importance even though the city continued to suffer until the Constitutionalists definitively occupied the city in August. Carranza had gained another point in his struggle against "tutelage," but the United States was not quite ready to abandon its traditional role of friendly advisor.

Secretary of State Bryan in early June resigned in a huff as a result of a difference with Wilson over the European situation, to be succeeded by Robert Lansing, who as counselor in the department had taken a line as meddling as Bryan's but perhaps more belligerent; therefore, the general posture of the administration toward Carranza changed not at all. One of Bryan's last official acts with respect to the Mexican situation was to send all U.S. agents in Mexico a statement issued by the president on June 2. After reviewing, in rather lugubrious terms, the conditions in the neighboring republic, Wilson harked to an oft-repeated theme: the United States could not "stand indifferently by" while Mexico destroyed herself, since the larger country had a "duty as friends and neighbors" to help bring the revolution to an end. The president then enunciated a new policy:

It is time, therefore, that the Government of the United States should frankly state the policy which in these extraordinary circumstances it be-

[80] Silliman to SecState, March 30, April 5, and April 9, 1915, files 812.00/14746, /14794, and /14824, NA, RG 59. In late May, Carranza did allow food shipments to Mexico City, even "at the risk of aiding the Zapatistas" (Arredondo to Carranza, June 3, 1915, ADN-DF 1915).

comes its duty to adopt. It must presently do what it has not hitherto done or felt at liberty to do, lend its active moral support to some man or group of men, if such may be found, who can rally the suffering people of Mexico to their support in an effort to ignore, if they cannot unite, the warring factions of the country, return to the constitution of the republic so long in abeyance, and set up a government at Mexico City which the great powers of the world can recognize and deal with, a government with whom the program of the revolution will be a business and not merely a platform. I therefore, publicly and very solemnly, call upon the leaders of the factions in Mexico to act together and to act promptly for the relief and redemption of their prostrate country. I feel it my duty to tell them that, if they cannot accommodate their differences and unite for this great purpose within a very short time, this Government will be constrained to decide what means should be employed by the United States to help Mexico save herself and save her people.[81]

For some days previously, the press had carried stories about the coming statement, the reported contents of which put Villa in a "defiant humor,"[82] but they elicited no response from Carranza.[83] Reactions differed when the president's message, with its gratuitous insults in the phrases "if such may be found" and "with whom the program of the revolution will be a business and not merely a platform," and with its tiresome threat of intervention, was widely distributed throughout Mexico. The Convention government in Mexico City, on its last legs and foreseeing ultimate defeat, made immediate and repeated attempts to convince Carranza of the necessity for laying down arms and establishing a new provisional government.[84] Hipólito Villa, the general's brother, interpreted it as distinctly favoring his brother. Villa believed, or feigned to believe, that only

[81] Wilson declaration of June 2, as published in Edgar E. Robinson and Victor J. West, *The Foreign Policy of Woodrow Wilson*, pp. 268–270.

[82] Cobb to SecState, June 1, 1915, file 812.00/15099, NA, RG 59.

[83] Arredondo on June 3 reported to Carranza that he and Charles Douglas had been able to have the message toned down from its original hostile note (ADN-DF 1915), but I find no other evidence to support the claim.

[84] Roque González Garza, the president of the Convention, passed a series of messages, through U.S. officials, to Carranza; but the Primer Jefe made no direct reply.

immediate cooperation among the contending groups would prevent massive armed intervention.[85] Carranza's Washington agent saw a great threat to his chief and urged him to make an immediate and favorable reply; otherwise Villa and the Convention would get an advantage.[86] And Silliman reported from Veracruz that Carranza's reply would be "appreciative, friendly and serene."[87]

When the First Chief did respond ten days later, he gave no indication of either friendliness or appreciation, nor did he address himself to Wilson. Immediately after reading the president's statement his first inclination was to reply directly to him,[88] but he soon abandoned that line of action; since the message was not addressed to him specifically, courtesy did not demand a direct answer. But he could, he thought, use Wilson's message as a lever in his own campaign, which at that time was going well. He therefore issued a public manifesto which, dated July 11 and delivered to the Department of State the following day with the request that it "be brought to the knowledge of His Excellency the President," made no reference whatsoever to Wilson's statement and only a short passing reference to foreign relations, in which he said he expected recognition for his government. The nub of his message contained no hint of a disposition to "accommodate" differences with the other factions: "I am therefore of the opinion that the time has come to call the attention of the warring factions still in armed opposition to the Constitutionalist Government to the futility of their attitude because of the recent definite victories gained by our army, as well as because of the conviction they must have of our sincerity and capability to realize the ideals of the Revolution. Therefore, I appeal to those factions to submit to the Constitutionalist Government in order to

[85] Obregón to Joaquín Amaro and other generals, June 21, 1915, ADN-Expedición Punitiva.

[86] Charles A. Douglas to Carranza, June 2, 1915, ADN-DF 1915.

[87] Silliman to SecState, June 4, 1915, file 812.00/15133, NA, RG 59.

[88] Arredondo, Douglas, and others in Washington made repeated requests for immediate action, and Carranza on June 4 told Arredondo: "I will proceed according to my convictions and the dignity of the nation. In accordance with these I will answer Wilson's note soon." The documents are in ADN-DF 1915.

expedite the reestablishment of peace and to consummate the work of the Revolution."[89]

Since the Carranza statement scarcely met the president's demands, and since all the other factions appeared willing—even anxious—to settle their differences peacefully, Lansing pressed his position. He instructed Silliman to inform Carranza "casually and in an unofficial and personal way" that he was waiting for some indication of a conciliatory attitude and that the reward for it might be recognition.[90] Silliman dutifully carried out his instructions even though he probably knew what the response would be; as he reported to the department, Carranza was "perplexed" by the Washington view and would "under no circumstances . . . treat with Villa; that there was no expediency that could induce him to make any offer whatever." Furthermore, the "intimation of possible recognition did not in the least affect his impassive face. He did not want recognition conditioned on conciliation."[91]

Obviously another tack was necessary if U.S. influence were to have any effect on the termination of the struggle. Lansing was so distraught that he recommended a course of action based upon the conviction that "nothing can be accomplished through them [the various leaders] to restore peace and stable government." He felt that "Carranza, Villa, and other factional leaders" had to retire and that negotiations should be carried on "through their lesser chiefs." His weapons: "withdrawal of moral support" and an arms embargo.[92] On this general assumption, and carrying out a suggestion earlier made by Leon Canova,[93] Lansing and Wilson began maneuvering to bring the other American nations into the play. In early July, Lansing

89 Arredondo to SecState, June 12, 1915, file 812.00/15215, NA, RG 59, enclosing a copy of Carranza's manifesto.

90 Lansing to Silliman, June 18, 1915, file 812.00/15261a, NA, RG 59.

91 Silliman to SecState, June 22, 1915, file 812.00/15288, NA, RG 59.

92 Lansing to Wilson, July 5, 1915, file 812.00/1540 1/2a, NA, RG 59.

93 Canova to Lansing, June 11, 1915, file 812.00/15283 1/2, NA, RG 59, suggested that the Caribbean nations, in which a large number of Mexican refugees resided, might be induced to make some representations to Carranza, and that these might then be used as a base for multilateral action.

conferred with the Washington representatives of Argentina, Bolivia, Brazil, Chile, Guatemala, and Uruguay and in the following weeks received commitments from all six governments to give aid and support to the United States in attempting to establish a government based upon conciliation among *all* the military leaders, not merely the three or four at the top. Under date of August 11 the seven representatives, including Lansing, invited nearly a hundred military leaders in Mexico to accept their good offices for the purpose of arranging a conference either inside or outside the country for the purpose of establishing a government that would warrant recognition from other nations.[94]

The response from the Conventionists, including the Villa and Zapata groups, was indeed gratifying; they were perfectly willing to attend a conference arranged by the seven diplomats; most of them accepted individually, while many indicated they would follow the wishes of their superiors. For about ten days Carranza made no reply at all, and when he did it was only for the purpose of clarifying a minor point: Were the seven diplomats speaking as representatives of their governments in their official capacity, or as private individuals?[95] The question appeared to be innocent enough, but when all the men assured Carranza on September 3 that they did have the authority of their governments behind them, the Primer Jefe revealed the real reason behind the question. Since the diplomats had signed the invitation in their official capacities, Carranza said, he could not "consent to a discussion of the domestic affairs of the Republic by mediation or on the initiative of any foreign government whatever."[96] The First Chief's answer, which he undoubtedly

[94] The statement is published in *Foreign Relations, 1915*, pp. 735–736. The invitations were delivered by the U.S. consuls in their districts, each consul being instructed to use his discretion as to the "prominent military and civil authorities" to receive them. The exact number to whom the invitations were delivered is in doubt, but the department received over eighty replies.

[95] Acuña to Lansing and others, as transmitted by Silliman to SecState, August 24, 1915, file 812.00/15898, NA, RG 59.

[96] Transmitted by Silliman to SecState, September 10, 1915, file 812.00/16988, NA, RG 59.

wrote but which appeared over the signature of Jesús Acuña, whom one U.S. official characterized as "an inexperienced boy,"[97] was excessively polite but firm. Mexican domestic affairs were of Mexican concern alone and "the acceptance of the invitation . . . would deeply affect the independence of the Republic and set a precedent for foreign intervention in the settlement of . . . internal questions." Such an action would be unthinkable. But, he concluded, if the diplomats wished to come to Mexico "for the purpose of discussing Mexican affairs from an international standpoint, with the sole object of determining whether . . . Venustiano Carranza exercises a de facto government," he would be delighted to make the arrangements to meet in a safe and convenient place.

And in this contest of wills Carranza had developed an extremely strong position. The reports from Mexico City, which his forces reoccupied in early August, were exceptionally good, with quiet and order prevailing. Constitutionalists had pushed Villa back on every front, and the Centaur of the North was even then having to contend with Tomás Urbina's defection.[98] A feeler that Lansing put out to woo Obregón away from Carranza had come to nought.[99] Without exception the Constitutionalist officials who had answered the diplomats' invitation had referred the question to Carranza, and only a few even commented on the contents.[100] Some of the Latin American diplomats who joined to extend the invitation had second thoughts, fearing that such mediation by an international group might indeed

[97] Canada to SecState, August 30, 1915, file 812.00/16016 1/2, NA, RG 59.

[98] Villa accused Urbina of keeping money that should have been sent to him, whereupon Urbina defected. In early September, Villa captured and executed him.

[99] Lansing hoped to have Obregón and General Scott, for whom Obregón had great respect, meet to discuss Mexican politics, with the obvious intent of convincing Obregón to intercede with his chief to mollify his stand (see Lansing to Consul Hanna, Monterrey, August 13, 1915, file 812.00/15717, NA, RG 59).

[100] Jacinto B. Treviño's long reply may be found, in both Spanish and the English translation, as an enclosure of Vice-Consul, Monterrey to SecState, August 20, 1915, file 812.00/15760, NA, RG 59. Replies from others are published in Isidro Fábela, ed., *Documentos históricos de la revolución mexicana*, III, 236–290.

set a precedent for intervention.[101] Finally, Carranza's irritation over U.S. meddling, which he showed in myriad ways,[102] began to have an effect in the Department of State. By mid-September no one in Washington really believed that a government could be established in Mexico through conciliation; one of the contending forces would ultimately have to be recognized, and of those forces only Carranza's gave any signs of vitality. The question was no longer one of alternative governments to recognize; it was simply whether to recognize Carranza. Lansing, nevertheless, remained reluctant to abandon a course of action he had instituted three months earlier, and he continued to discuss the question with the other six diplomats well into October.[103] But the longer he conferred the more obvious was Carranza's strength; by the first week in October the Constitutionalists effectively controlled all the nation save for parts of Chihuahua, Sonora, Morelos, and Oaxaca. Faced with the hard fact of the Constitutionalist victory, Lansing could do little but recommend de facto recognition for the First Chief, with no conditions and no commitments.[104]

When Carranza stood in the municipal palace in Torreón on October 19 to listen to Special Agent John Belt read a message from Lansing announcing recognition,[105] he had established the principle

[101] Ambassador da Gama admitted as much to David Lawrence, who had Lansing's ear (Lawrence to Lansing, October 1, 1915, file 812.00/16347 1/2, NA, RG 59).

[102] One way of showing his irritation was to refuse to grant a personal interview to Silliman, whom he liked. One confidential agent reported on August 30 that Silliman had not seen Carranza in weeks and that U.S. influence with Carranza was "virtually zero" (see Canada to SecState, August 30, 1915, file 812.00/16016 1/2, NA, RG 59).

[103] The details of the conferences, including stenographic notes, may be found in the 812.00 series for August, September, and October, NA, RG 59. A sufficient number of the documents have been published in *Foreign Relations, 1915*, to present a rather clear picture.

[104] Carranza was materially aided by Lansing's conviction that Germany would benefit from continued turmoil in Mexico, and that it was therefore mandatory for the United States to recognize and give aid to the strongest group.

[105] Carranza was then on tour through the country.

that Mexico as a sovereign nation had a right to determine its own fate without interference from other nations singly or in combination.[106] It was probably his greatest single contribution to Mexican freedom.

[106] The sterile and unfortunate Punitive Expedition in 1916–1917, brought on by Villa's raid on Columbus, New Mexico, was in no way an attack on the principle of national sovereignty. The documentation on that affair from the U.S. point of view may be found in the 812.00 series, NA, RG 59, and particularly in army files, NA, RG 94: file 2394312 deals with the early phases of the situation, including the Obregón-Scott meetings, and file 2416172 deals specifically with the battle of Carrizal and includes affidavits from all the U.S. survivors. The ADN documentation is rich on the subject from the Mexican side but includes little about the diplomacy. Volume II of Fabela, *Historia diplomática de la revolución mexicana*, and *Labor internacional*, contain most of the published diplomatic correspondence from Mexico. For an excellent secondary account see Clarence C. Clendenen, *The United States and Pancho Villa*, pp. 234–295.

9. A NEW CONSTITUTION

A section in the Plan de Guadalupe provided for national elections "as soon as peace is consolidated" after the triumph of the Constitutionalist army, but a recurring theme after mid-1913 was the proposition that civil and representative government would be reestablished only after reforms had been instituted by decree.[1] The December, 1914, additions to the plan played upon that theme and expanded it by giving the First Chief dictatorial powers to issue decrees, to appoint and remove "freely" all state and national officials, to convoke municipal elections after "the Supreme Chieftainship is reinstalled in the City of Mexico," and ultimately to supervise the election of a national congress to which the Primer Jefe would report. Only after that congress had an opportunity to study Carranza's reforms and to "ratify, amend, or complement, and raise to con-

[1] Many U.S. agents so reported after consulting with Carranza and others. Hale was particularly impressed by this determination and accurately forecast a long delay between the culmination of fighting and the reinstitution of constitutional government.

stitutional rank those which should have that character" would constitutional order be established. Carranza, in retrospect, viewed the hasty peace made by Madero with the government in 1911 as a disaster that finally destroyed Madero himself, and he had no intention of making the same mistake. He was determined to eliminate, insofar as it was possible, any danger to the new regime when it came to power through election.

Carranza could have returned his government to Mexico City any time after the middle of August, 1915. By that time Constitutionalist forces had secured the city, hemmed the Zapatistas into an ever-narrowing circle, and opened communications to the north and west. Carranza's men had cleared central Mexico, as far north as Zacatecas, and the complete west coast, except for a portion of Sonora, of all effective enemy resistance. But the First Chief was in no hurry to return to the capital city with his government; once there he would feel impelled to begin the process of establishing civil government, and that he did not wish to do until victory was an achievement rather than merely an immediate prospect. But in the early fall the omens for peace improved. Villa, unable to withstand Obregón's power, by the first week in October abandoned the entire north save for Chihuahua, and even there his organization seemed to be crumbling and many of his top-echelon commanders were defecting. Urbina was dead, Angeles was in the United States, and the Madero brothers were discouraged. Villa himself was then in the process of concentrating his forces in northern Chihuahua in order to move his base of operations to Sonora,[2] where the remnants of Maytorena's army still occupied Nogales and a few other sites, and Carranza agents were negotiating with the Villa commander in Ciudad Juárez to surrender that city. With complete victory only a step away, Carranza decided it was time to move.[3]

On October 2 State Department Special Agent John W. Belt re-

[2] One of the documents captured after the Columbus raid was a long letter from Villa to Zapata dated January 8, 1916, in which he summarized his activities after early October; it is a part of the 237763 file, NA, RG 94.

[3] Zapata still controlled much of Morelos and parts of the adjoining states, but Carranza never considered him to be a real threat to his government, merely an enormous nuisance.

ported from Veracruz that the First Chief planned an extensive journey with stops at Tampico, Monterrey, Torreón, Chihuahua, Zacatecas, and Guadalajara before returning to Mexico City.[4] Carranza never clarified the object of his trip, but he certainly had no well-planned itinerary for a tour that ultimately extended over a six-month period during which he and his retinue passed in triumphal march through twelve states, visited dozens of cities, and stopped at hundreds of smaller towns. Traveling first to Tampico, and accompanied by most of his high government officials, the First Chief by slow stages in early October passed through Monterrey and Saltillo on the way to Torreón, where he happened to be at the time he received notification of his de facto recognition on October 19. There Obregón joined him in what John Belt described as a "most clever political move" in view of some persistent rumors that the two leaders had come almost to the point of an open break.[5] After nearly two weeks in Torreón, Carranza and his numerous escorts—members of his government, his own military guard, the governor of Coahuila and his staff, Obregón and his aides, a military band, and a small army, for a total of about fifteen hundred persons[6]—left the Laguna city for the border, stopping in Monclova for four days. On November 2 he arrived in Piedras Negras, where for the next five days he made speeches, attended banquets, and held audiences; among those who paid their respects was John Lind. While there, Carranza allowed Obregón and Cándido Aguilar to cross the international boundary to fraternize with newspapermen and prominent local citizens, but he, himself, true to the rule he had established nearly two years before, never stepped out of his own country.

After a very satisfactory and flattering stay in that border city, Carranza returned to Monclova, making a side trip to his home in

[4] Belt to SecState, October 2, 1915, file 812.00/16350, NA, RG 59. Belt accompanied Carranza for some weeks in Silliman's absence. One or the other reported almost daily on the First Chief's moves; the documents are in the 812.00 file, from October through April.

[5] Belt to SecState, October 22, 1915, file 812.00/16568, NA, RG 59.

[6] So estimated Consul Blocker in Piedras Negras when Carranza arrived in that city (Blocker to SecState, November 2, 1915, file 812.00/16675, NA, RG 59).

Cuatro Ciénegas, and then continued to Saltillo, where he told Silliman that he planned to visit all the states and that it would be "near the end of the year" before he arrived in Mexico City.[7] He left his old state capital on November 18, spending the next month in travel to Nuevo Laredo and Matamoros and points in between before returning on December 19. Four days later he departed for San Luis Potosí, arriving there on Christmas Day; with the frequent stops, he needed nearly two full days to cover the three hundred miles. The local leaders in San Luis had never been strong Carrancistas, and their attitude toward him was cold to the point of hostility; he was, according to one reporter, "much displeased with his reception."[8] On December 30 he arrived in Querétaro, where he had originally planned to stay only a few days but where he spent nearly six weeks; while there, he ordered his governors to begin making plans for municipal elections,[9] and he also authorized any citizen of the Republic to execute Villa without trial, since he was "outside the law."[10]

In February he renewed his journey, going first to Guanajuato and then to Guadalajara, where his tour probably reached the apex of pomp; his official family consisted of not only four members of his cabinet and the local governor and commandant, but also seven other governors and three other commandants.[11] Obregón, on his way to Sonora for his own wedding, came along for good measure. After a few days in the western capital Carranza visited Colima and then Manzanillo, remaining there for some days before returning to Guadalajara, where on March 10 he received his first information about Villa's Columbus raid. He left immediately for Querétaro, the site of his temporary capital until he returned to Mexico City, at

[7] Silliman to SecState, November 15, 1915, file 812.00/16798, NA, RG 59.

[8] Thomas Dickenson to SecState, December 29, 1915, file 812.00/17052, NA, RG 59.

[9] Silliman to SecState, January 14, 1916, file 812.00/17101, NA, RG 59.

[10] Silliman to SecState, January 19, 1916, file 312.115C96/60, in *Foreign Relations, 1916*, p. 465.

[11] Cabinet ministers heading Gobernación, Foreign Relations, Hacienda, and Development and Communications; governors of Nuevo León, Tamaulipas, Coahuila, San Luis Potosí, Guanajuato, Veracruz, and Tabasco.

last, on April 15. But while in Querétaro he made two significant changes in his government; on March 13 Obregón took the oath of office as secretary of war and marine just before Cándido Aguilar took the same oath as secretary of foreign relations.[12]

The peace that seemed so close in October still eluded Mexico in April. To be sure, Villa in Sonora had been routed and his great army almost destroyed in a series of battles in November and December. Back in Chihuahua, with only a handful of men and embittered against both Carranza and the United States, the wily bandit-revolutionary roamed the countryside venting his spleen on all who refused to cooperate. In January he created a serious problem when he directed the execution of sixteen U.S. mining engineers at Santa Ysabel, and in March he led a raid on Columbus, New Mexico, which brought about the Punitive Expedition with all its consequent troubles for both Mexico and the United States.[13] Throughout that year and the next he appeared and disappeared like a will-o'-the-wisp, occasionally commanding armies of five thousand or more men who, after a successful attack on a town or a city, dispersed in small groups, hid their arms, and awaited another summons from their leader. Constitutionalist forces presumably controlled the state but, as Consul Letcher pointed out, it appeared as though Mexico had "entered upon another of the hopeless cycles of revolution with the usual phenomena apparent, namely, the government in charge of the cities and larger towns and the opposition holding the countryside and marauding at will."[14] Before the end of 1916 Villa had captured, and subsequently evacuated, every major city in the state except Ciudad Juárez, and he ended the year by capturing and looting Torreón. The government seemed helpless. Villa knew the countryside too well and had too many followers, and the Carranza officers were too inept. General Francisco Murguía, to whom Obre-

[12] Ignacio L. Pesqueira circular of March 14, 1916, ADN-DF 1916.

[13] In short, after Carranza appeared to have given permission but actually had not, Pershing led an expedition into Mexico to attempt Villa's capture. The expedition was an utter fiasco and accomplished nothing save to bring the two nations to the brink of war, particularly after a clash between U.S. and Mexican troops at Carrizal in June. Pershing withdrew in January, 1917, empty-handed.

[14] Letcher to SecState, February 9, 1916, file 812.00/17268, NA, RG 59.

gón in late November assigned the task of pacifying the state, complained bitterly that Villa fed on the discontent engendered by government military and civil officials. Most of them, he contended, were corrupt, greedy, and inefficient in every way except that of stealing; as a consequence the majority of the people felt they could enjoy greater freedom and protection under Villa than under the Carranza government.[15]

But Villa was not the only man in arms against Carranza, nor was Murguía the only Constitutionalist who accused his colleagues of dishonesty. From Durango, Zacatecas, Sinaloa, Guanajuato, San Luis Potosí, Tamaulipas, and a host of other states came a steady stream of reports concerning bandit-revolutionary raids that disrupted communications, undermined the economy, and hindered the return to constitutional government. From many states, too, came reports of dangerous friction among the Constitutionalists. Governors quarrelled with commandants, generals quarrelled among themselves, civilians upbraided military men, and officials accused other officials of corruption, brutality, and sloth.[16] Furthermore, most states reported food shortages, high prices, unemployment, pestilence, and general economic malaise. The outward signs were scarcely propitious for a return to an orderly and representative political system. In February one pessimistic U.S. consul reported: "There is now a very pronounced sentiment among the more intelligent Mexicans, that the defacto [*sic*] Government will not be able to handle the situation. They are able enough to expound the theory of reform and progress, but in practice they are woefully wanting. Mexico at present can be compared to kindergarten without teachers or mature persons."[17] Perhaps the judgment was too harsh, as was Leon

[15] Murguía to Carranza, December 13, 1916, ADN-Coahuila 1916. Murguía was bluff, tough, and completely devoted to Carranza.

[16] The ADN is filled with these complaints by officials against other officials, as well as with thousands of reports of armed activity.

[17] Gaston Schmutz (Aguascalientes) to SecState, February 9, 1916, file 812.00/17281, NA, RG 59. Schmutz was notoriously unsympathetic to the Constitutionalists from the beginning, and to the Mexicans in general. In a later report (February 17, /17326) he insisted that the foreigners constituted the only able and honest group in the country.

Canova's when he said bitterly that Carranza "frittered away his time travelling around the country" instead of taking the steps necessary to order the economy, suppress brigandage, and institute popular government.[18] In any case, the panorama in early 1916 was not such that Carranza and his advisors could visualize an immediate return to popular, representative, and constitutional government.[19]

Carranza's return to Mexico City in mid-April did nothing to instill greater efficiency or honesty among his military and civilian officials. In early June one U.S. representative reported that a "conservative" assessment of the situation was "financial chaos threatened and impending, graft principally through army rampant, executive inefficiency pronounced, beneficial coordination [in] departments lacking, foreign treaty rights through ignorance or design being disregarded, State Governments usurping Federal authority, aggression against property and vested privileges prevalent, public confidence almost disappearing, food supply insufficient and precarious, bandits operating boldly and successfully and political antagonism to general Government gaining in strength."[20]

In spite of this dolorous picture, the First Chief decided in mid-June that the "armed struggle [was] concluded insofar as it may have assumed any truly political character," and that the time had arrived to begin the process of returning to a "legal order."[21] He therefore decreed that the long-heralded municipal elections would take place on the first Sunday in September, and that the newly chosen officials would serve from October 1, 1916, to December 31, 1917. While Carranza allowed the state governors—his own appointees—to establish the election procedures for their own areas, he ordered them to limit eligibility for candidacy in two important

[18] Canova confidential memorandum, February 14, 1916, file 812.00/17271 1/2, NA, RG 59.

[19] The Carranza government was, in fact, issuing multitudinous decrees covering every aspect of Mexican society, but decrees could not restore value to fiat money, or stop the ravages of typhus then reaching epidemic proportions.

[20] Special Representative James L. Rodgers (Mexico City) to SecState, June 6, 1916, file 812.00/18332, NA, RG 59.

[21] Decree of June 12, 1916, in Jesús Acuña, *Memoria de la Secretaría de Gobernación*, pp. 349–350.

respects. No military man in active service could be a municipal officer; presumably he could be on active duty at the time of the election, but he would have to leave the service prior to assuming his municipal post. More importantly, no man would be eligible if he "had aided with arms or by serving as public employees, those governments or factions hostile to the Constitutionalist cause." Thus, by a stroke of the pen the First Chief eliminated from consideration every man who had served in a municipal post after February 22, 1913, except those designated by Carranza himself, as well as those who had served at any time in any armed force opposed by Carranza, and any man who had served in any public capacity under the areas of Huerta, Zapata, Convention, or Villa control. Strictly enforced, it would have meant that anyone who taught in the schools in Hermosillo during early 1915 would have been ineligible to hold a municipal office. Carranza justified the restriction on the ground that he had to be certain "to eliminate the possibility that the election of those municipal authorities might fall on persons who have been armed enemies of the Cause or who . . . have served [those enemies] even in private occupations." On September 3 the elections were held "throughout the Republic with absolute freedom and without obstacle," according to the Primer Jefe.[22] A decree issued the following day suppressed the powerful and often corrupt office of *jefe político* and completed the establishment of the "autonomous municipality" by providing a more nearly adequate fiscal base.[23]

According to schedule the next step in the return to constitutional order was to have been the election of a national congress, to whom Carranza was due to report. But in view of continued rebel activity within Mexico and the obvious counterrevolutionary plotting among the exiles, Carranza and his advisors decided to alter the plan. In other times, he said in a decree of September 14,[24] reforms instituted

[22] Venustiano Carranza, *Informe . . . encargado del poder ejecutivo de la República*, p. 62.

[23] Decree of September 4, 1916, in Acuña, *Memoria*, pp. 355–356.

[24] As a part of the preamble to the decree. This decree, along with two of September 19, establishing the procedures for selecting the delegates to the convention, are in ibid., pp. 356–368.

during a period of revolution had later been incorporated into the constitution, and this procedure he had originally planned to follow. But with so many little revolutionary bands operating for the ostensible purpose of creating a new order of things, he feared that the malcontents would use any excuse to attack the established government. In order, then, to eliminate "all pretext for continuing to alter public peace and conspiring against the autonomy of the nation, and at the same time to avert any delay in indispensable political reforms," it was necessary to convoke a constitutional assembly, freely elected, for the sole purpose of writing a new constitution. To that assembly he committed himself to present a draft that the delegates could "discuss, approve or modify," and that would have incorporated within it all the reforms instituted by decree.

His schedule called for an election on October 22, the preliminary sessions for organization from November 20 to 30, and the substantive sessions from December 1 to January 31, 1917. He selected Querétaro, the scene of Maximilian's last defeat and his execution, and his own temporary capital earlier in the year, as the site for the momentous task. Under his decree every electoral district in the nation, as it existed in the 1912 election, was to select a delegate and an alternate, their necessary qualifications being the same as those established for a member of congress under the Constitution of 1857 but with the predictable ban on any who had served "governments or factions hostile to the Constitutionalist Cause." The decree also barred any "individual exercising authority" from being chosen "in the place subject to his jurisdiction." In recognition of the enormous displacement of persons during the revolution, Carranza broadened the definition of "citizen of the state"—a requisite for candidacy—to include anyone born in the state, anyone who had lived there for six months prior to the election, or anyone who had qualified as a citizen there at the time of the Huerta coup. This meant, in short, that a man could represent a district he had not seen in years, or one to which he had been sent recently under military orders. The decree explicitly allowed the formation of political parties of any shade or posture but banned those organized for the purpose of electing "individuals of a particular race or creed."

Five days after the above decree, Carranza issued an electoral law based upon universal manhood suffrage. The decree spelled out the methods for gathering lists of qualified voters, giving proper surveillance of the polling places, casting ballots, and final counting and registering of the vote. Armed men were not to be stationed within a block of the polls, no one was to electioneer in the immediate area, and no one was to cast his ballot while either in uniform or bearing arms. On the face of them the provisions seemed to guarantee a completely open election in which even the defeated enemies could organize political parties and vote although they could not be candidates. But one thing the First Chief refused to do despite heavy pressure from his advisors: he would not declare a general amnesty under which thousands of exiles and expatriates could return and safely take part in the political process. A few months later he gave his reasoning for his adamant stand. Everyone had a right to expect, he said, that once the armed conflict terminated, those who had been defeated would with "the best good will accept the new order of things." But, he continued,

> far from this the expatriates, the Huertistas as well as those of other political coloration, instead of bringing their hostility to the Constitutional Government to an end, have continued and still continue that hostility; there are proofs that they have been the ones who have brought on all the attacks which have been the cause of difficulties between the Government of the United States and that of this Republic, with the unpatriotic object of bringing about intervention into the affairs of this country, and they and they alone are the ones who are encouraging all the little bandit gangs who are roaming the nation, robbing, murdering, burning and, in a word, causing all the ills they can.[25]

[25] Carranza, *Informe*, pp. 72–73. In his reference to the United States, Carranza was concerned not only with the Villa raid and the Punitive Expedition. During much of 1916, and well into 1917, bands from Mexico entered the United States, robbing and occasionally killing. U.S. troops pursued some of these into Mexico and brought the two nations close to war. There is some evidence to suggest that these groups received funds and encouragement from expatriates along the border, particularly from Vázquez Gómez, Villarreal, Blanquet, Rasgado, and Félix Díaz. But most evidence suggests that only the Villa raid on Columbus was politically motivated.

With only a month to prepare for the elections, those who h particular interest in the outcome began a flurry of activity. Poli parties mushroomed at the local level, most of them carrying name of either "liberal" or "constitutional" or both, and all of t dedicated to the election of a particular slate of candidates in immediate region; nothing even resembling a national party veloped. Long before the election it had become obvious t observers that three men had gained the political spotlight: Car za, Obregón, and Pablo González. Carranza clearly hope dominate the convention; his leadership had earned him that h he thought, and he encouraged his staunchest supporters and cl advisors to become candidates. Pablo González, either throug spect for his chief or through timidity, wanted no part of a d challenge to Carranza and therefore neither took part in the c paign nor allowed his friends to work in his behalf.[26] Obregón the other hand, encouraged his supporters to band together to delegates even though he himself refused to become a candid Most of the little temporary organizations that called themse political parties, then, leaned heavily in favor of either Carranz Obregón, without an overt alliance with either.

On paper all participants were to have a completely free hand ing the electoral process, but the practice seldom measured u the theory. In the main the pressures were quietly applied; in of the general ignorance and indifference this practice sufficed. to assure the selection of men truly representative of the dist on occasion more direct action became necessary, as was the cas Mexico City when police raided and closed one party conven because the delegates had the temerity to nominate a slate displeased the First Chief.[27] In some districts a number of candid campaigned—in one rural district in Puebla thirty-one aspir contested the one seat[28]—but in most districts only one or two

[26] Félix Fulgencio Palavicini, *Mi vida revolucionaria*, pp. 291–292. Palav was Carranza's minister of education when the campaign began.

[27] So reported Charles Parker in a confidential message to SecState, Oc 10, 1916, file 812.00/19487, NA, RG 59.

[28] Gabriel Ferrer de Mendiolea, *Historia del congreso constituyente de 1 1917*, p. 42.

peared. About one-eighth of the districts had none at all because rebel or bandit activities made elections impossible.

Only a small proportion of the eligible voters cast their ballots in what most observers characterized as a generally orderly election;[29] "there was not a single case of blood-letting," according to one authority.[30] The victors included a fair sprinkling of military men who had at one time acted as governors of states under a Carranza appointment, and a goodly number of Carranza's closest collaborators; among the latter were three cabinet ministers and three of his closest advisors who occupied subcabinet posts. But also among those elected were a great number whose names had never been prominent nationally and who had never taken part in the revolution, in either a military or a civilian capacity.[31]

Whether the men who began to arrive in Querétaro in mid-November really represented the Mexican people has always been the subject of debate. The Carranza decrees of October certainly limited the representative nature of those finally chosen. The widespread lethargy, because of either apathy or inexperience, did little to assure the selection of men truly representative of the district, particularly in areas outside the major concentrations of population.

29 The exact proportion cannot be computed for lack of evidence. Immediately after the election Carranza ordered that all certified results, with the proper documentation from each voting booth, be sent to the Ministry of Gobernación for safekeeping until the convention met. But either by design or through ignorance, most of the election officials failed to do so. Some sent the documents to the governor, some to municipal officials, some to the elected delegate, and some to Gobernación. The result was that most records were either destroyed or lost. But those complete records which did reach the credentials committee indicate a participation of less than 30 percent overall, and less than 10 percent in some districts. The reports of the committee may be found in the *Diario de los Debates del Congreso Constituyente, 1916–1917* in those sections devoted to the sessions of the Electoral College. The reports to the Department of State uniformly indicate a light vote.

30 Ferrer de Mendiolea, *Historia del congreso constituyente*, p. 42.

31 Complete rosters, both by alphabetical order and by states, may be found in ibid., pp. 161–187, and *Diario de los debates*, II, 1233–1249. Djed Bórquez [pseud. for Juan de Dios Bojórquez], *Crónica del constituyente*, pp. 736–744, gives an incomplete alphabetical list in which he characterized each delegate as "leftist" or "rightist."

Furthermore, Carranza's definition of "citizen" created the anomalous situation of allowing a virtual stranger in a district to be elected as a delegate. And despite Carranza's careful election law, some men were frightened away from the polls, and others voted as they were instructed. All these conditions made it appear that the delegates were of a single mind and mold, representing a single view, and that the view was Carranza's. Yet after the convention met, the tremendous spectrum of political and social philosophy became clearly evident; even Zapata had his champion.[32] But the spectrum did not include the old conservatives; those philosophically attached to the *porfiriato* had no spokesmen in Querétaro.

Delegates began arriving at the convention site days before the scheduled November 20 opening, and before that date a major quarrel developed over the question of the eligibility of some of Carranza's most devoted followers.[33] The First Chief's decree banned as delegates those who had aided the enemy by "serving as public employees" under opposition governments, but Carranza had brought into his government a number of men who had been members of the Bloc Renovador elected in 1912 to the lower house, and who had remained in the Chamber of Deputies under Huerta. They had been "public employees" under Huerta, most of them had voted to accept Madero's resignation in order to save his life, and they had accepted payment from the Huerta government. But they gave little aid and comfort to the dictator; it was this group which consistently blocked Huerta in the legislature and which finally forced the October crisis and the subsequent dissolution of the congress. A few of the bloc had slipped out of Mexico City and joined the revolution between February and October, but most of them had remained and had been jailed by Huerta; they were freed only after Huerta fled nine months later. Twenty-eight of the original members were elected as delegates and three as alternates; fourteen of the twenty-

[32] Colonel Luis T. Narro of Puebla, who insisted that many of the Zapatista leaders were more honorable and honest than some of the convention delegates.

[33] Unless otherwise indicated, all information concerning the organization and the debates of the Constitutional Congress comes from the *Diario de los debates*. No citations will be made except to quotations.

eight had been imprisoned by Huerta, and only a few had served Carranza in other than a civil capacity, but they were his closest advisors. Of those elected, four became prime targets even before the first meeting:: Alfonso Cravioto, José Natividad Macías, Félix F. Palavicini, and Luis Manuel Rojas. The ardent Obregonistas knew them to be passionate Carrancistas and believed them to be malevolent influences whose advice to Carranza had been responsible for internal bickering and for the failure to solve many outstanding economic problems. Obregón himself particularly despised Palavicini because some of his antics in Veracruz had created a critical situation, which for a time threatened the necessary supply of arms for the Villa campaign.

The burden for developing the case against the "renovators" was gladly accepted by Carranza's Minister of Gobernación Jesús Acuña;[34] his animosity for Palavicini was even greater than Obregón's. He gave special instructions to Manuel Aguirre Berlanga, his immediate inferior in Gobernación and a delegate to the convention, to challenge the credentials of the first "renovator" whose name came before the assembly; his principal target was Palavicini, but he was willing to eliminate them all. But Palavicini, early on the scene, became aware of the maneuvering and so informed Carranza.[35] On November 20 the First Chief dispatched a long communication to Aguirre Berlanga averring that the "renovators" who had remained in the Huerta legislature had done so at his specific order, transmitted to them by Eliseo Arredondo, because they could give greater service to the revolution by obstructing Huerta in Mexico City than they could by taking the field. Since he had given his assurance of the impeccable revolutionary antecedents of the men in question, Carranza assumed the issue to be dead. But he was wrong.

Interrupted train service between Mexico City and Querétaro delayed the opening of the first preliminary session, but at 10:30 A.M.

[34] Prior to his post in Gobernación, Acuña had been in charge of foreign affairs. When Palavicini's credentials were challenged on November 28, and Acuña's part in the affair became public, Carranza abruptly dismissed his minister of *gobernación* with the curt note that he had "lost confidence."

[35] Palavicini, *Mi vida revolucionaria*, pp. 292–293.

on November 21 the convention began when 140 of the possible 246 delegates met in the auditorium of the Palace of Fine Arts.[36] By prior agreement,[37] the temporary presidency fell to the first name on the alphabetical list of the elected delegates, Antonio Aguilar,[38] whose only duty was to preside over an election of officers who would function during the preliminary sessions. The new officers, with Manuel Amaya of Nuevo León as president, then supervised the election of members of two credentials committees, one of fifteen to examine the credentials of all other delegates, and one of three to weigh those of the first credentials committee. By careful caucusing and the preparation of a slate, the dedicated Obregonistas completely dominated the major credentials committee,[39] electing thirteen of fifteen; they made no attempt to control the second committee, which went unanimously to the dedicated Carranza group. Selection of the officers and the two committees consumed the entire first session, which adjourned at about ten o'clock that night.

For the next three days the committees examined credentials while the remainder of the delegates took a temporary respite from work, but on November 25 the second committee made its report. Fourteen of fifteen delegates, the chairman said, had submitted valid credentials which could not be questioned; even four "renovators," including Alfonso Cravioto, were cleared of any stigma for having served the Huerta legislature. But the committee found Carlos M. Esquerro of Sinaloa to be ineligible to sit in the convention, since he had served the Gutiérrez government for twenty days. The fact that he had been a "renovator," had fled Mexico City in March, had joined Carranza in October, had stayed with him during

[36] The number of electoral districts was 246, but 28 held no elections. The Carranza decree stipulated the quorum as one-half plus one, which was interpreted to mean of the total districts, which meant 124.

[37] In a Carranza decree issued after the election.

[38] Julián Adame of Zacatecas actually headed the list, but he had not arrived.

[39] The word "Obregonistas" is used for want of a better term. The convention included a relatively small number of passionate Carranza supporters who believed it an act of lese majesty to question any of his acts. Obregón had no such following, but those in the convention who were willing to challenge Carranza came to be termed Obregonistas or, later, "leftists."

the remainder of 1913 and most of 1914, and had rejoined the Constitutionalists after his short stay with Gutiérrez did not mitigate his gross error in having served the Convention government, said the committee report. But the issue was clearly not his antecedents, but his political posture; he was a dedicated Constitutionalist, but not a passionate Carrancista. If Esquerro could be eliminated on those grounds, then other Obregonistas could on others; the decision on his case was a test of strength, the outcome of which would determine the complexion of the convention. Most of the delegates recognized it for what it was, and for four days, off and on, the battle raged, with recriminations becoming more and more bitter. But the Esquerro supporters had the majority and forced the committee to submit a recommendation on November 28 that he be seated; the committee did so with ill grace:

> The Commission modifies its report in the sense desired by the majority of this Assembly, in order to obey parliamentary rules and practices, but it gives full responsibility to this House for violating the law imposed by the First Chief of the Army; a law made precisely to close the doors, at least for the moment, on those who turn their backs [on their friends] in order to give a fraternal embrace to our enemies; on those who cry out with frenetic emotion in the moment of apparent triumph, . . . "Long live Villa! Long live Angeles! Long live Robles! Long live Urbina and all those who have triumphed with the Convention!"[40]

In this bitter statement the committee was not striking primarily at Esquerro; it was striking at all those who were willing to challenge Carranza's leadership, even in the slightest degree. On the vote, Esquerro received 111 votes to be seated, while 50 delegates opposed his taking a seat. The members of the convention, obviously, had no intention of following Carranza's dictates blindly.

Palavicini carried the fight against Esquerro, but the Sinaloan, within little more than an hour after receiving an affirmative vote, had an opportunity to strike back. It so happened that Esquerro was the chairman of a subcommittee that examined Palavicini's credentials, and he brought in a report that recommended rejection of

[40] *Diario de los debates*, I, 118.

Palavicini's credentials on the ground of electoral fraud. As in the Esquerro case, the reason given for the recommendation had little to do with the real issue; Palavicini and what he stood for comprised the issue, not electoral fraud. During four hours of vicious debate, filled with invective and passion, Rafael Martínez de Escobar undertook not only to prove the allegations of electoral fraud but also to convince the delegates to reject Palavicini on the grounds of political immorality, while Palavicini in his own defense tried to impress upon the group that he was the victim of a dirty conspiracy against the First Chief himself. During the course of the charges and countercharges the gap between Palavicini and his group on the one hand and the Obregonistas on the other not only became clear, but also widened. Martínez de Escobar used logic and brutal attack as his weapons; Palavicini depended upon oratorical skill, knowledge of law and literature, and contemptuous wit. Martínez de Escobar, in reviewing Palavicini's history, accused his opponent of being a turncoat, of being completely devoid of any set of principles revolutionary or otherwise, and of switching sides as the situation warranted. He was a revolutionary for profit, said the speaker, because "he needed to have an automobile; a revolutionary because he needed to have a great house; a revolutionary because he needed fine food for his palate." If, said Martínez, "we were to strip Mr. Palavicini, we would find that from his head to his toes Mr. Palavicini is, politically, a black spot, a sinister blot." After an hour's peroration in which he put particular emphasis on Palavicini's failure to denounce Huerta, he concluded:

> And so, I repeat, it is necessary that Mr. Palavicini not be accepted as a deputy to the Constituent Congress and that the report be voted upon favorably, because Mr. Palavicini will serve only as a hindrance to this Congress; because Mr. Palavicini will not work for radical change, and in a moment of forgetfulness he will be converted into a defender of clerical privileges. We must support the report of the Commission, which is based upon a political criterion and it is based upon a legal criterion; for these reasons I ask this honorable Assembly not to admit impostors such as Mr. Palavicini into the bosom of the Constituent Congress.[41]

[41] Ibid., pp. 31, 32, 37.

In his two-hour defense (a rule of debate limited any single presentation to thirty minutes but was seldom enforced) Palavicini began on a contemptuous note by comparing Martínez de Escobar to one of "those poor worms who are unable to fly because they have not passed the stage of a chrysalis, who have not yet become butterflies and will never be able to dream of having the strong wings of a condor; they creep and they sting." The entire set of allegations, he said, was part and parcel of an "intrigue" set in motion by Obregón and Acuña, with Esquerro, Martínez de Escobar, and others acting as their lackeys. Esquerro's credentials, "dripping with fraud and exuding Villaism," had been accepted, and yet this man had the temerity to challenge his credentials because of some perfectly innocent irregularities. On one occasion Palavicini referred to Martínez de Escobar as a flea, on another as a pumpkin, and on still another as an inept child who could only fulminate. Between these attacks on others, the speaker reviewed his own history as a revolutionary and found himself to be dedicated, honest, courageous, loyal, principled, steadfast, and all the other things his enemies were not. Gerzayn Ugarte, another "renovator" and Carranza confidant, came to his friend's defense in terms no less insulting; tempers flared and at one point a physical combat almost ensued. The debate might have continued into the next day had not Cándido Aguilar, Carranza's foreign minister and a revolutionary of recognized merit but utterly loyal to his chief, demanded a closed session; there he said that Palavicini was a "dead politician" and not worth fighting over. Then he added: "It bothers me that we are losing time in discussing his credentials, when at this moment we have Francisco Villa occupying the capital of Chihuahua; when at this moment there are intrigues in the United States to prevent the signing of a [new] constitution, and not only in the United States but in Mexico as well . . . The American Government does not under any circumstances want this constitution completed."[42]

Aguilar's statement, with its implied threat of intervention com-

[42] Palavicini's long reply in his defense, along with the other statements quoted, may be found in ibid., pp. 136–154.

ing from the United States, effectively stopped the debate; in a blaze of patriotic fervor the arguments came to an end with the delegates rejecting, by a vote of 142 to 6, the committee's recommendation. The next day, with little debate and by voice vote, the convention seated the controversial Palavicini.[43] The score was even.

The acrimonious debates over Esquerro and Palavicini settled no issues but they did serve to make it clear that the convention was not a simple Carranza or Obregón agency; it was an assembly of independent-minded men. The debates also, unfortunately, exacerbated feelings on both sides to such an extent that mutual distrust made effective work in the convention difficult. The Esquerros and the Martínez de Escobars would put no faith in any argument raised by the Palavicinis or the Ugartes, nor would the latter listen to the points raised by the former. But the time consumed in the debates at least had one salutary effect; it made the delegates realize that if they continued in the same manner they would never finish the job; accordingly, in a flurry of hard work and apparent good will on November 29 and 30 the examination of credentials went smoothly and rapidly. By early evening on November 30 some credentials still needed processing, but the convention had seated 182 delegates, including Macías, Rojas, and Cravioto. Credential committee reports continued to come in after the convention began its substantive sessions; nine such meetings occurred, the last on January 25. By the time the last delegate had been seated, four had been denied seats on the grounds of their having served Huerta, two for having been in some vague way "enemies of the revolution," one for continuing in command of troops during the election in his district, one for electoral fraud, and one for being a Spaniard and not a Mexican citizen. In each case the alternate or the defeated candidate was approved, and officially the convention was composed of 218 delegates. But only 193 ever took their seats, and seldom were there more than 160 on the floor at any given moment.[44]

[43] The final action may be found in ibid., pp. 194–195.

[44] Two hundred nine signed the completed constitution, but only because in some cases both delegate and alternate had taken an active part and therefore earned the honor. For example, Cándido Aguilar attended the early sessions,

The last act of the preparatory sessions, on the evening of November 30, was the election of the permanent officers of the convention, which was to begin its deliberations the following day. The balloting, again after caucusing, went quietly and without discussion. Rojas emerged as president, to be aided by two vice-presidents, four secretaries, and four vice-secretaries. After the new officers were properly installed and all the delegates had taken the simple oath devised by Carranza, eleven delegates spoke for longer or shorter times about the glorious work that remained to be done; most of it was sheer oratory for its own sake, but Cándido Aguilar attempted to bring a degree of sanity and cooperation:

> I come not to make a speech, since others have done it; I come to fulfill an act of patriotism, I come to propose to the honorable assembly that we forget all the attacks which have been made; I come to say that when I attacked Aguirre Escobar, I did it because I thought it my duty; I come also to say that Aguirre Escobar is an honorable man. Gentlemen: We must bring to an end this struggle of personalisms in which we have been involved. Beginning tomorrow we must undertake a distinctive work. We must surrender ourselves to the task of constitutional reform. I suggest to all . . . that they withdraw all the insults, all the injurious remarks, which they have made.[45]

A voice of quiet reason and of diplomacy, it went unheeded; the insults, the injuries, the "personalisms" continued.

In the meantime Carranza, with his great sense of drama and history, departed from the National Palace in Mexico City at 8:00 A.M. on November 18 with a cavalcade of fifty men to make the long trek to Querétaro by horseback.[46] Following the path used by Maximilian in his retreat from Mexico City to Querétaro before his final capture and execution in 1867, the First Chief arrived at the convention site shortly after noon on November 24. There he held court, plotted strategy with his friends but made no overt attempt to interfere in

---

took leave to attend to the problems of the foreign ministry, and returned in January. Both he and his alternate Carlos Gracidas signed.

[45] *Diario de los debates*, I, 225.

[46] Obregón accompanied the First Chief into the suburbs but returned to his office by automobile.

the credentials quarrel, and waited for the formal opening. With all in readiness, on the afternoon of December 1 he appeared at the convention hall, properly escorted, to present his draft constitution and to deliver a two-hour explanation of the changes he had incorporated.[47] He had committed himself, he said, to present a draft in which "the liberal spirit and the form of government established [in the Constitution of 1857] would be preserved intact; that the reforms would be limited to eliminating the inapplicable parts, filling in the deficiencies, dissipating the obscurity of some of its precepts, and cleansing it of all the additions which were inspired only by the intent of using them to enthrone dictatorship."[48] Throughout his presentation he put great emphasis on the need to give adequate protection under the law to all, equally; in the process he dwelled more on the inequities of the past than on the changes he proposed. He made passing reference here and there to modifications incorporated, but spent more time discussing innovations not included; he spoke for a full fifteen minutes, for example, justifying his failure to include provisions for a parliamentary or cabinet form of government. And when he had concluded his speech the delegates could have said of him what Carlos Esquerro said about Palavicini on one occasion; he spoke a great deal and said little.[49]

His draft constitution reflected little of the turmoil that had been going on for the past four years; it was indeed simply a rewording and a reorganization of the Constitution of 1857 as it had been amended over the years, with a few of the "deficiencies" corrected. The most significant changes were in the purely political articles and had no surprises: no reelection for the president or for state governors, direct rather than indirect election for all officeholders chosen by the electorate, the elimination of the vice-presidency and a change in the procedure for selecting a successor to the president in case of his death or resignation, and a number of restrictions de-

[47] José Natividad Macías and Luis Manuel Rojas did most of the actual drafting, but they insisted that the ideas were Carranza's.

[48] *Diario de los debates*, I, 262.

[49] Carranza was a master of prolix prose, particularly in his formal addresses and in the preambles of his decrees; but he could also be curt and succinct.

signed to prevent officeholders from using their positions to assure their election to other positions. He included a few items with social and economic implications: lay education, freedom for all religions, ejidal lands to be worked in common "until they are divided by law," and protection against monopolies on articles of prime necessity. He even added a droplet of xenophobia by barring foreigners from owning real property without first renouncing any protection from their own governments. But in view of the pattern that had developed during the preconstitutional period, the draft was more remarkable for what it did not include than for what it did. He added not one new word with respect to the subsoil, the nationality of priests, the ownership of property used by religious organizations, the agrarian question, or the rights of labor and labor organization. The draft may well have been an improvement over the existing one in terms of clarity and organization, but in no sense could the changes be characterized as fundamental. Had the constitution that ultimately emerged followed closely the draft in all its provisions, without significant additions, it may not have been worth the roughly 150,000 man hours and 2 million pesos it cost.[50]

Although Carranza presented his draft to the convention on December 1, the members had no opportunity to see it until December 6, when they received the printed copy. In the meantime a test of strength occurred. Following the rules adopted, on December 5 the convention officers presented, for the assembly's approval or rejection, the nominees for the nine working committees, the most important of which was the Commission on the Constitution, charged with the responsibility of presenting a draft of each article, working from the Carranza draft as a guide. For that committee the board presented the names of José Natividad Macías, Guillermo Odorica, Gerzayn Ugarte, Enrique Colunga, and Enrique Recio. The proposal was an obvious attempt at compromise, but stacked in favor of the Carranza claque; the first three were "renovators" closely attached to Carranza, and the others were younger men of an Obregón affilia-

[50] My estimates, based upon the number of people, the number of hours spent in debate, the daily allowances, and the travel expenses, as well as secretarial and printing costs.

tion. As soon as the discussion started, Esteban Baca Calderón read a statement which began: "With all due respect and consideration for my companions, I would like to make this point: I think I interpret at this time the feelings, if not those of all the Assembly cerainly a great part of it; we have—those who have the same view as I—looked with profound distrust upon José Natividad Macías, very honorable, very respectable, very illustrious, and very wise; but this distrust is very much our own."[51]

In the ensuing debate the Carranza clique upheld the nomination on the grounds that Macías had helped draft the constitution and that he was certainly the most knowledgeable man there on constitutional law and practice. But the opposition objected to Macías because he *had* aided in the drafting. One speaker wanted "new elements not enamored of the ideas" in the draft; it was, he said, "an undeniable psychological fact that the author of a proposition must defend it to the utmost, against wind and tide, simply because he is the author of the proposition."[52] In view of the opposition, the board withdrew the nominations and on the following day, just before the reading of the draft constitution, allowed an open election. For this eventuality the opposition had prepared themselves, and they carried the day; the convention elected Francisco Múgica, Luis G. Monzón, Alberto Román, and the two earlier nominated—Colunga and Recio. It was a solid, unanimous Obregonista committee, chosen by an enormous majority; Colunga, Múgica, and Monzón each received more than 90 percent of the votes cast. The votes for Macías and Ugarte were too few to record.

One factor in this overwhelming majority was the propensity for contempt and intellectual arrogance that Palavicini, Macías, and many of the others closely allied to Carranza persistently demonstrated. On one occasion Palavicini said to one delegate, a metallurgical engineer: "I don't know whether you know arithmetic." Ugarte showed the same disdain by saying that "surely, in questions of law, an attorney knows more than a shoemaker." On another,

[51] *Diario de los debates*, I, 321. The laudatory terms had been used about Macías during the credentials debates.

[52] Ibid., p. 323.

Macías heaped scorn on Rafael Martínez because, he said, Martínez was "so terrified by all the sufferings which have befallen the laboring classes" that he could not even understand the written word. This was their pattern of operation. Anyone who disagreed, even in the slightest, became the victim of sarcasm and vitriolic wit. They did not reserve their waspishness for their ideological opponents only; many who agreed completely with the draft, and who were willing to accept it as it stood with a few minor changes, were treated in the same fashion. They were brilliant men, but their personalities unfortunately undermined their effectiveness in the convention setting.[53]

After Secretary Fernando Lizardi droned through a two-hour reading of the draft constitution—why it was thought necessary to read it aloud, when each delegate had a printed copy, is a mystery—the convention took a four-day respite to allow Múgica's committee to study the draft and bring in its first recommendations. On December 11 the committee presented a preamble, Carranza's draft articles 1 and 2 without change, a sharply altered article 3, and Carranza's article 4 with an addition that would prohibit the sale of alcoholic beverages and the maintenance of gambling houses.[54] Within the next few days the preamble,[55] and articles 1, 2, and 4 were approved without serious contest, although the Múgica addition was removed from article 4. But article 3 raised a storm. Carranza's article read: "There is to be full liberty of instruction, but that given in official educational establishments will be secular, and the instruction im-

[53] Palavicini carried his animosity with him when the convention completed its work. As a director of a newspaper, he was frequently acerbic in his comments about those of whom he disapproved.

[54] The first twenty-nine articles are a part of a section entitled "Individual Guarantees." Article 1 guaranteed constitutional protection to all, article 2 prohibited slavery, article 3 concerned education, and article 4 concerned the right to work in a licit profession, commerce, industry, or other activity. Múgica's committee, and many other revolutionaries, objected violently to both drinking and gambling.

[55] A long wrangle developed over the name of the nation, whether it should be the "United Mexican States," or the "Mexican Republic"; at issue was a concept of federalism, but the arguments were reminiscent of those of the early nineteenth century.

parted by these institutions will be free at both the upper and lower primary levels."[56] The Múgica version more nearly coincided with the thinking on religion and education since 1913: "There will be liberty of instruction; but that given in official establishments of education will be secular, as will be the upper and lower primary instruction given in private schools. No religious corporation, minister of any cult, or any person belonging to a similar association may establish or direct schools of primary instruction, nor give instruction in any school [*colegio*]. Private primary schools may be established only subject to the supervision of the Government. Primary instruction will be obligatory for all Mexicans, and in official establishments it will be free."[57]

This radical departure from the draft article, of course, shocked and enraged Palavicini, Macías, and their group, who fought bitterly to defeat it and substitute the original. As a group they were anticlerical, some of them violently so, but they believed that every parent ought to have the right to choose the school for his child; they also refused to consider the parochial schools as a danger to the public educational system. They used every trick they knew over a three-day period, which consumed between fifteen and twenty hours of debate; they even insisted on inviting Carranza to the opening debate in the hopes that his presence would influence both the nature of the debate and the final vote. Carranza came, he sat and listened, and he left without comment—and without effect. As it became more and more obvious that the committee had majority support, the minority speakers became more furious and more insulting, as well as more lofty and abstract in their arguments. Both groups, of course, insisted that they were Carranza's true friends and that their opponents were traitors to both the Primer Jefe and the revolution. Both groups insisted that they upheld the true revolutionary tradition. As the debate ground on, the opposition did force the committee to withdraw the recommendation to make some changes, but when it was all over, Múgica and his group won a solid

[56] The draft constitution may be found in *Diario de los debates*, I, 345–364.
[57] Ibid., p. 371.

victory; by a vote of 99–58, the convention approved article 3 to read: "Instruction is uncumbered; but that given in official establishments of education, as well as that in the upper and lower levels of primary instruction in private establishments, will be secular. No religious corporation, nor minister of any cult, may establish or direct schools of primary instruction. Private primary schools may be established only subject to supervision by the government. In official establishments primary instruction will be gratuitous."[58] The words differed from the Múgica draft, but the meaning was essentially the same except for the provision of obligatory attendance; the delegates thought that provision more properly belonged as a part of the duties of Mexican citizenship, and it appears in article 31. Antonio Villarreal had long since departed the camp of the Constitutionalists, but he would have applauded this article which would prevent "the pure white soul of childhood, the idealistic burning spirit of youth" from being "deformed" by clerical teachings.

Article 5, which Múgica's committee handed the assembly on December 12, provoked even greater discussion than article 3, and it ultimately was responsible for a new section in the constitution. Carranza's draft, which differed only minutely from that of the revised 1857 constitution, prohibited forced labor except that imposed as a penalty by a court, forbade any contract that limited personal or political freedom, limited personal labor contracts to one year's duration, and barred monastic orders, since they were in contravention of the above principles. The Commission on the Constitution changed few of Carranza's words, but made a significant addition: "The maximum work day will be eight hours. Night work for women and children is prohibited in industries. A weekly day of rest

[58] The constitution as it was originally completed and signed on January 31, 1917, may be found in *Diario de los debates*, II, 1181–1222, and in Ferrer de Mendiolea, *Historia del congreso constituyente*, pp. 189–251. Felipe Tena Ramírez, *Leyes fundamentales de México, 1808–1964*, gives the constitution as it had been revised to the latter date, but includes in the appendix the original version of the revised articles. *Foreign Relations, 1917*, pp. 950–981, has a not-too-accurate translation. The March, 1917, issue of the *Annals of the American Academy of Political and Social Science* has a more accurate translation, which is compared, article by article, with that of 1857.

is established as obligatory."[59] When the debate began on December 19, the recommendations brought an immediate and volatile response from the delegates, dozens of whom sought permission to speak either for the article or against it. The members deluged the committee with proposed additions and changes, some in written form to the committee chairman and some in oral form from the floor. As the debates ground on and on, and as the committee withdrew and resubmitted the article frequently in an effort to obtain a consensus, it became obvious that no agreement could be reached; it was also obvious that the convention generally sympathized with the idea of limiting the length of the work day, protecting women and children, and guaranteeing a weekly day of rest. Finally young Froylán Manjarrez of Puebla made a suggestion on December 26:

When the Secretary of this honorable Congress read us the list of those inscribed to speak for and against [the article], a feeling of animadversion against the Assembly itself began to inundate my spirit; I thought that there were very few of us here who were friends of the worker; but fortunately all of those who have come to impugn the recommendation have accepted the thesis of improvement for the working classes, wanting certain modifications, or, better said, putting certain additions to the recommended article. . . . [the worker needs protection, and] precisely because there are so many points which must be treated with respect to the worker, we do not want them all to be in article 5; it is impossible. We must make it more explicit in the text of the constitution, and I say to you it is absolutely necessary to request the committee to present us with a proposal for an entire title, an entire part of the constitution.[60]

Múgica's committee was too burdened with the study of the draft before it to give the necessary time to write a completely new article; the work pressure on the committee had been so great, in fact, that the convention had designated a second Commission on the Constitution only a few days previously to lighten the burden.[61] But

[59] *Diario de los debates*, I, 556.
[60] Ibid., pp. 687–688, 689.
[61] Consisting of Paulino Machorro y Narváez, Hilario Medina, Arturo Méndez, Heriberto Jara, and Agustín Garza González. The last became gravely ill and left Querétaro on January 8; his post on the committee was not filled.

something had to be done about the article; the feeling of the delegates was too strong to be ignored. Now it so happened that the cabinet minister under whose general jurisdiction labor questions fell was a delegate, as was his secretary in the office. A civilian with a distinguished revolutionary career and widely known for his devotion to land reform and social justice, Minister of Fomento Pastor Rouaix enjoyed the respect of both principal factions but was identified with neither. A few days after Manjarrez's suggestion, upon which the convention took no official action, Rouaix met with his secretary Rafael L. de los Ríos, his chief of the labor section José Inocente Lugo (not a delegate), and Macías to discuss the possibility of such a new article. Before the end of the year the four instituted regular morning meetings, inviting other delegates to come and express their views.[62] The informal sessions had no legal or official standing; Rouaix kept no minutes, called no rolls, recorded no votes. Through the first ten days of January the group—sometimes as many as fifty and other times as few as five—drafted and redrafted, attempting to incorporate every needed guarantee to labor into one comprehensive article. On January 13, Rouaix presented the proposal, signed by seventy delegates who represented every shade of political opinion and every section of the nation. After much discussion and some slight change,[63] the convention on January 23 unanimously approved it; at the same time it also approved a slightly modified article 5, which followed the Carranza draft closely.

The proposal submitted by Rouaix, as reformed and accepted by the assembly as article 123, constituted the most enlightened statement of labor protective principles in the world to that date. The second longest article in the constitution and the only one enjoying a separate title, it instructed the states and the national government to enact labor legislation within a stipulated framework. It provided

[62] The account for these informal meetings, and their outcome, is taken from Pastor Rouaix, *Génesis de los artículos 27 y 123 de la constitución política de 1917*, pp. 103–141.

[63] The draft, which had support from Rojas, Palavicini, Cravioto, Macías, and Alfonso Cabrera, as well as from such "Jacobins" as Jara and Calderón, was referred to the second Commission on the Constitution. This committee made some changes and submitted it to the convention.

for a maximum of eight hours for regular work, seven for night work, and six for children between the ages of twelve and sixteen, as well as one day of rest each week. It gave protection to mothers before and after parturition. It required a minimum wage, to be determined on the basis of local conditions but sufficient to "satisfy the normal necessities of life of the worker, his education, and his honest pleasures, considering him as the head of a family." It stipulated wage payment in legal tender, double pay for overtime, equal pay for equal work regardless of sex or nationality, and the right to organize and to strike. It required management to install proper safety devices, to furnish adequate housing at low cost and schools when the enterprise was in an isolated area, and to accept the responsibility for accidents or job-related illnesses. The article established a method for settling conflicts between labor and management, with both taking part in the procedure. It prohibited dismissal without just cause, abolished debt peonage, and, finally, it encouraged the formation of mutual insurance societies and cooperative housing organizations.

In the meantime the two committees responsible for using Carranza's draft as a base for making recommendations continued their normal work routine, but by mid-January it had become clear that the schedule would have to be stepped up if the congress hoped to complete its labors by January 31. By January 14 only half the Carranza articles had come before the convention, and of those only about 80 percent had been approved. Beginning on that date, then, the congress began meeting twice a day instead of once; on some days the debates ran until well after midnight. After that date, too, the commissions on the constitution presented great blocks of the proposed constitution to the assembly, and the delegates in turn voted on as many as six or eight articles simultaneously; most of the recommendations received unanimous or near-unanimous approval. In the earlier days each proposal made by a committee was accompanied by a lengthy printed statement of justification, which gave the delegates a summary of the committee's thinking; but in the last hectic two weeks the assembly dispensed with this practice—the printers could not keep up—and on many occasions a committee presented an article with no statement at all, and the convention accepted the proposal without a single word of debate. The convention took on an air of frenzy, with the delegates frequently shouting at one another, often stomping their feet to drown out the voices of the debaters, and repeatedly demanding the vote.

In that atmosphere of tension, fatigue, and impatience, two of the most important, and later most controversial, articles in the entire constitution came before the convention in the waning days. The first of these, in convention chronology, was article 130.[64] A part of the Carranza draft under General Provisions, it brought into one block all the anticlerical portions of the Constitution of 1857, with amendments. The Carranza draft provided for separation of Church and State, forbade the government to establish or prohibit any religion, stipulated marriage as a civil contract, gave to the national government dominion over religious questions, and allowed for a nonreligious oath. On the afternoon of January 26 the delegates had their first opportunity to see the committee's recommendations, which accepted the Carranza proposal almost without word change but added to it a great sweep of provisions that reflected the attitudes of some of the most anticlerical of the revolutionaries. The additions denied juridical personality to any church, made all ministers members of a profession and therefore subject to regulation, gave the states authority to limit the number of ministers of any faith, and limited ministerial functions to Mexicans by birth. Furthermore, the proposal forbade any kind of political activity by ministers, denied them the right to criticize government acts or personnel, limited the right to construct new churches, prohibited church-related publications ("by their title or simply by their ordinary tendencies") from making any comment on the government or its policies, banned political parties of a clerical affiliation, circumscribed the rights of priests to inherit property, and proscribed

64 During the debates, and as presented to the convention, this appeared as article 129 instead of 130. The discrepancy came from the fact that the labor article, ultimately under the number 123, was a new one without a number assigned officially. The Commission on Style finally put the articles in proper sequence, with proper numbers.

the application of a seminary course to any other professional degree. And, finally, those charged with an infraction of any of the above could not take their case before a jury. These provisions, in conjunction with those in articles 3, 5, 24, and 27,[65] hedged in the Church to such a degree that it lost all freedom of activity except in the most narrowly defined concept of dogma.[66]

Debate on the article began at about midnight on January 27, with a number of delegates both for and against inscribed to speak. But no one really spoke against the general concepts behind the provisions, though some did object to specifics. Palavicini, for example, wanted to allow foreign ministers for all faiths except Catholic and Protestant, the only ones of sufficient strength in Mexico to constitute any danger. One speaker could see no justification for allowing the states to limit the number of ministers. But most objections came not from the stringency of the recommendations but from their moderation. Modesto González Galindo from Tlaxcala wanted to ban oral confession, since, he said, "this secret [confession] which they [clerics] accept as dogma is not precisely a religious practice, it is not precisely an article of faith. They have taken secret oral confession in order to conspire against the Government and against republican institutions. In the Constitutionalist revolution this question was viewed practically; the revolutionary officers who triumphantly entered each town in the Republic went about removing the confessionals and publicly burning them, and they did this because they knew that the ministers of the Catholic religion had used that furniture to conspire against the revolution."[67] Nor was Francisco Múgica completely satisfied. He had no specific proposal to make, but the Mexicans would be justified, he said, in any effort "not only to persecute, but even to eliminate this hydra

[65] Article 3 eliminated clerical teaching at the primary level, 5 forbade monastic orders, 24 prohibited outdoor religious ceremonies, and 27 barred church ownership of real property and limited the right of clergymen to own such properties.

[66] Ostensibly the article applied to churches and clerics of all faiths, but it was aimed at the Catholic church and clergy. The prohibitions have never been fully applied to any other group.

[67] *Diario de los debates*, II, 1045.

known as the clergy . . . We have been too tolerant with this rabble which has come to make sure that Mexican society is held back."[68] After about two hours of debate, in which the speakers vied with one another in denouncing the clergy, the assembly voted unanimous approval.[69]

What has proved to be the most significant of all the constitutional articles received even less serious and sustained attention by the mass of the delegates than did the religious provisions; only a few delegates even had an opportunity to read the provisions regarding property and property rights before they became a part of the constitution. Carranza's draft article 27 made only a few additions to that of the 1857 constitution. It provided for expropriations of property on the ground of public utility, barred any church or church affiliate from owning or administering any property other than that intimately related to its religious function, made a passing reference to *ejidos*, limited public ownership of real estate, confined corporate property to that needed for its direct operations, and allowed banks to accept real estate mortgages. In view of the stir over land reform, public control of the subsoil, and foreign ownership of property, the article fell far short of the demands, and it fell to Múgica's committee to meet the desires of the majority of the delegates. But a redrafting constituted, in effect, the writing of a new article or series of articles, which would include a reexamination of the entire concept of property and of agrarian reform; Múgica's committee simply did not have the time to undertake such a massive task. As a consequence Pastor Rouaix again volunteered to chair an informal and unofficial committee to work on the problem.

Using somewhat the same techniques he had applied in his drafting of the labor code, Rouaix began holding conferences on the property question even before article 123 had been completed; in his task he had the able assistance of Andrés Molina Enríquez, who

[68] Ibid., pp. 1057, 1058.

[69] During the same session in debate on article 24, which guarantees freedom of religious thought and worship, Enrique Recio from Yucatán and some others made a serious attempt to impose additional restrictions, one of which was to limit the exercise of the priesthood to married men of a minimum age of fifty.

was not only a minor official in Rouaix's ministry but also an old-line agrarian reformer who had agitated for changes in the tenure system long before Díaz's fall from power.[70] Working furiously for about ten days during the latter part of the month, Rouaix and seventeen others presented their proposal to the convention on the afternoon of January 25,[71] at which time it was referred to Múgica's committee. On the afternoon of January 29 that committee presented the draft proposal, which used the Rouaix project as a base but expanded upon it. Debate on the question began immediately, even though the delegates had at their disposal only four typewritten copies of the draft and therefore had to depend upon an oral rendition of each section. After some five hours of debate the assembly recessed for an hour to allow Múgica to make some changes in one section, and after an additional three hours—at one point the secretary had to warn the delegates to remain awake—the delegates cast a unanimous vote of 150 in the affirmative. Most of the debate was not debate at all; most of the discussion concerned clarification, since the delegates had no printed copy. On many of the significant portions there were neither questions nor discussion. The debates give a strong impression that the great majority of the delegates were prepared to vote in the affirmative without explanation or discourse. All they had to know was that the article encompassed wide-ranging agrarian reform and put severe restrictions on foreign ownership or utilization of either the soil or the subsoil. The delegates gave scarce heed to this most transcendental of all the constitutional provisions.

And what did the article include? It laid the groundwork for the most fundamental of social and economic changes and prepared the

[70] Molina Enríquez, who was not a delegate, is often given credit for drafting article 27, but the assertion is incorrect. He did act as secretary for the group and in this sense "drafted" the proposal, but the ideas came from a vast variety of sources; furthermore, the final Múgica draft differed considerably from the Rouaix proposal. The latter is published as an appendix to *Diario de los debates*, II, 1223–1229.

[71] Among the names attached were Macías and Rubén Martí, both conservatives.

way for governmental policies that engendered bitter fights both in and out of Mexico. It was an affront to a way of life in Mexico and to accepted international concepts of both property and foreign rights. It was not only the longest, it was the most nationalistic and the most bellicose, of all the constitutional articles.

It began by subordinating all property rights to the needs of the society; all private property could be subjected to "the modalities which public interest dictates" and could be used to "make an equitable distribution of public wealth." Stemming from this concept, all *latifundia* were subject to expropriation for the purpose of creating small private holdings or community properties; all "towns, hamlets [*rancherías*], and communities" that lacked lands had a right to demand and to receive them through either restoration or dotation. National and state governments were given a mandate to fix the maximum size of any landed holding and to divide the excess according to a given formula. Any lands expropriated for the purpose of establishing agricultural communities were to be paid for on the basis of the declared tax value, and the prior owner was obliged to accept twenty-year, 5 percent bonds in return. Furthermore, the nation was declared to be the owner of all waters, rivers, and lakes. These provisions, as detailed in the article, were designed to create a new agricultural pattern, with a new tenure system, not only to increase production but also to free the agricultural workers from the exploitations of the past.

But these provisions only began the parade of significant changes. The nation declared its direct dominion over all subsoil deposits, including "petroleum and all the hydrogen carbides, solid, liquid, or gaseous." National ownership of these deposits was "inalienable and imprescriptible," and concessions for exploitation could be granted only by the national government to individuals or corporations operating under Mexican law. Only Mexicans, either by birth or naturalization, had a right to obtain property of any kind, but the national government could extend such privilege to foreign individuals or groups if the recipients would appear at the Ministry of Foreign Relations and indicate that for the purpose of holding property they would consider themselves Mexicans and therefore would not invoke the aid of their governments in case of difficulty;[72] failure to conform to the promise would be justification for confiscation. Under no circumstances could a foreigner "obtain dominion over" land or water within a strip about sixty miles wide along the land frontiers or thirty miles along the coasts.[73] These provisions said, in essence, that foreign investments already in existence would be made the object of governmental control, and that new investments could come into the country only under narrowly circumscribed terms; they declared Mexico to be for the Mexicans.

Mexicans, too, were to feel the lash of more stringent control over property ownership or administration. The "religious associations called churches, of whatever creed," could not own, administer, or invest in real estate of any kind, and all those buildings previously used by any religious cult for any purpose passed immediately to the national government. No institution of public or private benefit—schools, eleemosynary institutions, and the like—could own property not closely related to its function, but it could lend money with real estate as collateral if the term were for ten years or less. The same general ban fell on business, industries, and financial institutions. And finally, any concession or contract made after 1876, the consequence of which had been to create any form of monopoly over "land, water or natural wealth," could be either revised or nullified by the national government.

This article, more than any other, showed most clearly the hopes and the fears facing the delegates at the convention. It showed not only a determination to create a new land-tenure system and to impose restrictions on foreigners, but also a deadly fear of wealth and vested interest. The drafters felt impelled to give the restrictions and prohibitions in absolute detail; when Palavicini mildly commented, not from the floor in debate but in a private conversation, that the details were more properly the province of Congress and statute

[72] Apparently no one at the convention thought about the problem of embassies or legations; in 1948 a change allowed foreign governments to purchase land and property for those purposes. To that time the provision was simply ignored.

[73] The article read 100 and 50 kilometers respectively.

law than of the Constitutional Convention and constitutional law, he raised a storm of protest. This fear, which pervaded the convention, was most pointedly expressed by Heriberto Jara; after surveying the history of past pressures on the national congresses, he said: "Who can assure us that in the next Congress all the evil influences will not come into play? Who can assure us that at the next Congress there are going to be sufficiently strong revolutionaries to combat this tendency, who will not answer to the siren's song but who will, with hand on breast, comply with their duty? No one can assure it."[74] And since no one could assure it for future legislators, the revolutionaries at the convention were forced to build a tight structure that would prevent overweening influence by the economically powerful and—to Jara and others the words were synonymous—the evil. Few of those who spoke on that night of January 29–30 objected to any of the restrictions or provisions; most of them wanted more. Samuel de los Santos of San Luis Potosí wanted to prohibit the building of any new churches. Bojórquez of Sonora wanted a provision for an agricultural bank. Luis T. Navarro from Puebla wanted to restrict private property rights even more. Federico Ibarra of Jalisco demanded the inclusion of a stipulated royalty percentage in the concession provision. Enrique Enríquez of México would have prohibited foreign ownership of real estate for any reason under any circumstance. And everyone agreed that the delegates had a tremendous responsibility to see that the aims of the revolution would not be lost or perverted by succeeding groups. Juan de Dios Bojórquez received heavy applause when he pointed up the question, with respect to land reform: "We have an exact obligation, an ineluctable obligation to go to the local Governments, to the Governments of the States, to demand, to ask in the name of the people, that the ideas we are going to accept here be put into practice. We need to justify this great revolution, we need to justify the spilling of so much fraternal blood, we must demonstrate that the promises were not in vain."[75] If anyone at the convention disagreed with Bojórquez, or with others of like mind, he did not raise his voice.

[74] *Diario de los debates*, II, 1095.
[75] Ibid., p. 1087.

Before completing the work at Querétaro, the delegates had one last task: to adopt some transitory articles to put into effect the constitution itself and to adopt a procedure for returning to constitutional government. Most of Carranza's draft proposals, with minor changes, were included but some new ones were added. In the final form the articles provided for an immediate publication of the new constitution, elections for president and Congress in the near future with Carranza authorized to decree the specifics, the installation of the new government with a special congressional session and the inauguration of the president on May 1, and the reestablishment of the Supreme Court by June 1. The fears expressed in the constitution itself came to the surface in the transitory articles. Until such time as the national and state governments passed legislation with respect to labor and agrarian reform, "the bases established in this constitution for such laws will be put into effect," said one article, while another gave preference in acquiring land to those who had taken an active part in the revolution, and still another declared void all previous debts entered into by laborers with their "employers, their aides or their intermediaries."

With the constitution and transitory articles completed, on the afternoon of January 31 all the delegates and the First Chief swore fealty to it amid an effusion of emotional enthusiasm. Carranza read a short statement, which was answered by a much longer one from Hilario Medina. When Luis Manuel Rojas declared the labors of the Constitutional Congress to be completed and that body dissolved, the hall rang with shouts of "Long live the Constitutional Convention!" In sixty-two elapsed days, by working nights, Sundays, and normal holidays, the convention produced the longest constitution ever drafted to that time, and to the 209 men who signed the final draft that accomplishment, had there been no other, was a source of great pride.

During the long two months—seventy-two days if the preliminary sessions are included—of convention debate the rancorous exchanges and the scurrilous personal attacks obscured some fundamental facets of the convention itself and gave rise to many misconceptions. When Walter Thurston reported in mid-December that the "civil" and the "military" had split,[76] he simply reflected a widespread belief, and when Bojórquez later gave all credit to the "Jacobins" for the constitution, he spoke from his own conviction and observation.[77] On the other hand, the ultraconservatives and ex-Huerta followers convinced themselves that a small minority of men in a convention that represented a small minority of the nation wrote an "illegal" constitution.[78] But a careful reading of the approximately million and a half words of the debates brings these contentions into serious question. In spite of the bitter exchanges over many articles, not only those discussed here, there was a remarkable coincidence of basic aims among the delegates. The question was not whether the constitution should reflect and help develop a new society based upon new concepts; it was not whether Mexico needed fundamental reform. The question was not one of *what* so much as *how*. When Palavicini, for example, suggested that the details of article 27 would be more properly a matter of congressional act, he voiced a perfectly legitimate concern over the respective provinces of constitutional and statutory law; but nothing in his career could be interpreted as indicative of rejection of agrarian reform. José Natividad Macías, considered by many as the very epitome of conservatism, helped draft both articles 123 and 27 in their preliminary form. Pedro Chapa, another of the "conservatives," also signed both drafts, as did Samuel de los Santos. That the delegates differed among themselves on the implications of wording, on the probable consequences of a phrase, on the necessity for certain prohibitions, and on a wide variety of other matters is plain to see, but their words and their voices made it clear that they were all revolutionaries.

The record of the convention demonstrates, too, that the resulting constitution came not from a small minority but from a great majority. In any body of deliberating men a small group of leaders soon emerges, and in this respect the Querétaro assembly followed the

[76] Thurston to SecState, December 13 and 17, 1916, files 812.00/20075 and /20090, NA, RG 59.

[77] In his *Crónica del constituyente*, under the pseudonym of Djed Bórquez.

[78] This view is consistently expressed by Jorge Vera Estañol in *Carranza and His Bolshevik Regime* and in *La revolución mexicana: Orígenes y resultados*.

norm. The two commissions on the constitution occupied key positions, and their members took leading roles in the debates; it thus appeared as though these men dominated the proceedings. But the committees held open sessions at which many delegates appeared, they frequently made changes demanded by the assembly, and in general they attempted to satisfy not only the majority but the minority as well. The votes on the articles attest to the committees' success in drafting compromises; by unanimous vote the delegates approved fully half the articles, while ballots on many others ran as high as 90 percent. Curiously enough, the closest votes came on relatively unimportant articles and not on the "revolutionary" provisions. Furthermore, at one time or another every delegate took part in the debates. The constitution was not merely an expression of majority will; it came close to representing a consensus.

The widely discussed civilian-military split was also something of a myth. It was true enough—too true, perhaps—that some members of the military made slighting remarks about the failure of some of the civilians to take up arms, and that some civilians made cutting remarks about the military organization. But civilians Cano, Colunga, Pastrana Jaimes, and Rouaix voted with military men Aguirre, Jara, Múgica, and Norzagaray; while civilians Cabrera, Macías, Palavicini, and Zambrano agreed with military men Cándido Aguilar, Nafarrate, Navarro, and Pesqueira. An examination of the debates, and the votes cast, fails to uncover any civilian-military conflict or even any general agreement among the military on a single question. The members with military experience and those without voted and spoke their convictions with respect to the goals of the revolution and the best manner of achieving them.

Given the background and the educational experience of the delegates, the constitution was an exceptional document. Very few of the members had university degrees, even fewer had training in law, and not many had ever read treatises on political philosophy or jurisprudence. The membership was unusually heterogeneous for a body charged with the task of drafting fundamental law. The continuum ran from hard-rock miners and textile workers on one end to highly successful professional men on the other, with small businessmen, landowners, newspapermen, poets, and teachers in between. The ages spread from twenty-five—the minimum—to sixty-plus; the most active were in their thirties or forties. Jara was thirty-six, Lizardi thirty-three, Rojas and Monzón forty-six, Múgica thirty-two. Many were rough and tough; Monzón, a teacher before he joined the Constitutionalists, always carried a pistol and a knife. Some were sweet and gentle and terribly concerned about humanity: Rafael Martínez became emotional when he discussed the plight of the laborer. And many had served prison sentences in miasmic jails. The membership was, in short, a cross section of the literate male population in their most productive years, all of whom had passed through the crucible of the revolution. This very heterogeneity, perhaps, gave spice and flavor to the final document; no matter what the subject under discussion, some member of the assembly had intimate and personal knowledge of the problem involved. Jara knew, from personal experience, the power of vested interests and foreign pressure; Cano knew, from his own experience, the miserable condition of the working man in a mine.

In its final form the constitution followed closely the precepts of the 1857 constitution, but it nevertheless deviated markedly from that document. Like its liberal forebear it provided for a federal system, separation of powers, no reelection, and a bicameral legislature with civil and political rights guaranteed, and in this respect it differed little from the U.S. Constitution except in minor details. And like its progenitor, as amended, it imposed severe restrictions on churches and clergy, required certain acts of the citizenry, set up a legislative watchdog in the form of a permanent commission, and prohibited monopolies. But unlike the earlier charter, it accepted as a fundamental assumption the positive role of government in social and economic affairs. While this concept is most clearly shown in articles 27 and 123, it appears in others as well. Government, as the agent of society itself, was perceived to be something more than a mere referee among the contending elements in the society, something more than an instrument to prevent the exploitation of one group by another. Society, and decency, demanded that changes be made, and government as the agent of that society had an obligation not merely to allow those changes but also to force them.

Unlike its parent, too, the constitution was imbued with a sense of belligerent nationalism. Only natural-born Mexicans could be harbor pilots, masters or first engineers of merchant vessels, or members of the navy. Only natural-born citizens could serve in the national Congress, occupy cabinet posts, function as justices of the highest court, or perform as state governors. Foreigners were restricted in their rights of ownership, employment, and profession. The men of the revolution came through that traumatic experience proud of their achievements, proud of being Mexicans, proud of their heritage, and they were determined to create a nation of their own, depending upon their own resources and beholden to no one. Their experiences during the previous four years had shown them that they could stand up against one of the world's great powers, and they wrote those precepts of exaggerated national sovereignty into the constitution.

The revolutionaries now had an instrument, but one to which many Mexicans objected strenuously,[79] and one that the international powers, when they had time to do so in the midst of war, eyed askance.

[79] The ink on the printed constitution was scarcely dry before the hierarchy in exile published a bitter attack on all the provisions touching on Church or clergy.

10. CONSTITUTIONAL GOVERNMENT AND CARRANZA

Don Venustiano soon discovered that governing under a constitution posed a great number of difficulties with which he did not have to contend when he governed by dictatorial fiat. Even before the Constitutional Congress completed its work, the evidence that a highly organized opposition was in the making began piling up. The Partido Liberal Constitucionalista, originally started in Mexico City for the purpose of electing Carranza's hand-picked delegates to the convention at Querétaro, fell under the control of a group of men who had once collaborated closely with Carranza, but who had become disenchanted to the point of bitterness. Jesús Acuña, Jesús Urueta, Rafael Zubarán Capmany, and Dr. Atl took turns, in the pages of *El Gladiator*, in lambasting not only Carranza's friends but also the First Chief himself until Carranza ordered the newspaper's suppression in early February.[1] Closing the paper served little pur-

[1] Rafael Nieto to Carranza, February 9, 1917, and César López de Lara to Carranza, February 9, 1917, both in ADN-DF 1917. López de Lara was the gov-

pose other than to make his opposition even more convinced of the necessity to bridle him, with the result that the PLC undertook a drive to become a national party with affiliates in every state. Carranza attempted to counter this move by instructing his governors not to furnish information that might be used for the purpose of establishing political alliances; the First Chief took the position that political parties in the various states should function "completely independently, without leagues from state to state."[2] Despite his best efforts, an embryonic national party of opposition had formed by the time the convention delegates took their leave.

Following the mandate given in the transitory articles of the constitution, on February 6 Carranza announced the procedures for the election of the president and the members of the national Congress, to be held on Sunday, March 11.[3] Carranza, realizing that he had been out-maneuvered in the recent convention elections, decided to follow the advice of some of his friends who, like Palavicini, regretted the "rebellious indiscipline of the [Constitutional Congress, which] . . . should have shown more subordination to the Chief of the Party." Alfredo Breceda suggested to him that it "would be unwise to have opposition in the next Congress," and Antonio Medina thought that all officeholders should be honest and intelligent, but gave as his prime criterion absolute subservience to the chief.[4] Secure in the knowledge that he would be elected president—he had no opposition for that office—Carranza bent his efforts to control the new Congress and therefore began maneuvering in a manner reminiscent of the Díaz days and completely at variance with the princi-

---

ernor of the Federal District, and it was he who carried out Carranza's order to suppress the paper.

[2] Carranza circular to all governors, February 10, 1917, ADN-Querétaro 1917. The order was prompted by information that the PLC was asking governors to give the names of local political clubs.

[3] The procedures were roughly equivalent to those used in the election for the convention (Venustiano Carranza, *Informe . . . encargado del poder ejecutivo de la República*, pp. 28–29).

[4] Palavicini to Carranza, January 25, 1917, ADN-Querétaro 1917; Breceda to Carranza, February 16, 1917, ADN-DF 1917; Medina to Carranza, March 31, 1917, ADN-Puebla 1917. These are merely random examples of a host of letters in the same vein.

ples established in the new constitution. He selected candidates for almost every state and sent emissaries to give those candidates support. He removed some provisional governors who demonstrated a complete impartiality and appointed others in whom he had more confidence. He used government money to subsidize candidates and to aid sympathetic newspapers. He discouraged men in public employment from supporting opposition candidates and discharged those who did, even while he encouraged or ordered both national and state functionaries to give aid to his candidates.[5] But the First Chief realized that he could not run the risk of outright imposition and therefore did not make the mistake of attempting to use military force; too many of the military were in the opposition camp. And when the newly elected deputies and senators met in the early days of April to organize into legislative bodies, Carranza had to admit to himself that he no longer had absolute power.[6] The limitations on that power became even more clear when, on April 13, the lower house rejected Palavicini's credentials as a deputy from Tabasco.[7]

The First Chief gave no overt signs of either disappointment or hostility. On April 15 he appeared before a joint session to give, at long last, the promised report of his stewardship over the past four

[5] Examples to substantiate these statements: Carranza to López de Lara, February 8, 1917 (naming candidates, and instructing López de Lara to give them financial aid); Carranza to Pablo González and Rafael Nieto, February 8, 1917 (instructing them to maintain control of *El Universal*); Enrique Muñoz to Carranza, February 4, 1917 (repeating instructions Carranza had given to Provisional Governor Antonio Norzagaray of Aguascalientes); Carranza to Andrés Osuna, January 25, 1917 (ordering him not to accept the presidency of the PLC); Juan Barragán to Carranza's secretary, Gerzayn Ugarte, March 28, 1917 (asking that Carranza reimburse Cepeda for 3,500 pesos spent in propaganda); Manuel Mezta to Carranza, March 2, 1917 (reporting on a mission to Sinaloa in behalf of Carranza candidates); Pastor Rouaix to Carranza, February 14, 1917 (concerning Carranza's instructions for Durango); Carranza to Provisional Governor General Pablo A. de la Garza, February 10, 1917 ("recommending" that de la Garza give "guarantees" to a candidate; de la Garza was soon replaced by Alfredo Ricaut). All these, and many similar, are in the various files of the ADN for 1917.

[6] Accounts of the elections indicate a good turnout and a peaceful casting of ballots.

[7] Félix Fulgencio Palavicini, *Mi vida revolucionaria*, pp. 397–435, discusses the credential fight and its background.

years. Forty-year-old Deputy Eduardo Hay made a short and pleasant reply, after which the Primer Jefe left the congressional halls amid the plaudits of the crowd. Two weeks later, in a ten-minute ceremony before a joint session and witnessed by the members of the diplomatic corps,[8] Venustiano Carranza took the oath of office as constitutional president; characteristically, he himself read the oath, rather than having it administered to him. Thus the fifty-eight–year-old Carranza ostensibly surrendered his dictatorial powers as First Chief and assumed all the limitations implied in a constitutional regime; "Old Whiskers," as he came to be called by his enemies, at last had a legal claim to govern; and he serenely returned to the National Palace through an immense and cheering crowd.

Carranza may have been serene when he returned to his office, but the political pot was aboil. Soon after the congressional elections, he had issued a decree by which the states, as well as the national government, would return to constitutional rule. As soon as conditions warranted in each state, he said, the provisional governors would fix the date for state elections, with the new state legislatures constituting themselves as constituent assemblies for the purpose of making the changes necessary to conform to the new national charter. Under existing conditions such elections were impossible in many states. Villa's continued depredations in Chihuahua demanded a military government instead of civil institutions, while in Morelos the Zapatistas controlled all but the larger towns. Félix Díaz and a group of others, including Juan Andreu Almazán and Higinio Aguilar, kept Oaxaca, Chiapas, and Tabasco in an uproar and therefore obviated elections in those states. Salvador Alvarado, the provisional governor of Yucatán, generally abided by Carranza's wishes, but he had carved out a little empire of his own and hated to give up the wealth coming from henequen. In the remainder of the states elections were either held or attempted during the early summer, and in most cases

[8] Most nations had reestablished full diplomatic relations with Mexico, recognizing Carranza, in 1916; the United States delayed naming an ambassador until after the completion of the constitution. In the inaugural ceremonies, the diplomats had their choice of seats, depending upon their sympathies with respect to the European war.

Carranza managed to achieve the election of governors friendly to him. In San Luis Potosí he designated Alfredo Breceda to act as provisional governor to assure the election of his favorite, Juan Barragán, who used some strong-arm tactics during the campaign.[9] In Nuevo León he depended upon General Alfredo Ricaut to sustain the candidacy of Nicéforo Zambrano,[10] a relative, and he sent nephew Emilio Salinas to Querétaro as provisional governor to supervise the election of collaborator Ernesto Perrusquía, who was under fire in Mexico City because of his sudden wealth.[11] He looked with considerable favor upon the candidacy of son-in-law Cándido Aguilar for governor of Veracruz,[12] and equally favored the election of Alfonso Cabrera, his finance minister's brother, in Puebla.[13] In the new state of Nayarit—the old territory of Tepic—General José Santos Godínez emerged victorious over Esteban Baca Calderón,[14] and in Guanajuato long-time supporter Agustín Alcocer took office.[15] Most of these electoral contests were accompanied by charges of fraud, of military pressure, and of official imposition, but they were surprisingly free from any real violence.

[9] Among other things, Barragán forcibly—and without recourse to law—closed an opposition newspaper, arrested the editor, and threatened the publisher with bodily harm unless all publicity attacks ceased (S. M. Santos to Carranza, April 21, 1917, ADN-San Luis Potosí 1917).

[10] The documentation on Zambrano's election may be found in ADN-Nuevo León 1917. Among the most interesting documents is a letter from Zambrano to Carranza, shortly after his election, asking for a concession to import duty free fifty to a hundred thousand pesos of merchandise as compensation for the costs of the campaign. Carranza granted the request.

[11] The documentation is in ADN-Querétaro 1917. Perrusquía was in Finance and was accused of using his position to make a fortune (A. Fernández to Carranza, April 21, 1917, ADN-DF 1917).

[12] The best documentation on the election may be found in ADN-Veracruz 1917, which has messages from Provisional Governor Jara, Aguilar, and Gavira to Carranza, and Carranza's message to them.

[13] ADN-Puebla 1917 has correspondence between Carranza and the various candidates and supporters.

[14] ADN-Nayarit 1917 and ADN-DF 1917 have ample documentation on the election. General J. J. Ríos considered Godínez's election "a shame and . . . a joke of the revolutionary promises" (Ríos to José J. Méndez, November 7, 1917, ADN-DF 1917).

[15] ADN-Guanajuato 1917 contains the documentation.

In some states the gubernatorial contests brought near rebellion, and in a few actual warfare. In Sinaloa six men entered the lists,[16] with Obregón favoring either José Salazar or Fortunato de la Vega. Unfortunately for the Obregón forces, they could not cooperate among themselves, and four of the six candidates considered themselves to be Obregonistas. When the vote went to Carranza favorite Ramón Iturbe, the losers complained bitterly to Carranza that Iturbe had gained his position only by fraud, and one of the losers stated that he would not allow Iturbe to occupy his office for a month before he evicted him. Municipal presidents and councils refused to recognize Iturbe's authority, the local garrison openly flaunted his orders, and an armed uprising appeared to be imminent. In these circumstances, Obregón, who had left Carranza's government "for reasons of health" and who obviously had every intention of standing for election in 1920, volunteered his services as a mediator and managed to assuage some of the hostile feelings for the time being. Iturbe took office with Carranza's blessing and Obregón's tolerance, but the situation remained tense.

In Coahuila the Carranza steam roller brought outright rebellion on the part of one of his most devoted followers of the past.[17] Provisional Governor Gustavo Espinosa Mireles resigned that post in April so that he might run for the regular term, even though one of Carranza's fellow Coahuilans had warned that a dangerous situation was created because public opinion held Espinosa Mireles to be the "official" candidate. The other principal contestant for the position was Luis Gutiérrez, who in late 1914 had broken with his brother in order to remain loyal to Carranza; Gutiérrez had strong support from Francisco Coss, the man to whom Carranza had looked for protection when he fled Mexico City in early November, 1914.

[16] ADN-Sinaloa, Sonora, and DF 1917, all have documentation on the election, with correspondence from Carranza, Obregón, Flores, Mezta, Moreno, and Iturbe (the last four were candidates) the most interesting.

[17] The extensive documentation on the Coahuila election and the subsequent rebellion may be found in ADN-Coahuila 1917, with some in DF 1917. It includes letters from Coss, Gutiérrez, Neira, Espinosa Mireles, Diéguez, Urbano Flores, and J. L. Arredondo, as well as an open letter printed over the names of the Gutiérrez brothers and Coss, giving their rationale for the military movement.

Serious quarrels began almost immediately, with each candidate accusing the other of making insulting remarks and of using tactics more suitable to bandits than serious politicians. Within three days after Espinosa Mireles surrendered his position to the new acting governor, General B. Neira, one of Neira's men killed a Gutiérrez supporter; Neira insisted that the death came from an attempt at robbery and had no political implications. As the campaign dragged on through the summer months the clashes became more frequent and the charges more scurrilous. Neira accused Gutiérrez's followers of using arms to prevent Espinosa Mireles from campaigning, of preaching sedition, of using amnestied Villistas as propagandists, and of threatening voters on election day. Gutiérrez and his followers accused Neira and Espinosa Mireles of perverting the revolution, of mistreating the loyal and true revolutionaries to the benefit of those who had taken little or no part in the fighting, and of using armed men at the polls to prevent a proper vote. Whether Espinosa Mireles obtained the majority of the votes cast will never be known, but General Neira surrendered the office to him in late August. Gutiérrez and Coss bided their time, with Gutiérrez first making a trip to Mexico City to object to the imposition. In mid-December the two generals disavowed their support to both the president and the governor and began a short-lived and completely abortive military movement, which only a few dozen of their closest friends joined. Carranza may not have had the power he enjoyed in the previous year, but at the same time few people were willing to risk a renewed revolution in the name of democracy, when it was clear that all parties involved had been equally guilty.

In Michoacán the situation was almost as bad,[18] but it did not result in revolution, probably because none of the three candidates was an obvious Carranza choice. On April 12 Provisional Governor José Rentería Luviano announced that the elections would be held on May 6, an obvious attempt to follow the letter of the law but to undermine its meaning, since the slightly more than three weeks be-

[18] ADN-Michoacán and DF 1917 both contain extensive documentation in the form of messages from the three candidates as well as the governor and many supporters of one or another of the candidates.

tween announcement and election would scarcely assure a free and democratic election. Rentería Luviano apparently had ambitions of his own for the immediate future: he wanted to remain in the position of governor, either provisionally or constitutionally. Since he could not follow the latter course, he decided to play no favorites, but to make campaigning difficult for all other candidates: Pascual Ortiz Rubio, Francisco Múgica, and Antonio de P. Magaña. In the face of demands that greater time be given for campaigning, Rentería Luviano postponed the election until July 1, at which time Ortiz Rubio received a clear majority—with both Múgica and Magaña claiming fraud, of course. But the results of the election seemed to be endangered not from the over-eager partisans of the losers but from the intransigence of the provisional governor. For a time he refused to call the new legislature into session, attempted to frighten Ortiz Rubio out of the state, and at one point informed the victor that he would not be allowed to occupy the gubernatorial office. But under pressure from Carranza he reluctantly acceded to the electoral process; Ortiz Rubio took the oath of office on August 8.

In Tamaulipas the bitter campaign for the governorship over a two-year period led to armed clashes resulting in many deaths, two postponements, frequent changes in the provisional governorship, an election in which each side claimed victory and established a government, the voiding of the election by the Carranza administration, and finally a rebellion.[19] The Carranza-backed candidate was César López de Lara, the Carranza-appointed and loyal governor of the Federal District, who began his campaign in early April. Luis Caballero, the opposition candidate with PLC support, had given magnificent service during the revolution against both Huerta and Villa, spending most of his time in his native state or its immediate environs. Extremely popular, he enjoyed the full support of all the most important municipal officers as well as the majority of the military men. When López de Lara appeared in Tampico for his first speech on April 15 he brought along with him a military guard of some two

[19] The documentation is in ADN-Tamaulipas, DF, Guanajuato, and Querétaro for 1917 and consists of hundreds of messages from many individuals as well as the principals.

hundred men and a military band of about forty pieces, but before he spoke his first word Caballero's brother-in-law attempted to shoot him; in the ensuing melee a number of people were gravely wounded. Two days later a repetition occurred in Ciudad Victoria, with two men dead and a number injured. In both cases, of course, each group accused the other of responsibility for the affair, and each protested to Carranza over the lack of "guarantees"; Provisional Governor Gregorio Osuna, on Carranza's instructions, ordered a suspension of all political activities and demonstrations, but he admitted to his superior that he could do nothing, since Caballero controlled the state. Two months later the situation had worsened, with the contending forces on the point of open warfare; under these circumstances Carranza appointed Alfredo Ricaut, one of the original signers of the Plan de Guadalupe and fresh from his provisional governorship in Nuevo León, where he had supervised Nicéforo Zambrano's election, as acting governor of the state. Because of the obvious impossibility of holding anything approaching a peaceful and fair election, Ricaut postponed the contest until the following February in the hope that passions would cool during the interim. In the meantime Carranza sent Manuel Diéguez to the state as the commander of the federal forces there, with strict orders to prevent violence.

But the electoral hiatus did nothing to relieve the tensions, and in January, 1918, conditions degenerated into the situation of the year before: armed clashes in Tampico, Ciudad Victoria, Villagrán, and other places; military pressures throughout the state; frequent denials by municipal authorities of the right to make speeches; and, finally, terrorizing at the ballot boxes. Since both sides claimed victory—and since Caballero probably gained the majority—Carranza through Minister of Gobernación Aguirre Berlanga ordered Ricaut to seal the legislative chamber in Ciudad Victoria to prevent the claimants of either party from taking control until the central government had an opportunity to determine the outcome. Despite the seal, the Caballero deputies broke into the chamber, organized themselves as the state legislature, and declared Caballero to be the constitutional governor of the state. A conference between Caballero and Ricaut, with others attending, came to naught other than a signing of a joint statement that Caballero claimed the governorship and that Ricaut denied the claim. For a few weeks during March and April the uneasy situation continued,[20] but in late April the national government declared Caballero in rebellion. Unlike the Coss-Gutiérrez movement in Coahuila, the Caballero rebellion assumed serious proportions that necessitated a continuation of the provisional form of government. An election in 1919 finally put Emilio Portes Gil in the governor's chair, and in January, 1920, Caballero gave up the fight and surrendered.

A consideration of the 1917 gubernatorial elections as a group shows some interesting facets of Mexican political life after four years of revolution.[21] In the first place, Carranza had more than a transitory interest in the contests and frequently made a mockery of his oft-repeated principle of state sovereignty by carefully desig-

[20] General Emiliano P. Nafarrate, a strong Carrancista, became a victim of the tensions when he was gunned down in Tampico by a police agent during a quarrel.

[21] The list of governors, with a starred indication of Carranza addiction, follows:

Aguascalientes	Lic. Aurelio González*
Campeche	General Joaquín Mucel*
Coahuila	Lic. Gustavo Espinosa Mireles*
Colima	General José Felipe Valle*
Durango	General Domingo Arrieta (illiterate)
Guanajuato	General Agustín Alcocer*
Guerrero	General Silvestre G. Mariscal
Hidalgo	General Nicolás Flores*
Jalisco	General Manuel Diéguez*
Michoacán	General Pascual Ortiz Rubio
Nuevo León	Nicéforo Zambrano*
Puebla	Dr. Alfonso Cabrera*
Querétaro	Ernesto Perrusquía*
San Luis Potosí	General Juan Barragán*
Sinaloa	General Ramón Iturbe*
Sonora	General Plutarco Elías Calles
Veracruz	General Cándido Aguilar*
Zacatecas	General Enrique Estrada
Nayarit	General José Santos Godínez*

Most of these were elected for four-year terms. Many of them took leaves from their offices to undertake military missions for Carranza.

nating the man whom he would support for the position. Barragán, Aguilar, Perrusquía, and Alcocer all resigned from positions close to him in order to run for the governor's office in various states, and López de Lara continued as governor of the Federal District during his long campaign. Furthermore, some political hopefuls withdrew in the face of a Carranza scowl.[22] Second, in his campaign to put trusted men into the governorships he was considerably more successful than in his congressional efforts; of the nineteen governors elected before the end of the year, fourteen were close allies, while only three—Calles of Sonora, Enrique Estrada of Zacatecas, and Silvestre G. Mariscal of Guerrero—could be considered as clearly oppositionist, and one of these he successfully removed within a matter of months.[23] Third, not all provisional governors saw the return to constitutional government as an untarnished blessing; Alvarado in Yucatán, despite peaceful conditions, managed to delay elections for about two years in spite of Carranza's frequent orders. Fourth, and perhaps most importantly, *each* candidate and his supporters firmly believed that he would emerge victorious in a free election and accepted as an article of faith that his failure to obtain a majority was in itself prima facie evidence of corruption. In this conviction all candidates, to protect against unwarranted pressure and electoral fraud, surrounded themselves with armed men who constantly harassed their opponents. This conviction, too, led all candidates to stoop to any possible political trick or political pressure. Barragán and others forcibly closed newspapers that printed unfa-

[22] For example, Eleuterio Avila announced his candidacy for the governorship of Yucatán without consulting Carranza but withdrew when he found that Carranza's attitude "was not what [he] had hoped for." He had quarrelled with Luis Cabrera in December, 1914, and Carranza did not forget it (Avila to Carranza, August 28, 1916, in ADN-DF 1917). Carranza also, when it appeared that Jesús Agustín Castro's candidacy in Durango might create dissension among his own partisans, effectively eliminated that general from the contest by making him the subsecretary of war.

[23] While Silvestre Mariscal was in Mexico City in early 1918 on a state mission, he was arrested because he had given an alleged improper military order. He was never allowed to return to his office, in spite of protests from his state. The correspondence in the case is in ADN-DF and Guanajuato 1918.

vorable comments;[24] all candidates accused their opponents of being novo-revolutionaries, Villistas, reactionaries, bandits, clericals, or any other form of low person that might occur to them, without the slightest regard for truth. It would appear, from the campaign charges, that not a single candidate for governor had given any service at all to the triumph of the revolution. But the most interesting political trick occurred in Michoacán where the Ortiz Rubio supporters published and widely disseminated, two weeks before the election, a black-bordered announcement of candidate Antonio de P. Magaña's death; the false notice may have had some effect, since Magaña polled the fewest votes among the three candidates. And, last, those who had carried the military struggle were, apparently, the heroes of the hour; fourteen of the nineteen victors were generals.

The delegates to the Constitutional Convention had written into that charter a magnificent set of democratic principles that guaranteed complete freedom of political participation and a set of civil rights protections even more generous than those in the U.S. Constitution and laws. But events in 1917 proved conclusively that the drafters of that charter had been much more interested in preparing an ideal for the future than in enunciating a system with which they could live immediately. Democracy in any real sense of the word simply did not exist in Mexico in late 1917, but the wonder is not that Carranza skirted the constitution, but that he was not more overt in behalf of his own power and that of his friends. He certainly had encouragement, not only from his partisans but also from his opponents, through example. Governor Calles of Sonora, for example, insisted in early January, 1918, that he be allowed to suspend indi-

[24] Barragán was an ardent supporter of press freedom—as long as it did not allow criticism of him or his friends. Some four months after his election he became concerned about the mounting opposition campaign in many PLC-sympathizing newspapers, and he urged Carranza to suppress the critics, diplomatically but firmly. He closed his letter by saying: "In this state at various times the opposition have attempted to publish newspapers, but they have not been able to do so and the public has not said one word against me for not permitting their appearance" (Barragán to Carranza, October 14, 1917, in ADN-San Luis Potosí 1917).

vidual guarantees in his state in order "to end once and for all the constant conspiracies against the Government," and he could not understand the president's refusal to grant the permission.[25] This lack of faith in, or misunderstanding of, the entire process of political democracy with its concomitant personal guarantees was perhaps best summed up, unconsciously, by Heriberto Barrón in early 1918. Barrón, a newspaperman, had been on the revolutionary fringes for years and had always been jealous of his prerogatives as a writer to publish the truth as he saw it. Something of a Carranza sycophant, he constantly bombarded the president with long letters protesting his utter loyalty not only to Carranza but also to truth and beauty. But he not only recommended to Carranza that he close the newspaper *Excélsior* because of some unsympathetic articles;[26] he went considerably further. In February the Supreme Court remanded to the inferior courts a case involving two military men accused of sedition; Barrón saw in the act a failure to follow the wishes of the executive. In commenting on the case to Carranza, he concluded: "It is not my desire to censure the Court, but to call attention forcefully to the fact that the Court is trying to proceed in the application of laws and guarantees given by the Constitution, under the absurd criterion that we are in a normal and tranquil period, when the abnormal and disturbed period [in which we find ourselves] requires a criterion diametrically opposed to a legal application; what is needed is strong support to the Executive."[27] Barrón favored law and constitutional guarantees as long as he benefited, but he opposed those guarantees when they gave comfort to his opponents. In 1917–1918 this norm reigned supreme in the political process; without exception every man in Mexican political life subscribed to it to a greater or lesser degree.

The din of the gubernatorial elections had scarcely subsided before congressional elections brought renewed agitation. The deputies elected in the spring of 1917 counted their term from the previ-

25 Calles to Carranza, January 2 and 14, 1918, and Carranza to Calles, January 19, 1918, all in ADN-Sonora 1918.

26 Barrón to Carranza, January 18, 1918, in ADN-DF 1918.

27 Barrón to Carranza, February 9, 1918, ibid.

ous September, to serve until September, 1918; the same applied to half the senators. Therefore, in order to put congressional terms on a regular base, a new electoral law in later 1917 established the fourth Sunday in July—July 28—as the off-year election date. The campaign for the seats began in early 1918. Internal conditions were no more conducive for free and democratic elections than they had been the year before; if anything, they were worse. Villa's strength grew and waned by the month,[28] Peláez still controlled much of the oil zone; Félix Díaz and his companions still disrupted economics and politics in the southeast; innumerable little bandit-revolutionary bands traversed the countryside in Querétaro, Guanajuato, Nuevo León, Michoacán, Jalisco, Guerrero, and Puebla; and Zapata showed as much if not more strength than he had the year before. In addition, the rancors generated during the previous year's elections had certainly not subsided, economic conditions in most sections had deteriorated, and the PLC had become better organized and more strident in its criticisms of Carranza's authoritarianism and his inability to bring either peace or prosperity.

In this gloomy atmosphere the country experienced a variation on the theme of the previous year. Again Carranza aided his favorites,[29] again pressures were applied from all directions, again bloody clashes occurred, again all candidates accused their opponents of fraud, imposition, and corruption—and again the heavy majority in Congress leaned in the direction of the PLC and its oppositionist policies. This was the legislature with which Carranza had to work for the remaining two years of his term; it was a congress he often tried to circumvent but never learned to manage. The chamber,

[28] On an average of once a month throughout this year and the next, a government spokesman would proclaim Villa officially no longer a danger; but he always reappeared with thousands of men under his command, and late in 1918 Felipe Angeles rejoined him.

[29] Hundreds of candidates or potential candidates sought help from the president. One of the most poignant pleas came from a veteran of the wars against Maximilian; elderly and infirm, he wanted to move to Mexico City, where his daughter lived, and he wanted help from Carranza: "A seat in the next Congress would take me to her side; or perhaps, sir, you could assign me to another post" (Ramón Guzmán to Carranza, July 6, 1918, in ADN-Puebla 1918).

which had the larger opposition majority, was particularly obstreperous; it consistently held up or refused to act upon Carranza's proposals, and it frequently challenged the president's powers.

During Carranza's tenure as constitutional president, Mexican officialdom, from the highest to the lowest, made only sporadic attempts to enforce the prohibitions or to effectuate the mandates written into the constitution. The religious articles stirred up the most immediate controversy. Fourteen exiled members of the episcopate, including the archbishops of México, Michoacán, Durango, Yucatán, and Linares, in late February issued a strongly worded "protest" denouncing every portion of the new charter that in any way limited the activities of ministers or church.[30] The clerics questioned the validity of a constitution "drawn up and published by a group of politicians who did not abide by the indispensable conditions . . . placed in the Constitution of 1857 with respect to amendments; among whom in the assembly which drafted this code there were no representatives of other political groups in the country, these being formally excluded; and finally, who abolished beforehand, no one knows with what authority, the then existing constitution." They did not limit their objections to the new provisions; they also objected to the inclusion of the portions that had been a matter of constitutional law since the Juárez period. They said, in essence, that they wished to return to the state of affairs that had existed prior to 1857, and they would "disavow any act or manifesto, even though it emanates from persons in our dioceses who might be invested with ecclesiastical authority, if it is contrary to our declarations and protests."

The protest caused no great stir in governmental circles for some months. It apparently circulated freely and unchallenged within the country until July when, on orders from Guadalajara Archbishop

[30] "Protesta que hacen los prelados mexicanos que suscriben, con ocasión de la Constitución Política de los Estados Unidos Mexicanos publicada en Querétaro el día cinco de febrero de mil novecientos diecisiete," dated February 24, 1917, in ADN-Querétaro 1917. The "Protest" was published in San Antonio, Texas, under circumstances suggesting that the Mexican prelates may have had the assistance of some of their U.S. colleagues.

Francisco Orozco y Jiménez, eight priests, one of whom officiated at the cathedral, read it in its entirety during Sunday mass.[31] The reading of the protest triggered street demonstrations, which in turn brought a sharp reaction from the notoriously anticlerical state and local government officials.[32] On July 17 the cathedral and the seven other churches in which the protest had been read were closed and sealed by state authorities, and police agents renewed their search for the archbishop, who had been in hiding for months. During the following months various groups appealed to the central government for a reopening of the sealed churches, but Carranza did not wish to become too intimately embroiled in the affair and allowed the local authorities to continue their policy. During July and August the state authorities issued frequent frightening statements to the effect that Orozco y Jiménez would be executed if he were apprehended, but by September it began to appear that perhaps the government did not actually wish to find the archbishop; as a fugitive he was a minor nuisance, but as a prisoner he would be an acute embarrassment. On October 20 the governor allowed a resumption of religious services in the cathedral,[33] and in the following months he gradually extended the same privilege to the other seven churches. By early 1918 the state administration and the local clerics and their avid supporters had reached a tenuous understanding, never formalized either orally or in written form, but generally understood nevertheless; for the moment, at least, neither side would press the issue. But the state authorities adamantly refused to question the validity of existing law and steadfastly denied—when asked—to foreign ministers the right to perform religious acts.[34]

[31] Silliman to SecState, July 17, 1917, file 812.404/145, NA, RG 59, and later dispatches from the same source, report on the issue.

[32] General Diéguez, the governor, was outspoken in his contempt for both clergy and church and surrounded himself with men of the same brand of thought.

[33] Silliman to SecState, October 20, 22, 1917, files 812.404/161 and /163, NA, RG 59.

[34] In the latter part of the year and in early 1918, many foreign Protestant ministers became exercised over the prohibition against foreign clergy. Episcopal Bishop Henry Aves in Guadalajara attempted to obtain from the state government an exception; he was told bluntly that the prohibition in article 30 would

In the meantime another aspect of the religious issue came before the central and local governments with a steady and rising pressure. During the active days of the military struggle, military commanders with or without orders from the Primer Jefe had "intervened" Church properties of all sorts in most areas of the nation, putting some of them to public use and leaving others closed and idle. In Morelia alone, in early 1917, state government offices were housed in buildings that had once been eleven Catholic schools, a hospital, and an orphanage;[35] in Jalisco the government had seized a number of churches and converted them into workshops, barracks, and storehouses.[36] In addition to these obviously clerical properties, admitted by all to be such, the government had seized innumerable private properties on the grounds either of temporary need or of "enemy goods." A decision had to be made with respect to the ultimate disposition of both these types, and for both the caretaker administration and the recommendation regarding final disposition, Carranza created a special office as an adjunct to the Ministry of Finance. Even before his inauguration as constitutional president, Carranza began to order the return of some of the properties, both to individuals and to the Church,[37] but the demands for rapid action were incessant and insistent.[38] In mid-May, Minister of Finance Luis Ca-

be applied with vigor. But it is clear that Protestants did continue their services, and that they were not expelled, either from Jalisco or other states. The reports may be found in the 812.404 series, NA, RG 59. An interesting sidelight is that Aves, who had been in Guadalajara for twelve years, could not speak Spanish and therefore hardly constituted a threat to the government.

35 A list of the properties is given in Samuel R. González to Carranza, January 9, 1917, ADN-Michoacán 1917. One of the school buildings, in which the state government had established a normal school, was returned to church use in mid-January.

36 Numerous pleas to Carranza in 1917 requested the return of certain churches to the religious. Almost without exception, these pleas—some of them with hundreds of signatures—came from women. The documents are in ADN-Jalisco 1917.

37 Legally, of course, properties were not "returned" to the Church; they continued to belong to the nation but were turned over to the Church for religious uses.

38 From all parts of the country such requests came. Among the more interesting are those coming from the Madero family, most of whose properties were

brera pinpointed the problem. It was absolutely crucial, he said, that extreme care be taken with respect to every intervened property in order to ascertain with surety whether it belonged to the Church. Those properties actually controlled by the Church, whether overtly or covertly, belonged to the nation and could be used in any fashion deemed fit, without the payment of an indemnity; properties belonging to individuals, on the other hand, could not be confiscated except under special laws. Cabrera stated as a fact that vast holdings in Durango, Michoacán, Guanajuato, and Puebla actually belonged to the Church even though they appeared to be the holdings of corporations or of individual clerics. The nub of the problem, then, was to distinguish between bona fide private property and Church property. For those holdings registered in the name of an individual cleric he had a simple formula: "It could be accepted as a norm that the properties belonging to clerics, which have come to them by gift or succession from non-relatives or from other clergymen, are to be considered as belonging to the church, and therefore should be confiscated."[39]

And Cabrera's ministry did exercise care in examining the titles. In one case his investigators traced the ownership of a hacienda through three generations and four persons in order to demonstrate that the titular owner was in fact a Church agent.[40] But the biggest single haul of Church property occurred in Puebla, where, in early 1918, the government confiscated both urban and rural holdings belonging to a company incorporated under the name of "La Piedad." The government proved, to its own satisfaction at least, that the

---

seized in 1915–1916 (see particularly Carolina viuda de Madero to Carranza, January 18, 1917, ADN-Nuevo León 1917, and Julio Madero to Cabrera, March 17, 1917, ADN-DF 1917). Julio, who had served on Obregón's staff, was an executor for the estates of both his brother Francisco I. and his father Francisco. Julio listed the value of his father's intervened properties as about four million pesos.

[39] Cabrera to Carranza, May 12, 1917, ADN-DF 1917.

[40] Undated SecHacienda memorandum, ADN-Jalisco 1917. The hacienda, at Lagos in Jalisco, had passed from Eulalia Rosas to Father Pablo Anda to church sacristan Manuel Barrientos to Petra Oláez through a combination of legacy and purchase. Hacienda contended that in each case the action was fraudulent.

company had been formed with Church money, that clerics determined the policies of the company, and that the major activities of the company were religious in nature. The total value of the holdings ran into millions of pesos.[41]

But in general, during late 1917 and early 1918, the overt anticlericalism of the earlier period tended to dissipate. Except in Jalisco the question of ministerial citizenship was seldom mentioned, in most states the clerical schools resumed operation, the government returned temples to Church jurisdiction, and religious life returned to normal even though many officials, according to the British vice-consul in Gómez Palacio, considered "that an irreligious attitude [was] an indispensable adjunct to the pose of culture and enlightenment."[42] The incidents between Church and State were isolated, not generalized, with enforcement of the constitution depending upon the whim of the local officials. Calles in Sonora expelled some priests for antirevolutionary activities,[43] Alvarado of Yucatán exiled seventeen priests for presumed political activities,[44] but only in Jalisco did a direct conflict take place.[45] In August, 1918, the state government decided to effectuate that portion of article 130 which gave the states the authority to limit the number of priests. Demanding prior registration as a condition for performing religious services, the decree cut to about one-third the number of priests allowed to officiate.[46] The clergy, claiming that under those circumstances they

[41] Although the government took over the administration of the properties in April, 1918, the final disposition of the case was not completed until 1921.

[42] Consul Hanna to SecState, November 8, 1917, file 812.404/165, NA, RG 59, enclosing a letter of October 23 from the British vice-consul. In the absence of a U.S. agent in the region, Hanna had asked the British agent to give him information.

[43] Manuela Márquez to Calles, April 10, 1917, ADN-Sonora 1917. She protested Calles's action and attempted to prove that the priests in question were loyal Constitutionalists.

[44] Consul Gaylord Marsh (Progreso) to SecState, October 30, 1917, file 812.404/166, NA, RG 59.

[45] Espinosa Mireles to Carranza, February 13, 1918, ADN-Coahuila 1918, gives the history of the affair and justifies his action against Bishop Jesús María Echavarría.

[46] The development of the crisis may be followed in the 812.404 series, NA,

could not perform their functions, left their churches throughout the state. A Catholic youth group organized a boycott of businesses,[47] encouraging all devout Catholics to purchase only those things absolutely essential to maintaining health and vigor. The government countered by expelling Archbishop Orozco y Jiménez from Mexico, but the clerical strike and the civilian boycott continued with devastating effect; in early 1919 the state administration rescinded the offensive decree and religious peace returned.[48]

The Jalisco crisis deeply disturbed the president. He had never been convinced of the need for the more intransigent anticlerical provisions in the constitution, and the actions by the state government seriously threatened not only state but also national equilibrium. The boycott came at a time when influenza ravished the state, already suffering from crop failures. Furthermore, the situation put his government in an embarrassing position, since both state government and proclericals demanded from him support for their contentions; under these circumstances he could do little but cite the law as it existed.[49] But the potentially explosive circumstances in Jalisco, and the brooding uneasiness throughout the country on the religious issue,[50] convinced him that his original judgment had been correct; that Mexico neither needed nor would peacefully accept the stringent regulations imposed by the constitution. Therefore in the fall of 1918 he brought two proposals for constitutional change before Congress. On November 20 he requested a new article 3, which would follow exactly the thought of his proposal at Querétaro,[51] and a few

RG 59; for a short antigovernment exposition, see Antonio Ríus Facius, *La juventud católica y la Revolución Mejicana, 1910–1925*, pp. 125–134.

[47] The Asociación Católica de la Juventud Mexicana, a Catholic action group, was dedicated to implementing the precepts of *Rerum Novarum*.

[48] The new governor was Luis Castellanos y Tapia.

[49] Carranza did not agree with Diéguez on his anticlericalism, but since the governor was completely loyal to Carranza the president felt obliged to give him support.

[50] Carranza was constantly bombarded, from all states, with petitions against the various articles relating to religion; most of these concerned article 3 and those parts of article 130 which forbade foreign ministers and allowed the states to set the number of clergymen.

[51] The proposed change appears in *Diario Oficial*, November 21, 1918.

days later he recommended that article 130 be changed in three significant provisions.[52] He hoped to rescind the prohibition against foreign ministers, to withdraw the authority given to the states to limit the number of priests, and to redefine clerical property so that only real estate would fall under the ban of ownership. In order to amend the constitution in the sense he desired, Carranza needed the support of two-thirds of the members of Congress as well as a majority of the state legislatures.[53] He could count on neither. Articles 3 and 130 remained a part of the constitution, in exactly the form emanating from Querétaro, during the remainder of Carranza's term in office, but he made no attempt to enforce the prohibitions and the state governors, in the majority strong Carranza supporters, followed the national lead. Despite constitutional mandates and prohibitions, as far as practice was concerned the Church in early 1920 found itself in a situation not materially different from that of 1910.[54]

Writing a complicated constitutional article for the purpose of creating a new land-tenure system proved to be much easier than actually distributing land. By the time the constitution became fundamental law on May 1, 1917, hundreds of villages throughout the nation either were in actual occupation of seized lands, or they were clamoring for restitution or dotation, but few had any legal claim to the land they occupied. Effective and rapid land distribution depended upon dedication by both state and national leaders, and upon a willingness on the part of administrators at all levels both to cut bureaucratic red tape and to work closely with the new *ejidatarios* to make them aware of their responsibilities and their rights. It also depended upon a conviction that the new tenure system would have no deleterious effect upon agricultural production. Beset as the nation was with warring factions, with the enormous destruc-

[52] In *Diario Oficial*, November 27, 1918.

[53] Article 135 stipulates the procedures for amending the constitution.

[54] In many ways the clergy and the proclericals were more circumspect. The prohibition against political parties with a religious affiliation was generally honored, and only on rare occasions did a church-affiliated publication comment on political questions. Furthermore, some church schools never reopened, many temples and other church buildings remained in government hands, and in some states no foreign clergy officiated.

tion of physical facilities resulting from the fighting, with a shortage of manpower, and with food shortages threatening to produce famine, many public officials—including Carranza—doubted the efficacy of wholesale land distribution. Furthermore, government officials at all levels differed in their perceptions of land reform despite the emphasis on the *ejidos* written into article 27. Adolfo de la Huerta, as governor of Sonora, put greater emphasis on the establishment of agricultural "colonies" of small independent landholders than he did on ejidal development,[55] Provisional Governor Espinosa in Guanajuato encouraged the *hacendados* to sell their lands in medium-sized plots to individuals,[56] and some of Carranza's advisors wanted to emphasize improved owner-renter relations to guarantee a proper distribution of income.[57] The *hacendados* themselves, quite naturally, proved to be uncooperative, as did some of the governors. *Hacendados* in Veracruz, according to National Agrarian Commission President Eduardo Hay, were charging rent to *ejidatarios* two years after the villagers had received land on a provisional basis,[58] the governor of México refused to allow new *ejidatarios* to occupy lands allotted them by the central government,[59] and the provisional governments of both Michoacán and Hidalgo refused to act on village requests even though they had complete documentation.[60] The result of this sloth, indifference, or hostility was that very little was accomplished during the first year of constitutional government; by mid-February, 1918, only ninety-seven villages had received land by restitution or dotation.[61]

[55] De la Huerta to Carranza, March 12, 1917, ADN-Sonora 1917, reporting on the development of such colonies on the Colorado River.

[56] Feliciano Ayala and others to Caja de Préstamos, January 24, 1917, ADN-Michoacán 1917, concerning the division of haciendas near Acámbaro.

[57] Miguel Mora to Carranza, September 28, 1917, ADN-Jalisco 1917. He proposed that the state agrarian commission serve as a watchdog over the settlement of accounts as soon as the harvest had been completed.

[58] Eduardo Hay to Carranza, January 20, 1917, ADN-DF 1917.

[59] Jesús Martínez and others to Carranza, May 30, 1917, ADN-DF 1917.

[60] Múgica to Carranza, June 7, 1917, and Juan G. Bodillo to Carranza, June 8, 1917, in ADN-Michoacán and DF 1917, respectively.

[61] *La Revista Agrícola,* March 15, 1918, p. 47; the report was as of February 11.

Carranza himself was never particularly entranced with the possibility of effecting an agrarian revolution through the medium of the *ejido*; as a successful medium-sized landholder,[62] he was more attracted to private ownership than to community utilization. With many of his governors and other officials protesting almost daily about the slow pace of agrarian reform,[63] and without any enabling legislation on the statute books for article 27, in mid-1918 Carranza sent his Minister of Fomento Pastor Rouaix on a tour of the country to determine the nature and extent of the land problem, and then in October instructed him to draft a bill for submission to Congress; the proposal is perhaps the clearest exposition of Carranza thinking on the agrarian question.[64]

The draft proposal was based on the assumption that the ultimate aim of agrarian reform was the creation of a class of small landholders who owned their own properties, not on the restoration of the community-property concept; a further assumption was that the nation would make no free gifts of land. According to the bill,[65] all lands acquired by villages under the 1915 decree were to be divided into equal parcels for distribution among the villagers. After the costs to the government for the expropriation had been determined, each of the parcels would be given a proportionate value; any villager could then claim a parcel by agreeing to pay the set price, with a 10 percent down payment to be followed by nine annual installments, at a 5 percent rate of interest. Lands so acquired could not be alienated except by legal succession, the failure of the owner either to work the land steadily or to make his payments on time

62 On June 27, 1918, the state treasurer of Coahuila notified Carranza that the tax value of his properties in the state amounted to 35,000 pesos; the real value in normal times was probably two or three times as great, but this put him in the medium-sized rather than the large landholding class.

63 Among the governors who indicated some impatience were Cándido Aguilar, Ortiz Rubio, Alfonso Cabrera, Domingo Arrieta, and Espinosa Mireles. Other officials who were pressing for action were Minister of Fomento Rouaix, Francisco Field Jurado, C. Ocampo, and Flavio Bórquez.

64 Rouaix to Carranza, October 14, 1918, ADN-DF 1918, submitting a draft proposal to be discussed by the council of ministers.

65 Apparently the proposal never came before the national Congress, probably because of objections raised by members of the cabinet.

would be grounds for reassigning the parcel to another villager on the same terms, and any parcels not claimed at the time would be held in reserve for later assignment as young men came of age. The posture here was clearly Carranza's own, and at wide variance with the views of a majority of those who had fought for agrarian reform; the plan was also completely unrealistic. During his journey to the north, Rouaix had visited a number of *hacendados* in Coahuila and Chihuahua who were willing to sell their land to the government; his estimate was that such lands, irrigated, could be sold at about 500 pesos a hectare.[66] Estimates of land values in central Mexico ranged from 50 to 500 pesos a hectare, with an average of about 100 pesos a hectare for good arable land. Even if the expropriation costs were only half that price, a five hectare plot—and most observers agreed that this would be the minimum size—would cost between 250 and 1,000 pesos. Under the Carranza proposal, then, a man would need at least 25 pesos in cash, as a down payment, to claim a parcel. But Francisco Múgica reported that in Michoacán the agricultural laborers received a wage of about thirty centavos a day;[67] with a maximum of two hundred working days a year, the farm laborer therefore earned some 60 pesos, all of which he needed to feed his family. Under these circumstances it was feckless to believe that the average head of family in an agricultural village could find 25 pesos in cash to use as a down payment.

Despite the president's lack of enthusiasm for ejidal restoration, and even though he put greater stock in attracting foreigners to establish agricultural colonies,[68] the program inched forward under an unchanged article 27. *Hacendados* protested bitterly about the expropriation of lands, which had "been in the family since 1542," as

[66] Rouaix made a series of reports on his journey; most of them are in ADN-Coahuila and Chihuahua 1918.

[67] Múgica to Carranza, June 7, 1917, ADN-Michoacán 1917; he urged Carranza to order Governor Rentería Luviano to establish a minimum wage of one peso. Múgica's estimate was that the daily wage was insufficient to buy food.

[68] Carranza in early 1920 authorized the Ministry of Agriculture and Development to pay internal travel expenses for immigrants intending to establish colonies.

one Guanajuato owner claimed,[69] and over being paid "in paper which for the property owner [had] a value of X," according to a Jalisco *hacendado*,[70] but during 1919 and early 1920 a pattern of ejidal development began to emerge, hesitantly and tentatively. In all the states in the central region, local agrarian commissions examined and approved applications for either restitution or dotation. Members of Congress and local political leaders prodded both the president and the National Agrarian Commission to approve the requests for bona fide agricultural villages; before the end of his term of office, Carranza's government had allotted definitively over 200,000 hectares—nearly half a million acres or eight hundred square miles —to *ejidos*. This constituted only slightly more than one-half of 1 percent, but the principle of community property, as a gift from the national government, had been firmly established. Many details remained to be clarified, but the principle was never again seriously challenged.

The vaunted promises included in article 123 remained just as dormant for the vast majority of Mexican laborers as did those of article 27 for 99 percent of the agricultural laborers. A year passed before the first state passed a labor law adhering to the principles laid down in the constitution: in mid-January, 1918, Veracruz put on the statute books a comprehensive law that in some ways surpassed the guarantees given in the constitution. During the next two years many other states followed suit, but unfortunately the welter of conflicting precepts from state to state caused greater confusion than elucidation, and even more unfortunately—from the laborer's point of view—few states made any attempt at rigid enforcement.[71] At the national level the situation was even more doleful. Deputy Octavio Trigo of Chihuahua on October 10, 1918, did introduce a comprehensive bill covering indemnities for on-the-job accidents,[72]

[69] Unsigned, undated memorandum, ADN-Guanajuato 1917, concerning lands in the Bajío, near Apaseo el Alto.

[70] J. González to Carranza, September 1, 1919, AGN-Jalisco 1919.

[71] The state labor laws are discussed, state by state, in *Monthly Labor Review* in various issues beginning with December, 1922, and ending in August, 1924.

[72] Proyecto de Ley sobre accidentes del trabajo, October 10, 1918, in ADN-DF 1918.

but it never became law, and those areas subject to national labor jurisdiction—the Federal District and the territories—continued without any labor law of any kind in spite of the fact that the Federal District had the highest concentration of industrial workers in the nation.[73] Whatever gains labor made during the Carranza period came as a result of its own efforts, not as a result of affirmative actions by the various governmental agencies.

And labor did make some gains, often against great odds. When a strike began in the Tampico oil region in 1917, Carranza ordered the governor to "take the necessary actions to give all guarantees to lives and properties,"[74] which General Osuna interpreted to mean to prevent a work stoppage. A few months later members of the army fired on petroleum strikers at Minatlitán, and when the president of the union protested to Carranza the local commander reacted by arresting the labor leader on the grounds of "making unjust accusations against the garrison, and of defaming the army";[75] neither national nor state law provided for prosecution on such charges. Regardless of the generally unsympathetic stance of government officials, the oil workers continued to demand increased wages and improved working conditions, and when the arbitration and conciliation board could come to no agreement in Tampico during October another strike began; Provisional Governor Ricaut promptly arrested the "agitators and Peláez accomplices,"[76] who happened to be the labor leaders. The oil workers were not the only labor group in a bellicose mood. In the spring of 1918 the textile workers in the Orizaba region went on strike, soon to be joined by the streetcar employees; on this occasion Governor Cabrera proved to be sympathetic to labor's de-

[73] The national government did establish boards of arbitration and conciliation in November, 1917, and decreed one day of rest per week in December, 1919, but did not pass a comprehensive law.

[74] Carranza to Acting Governor Gregorio Osuna, April 30, 1917, ADN-DF 1917. He also instructed the state commandant in the same vein.

[75] Ignacio Gómez to Carranza, June 3, 1917; Carranza to General Rafael Maldonado, June 5, 1917; and Maldonado to Carranza, June 7, 1917, all in ADN-Veracruz 1917.

[76] Ricaut to Carranza, October 23 and November 25, 1917, ADN-Tamaulipas 1917; Acting SecState to Ambassador Fletcher, November 16, 1917, file 812.504 /148, NA, RG 59.

mands.[77] Other groups went on strike in Guanajuato, Querétaro, and the Federal District. The issue, of course, was the same as that in 1915–1916: the increasing gap between the cost of living and the wages paid. The Mexican equivalent of the NAM had a simple answer; in a bitter denunciation of the workers in general and the Orizaba syndicate in particular, its spokesman said:

> The syndicate is an instrument of oppression; it forces the closed shop, forcibly collects dues, prevents the dismissal of incompetent workers, and orders unjustified strikes. The money it collects is not used for the purposes stated, but only for the engendering of hatred against the industrialists. The law [article 123] which allows the development of such associations does not—or should not—leave the syndicates free to take such actions of arrogance and power. The only manner of curbing such power, and of guaranteeing life, property, and the freedom to work, is to station a strong garrison of Federal troops in Orizaba.[78]

That far Carranza was not yet prepared to go.

Carranza himself was never unsympathetic to the plight of the laboring man, but he was adamantly opposed to the development of "labor" as a special class within the Mexican society, with special dispensations and with special powers. But since 1910 the laboring groups had come of age, in part as the result of encouragement and aid from organized labor in the United States and in some of the European countries; Carranza had to contend with a militant and demanding group of labor leaders, who in some industries had sufficient influence over the rank and file to cause serious difficulties to both the economy and the government. During 1917 the multitude of unions and syndicates had attempted to organize a national association, but doctrinal differences and personal ambitions had prevented any effective action, and late in the year no effective national organization existed. This failure on the part of the independent groups to meld into a strong national union displeased Carranza not at all; he would have preferred that condition to remain. But the

[77] Alfonso Cabrera to Carranza, February 26 and March 5, 1918, ADN-Puebla 1918; Pedro Cortina to Carranza, March 11 and March 13, 1918, ADN-DF 1918.

[78] Confederación de Cámaras Industriales de los Estados Unidos Mexicanos to Carranza, October 23, 1918, ADN-Veracruz 1918.

viejo barbón well knew that eventually a national organization would emerge, and in order to protect himself against the power of such an independent entity he decided to aid in the development of a creature he could control. For his agent he selected Espinosa Mireles.

Governor Gustavo Espinosa Mireles of Coahuila was a dedicated Carrancista of a somewhat conservative bent,[79] who owed his position in politics to Carranza's sponsorship and who as a consequence was anxious to do the president's bidding. At Carranza's request,[80] in March, 1918, the Coahuila governor invited all labor unions and syndicates throughout the nation to send delegates to a great convention to meet in Saltillo on May 1 for the purpose of developing a national organization; the national government paid all the expenses of all delegates, with the obvious hope of controlling both a statement of principles and the organization itself. When the delegates met they certainly did not represent all organized groups—the major groups from the Federal District, among others, refused to attend—but they could certainly claim to be national in scope.[81] They came from eighteen states, they belonged to unions in every industry, and they covered the ideological spectrum from simple trade unionism of the Gompers style on one end to radical anarcho-syndicalism on the other. From the twelve-day meeting, often tumultuous, sometimes bitter, and always machiavellian, the Confederación Regional Obrera Mexicana (CROM) emerged under the leadership of trade unionist Luis Morones,[82] a shrewd and tough laboring man as much inter-

[79] That is, conservative within the files of the revolutionary forces. He could scarcely be classified as "conservative" in comparison with Manuel Calero, Toribio Esquivel Obregón, or Emilio Rabasa.

[80] I have found no concrete evidence of this request, but peripheral evidence is so strongly suggestive that one can assume such an action, probably transmitted verbally. Only a few days after issuing the invitation on March 22, the governor made a hurried trip to Mexico City, at Carranza's behest.

[81] For an account of the proceedings, see *Informe del Tercer Congreso Obrero Nacional verificado en Saltillo, del 1 al 12 de mayo de 1918*.

[82] At that time Morones was greatly influenced by Samuel Gompers, who even then was attempting to convince Morones to marshal Mexican labor opinion in favor of the Allies in the war (see Sinclair Snow, *The Pan American Federation of Labor*).

ested in his own self aggrandizement as he was in labor improvement.[83] The statement of principles, somewhat turgid and frequently inconsistent, emphasized class war, direct rather than political action, control of industry by the workers, and free land for the peasants, but the specific demands for wages, working conditions, and other items of immediate concern to the working man were scarcely revolutionary. One scholar has characterized the program as being "as mild as even the most conservative government could ask for, eloquent evidence that the leaders were not interested in thorough-going revolutionary methods."[84] But when the delegates began their homeward treks, President Carranza and Governor Espinosa Mireles had to make an uncomfortable admission; their maneuverings had not been so successful as those of Morones. The subservient national organization had failed to materialize, and Carranza could expect cooperation from the new leadership only if it benefited labor—and Morones.

Morones never took seriously the bombastic phrases of the CROM denunciation of political action. He was above all else a practical man of politics who had an unerring sense of where power lay and how to use it. Soon after the formation of the new national confederation he surrounded himself with a small semisecret group of like thinking, dubbed the Grupo Acción, which concerned itself not only with direct action but also with political action; its primary concern was to weigh the political alternatives and to choose that which might be most beneficial.

By the beginning of 1920, then, Mexican labor had made some gains, but the Promised Land of article 123 was still far away. To be sure, the most vicious practices of the *porfiriato* had long since disappeared. Debt peonage no longer existed. Shop foremen no longer physically mistreated the workmen, the old-style company store was dead, and only on rare occasions did management engage in the ear-

[83] For an adulatory and not always accurate biography of Morones see Joseph H. Retinger, *Morones of Mexico*.

[84] Marjorie Ruth Clark, *Organized Labor in Mexico*, p. 61. But if Clark is no more accurate in interpretation than she is in detail, the evaluation should not be taken seriously.

lier general practice of paying in chits or scrip.[85] Furthermore, labor had a legal right to organize and to strike, and these rights the workmen exercised even though striking was sometimes perilous.[86] On the other hand the minimum wage, in those few areas where it was established and enforced, fell far short of being "sufficient to satisfy the normal necessities of life," and the average workday continued to be in excess of eight hours. Laborers still worked in dangerous and squalid surroundings, they still suffered accidents without compensation, and they were still subject to arbitrary dismissal.[87] But they also had the assurance of article 123 behind them.

Even in those areas dearest to his political and economic philosophy Carranza could do little during his administration. He was a firm adherent of government control over the subsoil deposits and of rigid control over foreign enterprises, but, by the time he began the doleful trek that ended at Tlaxcalantongo,[88] national ownership and control over the oil deposits was no closer to a reality than it had been when the delegates at Querétaro voted their defiant article 27. A combination of domestic and foreign pressures effectively stymied any legislation designed to put subsoil deposits under strict government control. The major domestic pressure, of course, was the continued control that rebel Manuel Peláez exercised over the area in which the productive wells were situated; Peláez never occupied the

[85] Francisco Murguía in Chihuahua ordered the arrest and retention, without trial or hearing, of a mine manager because he paid part of the wages in scrip that local banks and merchants discounted 20 percent. When the manager made arrangements to pay in legal tender, Murguía ordered his release (Murguía to Carranza, November 26, 1917, ADN-Guanajuato 1917).

[86] In mid-1919 the teachers in the Federal District went on strike because their wages had not been paid, and a few days later the streetcar operators joined them in sympathy. Carranza ordered the army to operate the streetcars, using weapons if necessary to maintain service, and in the subsequent reorganization of the school system many teachers discovered that their jobs had disappeared.

[87] A group of streetcar workers from Puebla complained to Carranza in April, 1918, that they had been discharged because they had taken the lead in organizing a syndicate (Cástulo Buendía, Enrique Escalante, and others to Carranza, April 1, 1918, ADN-DF 1918).

[88] The small village in which Carranza was killed on the night of May 20, 1920.

refining-shipping point of Tampico, but in the vast petroleum hinterland his word was law, and the companies recognized it as such.[89] But the question was not merely one of Peláez's control. For his own purposes Peláez had convinced many small landowners, including the indigenes in the Pánuco region, that the subsoil provisions of article 27 would deprive them of their lands and whatever income they derived from the oil exploitations in the region. The rumor became so widespread, and the feeling so intense, that, even before Carranza took office as constitutional president, Nicéforo Zambrano of Nuevo León advised him to urge Congress to suspend that portion of article 27, at least for the moment.[90] The president made no such recommendation when the national Congress began its session in May, 1917, but neither did he urge immediate enabling legislation for the article. For the next three years Peláez continued his operations in the oil regions, circumscribed in an ever narrowing circle. But as long as he controlled some of the oil region the government was in an embarrassing situation and could hardly press for comprehensive enabling legislation.

More potent as a deterrent to legislation was foreign pressure. By the time Carranza took the oath of office as constitutional president, World War I was reaching its most critical stage for the allies, and it was generally assumed that neither the United States nor Great Britain would allow any disruption of the flow of oil so necessary to the two navies.[91] The United States had persisted in objecting to the

[89] Peláez regularly collected money from the companies for "protection"; Carranza objected strenuously and accused the companies of aiding the rebels, but he had to admit that the oilmen had no alternative.

[90] Zambrano to Carranza, February 19, 1917, ADN-DF 1917.

[91] There remains a distinct difference of scholarly opinion on the necessity of Mexican oil for the British navy. Peter Calvert (*The Mexican Revolution, 1910–1914*) implies that it was helpful but not essential, while Lorenzo Meyer (*México y Estados Unidos en el conflicto petrolero, 1917–1942*) strongly suggests that it was critical. Luis Liceaga (*Félix Díaz*) states unequivocally that the United States was prepared to occupy the oil fields if necessary. I have found no conclusive evidence of such preparation, but the accusation was widely believed in Mexico. Juan B. Rojo reported (Rojo to Carranza, June 25, 1917, ADN-DF 1917), for example, that a Navy Department official testifying before the Senate Naval Affairs Committee had stated that the oil was so important that forceful seizure would be justified.

decrees issued in 1915 and 1916 and periodically requested a clarification of the status of foreign companies operating in Mexico;[92] the possibility of a retroactive application of article 27 made both the companies and their governments somewhat nervous. At the moment the Carranza government could ill afford to challenge the British and U.S. interests directly; the stakes were too high and the chances of failure too great. The more militant members of the new Congress, of course, hoped to put all articles of the new constitution into immediate effect and were ready to discuss enabling legislation, but by the terms of the transitory article that called the special session, the Congress could discuss only those bills presented by the executive. Since Carranza was obviously dubious about such legislation, Congress in early June "invited" the president to prepare a bill.[93] Some months earlier Minister of Industry and Commerce Alberto Pani had taken the first step in gathering data necessary to draft a law;[94] among other things he asked the petroleum companies to make whatever observations they might care to with respect to the eventual enforcement of article 27. When these suggestions proved to be "completely outside the revolutionary criterion,"[95] Pani drafted a bill to be presented to the National Congress of Industries in the fall of 1917 for the consideration of that group. But the industrialists proved also to be "adverse . . . to any modification of the regimen established, and the situation of the companies formed, during the Porfirian dictatorship."[96] Late in the year the draft and the relevant data were handed to the permanent commission for study. At every step in the process the U.S. government protested what appeared to be a policy devoted to a confiscation of the rights obtained by the oil companies in the earlier era.

In the meantime the Mexican government moved in on the oil companies from another direction. By a preconstitutional decree of

[92] The most useful archival material on this subject is file 812.6363, NA, RG 59.

[93] Fletcher to SecState, June 11, 1917, and June 27, 1917, files 812.011/53 and 812.6363/288, NA, RG 59.

[94] On April 26, 1917.

[95] Alberto J. Pani, *Apuntes autobiográficos*, I, 263.

[96] Ibid.

April 13, Carranza attempted to establish the principle of a royalty payment, without actually using the word. According to the decree,[97] the government would collect a 10 percent tax on all production, with the value of the oil fixed in the decree and depending upon the specific gravity: the lighter the oil the greater its value. Every two months the Ministry of Hacienda was to determine the value, as the world market price shifted.[98] The "special stamp tax," as the decree defined the new schedule, appeared to both the oil companies and the Department of State as a "confiscation of American rights by retroactive legislation," and they protested it as such.[99] But Ambassador Fletcher was not in whole-hearted agreement with his superiors.[100] He pointed out that financially the government was in a "difficult position" inasmuch as the economy was halting and debts were high; the national government needed increased income: "Money must be raised and petroleum and mining taxation bearing largely upon foreigners seems popular perhaps because of Mexico's inability to secure foreign financial assistance. . . . This instruction [of protest from Lansing] would seem to involve a change in our present policy with regard to Mexico."[101]

At the same time, Carranza's government gave the oil companies another cause for concern. As soon as it became clear, in January, that the new constitution would nationalize the subsoil, some oil companies began a flurry of leasing activity,[102] which continued un-

[97] Fletcher to SecState, April 19, 1917, file 812.6363/275, NA, RG 59. The tax was to take effect on May 1, the beginning of the constitutional term.

[98] The changing rates may be found in *El Economista* during succeeding months. The first such change, as published in *El Economista*, June 12, 1917, lowered the value—and therefore the tax—by about 10 percent. The value was that computed for the oil as it was loaded at the oil ports, and was certainly not excessive; the best grade crude was set at about fifty cents (U.S.) per barrel, when the average value at the well in the United States was about $2.00. In 1917 total production reached 55 million barrels.

[99] Lansing to Fletcher, June 6, 1917, file 812.011/48a, NA, RG 59.

[100] Henry P. Fletcher was designated as ambassador in February, 1917, and presented his credentials in March.

[101] Fletcher to SecState, June 7, 1917, file 812.011/49, NA, RG 59.

[102] On January 30, for example, the Mexican consul in New York reported that one company had, only a few days before, paid a Mexican citizen about $200,000 for a lease "in flagrant violation" of Carranza's earlier decrees and the

til May 1, the date upon which the constitution went into effect. But by an order to his petroleum inspectors of June 24, Carranza took the position that the basic prohibitions of the constitution went into effect on the date of publication, or February 5, and refused to grant drilling permits on leases acquired after the date of promulgation. Alberto Pani stated the Mexican case quite succinctly: "Leases, or contracts of whatever nature relating to the exploitation of these [hydrocarbon] mineral products, entered into on dates prior to the promulgation of the Constitution are presumed to have been made in good faith; but not those made subsequent to that date."[103] In the face of renewed protests made by the United States, in early August the Mexican president relieved the pressure somewhat by assuring Ambassador Fletcher that Mexico had no intention of taking over properties in production before February 5 and stated that under no circumstances would there be confiscation.[104]

Carranza may not have been willing to challenge the Great Powers directly, but neither did he want to drop completely the question of national ownership and control of the natural resources. Under emergency fiscal powers that the national Congress had granted him the year before,[105] on February 19, 1918, Carranza issued a new tax decree that not only established a clearly identified royalty but also stated that the uncaptured oil belonged to the nation and that drilling could be done only as the result of a special permit to be issued by the government; the provision applied whether the land had been acquired before or after February 1.[106] The owners of leases of the land had first choice, but others could "denounce" the land if the

---

spirit of article 27—not yet approved but in the offing (Juan T. Burns to Sub-Sec Foreign Relations, January 30, 1917, ADN-DF 1917).

[103] Pani to Fletcher, June 28, 1917, as enclosure in Summerlin to SecState, July 9, 1917, file 812.6363/292, NA, RG 59.

[104] Fletcher to SecState, August 2, 1917, file 812.63/481, NA, RG 59.

[105] Congress granted Carranza broad fiscal powers on May 17, 1917, allowing him to take emergency measures to meet the critical problem of salaries. During the next two years the PLC made frequent attempts to rescind that power and finally did so.

[106] The decree may be found in published, translated form in *Foreign Relations, 1918*, pp. 702–704.

owner failed to make a request within a stipulated time limit;[107] other than in the new tax schedule, the decree did not affect the wells already in production. Accepting as a principle the right of the Mexican government to demand that landowners obtain drilling permits, of course, would have relegated the owners of the oil lands to a position of mere concessionaires; the oil lands would be of less value without the unencumbered right to drill. Throughout 1918 and 1919 the quarrel between Mexico on the one hand and the companies and the U.S. government on the other continued. A conference between Mexican officials and oil company representatives in June, 1918, produced minor changes but did not change the principle,[108] and correspondence between the two governments "merely reiterated their respective positions."[109] Mexico held fast to the principle, but found it necessary to extend the time limit at frequent intervals and even, finally, to issue drilling permits for those lands held prior to February 5, 1917.[110] Neither side had budged from its contention with respect to Mexican ownership of the subsoil.

U.S. involvement in World War I compounded the strains on Mexican-American relations. It also gave Carranza certain advantages in his diplomatic dealings, for the United States at all costs needed peace in the Western Hemisphere. The preposterous Zimmermann telegram,[111] in which the German government early in 1917 instructed its ambassador in Mexico to offer help in recovering territory lost to the United States in 1848 if Mexico joined the

[107] That is, request permission to drill. In August, Carranza announced that any private individual could seek such permits.

[108] Pani, *Apuntes autobiográficos*, I, 264. Pani and Rafael Nieto from Finance represented Mexico; James H. Garfield and Nelson Rhoads spoke for the companies.

[109] C. Dennis Ignasias, "Reluctant Recognition: The United States and the Recognition of Alvaro Obregón of Mexico, 1920–1924," pp. 20–21.

[110] For some period of time it appeared as though the lack of new wells would bring a decline in production and in January, 1919, a number of the companies requested provisional permits with the stipulation that the issuance of such permits would in no way be interpreted as a retreat from principle. A year later, in January, 1920, Carranza acceded to the request. Production, incidentally, never declined; it increased dramatically.

[111] The best study is Barbara Tuchman, *The Zimmermann Telegram.*

war against the Allies,[112] outraged American public opinion against Germany. It also caused concern in Washington over what Carranza might do. As a matter of fact Carranza was sorely tempted to pursue the matter.[113] He was dissuaded by close advisers—including Obregón, who told him, "Germany, like the clergyman at the bedside of the dying man, will recommend our country to the mercies of Providence. That and nothing more."[114] Carranza sidestepped the offer; he even told Ambassador Fletcher during the first week of March that he had received no proposal from the Germans—but refused to say what Mexico's answer to such a proposition might be.[115]

Although the First Chief proclaimed strict Mexican neutrality after the United States declared war in April, [116] he let it be known—no doubt with a calculating eye on Washington—that his sympathies were with the Germans. He told students at the National University in May that, while the United States had been a scourge to its southern neighbors for years, "good and noble Germany" had never molested Mexico and Latin America. Mexico's interests, he said, lay "solely and resolutely with the Central Powers"; the Allies, if victorious, would repay U.S. aid by leaving the Americans a free hand in the southern republics.[117] U.S. diplomats close to the situation did not believe, after April at any rate, that Mexico would

[112] The idea of using U.S. territory as a bait may have originated two years before, when German agents were involved in a counterrevolutionary scheme to restore Victoriano Huerta to power; the plotters' "Plan of San Diego" called for restoration of Mexican territories lost to the United States (see Michael Meyer, "The Mexican-German Conspiracy of 1915," *The Americas* 23, no. 1 [July, 1966]: 76–89).

[113] See for example Roberto Guzmán Esparza, *Memorias de Don Adolfo de la Huerta según su propio dictado*, p. 101, and E. J. Dillon, *President Obregón: A World Reformer*, p. 166.

[114] Dillon, *President Obregón*, p. 166.

[115] Fletcher to SecState, March 10, 1917, in *Foreign Relations, 1917*, pp. 238–239; also Cándido Aguilar to Carranza, March 10, 1917, ADN-DF 1917.

[116] Fletcher to SecState, April 15, 1917, in *Foreign Relations, Supplement 1, 1917*, p. 255.

[117] Stenographic transcript of Carranza speech at National University, May 15, 1917, in ADN-DF 1917.

enter the war,[118] but Woodrow Wilson was determined to avoid any altercation with "that pedantic ass, the First Chief" (as he referred to him in a note to Robert Lansing).[119] To that end the administration became conciliatory on several points. In July the State Department granted permission for Carranza to take delivery on 2.7 million rounds of ammunition (already paid for but embargoed since 1916),[120] and in August the department told Carranza it would not block his efforts to negotiate a loan from U.S. bankers.[121] Carranza occasionally reciprocated with conciliatory words. Late in 1917 he assured American officials that they could rely not only on his neutrality but also on neutral cooperation—raw materials needed for the war effort would continue to flow.[122] His actions, however, were anything but amicable. He not only harassed the oil companies, he also browbeat the United States into selling him machinery and continually vexed Washington by his unyielding stands on matters involving American investments—correctly convinced that he had little to fear.[123] U.S.-Mexican relations by the time the armistice was signed were frigid; if no worse than before the war, there were no indications that they would improve in the foreseeable future.

While diplomats, politicians, and businessmen wrangled, the Mexican populace during Carranza's administration groped desperately to find simple personal security. If there was less danger of meeting with violent death after 1917 than in the four years before, the threat of sinking into material destitution and dying of starvation or disease was for many starkly real. Food production was critically low. Corn in 1918 dropped below two million tons,

[118] See for example Fletcher to SecState, April 25, 1917, file 862.20212/273, NA, RG 59.

[119] Wilson to Lansing, April 9, 1917, file 711.12/36 1/2, NA, RG 59.

[120] Acting Secretary of State Frank Polk to Consul Dawson, July 21, 1917, file 812.113/8386, NA, RG 59. Carranza insisted he needed the cartridges for internal security operations and pledged that they would not fall into Villa's hands.

[121] Lansing to Fletcher, August 8, 1917, file 812.51/312, NA, RG 59.

[122] Guzmán Esparza, *Memorias de Don Adolfo de la Huerta*, pp. 102–103.

[123] Howard Cline, *The United States and Mexico*, pp. 183–188, has a handy and succinct summary of U.S.-Mexican wartime relations.

less than during the hungry last decade of the *porfiriato*; beans, the other great staple, were at only 65 percent of the 1910 figure,[124] and the pattern was similar for most other comestibles. Some of the decline was due to adverse weather conditions, more of it to a general refusal of food growers to risk large-scale production while land tenure and markets were highly uncertain and new armed outbreaks were always a possibility.

State and local officials in 1918 reported desperate conditions. Governor Espinosa Mireles of Coahuila wired Carranza in February that hundreds of people were entering his state daily from Nuevo León, Zacatecas, Durango, and San Luis Potosí in search of food, thus aggravating the already severe grain shortage.[125] Murguía of Chihuahua in March told the president he was stopping all exports of grain and cattle to the United States because of scarcities (he added bitterly that Mexicans were being shot by U.S. border patrols while trying to bring food across the boundary to their families).[126] In June, Ciudad Juárez was completely without meat.[127] Other governors told of similar or worse conditions in their states.[128] To complete the desolate picture, a disastrous epidemic of "Spanish flu" in late 1918 and early 1919 almost paralyzed the country.

Unemployment was high, job security was nonexistent and wages for most workingmen hovered at a subsistence level—or fell below. The situation in the mining industry was in many respects typical. The companies, most of them foreign owned, had begun to revive in 1916 and hoped to get back to regular production after normal

[124] See table 6, p. 372, in Charles C. Cumberland, *Mexico: The Struggle for Modernity*.

[125] Espinosa Mireles to Carranza, February 22, 1918, ADN-Coahuila 1918.

[126] Murguía to Carranza, March 12, 1918, ADN-Chihuahua 1918. The United States had prohibited most food exports as a war measure. In July, Washington relaxed restrictions on sales of corn, pork, and other edibles to Mexico (see State Department circular to consular agents in Mexico, July 22, 1918, file 711.12/132a, NA, RG 59).

[127] Murguía to Carranza, June 8, 1918, ADN-Chihuahua 1918.

[128] See ADN, various states, for 1917 and 1918. U.S. consular reports for the same period tell of hunger and malnutrition in most parts of the country, worsening until late in 1918 and then leveling off or improving slightly.

government was reestablished, but many held back after seeing the new constitution. During the first part of 1917 they jockeyed and stalled while workers sat idle. The American Smelting and Refining Company told Mexican officials early in 1917 that it was considering reopening and modernizing its Monterrey plant but that labor clauses in the new charter might mean trouble and the company wanted assurances that it could operate "without extraneous intervention."[129] In April the Chispas mines in Sonora closed, throwing a thousand Mexicans out of work—reportedly to protest the new laws and to pressure the government.[130] Cananea Consolidated shut down in June after a dispute with Sonora officials; it had insisted that it be allowed to operate under its prerevolutionary agreements with the state.[131] Although Carranza after the middle of 1917 took a generally tolerant line with foreign mining interests—for example, abolishing tariffs on machinery and parts and scaling down other taxes—[132] local conditions often made normal operations impossible. In Durango ruined rail lines and bandit activity in 1917 forced near-total suspension of work.[133] There was a general recovery in the industry after 1917 but it gained momentum slowly—in 1918 and 1919 only around 12 percent of the mines and 21 percent of the processing plants were operating.[134] By early 1920 both production and prices were rising dramatically—but the Mexican worker benefited little if at all. His peso wage was not significantly higher than it had been before 1910, while inflation drove his real wage to desperate lows. And by the middle of the year sharp drops in world mineral prices threw the industry into a new depression.

The government wrestled dispiritedly with the problem of public

[129] Representatives of American Smelting and Refining Company to Carranza, February 3, 1917, ADN-DF 1917.

[130] Calles to Carranza, April 17, 1917, ADN-Sonora 1917.

[131] Juan D. Rojo to Carranza, June 22, 1917, and Calles to Carranza, September 3, 1917, in ADN-Sonora 1917.

[132] Marvin D. Bernstein, *The Mexican Mining Industry, 1890–1950*, p. 120.

[133] Vice Consul Homer C. Coen to SecState, February 17, 1917, file 812.63 /372, NA, RG 59.

[134] Bernstein, *The Mexican Mining Industry*, p. 118.

finance. The national debt was astronomical—Swiss bankers estimated it at 722 million pesos in December, 1919.[135] Although revenues rose handsomely during most of Carranza's term, mainly from oil and mineral taxes, the demands on the treasury were backbreaking. Military expenditures annually ate up the lion's share of the budget.[136] Much of this was boondoggle or outright thievery but much of it was legitimate. There was literally not a day during Carranza's presidency when someone, somewhere in Mexico was not in arms against the government; pararevolutionary activity and banditry refused to disappear. Most of it was not a real danger to the government but it caused a steady and massive drain on an already blighted economy.[137]

Carranza in his plight did have some occasional solace: in early April, 1919, Pablo González engineered Emiliano Zapata's assassination, and in November government troops captured, tried, and executed Felipe Angeles.[138]

They were hard years. Most Mexicans could well wonder whether the revolution had not been a tragic mistake. Despite the establishment of a new government and the return of peace to most parts of the country, good times did not appear. Few Mexicans could hold Carranza directly responsible; given the myriad domestic problems and the country's precarious international position, prob-

[135] The Swiss calculated the foreign debt at 607 million pesos, of which 189 million had been incurred by Huerta, and the domestic debt at 115 million—48 million of it Huerta's, 44 million contracted by the preconstitutional regime, and 23 million consisting of claims for damage suffered during the revolution (Mexican Consul General Manuel Bauche Alcalde [Bern] to Carranza, December 11, 1919, ADN-DF 1919).

[136] In March, 1918, slightly over 7 million pesos of the total federal payroll of 9.5 million went to the armed forces (see Presupuesto de sueldos para el mes de marzo de 1918, in ADN-DF 1918).

[137] During January, 1920, for example, eight of the seventeen train wrecks reported in Mexico were the work of outlaws (Director General of National Railways to Carranza, February 29, 1920, ADN-DF 1920).

[138] Angeles, firmly grasping and sometimes stroking a copy of Renan's *Life of Christ* throughout his trial, insisted that he had returned to Mexico and rejoined Villa only in order to convince that *caudillo* not to be so bestial in his treatment of prisoners; but he helped direct an unsuccessful attack on Ciudad Juárez on June 14. Carranza received hundreds of letters begging him to pardon Angeles.

ably no leader could have done much to improve conditions. On the other hand, Carranza gave little indication that he intended to fulfill many of the promises written into the Constitution of 1917. He was at heart a liberal gradualist, and the document's radical social provisions repelled him. He showed by his stands on labor matters and the religious question, for example, that he had no desire to take advanced positions. Whether the revolution was foundering during Carranza's presidency is debatable, but the president's attitudes caused growing unrest in the ranks of revolutionists who took the constitution very seriously indeed. Yet, Carranza could almost certainly have completed his term of office and retired gracefully and with honor in December, 1920. He failed to do so because he insisted on imposing a successor, and many important people, for both personal and ideological reasons, would not let him do this. Carranza believed he could work his will. He was not by choice a fighter for lost causes—more than once he had swallowed his towering pride and avoided battles he might lose. His judgment had usually been right in such matters; but as 1920 approached, it played him false, and the error cost him both his government and his life.

On January 15, 1919, Carranza spoke out on national politics.[139] The presidential election was still a year and a half away, but already there was much speculation about who would succeed him, and Carranza wanted to quell it. He expressed grave concern over what he termed a climate of growing divisiveness in the country. He appealed to all who had fought for the Constitutionalist cause to unite behind his government. The enemies of the revolution, he said, were still powerful; factionalism in revolutionary ranks would invite disaster, and just such a division, he averred, could result from a premature taking of sides in favor of one or another would-be presidential candidate. The pronouncement aroused suspicions that he was trying to keep the field clear of hopefuls so that he could name his successor with a minimum of opposition. Just who that might be no one could guess, but clearly it would not be the

[139] *Diario Oficial*, January 16, 1919.

man whom many revolutionists already eyed with high enthusiasm —Alvaro Obregón.

The "Hero of Celaya" had resigned as minister of war in May, 1917, and returned to his ranch in Sonora. There he ran a profitable business raising chickpeas but found time to receive friends and to make occasional trips in Mexico and abroad. No one believed his retirement from national affairs was permanent, and Obregón did nothing to discourage speculation that he would run for president in 1920. From the first he was the most prominent contender, and the coolness of his relations with Carranza precluded the possibility of official support.[140]

Obregón announced his candidacy on June 1, 1919.[141] His statement was a solemn warning that the revolution was in jeopardy, that unless there were fundamental reorientations the years of suffering and sacrifice would have been wasted. The problem was at heart a moral one; there was, he said, "a well-founded fear that the material interests accumulated by unscrupulous leaders during the Revolution constitute an insurmountable barrier to the implantation of those advanced principles proclaimed during the armed conflict." The revolution must shed its transitory and tarnished battle array, and only new leadership could accomplish this. His references to Carranza, although couched in respect, were an unmistakable call for the president to fade from the scene: "The historic figure of the First Chief of the Constitutionalist Army is in danger, if his work . . . remains barren and comes solely to offer, as its bitter fruit, the doleful result of our earlier revolutions: not permitting the country to liberate itself from its liberators." The key, he said, was effective suffrage, which would produce leaders answerable only to the people; if permitted to choose freely, the people would do right. In the coming elections, "either our nascent democracy will be definitely consolidated . . . or the seeds of the Revolution will be uprooted from their natural beds and sowed in grounds fertilized with abuse and immorality." He said that he was

[140] See Dillon, *President Obregón*, pp. 145–157.

[141] "Manifiesto a la Nación, lanzado por el C. Alvaro Obregón," in José Vasconcelos, *La caída de Carranza*, pp. 3–26.

not the candidate of any existing political party; he called instead for a new liberal coalition and offered himself as its leader.[142]

The pronouncement drew battle lines. Carranza was furious,[143] although, typically, he avoided breaking publicly with Obregón. Support for the Sonora hero's candidacy blossomed at once. A hundred federal deputies wired pledges of adherence.[144] Leaders of the CROM also were confident that he was their man; on August 6 they signed a pact with Obregón: The syndicates would support his candidacy; Obregón committed himself, if elected, to give special consideration to labor in general and to the CROM in particular. Among other things, he promised to create a Ministry of Labor headed by a man recommended by labor, to work for a comprehensive labor law, to make himself available for weekly consultations with CROM officers, and to seek the advice of labor leaders on matters of national policy.[145] As Obregón's fortunes waxed, Carranza's political hold weakened. By the end of October, Obregón partisans in the Chamber of Deputies had taken over the leadership of most committees,[146] and Congress proceeded to replace Carrancista members of the federal judiciary with its own choices.[147]

142 Although Obregón continued to avoid adhering to any existing party, he permitted the PLC to nominate him as its candidate and later accepted the formal backing of the Cooperatist party, headed by Jorge Prieto Laurens.

143 According to Miguel Alessio Robles (*Historia política de la revolución*, pp. 227–228), Carranza summoned various prominent Sonorans living in Mexico City and told them that he had been prepared to back Obregón as his successor but that now he could not do so.

144 Chargé d'Affaires George F. Summerlin to SecState, June 11, 1919, file 812.00/22842, NA, RG 59.

145 Clark, *Organized Labor in Mexico*, pp. 72, 73. The pact was secret until years afterward, but the CROM's all-out support of Obregón was very obvious. In December the Grupo Acción established the Mexican Labor party to help elect him; in March, 1920, as the campaign entered its final stage, the party assigned key personnel to mobilize worker and peasant support, and Morones personally joined Obregón on the campaign trail (ibid., pp. 73–74).

146 See Torres to Mario Méndez, November 1, 1919, ADN-Querétaro 1919.

147 See E. Ronorosa Anrade to Carranza, October 29, 1919, and Fidel Sapién to Carranza, November 18, 1919, in ADN-DF 1919. Congress had the right to do this, although it was a rebuff to the president; federal judges below the level

By now Carranza was ready to counterattack. Obregón must be stopped, and Carranza prepared to throw his weight behind a candidate of his own. His choice was an odd one. Ignacio Bonillas, Mexican ambassador to the United States, had been a Carranza loyalist since 1913. Of respectable but unspectacular reputation, he was largely unknown to Mexicans. No matter; Carranza had made his decision and meant to have his way. Early in November administration stalwarts organized the "Democratic National party." It was presided over by the president's trusted aide, Luis Manuel Rojas, who drafted a party manifesto, to be released at the proper time, presenting Bonillas to the electorate. Great care was taken to hide the official origin of the candidacy.[148] Bonillas would be offered as the civilian candidate, in contrast to the two generals—Obregón and the other hopeful, Pablo González.

González, after working for several months to organize support, launched his drive in earnest on January 13, 1920, as the candidate of the "Progressive party." He began a spirited but rather disoriented campaign. His support was diverse but gave the impression of being something less than revolutionary—backers included large numbers of *hacendados* and businessmen.[149] A number of army leaders also backed him, although Obregón enjoyed the support of the vast majority of the military. In all, González's campaign never developed a momentum that gave him a serious chance of winning.

In January, Carranza's offensive was in high gear. On the eighteenth the administration newspaper, *El Demócrata*, published the manifesto of the "Democratic National party" formally launching the Bonillas candidacy.[150] It warned darkly that the contest between

---

of the Supreme Court (which is elected) are chosen by Congress (article 73). The constitution specified that after 1923 judges could be removed only for bad conduct and after impeachment.

[148] See Rojas to Carranza, November 19, 24, 26, 1919, ADN-DF 1919.

[149] *El Universal*, February 1, 1920.

[150] *El Demócrata*, January 18, 1920. This was the first sure indication that Bonillas was in fact the administration's candidate. On January 7 the U.S. chargé d'affaires reported to Washington that, although it was known Bonillas would run, it was still uncertain whether he would do so with Carranza's support (Summerlin to SecState, January 7, 1920, file 812.00/23328, NA, RG 59).

Obregón and González could end in a fratricidal military conflict and unctuously called upon both to retire in favor of the ambassador. Obregón followers decried the manifesto as an attempt to subvert free elections.[151] Early in February seventeen state governors met in Mexico City at Carranza's behest to "confer" on ways to insure effective suffrage in the approaching elections and a peaceful transfer of presidential power. Ten governors refused to participate;[152] those who did, issued a statement on the tenth.[153] It noted that one party in the campaign (Obregón's) was accusing the federal government of attempting to impose a candidate and was evidently building that issue as an excuse to rebel. The governors deplored such tactics and pledged to conduct themselves in such a manner as to obviate any pretext for extralegal acts; they would refrain from taking a partisan position in the elections and would do all they could to assure a fair vote in their states. Adolfo de la Huerta, governor of Sonora, took immediate exception to the statement, which he said amounted to an attempt to force the states to approve the administration's presidential choice.[154] The pro-Obregón newspaper *El Monitor Republicano* vehemently resented the charge that Obregonistas were plotting rebellion; it branded the governors' action a move to intimidate liberals and independents and accused the government of persecuting Obregón supporters in various parts of the country.[155]

While the governors met, a convention of Obregón supporters also assembled in Mexico City. Its leaders included an impressive array of revolutionary leaders, among them Roque Estrada, Benjamín Hill, Felipe Carrillo, Miguel Alessio Robles, and Andrés Castro.[156] The delegates finished their work the second week of March, adopting a seventeen-plank platform headed by demands

151 See *El Monitor Republicano*, nearly every issue after January 19, 1920.

152 Missing were the governors of Sonora, Sinaloa, Chihuahua, Colima, Oaxaca, Tamaulipas, Zacatecas, Michoacán, Chiapas, and Tabasco.

153 *El Universal*, February 11, 1920.

154 Weekly report, Commanding General Southern Department to War Department, February 28, 1920, NA, RG 94.

155 *El Monitor Republicano*, March 3, 1920.

156 *El Universal*, February 1, 1920.

for effective suffrage, no reelection, and state and local autonomy.[157] Within the revolutionary framework, it was an unexceptional document; Carranza himself could not have quarreled with it in principle, however much he could resent its implied criticisms of his own stewardship. But platforms were now unimportant; the issue was power and who would wield it.

Ignacio Bonillas remained in Washington, and his maidenly reluctance to become a candidate was decidedly embarrassing to the Carranza administration. Bonillas said on March first that he would run only if the Mexican people wanted him, that so far only bureaucrats had encouraged him.[158] But two weeks later he somehow concluded that a popular call had come, and on March 18, just after crossing the border into Mexico, he announced his candidacy. He reached Mexico City on the twenty-first, where his public reception was dismally small and apathetic;[159] the only excitement surrounding it was the arrest of a number of Obregón supporters on charges of creating a disturbance.[160] Now Obregonista attacks on Bonillas rose to a roar. He was ridiculed as being tainted with gringoism because of his long residence in the United States—"'Mister' Bonillas" who had forgotten how to speak Spanish. It was charged that he had once been a sheriff in Arizona, then a Protestant minister in Texas.[161] Obregón partisans also stepped up their criticism of Carranza's administration; newspapers almost every day carried charges of graft and corruption in high places.

Matters were nearing some kind of climax. The possibility of an electoral decision that the losers would accept had all but vanished. Ingredients were there for an explosion, and the fuse was lit in the state of Sonora.

Sonora, sparsely populated, arid, poor, had long been a volatile

[157] *El Monitor Republicano*, March 14, 1920. There were also social planks, farther down the list. Point 10 called for legislation to implement article 123 of the constitution, and points 12 and 13 called for greater strides in land reform.

[158] Ibid., March 5, 1920.

[159] Ibid., March 22, 1920.

[160] They also included Miguel Alessio Robles and Basilio Vadillo, editor of *El Monitor Republicano* (ibid., March 22, 1920).

[161] Ibid., March 29, 1920.

force in Mexican geopolitics. Perhaps its remoteness from the core center of Mexico, its proximity to the United States, or its chronic troubles with the Yaqui Indians made it the different place it was. In any event, national leaders could seldom take its docility for granted. A bulwark in the struggle against Victoriano Huerta, it had produced far more than its share of leaders in the Constitutionalist revolution, and now it was about to demonstrate again its readiness to oppose leaders in Mexico City of whom it disapproved.

From the moment Obregón announced his candidacy, relations between Sonora and Carranza began to break down. In a move seen by Sonorans as a spiteful slap, Carranza on June 11, 1919, decreed that the waters of the Sonora River were federal property.[162] The cries of outrage still rang when Adolfo de la Huerta succeeded Plutarco Elías Calles as governor in September. De la Huerta, a thirty-seven-year-old native of the state, had achieved considerable prominence in the Constitutionalist movement despite his civilian status. A bank official before the revolution, he joined Carranza in 1913 and served in the cabinet during the preconstitutional period. In 1916 he was interim governor of Sonora, then during World War I he held diplomatic posts in Washington and New York. Afterward he returned to Mexico and was elected governor of his home state.[163]

It was de la Huerta who would preside over Sonora's progression into rebellion. Within weeks after he took office the breach between the state and Mexico City widened still further. De la Huerta had moved to settle the Yaqui problem. With Carranza's authorization he negotiated a peace treaty—which Carranza then refused to ratify.[164] It was not mere petulance on the part of the dour old leader; Sonora was by now Alvaro Obregón's prime bastion of support, its leaders and most of its citizens loudly championing their favorite son's cause, and Carranza was determined to show the obstreperous

[162] Jesús Romero Flores, *Anales históricos de la revolución mexicana*, II, 282.

[163] Carranza in May offered to back de la Huerta for president but the Sonoran refused—according to his biographer on grounds that to accept official endorsement would violate the principle of free elections (see Guzmán Esparza, *Memorias de Don Adolfo de la Huerta*, pp. 138–139).

[164] Romero Flores, *Anales históricos*, II, 282–284.

state that it could expect very short shrift if it insisted on distressing him.

By January the state's top men, all of them Obregonistas, were disassociating themselves from the national administration. Calles, who had joined the cabinet as secretary of industry and commerce in October, resigned, saying that in view of his close alliance with the Obregón party it would be improper for him to remain in the government.[165] There were growing indications that the Carranza-Sonora rift might become physical; also in January, Carranza replaced the federal chief of operations in the state with a general whom he considered more trustworthy,[166] and during the next several weeks he increased federal troop strength there.[167] American observers interpreted it as a move to ensure federal control during the elections.[168]

By March, as popular opinion continued to tip toward Obregón, it was clear that Carranza had been outdistanced politically, but his determination to have his way had diminished not one iota. He also knew that probably he would have to resort to armed action and that Sonora in that event would be the key. He decided to force matters. Giving as his reason that the Yaquis needed to be dealt with sternly, he ordered General Manuel Diéguez to prepare to enter the state with a large federal command, supported by a contingent under Francisco Murguía.[169] There followed a tense week of tongue-in-cheek exchanges between the state's governor and the president. In

[165] *El Universal*, February 2, 1920; Calles to Carranza, January 31, 1920, ADN-DF 1920. Only a week before, Calles had protested to Carranza against reports that he was using his office to forward the aims of "the political party to which I belong" (Calles to Carranza, January 22, 1920, ADN-DF 1920).

[166] Weekly report, Commanding General Southern Department to War Department, January 24, 1920, NA, RG 94. The new commander was General Juan José Ríos.

[167] Ibid., March 13, 1920.

[168] Ibid. Sonora was not entirely innocent in the military escalation. The Southern Command weekly reports throughout February and March stated that Obregón men in the state were stockpiling arms and ammunition in preparation for a confrontation with the federal government.

[169] Romero Flores, *Anales históricos*, II, 287.

a telegram to Carranza on March 30,[170] de la Huerta said there were persistent rumors that the federal administration intended to replace him with a military governor. He pointed out that the state was loyal and at peace; the Yaquis were quiet—although the arrival of Diéguez with new federal troops would unsettle them. He asked the president to reconsider his plans. Carranza replied that he had no intention of imposing military rule on the state, that any commander sent to Sonora would be acting in the national interest and under presidential supervision; rumors to the contrary were unfounded.[171] De la Huerta retorted (April 4) that the ugly rumors persisted,[172] and that, although he would like to be able to quiet them, this was difficult; he referred to editorials in *El Demócrata* that said it would be justified to send troops to Sonora to depose him because he was an Obregonista. He also noted that in 1919 when the Yaquis were in rebellion the state had difficulty getting adequate federal aid, whereas now, when the Indians were subdued, there would be an abundance of it. Again he urged suspension of the order.

On April 7, as municipal leaders in Sonora deluged de la Huerta with pledges of loyalty,[173] the state legislature resolved unanimously to inform Carranza that the sending of federal troops would be an attack on the state's sovereignty, with consequences for which the president would bear full responsibility.[174] De la Huerta followed this with a peremptory telegram;[175] he wished to know immediately, he told Carranza, what the government planned to do, and he warned that, unless the reply were satisfactory, "there will originate in Sonora a conflagration which will surely envelop the Republic." The answer showed Carranza at his imperious best:[176] he would "not debate with a state government the advisability or inadvisability of military movements dictated within my constitutional faculties"; a state that resisted the federal government's lawful military authority would be in rebellion, and indeed the recent action of the Sonora

170 Text in Vasconcelos, *La caída de Carranza*, pp. 148–151.
171 Ibid., pp. 152–153. 172 Ibid., pp. 154–160. 173 Ibid., pp. 167–170.
174 "Protesta del Congreso de Sonora," ibid., pp. 171–172.
175 Ibid., pp. 173–174.
176 Ibid., pp. 175–179.

legislature indicated that this was probably already the case; if Sonora believed its rights were being violated it should appeal to the Supreme Court—any other attempted remedy would be plain insurrection. Late on the evening of April 9 Sonora broke relations with the national government, and Carranza immediately announced that he was ordering twenty thousand regulars into the state.[177]

On the seventh the federal chief of operations in Sonora, General Juan José Ríos, had telegraphed his subordinate officers asking each for an immediate pledge of loyalty to the national government. When they replied almost to a man that they would side with Sonora, Ríos fled to the United States.[178] The next day Calles, who had taken charge of the state's military defense, wired Diéguez that the people had lost all confidence in the central government and that, if more federal troops entered Sonora, there would be civil war.[179]

Actually Sonora's situation was not so precarious as it appeared; its leaders had gambled on receiving support from other states, and they were not disappointed. Key military men in Sinaloa, Nayarit, and Jalisco began withdrawing allegiance from the federal government.[180] The first armed clash came on the fifteenth, when Angel Flores defeated a loyalist federal force at San Blas, Sinaloa.[181] After that the dam broke. On the sixteenth Arnulfo R. Gómez, joined by Peláez, rebelled in the Huasteca with 2,500 men; Enrique Estrada rose in Zacatecas; on the twenty-first General Porfirio Gómez deserted the government and quickly removed the region between Monterrey and Matamoros from federal control.[182] Pascual Ortiz Rubio in Michoacán joined the revolt.[183] Each day brought news of more defections from the federal army.

177 Consul Francis J. Dyer (Nogales) to SecState, April 10, 1920, file 812.00 /23557, NA, RG 59.

178 Juan Gualberto Amaya, *Venustiano Carranza: Caudillo constitucionalista*, pp. 421–423.

179 Vasconcelos, *La caída de Carranza*, p. 184.

180 Weekly report, Commanding General Southern Department to War Department, April 10, 1920, NA, RG 94.

181 Ibid., April 17, 1920.

182 Romero Flores, *Anales históricos*, II, 290.

183 Ibid., p. 289.

On April 23 the rebellion was formalized with the issuance of the Plan de Agua Prieta,[184] signed by Calles, Angel Flores, Francisco R. Serrano, and hundreds of military and civilian officials in Sonora. The plan accused Carranza of trampling popular rule and state sovereignty and of betraying the Constitutionalist revolution. It declared him deposed, and it annulled several recent state elections on grounds that they had been rigged with federal connivance. It promised to recognize officeholders elsewhere in the country provided they did not oppose the plan, and it welcomed all military men to take their places in the "Liberal Constitutionalist Army." The plan named de la Huerta supreme chief of the movement until the state governors could convene to elect one, failing which de la Huerta would retain the post; after Mexico City was occupied, Congress would choose a provisional president who would convoke national elections.

The man who would benefit most from the Agua Prieta rebellion nearly became its first victim. Alvaro Obregón was campaigning in the northeast when the Sonora crisis erupted. As popular enthusiasm for him had grown, so had government harassment. In Tampico several members of his entourage were beaten and jailed; in Ciudad Victoria local authorities pressured hotels and restaurants into refusing service to him and his staff; federal troops shadowed his campaign train.[185] The culmination came on April 2 in Matamoros, where Obregón was handed a summons to appear in Mexico City as a witness in the trial of General Roberto Cejudo, who was charged with treason.[186] Obregón saw the move for what it was—a final, desperate attempt to stop him from reaching the presidency. Friends begged him to ignore the order, but he went. When he reached the capital he received a message from Calles telling him that Sonora

[184] Text in Manuel González Ramírez, ed., *Planes políticos y otros documentos*, pp. 251–255.

[185] Jorge Prieto Laurens, *Cincuenta años de política mexicana*, pp. 84–87.

[186] Several rebel bands, totally unconnected with the Sonora quarrel, including the one led by Cejudo, had contacted Obregón. There is no evidence that he aided or abetted them, but the government claimed to have compromising evidence (see Alessio Robles, *Historia política*, p. 231).

was breaking with the federal government.[187] The news momentarily shook him; he remarked to friends that, although he supposed Calles and de la Huerta had good reasons for their move, it left him in a rat trap.[188] He now expected to be imprisoned and possibly killed.[189] Detectives followed him wherever he went.[190] Then on the night of April 11, the eve of a court appearance where he expected to be formally charged and detained,[191] he eluded police and fled in disguise to Guerrero.[192] There, after several anxious days, with only fragmentary reports of what was happening elsewhere in the country, support solidified around him. First, General Fortunato Maycotte, federal chief of operations in the state, then Ortiz Rubio and Roque Estrada, followed by other old friends, put themselves at his disposal.[193] On the twentieth, from Chilpancingo, Obregón issued a manifesto. He said that Carranza's attempts to subvert free elections by imposing Bonillas and blocking his own efforts to wage an honest political campaign had forced him to suspend his race for the presidency and assume the mantle of soldier; he placed himself at the orders of de la Huerta in the struggle to unseat Carranza.[194]

The rebellion spread. By the first of May most of the federal army had deserted to the rebels, and on the fourth Pablo González joined the stampede.[195] On May 7 Venustiano Carranza began his public and personal agony. That day the government left Mexico City and headed toward Veracruz, where Carranza hoped to repeat history. Six years earlier, holed up in the port city, he had ridden out the Villa onslaught, and now he would defy his new enemies with his back to the sea. A miracle might somehow happen.

The evacuation of Mexico City was an unwieldy, disorganized

[187] Prieto Laurens, *Cincuenta años*, pp. 87–89.
[188] Ibid., p. 89.
[189] Dillon, *President Obregón*, pp. 193–194.
[190] Alessio Robles, *Historia política*, p. 232.
[191] Ibid., pp. 232–233; Dillon, *President Obregón*, p. 193.
[192] Alessio Robles, *Historia política*, pp. 233–236.
[193] Ibid., pp. 235–236.
[194] Text in Vasconcelos, *La caída de Carranza*, pp. 202–206.
[195] Amaya, *Venustiano Carranza*, pp. 426–427.

scramble.[196] Cabinet ministers, Supreme Court justices, congressmen, civil servants—many accompanied by their families—crowded aboard trains that also carried the national treasury, artillery, and machinery for manufacturing arms and ammunition. The hapless Bonillas was also in the cortege. Cavalry units commanded by the still-loyal General Francisco Murguía undertook to escort the convoy to safety. But the refugees had barely cleared the outskirts of the capital when rebels began to close in. Moving only a few miles a day, the trains ground along while the troops fought off attacks that grew constantly more severe. On the thirteenth the long caravan reached Aljibes in the Puebla mountains and there it halted. The tracks ahead were torn up and most of the locomotives were out of fuel. In the afternoon Murguía beat back a determined assault, but the next day a ferocious attack turned matters into chaos, and Carranza and a handful of aides abandoned the trains and struck out into the mountains on horseback. On May 20 they reached the village of San Antonio Tlaxcalantongo. That night, as the exhausted fugitives slept, rebels stormed into the encampment and sprayed the huts with bullets. In one of them Venustiano Carranza died.

196 For a detailed first-hand account of the flight from Mexico City that ended in Carranza's death see Francisco L. Urquizo, *Páginas de la revolución*, pp. 175–271 passim.

EPILOGUE

On May 24, 1920, Mexico closed one chapter of its turbulent history and began another. The old chief was buried in Mexico City after a modest funeral—his daughters had to borrow money for the arrangements. Later generations of Mexicans would honor him as they did Madero or Obregón, but for the moment the nation's attention was fixed elsewhere. The same day, Congress elected Adolfo de la Huerta interim president of Mexico.

De la Huerta's six months in office were efficient and productive. He worked skillfully to pacify the country. Even Pancho Villa agreed to retire; with his archenemy Carranza gone he had lost his appetite for harrying the government. De la Huerta also presided over the election of Alvaro Obregón. Bonillas and González had withdrawn from the race after Carranza's death, for neither cared to stand against an irresistible force. A hastily organized "National Republican party," led by prominent Catholic laymen, nominated one-time Carrancista Alfredo Robles Domínguez, but it was pure gesture. The elections on September 5 were peaceful, and although the official returns gave Obregón a suspiciously lopsided 95 percent of the vote, few doubted that he was the popular choice.

Obregón took over an exhausted and disheveled country. Perhaps a million Mexicans had perished since 1910. The economy was blighted, finances a bedlam, demoralization widespread. But Obregón, capitalizing on the general willingness to accept direction and on his reputation as a shaper of events, went resolutely to work. He hoped to instill a new sense of purpose grounded in the activist philosophy that had prevailed at Querétaro in 1917. Working under severe handicaps, he mobilized what resources he could to begin fulfilling some of the constitution's promises. His energetic minister of agriculture, Antonio I. Villarreal, supervised distribution of 1.75 million hectares of land to nearly a thousand rural communities. It was a small step toward achieving the massive reform projected by the drafters of article 27, but it was a sevenfold advance over Carranza's reluctant tokenism. Public education received a larger share of the national budget than ever before in Mexico's history. José Vasconcelos and his dedicated phalanxes in the new education ministry labored feverishly to build and staff schools and libraries, and if immediate results were sparse, their efforts sparked a lasting enthusiasm for self-improvement. The government encouraged agrarian syndical activity and political involvement. This irritated the CROM, which correctly interpreted it as a move to counterbalance Morones's formidable influence, but Obregón kept the militant union's support by continuing to acknowledge its claim to a voice in national decision making.

Obregón realized that lasting advance depended on preventing the revolution from being crushed by foreign armed intervention. He maneuvered to assuage the ire of foreign investors over real or imagined grievances while at the same time defending what he deemed essential precepts of revolutionary nationalism. He did not resolve all differences, but he concluded an agreement with the United States in 1923 over the complex question of oil holdings. This won him U.S. recognition and probably saved his regime from a serious attempt to overthrow it. Late in 1923 Adolfo de la Huerta, angered by Obregón's refusal to back him for president, led a determined and almost successful revolt. Washington allowed arms shipments to Obregón and denied them to his enemies. He left office in 1924, the first Mexican president since Porfirio Díaz to complete a full term.

Obregón set directions that guided Mexican leaders for a generation. He established a firm commitment to the principles proclaimed in the constitution, but when necessary he subordinated it to a realistic appreciation of the obstacles that stood in the way of their fulfillment. In practical terms this meant that Mexico would advance under the revolutionary aegis, but that its leaders would not risk disaster by recklessly overplaying their hands. Moreover, they would employ any means, however ruthless, to insure their own survival and that of the revolutionary state. However much Obregón might have wished to see democracy become a reality he would not gamble; he lauded political freedom and scrupulously observed its outward forms, but he ruled as a dictator and handpicked his successor—as he had not allowed Carranza to do. Calles, who inherited the presidency in 1924, governed with an iron fist and although he relinquished office in 1928 he dominated the country for another six years through puppet presidents. Transfer of national leadership after 1934 was regular and orderly, but ratified in elections of often dubious honesty; and every president concentrated near-absolute power in his own hands and to all intents and purposes selected the man who followed him.

To some this disparity between democratic trappings and autocratic practice was sheer cynicism, but others accepted it as a necessary concession to reality in a country where allowing open political processes would invite a relapse into chaos. The dichotomy was systematized in 1928 by the creation of an official revolutionary party that encouraged broad public participation in political affairs while reserving ultimate control to the national executive. Defenders of the system insisted that it was the only way. The upheaval of the teens had shattered traditions of obedience to authority and spawned a huge and unruly military machine that took years to dismantle. For years freewheeling generals were willing to plunge the country into more civil war—not usually for ideological reasons but merely to place this or that *caudillo* in the presidential chair. Disgruntled power seekers rebelled in force in 1923, 1927, 1929, and 1938, and almost every year in between petty insurgents engineered local outbursts. Only after 1940 could governments depend on the loyalty of a chastened and professional army.

Some of the momentous problems the revolutionists grappled with during the Constitutionalist years—foreign investments, religion, labor, land—were resolved at least in part long after Carranza's fall. The revolution's xenophobia stemmed from foreign domination of Mexico's economic life, and moves to enforce the constitution's proscriptions on alien exploitation caused years of dangerous international contention. Not until Lázaro Cárdenas expropriated foreign oil properties in 1938 and Franklin D. Roosevelt recognized that American interests lay in gracefully accepting the act did the problem shrink to manageable proportions.

The hostility between the revolution and the Catholic church defied solution for two decades. Obregón, for the sake of internal harmony, left most of the constitution's anticlerical provisions in abeyance, but Calles's attempt to enforce them in 1926 touched off the tragic Cristero rebellion, which lasted three years and took thousands of lives. Church and government reluctantly agreed to a truce in 1929, but hatreds quickly resurfaced and regimes in the thirties resorted to tooth-and-nail persecution, which for a time seemed likely to destroy organized religion in Mexico. Only gradually, as it became obvious to both sides that neither could prevail absolutely, did the Church and the revolutionary state accept an informal arrangement that each could live with.

Organized labor, which hoped for so much from the revolution, had to wait until the constitution was fourteen years old before major precepts of article 123 were translated into a national labor code. Further guarantees came slowly, as worker groups became increasingly integrated into the institutional revolutionary family. Only by mid-century were governments implementing effective programs of health care, pensions, and other welfare measures for workingmen and for the population at large.

Land reform, the transcendent concern of millions of Mexicans, went through a torturous course of fits and starts and perplexed national leaders more than any other single problem. Land redistribution gained momentum throughout the twenties, then slackened; Cárdenas in the thirties gave it a massive new impetus, and later governments continued it in a businesslike and undramatic way until the process was essentially complete. The other function of agrarian reform—production—presented a dismal picture for decades. Only in the 1940's did agriculture begin to recover from the effects of revolutionary destruction and changed patterns of landholding, and probably not until 1950 did most Mexicans have as much to eat as they did in 1910.

The continuing problems accounted for the fundamental difficulty of deciding if and when the revolution ended. Various people who lived it or studied it disagreed on which event terminated the movement begun by Francisco Madero. Few believed it was Carranza's overthrow in 1920. The ruling revolutionary party half a century later insisted that the revolution was still going on. In this view, "revolution" became a synonym for efforts to promote material progress, national pride—almost anything that brought the good life to Mexicans. Others argued that "revolution" had by this time become but an empty slogan, useful only to time-serving politicians. Obviously, viewpoints depended on one's definition of the nature of the revolution.

Many early observers wrongly assumed that greed and vengeance alone motivated the revolutionists and that their triumph foreshadowed the enthronement of radicalism. This is not surprising. The leaders of the revolution—consciously, and a great many others less consciously—set out to obliterate much of Mexico's past, and that past was deeply entrenched. There followed a lengthy tearing-down process that both fascinated and repelled most who watched it. But the brutality, the anarchy, the radical rhetoric largely obscured the fact that the end goal of it all was essentially moderate. Certainly its leaders were revolutionaries—they meant to change Mexico into a nation that was both a twentieth-century state and a land of economic and social opportunity for every inhabitant. They meant to gain for Mexicans a new dignity and the material advantages that come from economic maturity. In this they differed not at all from other modern revolutionists. The difference—and it is a significant one—is that they proposed to transform Mexican society within a framework of political democracy. No revolutionist of importance questioned the basic tenets of democracy that grew from the Enlightenment. None opposed in principle the institutions that are part of the social structure of modern middle-class nations—churches, private business, banking, private education, and the like. None preached a classless society. The occasional excursions into messianic oratory on the part of a few leaders were not reflected in practice. The periodic lapses into dishonest and sometimes violent techniques were manifestations of expediency, not philosophy. The revolution had a rationale, but it did not have a limited, disciplined ideology in the sense that later Marxist-inspired ones, for example, did.

At the same time, while the Mexican revolutionists accepted democracy, some departed in an important way from basic assumptions held by many Western liberal democrats in the early years of the twentieth century. The Constitutionalists were united in their commitment to freedom, economic growth, and social mobility, but they divided over the question of what the function of government should be in making these things possible. Carranza's adherents accepted, with slight modifications, the principles of laissez-faire liberalism; government should referee and when absolutely necessary regulate certain aspects of national life, but only to enable natural growth to take its course. The group represented by Alvaro Obregón, which prevailed in 1920, rejected laissez faire as a general theory of national progress. They were convinced that Mexico could not afford to rely on the vagaries of "natural" forces; they refused to pin their hopes on some slow evolutionary process that might somehow, some day, produce good times. Instead they endowed the state with direct responsibility for the economic security and personal dignity of its citizens. They did not seek to destroy capitalism, but they did insist that it function so as to contribute to the greater social good—as defined by the state. After 1920 government intervened as a matter of course in nearly every sector of Mexican life, both for the purpose of destroying enclaves of traditionalist resistance to change, and to accelerate national construction.

The revolution destroyed the old and thus made possible the new. It pried Mexico loose from the vicious syndrome of backwardness characteristic of much of the twentieth-century world and set it on a course toward modernity. The goal had not been reached as the decade of the seventies opened. Many Mexicans did not yet enjoy the kind of life their revolution had promised them. And even the very real progress of the nation as a whole brought in its wake new and serious problems. Perhaps, as some claimed sixty years after Madero opened the floodgates, the revolutionary mystique had outlived its usefulness. But even those who sought new solutions took the revolution as their point of departure. The crucible of the teens forged something irreversible. If the present was less than perfect and the future uncertain, the past had been discarded forever.

MATERIALS CITED

Acuña, Jesús. *Memoria de la Secretaría de Gobernación correspondiente al período revolucionario comprendido entre el 19 de febrero de 1913 y el 30 de noviembre de 1916.* Mexico City: Talleres Linotipográficos de "Revista de Revistas," 1916.

Aguirre Berlanga, Manuel. *Génesis legal de la revolución constitucionalista. Revolución y reforma, Libro 1.* Mexico City: Imprenta Nacional, 1918.

Alessio Robles, Miguel, *Historia política de la revolución.* 3rd ed. Mexico City: Ediciones Botas, 1946.

———. *Ideales de la revolución.* Mexico City: Editorial "Cultura," 1935.

Amaya, Juan Gualberto. *Venustiano Carranza: Caudillo constitucionalista.* Mexico City, 1947.

American Journal of International Law. 1913.

Annals of the American Academy of Political and Social Science. 1917.

Atwater, Elton. *American Regulation of Arms Exports.* Washington, D.C.: Carnegie Endowment for International Peace, 1941.

Baker, Ray Stannard. *Woodrow Wilson: Life and Letters, 1913–1914.* Garden City: Doubleday, Page and Company, 1939.

Barragán, Juan. *Historia del ejército y de la revolución constitucionalista.* 2 vols. Mexico City: Talleres de la Editorial Stylo, 1946.

Bernstein, Marvin D. *The Mexican Mining Industry, 1890–1950: A Study of the Interaction of Politics, Economics, and Technology.* Albany: State University of New York, 1965.

Blakeslee, George H., ed. *Mexico and the Caribbean.* Clark University Addresses. New York: G. E. Stechert and Company, 1920.

Bojórquez, Juan de Dios. *Crónica del constituyente.* Mexico City: Ediciones Botas, 1938. [Published under pseudonym of Djed Bórquez]

Brayer, Herbert O. "The Cananea Incident." *New Mexico Historical Review* 13 (1938): 387–415.

Breceda, Alfredo. *México revolucionario, 1913–1917*. 2 vols. Madrid: Tipografía Artística Cervantes, 1920.

Calvert, Peter. *The Mexican Revolution, 1910–1914: The Diplomacy of Anglo-American Conflict*. Cambridge: Cambridge University Press, 1968.

Carranza, Venustiano. *Informe del C. Venustiano Carranza, Primer Jefe del Ejército Constitucionalista, encargado del poder ejecutivo de la República. Leído ante el Congreso de la Unión, en la sesión de 15 de abril de 1917*. Mexico City: Imprenta del Gobierno, 1917.

Casasola, Gustavo, ed. *Historia gráfica de la revolución mexicana, 1900–1960*. 4 vols. Mexico City: Editorial F. Trillas, 1964.

El Centinela. 1913. [Mexico City weekly]

Clark, Marjorie Ruth. *Organized Labor in Mexico*. Chapel Hill: University of North Carolina Press, 1934.

Clendenen, Clarence C. *The United States and Pancho Villa: A Study in Unconventional Diplomacy*. Ithaca, N.Y.: Published for the American Historical Association by Cornell University Press, 1961.

Cline, Howard. *The United States and Mexico*. 2nd ed. rev. New York: Atheneum, 1963.

La Convención. 1914. [Itinerant organ of the Convention government]

Cosío Villegas, Daniel, ed. *Historia moderna de México*. 7 vols. Mexico City: Editorial Hermes, 1955–1965.

Cumberland, Charles C. "Huerta y Carranza ante la ocupación de Veracruz." *Historia Mexicana*, no. 24 (1957): 534–547.

———. "The Jenkins Case and Mexican-American Relations." *Hispanic American Historical Review*, no. 4 (November, 1951): 586–607.

———. *Mexican Revolution: Genesis under Madero*. Austin: University of Texas Press, 1952.

———. *Mexico: The Struggle for Modernity*. New York: Oxford University Press, 1968.

El Demócrata. 1915. [Mexico City daily]

El Diario. 1913–1914. [Mexico City daily]

Dillon, E. J. *President Obregón: A World Reformer*. Boston: Small, Maynard and Company, 1923.

El Economista. 1917. [Mexico City weekly]

Esquivel Obregón, Toribio. *La influencia de España y los Estados Unidos sobre México*. Madrid: Casa Editorial Calleja, 1918.

Fabela, Isidro, ed. *Documentos históricos de la revolución mexicana*. 10 vols. Mexico City: Fondo de Cultura Económica, 1960–1966.

———. *Historia diplomática de la revolución mexicana, 1912–1917*. 2 vols. Mexico City: Fondo de Cultura Económica, 1958–1959.

Ferrer de Mendiolea, Gabriel. *Historia del congreso constituyente de 1916–1917*. Mexico City: Biblioteca del Instituto Nacional de Estudios Históricos, 1957.

Flandrau, Charles Macomb. *Viva Mexico!* Edited and with Introduction by C. Harvey Gardiner. Urbana: University of Illinois Press, 1964.

Fyfe, Henry Hamilton. *The Real Mexico: A Study on the Spot*. New York: McBride, Nast and Company, 1914.

González Ramírez, Manuel. *La huelga de Cananea*. Mexico City: Fondo de Cultura Económica, 1956.

———, ed. *Planes políticos y otros documentos*. Mexico City: Fondo de Cultura Económica, 1954.

González Roa, Fernando. *El aspecto agrario de la revolución mexicana*. Mexico City: Departamento de Aprovisionamientos Generales, Dirección de Talleres Gráficos, 1919.

Guzmán, Martín Luis. *Memorias de Pancho Villa*. 2nd ed. Mexico City: Compañía General de Ediciones, 1951.

Guzmán Esparza, Roberto. *Memorias de Don Adolfo de la Huerta según su propio dictado*. Mexico City: Ediciones "Guzmán," 1957.

Hale, Charles A. *Mexican Liberalism in the Age of Mora, 1821–1853*. New Haven: Yale University Press, 1968.

Hendrick, Burton Jesse. *Life and Letters of Walter H. Page*. 3 vols. Garden City: Doubleday, Page and Company, 1922.

Ignasias, C. Dennis. "Reluctant Recognition: The United States and the Recognition of Alvaro Obregón of Mexico, 1920–1924." Doctoral dissertation, Michigan State University, 1967.

El Imparcial. 1913. [Mexico City daily]

Informe del Tercer Congreso Obrero Nacional verificado en Saltillo, del 1 al 12 de mayo de 1918. N.p., n.d.

Liceaga, Luis. *Félix Díaz*. Mexico City: Editorial Jus, 1958.

Link, Arthur S. *Wilson: The New Freedom*. 2 vols. Princeton: Princeton University Press, 1956.

Lombardo Toledano, Vicente. *La libertad sindical en México*. Mexico City: Talleres Linotipográficos "La Lucha," 1926.

López Aparicio, Alfonso. *El movimiento obrero en México*. Mexico City: Editorial Jus, 1952.

Magaña, Gildardo, and Carlos Pérez Guerrero. *Emiliano Zapata y el agrarismo en México*. 5 vols. Mexico City: Editorial Ruta, 1951–1952.

María y Campos, Armando de. *Múgica: Crónica biográfica, aportación a la historia de la Revolución Mexicana.* Mexico City: Compañía de Ediciones Populares, 1939.

Maytorena, José María. *Algunas verdades sobre el General Alvaro Obregón.* Los Angeles: Imprenta de "El Heraldo de México," 1919–1920.

Mecham, John Lloyd. *Church and State in Latin America: A History of Politico-Ecclesiastical Relations.* Chapel Hill: University of North Carolina Press, 1934.

Mena Brito, Bernardino. *Carranza: Sus amigos, sus enemigos.* Mexico City: Ediciones Botas, 1935.

Mendieta y Núñez, Lucio. *El problema agrario de México desde su origen hasta la época actual.* 6th ed. Mexico City: Editorial Porrúa, 1954.

Mexican Oil Association. *Boletín de valores petroleros* 1, no. 2 (1913).

Mexico. Archivo General de la Nación. 1913–1920.

———. Archivo Histórico de la Secretaría de Defensa Nacional. 1913–1920.

———. *Boletín de Estadística Fiscal* (January, 1915). [Published in 1917.]

———. *Decretos y demás disposiciones del ejército constitucionalista: Febrero 19 de 1913 a abril 30 de 1914.* Chihuahua, 1914.

———. *Diario de los debates del Congreso Constituyente, 1916–1917.* 2 vols. Mexico City: Talleres Gráficos de la Nación, 1960.

———. *Diario Oficial.* 1918–1919.

———. *Mexico's Oil: A Compilation of Official Documents in the Conflict of Economic Order in the Petroleum Industry.* Mexico City, 1940.

———. Secretaría de Educación Pública. *Biblioteca enciclopédica popular: Documentos de la revolución mexicana.*

———. ———. *Boletín del petróleo.* Mexico City: Talleres Gráficos de la Nación, 1922.

———. Secretaría de Relaciones Exteriores. *Labor internacional de la revolución constitucionalista de México.* Mexico City: Imprenta de la Secretaría de Gobernación, 1918.

Meyer, Lorenzo. *México y Estados Unidos en el conflicto petrolero, 1917–1942.* Mexico City: El Colegio de México, 1968.

Meyer, Michael. "The Mexican-German Conspiracy of 1915." *The Americas* 23, no. 1 (July, 1966): 76–89.

Moheno, Querido. *Mi actuación política después de la decena trágica.* Mexico City: Ediciones Botas, 1939.

Molina Enríquez, Andrés. *Los grandes problemas nacionales*. Mexico City: Imprenta de A. Carranza e Hijos, 1909.

El Monitor Republicano. 1920. [Mexico City daily]

Monthly Labor Review. 1922–1924.

Obregón, Alvaro. *Ocho mil kilómetros en campaña: Relación de las acciones de armas efectuadas en más de veinte Estados de la República durante un período de cuatro años*. Mexico City: Librería de la Vda. de Ch. Bouret, 1917.

La Opinión. 1915. [Mexico City daily]

O'Shaughnessy, Edith. *A Diplomat's Wife in Mexico*. New York: Harper and Brothers, 1916.

El País. 1913–1914. [Mexico City daily]

Palavicini, Félix Fulgencio. *Mi vida revolucionaria*. Mexico City: Ediciones Botas, 1937.

Palomares, Justino. *La invasión yanqui en 1914*. Mexico City, 1940.

Pan American Petroleum and Transport Company. *Mexican Petroleum*. New York, 1922.

Pani, Alberto J. *Apuntes autobiográficos*. 2 vols. 2nd ed. Mexico City: Librería de Manuel Porrúa, 1950.

Pérez Lugo, J. *La cuestión religiosa en México: Recopilación de leyes, disposiciones legales y documentos para el estudio de este problema político*. Mexico City: Central Cultural "Cuauhtémoc," 1926.

Periódico Oficial [Aguascalientes]. 1914–1915.

Periódico Oficial del Gobierno del Estado Libre y Soberano de Coahuila de Zaragoza [Saltillo]. 21, no. 34 (1913).

La Prensa. 1915. [Mexico City daily]

Prieto Laurens, Jorge. *Cincuenta años de política mexicana: Memorias políticas*. Mexico City: Editora Mexicana de Periódicos, Libros, y Revistas, 1968.

El Pueblo. 1916. [Mexico City daily]

Quirk, Robert E. *An Affair of Honor: Woodrow Wilson and the Occupation of Veracruz*. Lexington: University of Kentucky Press, 1962.

———. *The Mexican Revolution, 1914–1915: The Convention of Aguascalientes*. Bloomington: Indiana University Press, 1960.

Rabasa, Emilio. *La evolución histórica de México*. Mexico City: Librería de la Vda. de Ch. Bouret, 1920.

Retinger, Joseph H. *Morones of Mexico: A History of the Labour Movement in That Country*. London: The Labour Publishing Company Ltd., 1926.

La Revista Agrícola. 1918.

Revista Mexicana. "El verdadero origen de la revolución constitucionalista." June 24, 1917.

Ríus Facius, Antonio. *La juventud católica y la Revolución Mejicana, 1910–1925.* Mexico City: Editorial Jus, 1963.

Robinson, Edgar E., and Victor J. West. *The Foreign Policy of Woodrow Wilson.* New York: The Macmillan Company, 1917.

Romero Flores, Jesús. *Anales históricos de la revolución mexicana.* 5 vols. Mexico City: "Biblioteca del Maestro" de *El Nacional,* 1939–1940.

Rouaix, Pastor. *Génesis de los artículos 27 y 123 de la constitución política de 1917.* 2nd ed. Mexico City: Biblioteca del Instituto Nacional de Estudios Históricos de la Revolución Mexicana, 1959.

Schmitt, Karl. "The Mexican Positivists and the Church-State Question, 1876–1911." *A Journal of Church and State* 8, no. 2 (Spring, 1966): 200–213.

Snow, Sinclair. *The Pan American Federation of Labor.* Durham: Duke University Press, 1964.

El Sol. 1914. [Mexico City daily]

Stephenson, George M. *John Lind of Minnesota.* Minneapolis: University of Minnesota Press, 1935.

Tannenbaum, Frank. *The Mexican Agrarian Revolution.* New York: The Macmillan Company, 1929.

Teitelbaum, Louis M. *Woodrow Wilson and the Mexican Revolution, 1913–1916: A History of United States-Mexican Relations from the Murder of Madero until Villa's Provocation across the Border.* New York: Exposition Press, 1967.

Tena Ramírez, Felipe. *Leyes fundamentales de México, 1808–1964.* 2d ed. Mexico City: Editorial Porrúa, 1964.

Toro, Carlos. *La caída de Madero por la revolución felicista.* Mexico City: F. García y Alva, 1913.

Tuchman, Barbara. *The Zimmermann Telegram.* New York: The Viking Press, 1958.

United States. Department of State. *Papers Relating to the Foreign Relations of the United States.* Washington, D.C.: Government Printing Office, various dates.

———. National Archives. (State Department). Record Group 59.

———. ———. Adjutant General's Office Records (War Department). Record Group 94.

———. ———. Punitive Expedition Records. Record Group 120.

———. Senate. *Investigation of Mexican Affairs. Report and Hearings before a Subcommittee of the Committee on Foreign Relations.* 62nd Cong., 2nd sess. Washington, D.C.: Government Printing Office, 1913.

El Universal. 1920, 1934. [Mexico City daily]

Urquizo, Francisco L. *Páginas de la revolución.* Mexico City: Talleres Gráficos de la Nación, 1956.

Vasconcelos, José. *La caída de Carranza: De la dictadura a la libertad.* Mexico City: Imprenta de Murguía, 1920.

Vera Estañol, Jorge. *Carranza and His Bolshevik Regime.* Los Angeles: Wayside Press, 1920.

———. *La revolución mexicana: Orígenes y resultados.* Mexico City: Editorial Porrúa, 1957.

Villa, Pancho. *Memorias.* See Guzmán, Martín Luis.

Womack, John, Jr. *Zapata and the Mexican Revolution.* New York: Knopf, 1968.

INDEX